Clinical Applications of Continuous Performance Tests

Measuring Attention and Impulsive Responding in Children and Adults

Cynthia A. Riccio

Cecil R. Reynolds

Patricia A. Lowe

John Wiley & Sons, Inc.

New York • Chichester • Weinheim • Brisbane • Singapore • Toronto

This book is printed on acid-free paper. ∞

Copyright © 2001 by John Wiley & Sons, Inc. All rights reserved.

Published simultaneously in Canada.

Library of Congress Cataloging-in-Publication Data:

Riccio, Cynthia A.
    Clinical applications of continuous performance tests : measuring attention and impulsive responding in children and adults / Cynthia A. Riccio, Cecil R. Reynolds, Patricia A. Lowe.
        p.   cm.
    Includes index.
    ISBN 0-471-38032-6 (cloth : alk. paper)
    1. Neuropsychological tests—Handbooks, manuals, etc.   2. Clinical neuropsychology—Handbooks, manuals, etc.   3. Performance—Testing—Handbooks, manuals, etc.   4. Attention-deficit/hyperactivity disorder—Handbooks, manuals, etc.   5. Impulse control disorders—Handbooks, manuals, etc.   I. Reynolds, Cecil R., 1952–   II. Lowe, Patricia A.

    RC386.6.N48   R53   2001
    616.89'075—dc21   00-043923

Printed in the United States of America.

10 9 8 7 6 5 4 3 2 1

4/26/06

Contents

Foreword

> The boundary between behavior and biology is arbitrary and changing. It has been imposed not by the natural contours of the disciplines, but by lack of knowledge. As our knowledge expands, the biological and behavioral disciplines will merge at certain points, and it is at these points of merger that our understanding of mentation will rest on particularly secure ground . . . Ultimately, the joining of these two basic disciplines represents the emerging conviction that a coherent and biologically unified description of mentation is possible. (Kandel, 1985, p. 832)

ALL TOO OFTEN individuals, whether clinicians or researchers, adapt and develop evaluation tools to meet the need of a particular type of client or to address a specific theoretical question. These evaluation tools may then be modified repeatedly and employed with different populations or to address theoretical issues for which they were not originally developed. Over time, within each specialty area, research accumulates with regard to one variation of the task or another and in its use with a given population. Multiple extensions of research result, radiating from a central idea or basic task. Understandably, many clinicians or researchers may become familiar with only one variation of an evaluation procedure that is specific to their individual practice or research agenda. Such a narrow perspective as to the value and scope of related procedures can lead to undesirable consequences, including misinterpreting the results of other variations of the procedure.

This volume represents a substantial effort at synthesizing and critically evaluating the research on the continuous performance test (CPT) that has accumulated over the past 50 years. This is quite an undertaking since over 300 papers have been generated across a range of populations and ages with multiple variations in CPT task demands and parameters. The resulting knowledge-base is impressive and can now be accessed in this single volume.

The conceptualization and procedures associated with CPT tasks are especially alluring in relation to Kandel's suggestion that the behavioral and biological sciences have points of merger. Why? Because there exists clear evidence that in many cases of neuropsychological disease or dysfunction, performance on CPT indices may be significantly impaired.

Thus for psychologists, the CPT may be viewed as tapping into more neurobiologically mediated processes, a point well addressed in this volume. However, to really appreciate the potential value and pitfalls in employing CPT procedures in research or clinical practice, we must have a critical understanding of the extant literature. It is for this reason that this volume is such a vitally important resource for clinicians and researchers alike.

As I read through this book, several clear messages emerge when all of the research is taken into account. First, any specific CPT may vary from another CPT procedure in not only the level of difficulty but in the task demands. Hence, interpretation of performance on any CPT can only be interpreted in relation to the research data regarding that particular CPT procedure. Clinical or theoretical hypotheses generated from one CPT procedure may not generalize to indices of performance derived from another variation of the CPT procedure.

Second, as is the case for all measures employed in clinical practice, standardization of administration must be the rule—both in practice and in the standardization process itself. In large part, the standardization and norming of CPT procedures has not been a particular strength of the literature, until recently. Standardization and appropriate task-specific norms are essential if the results of performance on CPT procedures are to have clinical or theoretical value.

Third, CPTs as a family of paradigms are clearly sensitive to a variety of central nervous system (CNS) disorders in both children and adults. There is a wealth of data available in this regard. However, sufficient evidence does not exist regarding the specificity of impairment for any particular CNS disorder or dysfunction. In this context then, performance in the impaired range on any CPT procedure should be viewed at best as a nonspecific pathognomonic sign of CNS dysfunction.

Fourth, in examining the literature, it is clear that a variety of CPT paradigms exist, some of which tap different sensory modalities and different aspects of cognitive processes. While related to my first point, this variability in procedures may be seen as desirable depending on the particular sensory or cognitive process believed to be deficient in that we may have available CPT procedures to assess attentional and executive control parameters in relation to those more specific sensory or cognitive processes.

Fifth, while performance on any given CPT procedure may most often be used in reaching a diagnosis of CNS dysfunction, performance measures from the CPT may be an optimal tool for use in the monitoring of attention and executive control in conjunction with treatment (medication or otherwise). Further, performance on the CPT may also be a useful tool for documenting disease progression, even when the initial behaviors of concern are not related to attention or executive control.

One of the most significant features of this book is the identification of the research needed to further develop the CPT as a more valuable tool for clinical diagnosis, the monitoring of treatment effects, and as a procedure for documenting disease progression in both children and adults. However, the authors of this volume also urge appropriate caution in the clinical use of CPT measures as a definitive diagnostic tool. The results of CPT procedures need to be interpreted clinically in relation to the constellation of performance on other behavioral, cognitive, and related neuropsychological measures and procedures.

Overall, this comprehensive and well-written volume fills a very significant void in the clinical and research literature in regard to the conceptualization and utility of CPT procedures in research and clinical practice. Not only have the authors accomplished a wonderful critical review of the literature regarding CPT procedures, but they have presented it in a carefully formulated way such that questions regarding the CPT can easily be addressed in one essential source. This is a major contribution to the literature.

GEORGE W. HYND
Research Professor and Director
Center for Clinical and Development Neuropsychology
The University of Georgia

Preface

DURING THE 1950s, a paradigm that has become known as the continuous performance test (CPT) was devised for specific research applications. This design was similar in some ways to measures of vigilance earlier in the twentieth century. The new design was quite successful and interested researchers in many areas of psychology, including the pure experimentalists as well as the applied researchers. The expansive research literature on the CPT suggests that variables measured by various CPT paradigms, of which there are many, are affected by many psychopathologies commonly encountered by psychologists as well as by trauma and physical disease.

During the 1990s, as a result of heavy marketing and the managed care movement, CPTs began to be used to establish specific diagnoses within psychology, most commonly Attention-Deficit/Hyperactivity Disorder (ADHD) and its subtypes. A few reviews of literature have been done dealing with specific aspects of CPT performance or a single psychopathology. Nowhere have we located a work that deals with the complexity of the various CPT paradigms themselves or with the multiple psychopathologies to which these paradigms have been applied. In fact, we were unable to locate a single study that compared CPTs with differing demands across populations. Our search for improved clinical and research applications of the CPT gave rise to the current volume.

In this work, we hope to provide a reference source for those who would apply various CPTs in their clinical practice as well as those who are engaged in research with these interesting and, now, mainstay paradigms. We begin with a description of the various neural substrates of CPT variables as they are now understood. The many inventive CPT paradigms are next described before we move to an assessment of the psychometric characteristics of some of the commercially available CPTs. We next look at the association of various demographic characteristics and other status variables to performance on CPTs. The use of various CPT paradigms in the diagnostic process itself is then reviewed for children, youth, and adults; findings here have been similar across age levels in some areas, yet quite disparate in others. Medication effects are assessed as well, and we find that many of the existing CPT paradigms are in fact quite sensitive to medication effects and therefore may be useful in monitoring treatment as well as assessing undesirable cognitive side effects of many psychoactive medications. The potential for the use of CPTs in monitoring other forms of treatment (e.g., attention training) is reviewed as well.

We hope to inspire additional, much needed research as noted and delineated throughout the book and summarized in our final chapter. Despite nearly a century of research on tasks associated with vigilance and more complex CPT designs, there is a great deal that remains to be done. Large-scale multisite studies specific to the use of CPTs in differential diagnosis and treatment monitoring continue to be needed. The CPT has sufficient promise to warrant grant support for these endeavors.

ACKNOWLEDGMENTS

We offer our appreciation to Jennifer J. Moore for her extensive work in developing the literature searches and reviews with us in the preparation of this volume. Our Wiley editor, Tracey Belmont, who pursued this volume with us and then showed tremendous patience as we continued to find literature and revise this work, also deserves our appreciation. We wish to thank Rafael Klorman for providing a much-needed figure from his research with the CPT and George Hynd for agreeing to write the Foreword for us. In addition, Cyndi would like to express her appreciation to Christine French and Monica Wolfe for their assistance in manuscript preparation and to her colleagues for their continued support. Cecil once again acknowledges his debt to Julia, who keeps him centered and without whose emotional support he could not be successful. Patricia would like to express her appreciation to family, friends, and the Warm Springs Counseling Center (WSCC) staff for their support, encouragement, and sense of humor throughout this endeavor. To those who read this work, we offer our appreciation for working through the often complex material that we have tried so hard to present in a logical fashion. We hope you benefit in some way from our efforts.

CYNTHIA A. RICCIO
CECIL R. REYNOLDS
PATRICIA A. LOWE

CHAPTER 1

Neurobiology of Attention and Executive Control

BEFORE DISCUSSING THE clinical uses and limitations of the continuous performance test (CPT), it is important to appreciate what we know about attention and executive control and their importance to clinical neuropsychology in terms of both assessment and rehabilitation. Problems with attention are inherent in a multitude of disorders, but most frequently noted in conjunction with Attention-Deficit/Hyperactivity Disorder (ADHD) and, in adults, schizophrenia. Attention problems in one form or another are associated with many neurological disorders. Hemineglect or hemiattention, for example, is a common manifestation of unilateral lesions due to stroke (R.A. Cohen, Malloy, & Jenkins, 1999; Mesulam, 1981, 1985a, 1985b). Neurological disorders associated with more diffuse damage (e.g., generalized seizures, Alzheimer's disease) and diffuse trauma such as anoxic encephalopathy often include behavioral manifestations of impaired attention as well as impaired executive control (R.A. Cohen et al., 1999). At the same time, impairment of attention is one of the more common symptoms of multiple sclerosis (R.A. Cohen, 1993b), with problems of slowed processing as well as attentional control. In this regard, attention can be seen as involving motor, cognitive, and social processes (Sohlberg & Mateer, 1989a, 1989b). Attentional deficits are also associated with other neurological disorders. The notion of attention and executive control function as related to the integrity of the frontal lobes is derived from clinical evidence and behavioral correlates of traumatic brain injury (TBI). The most common complaints of patients following TBI are attention and concentration problems, coupled with memory deficits. It has been argued that memory relies on the neural traces of attention and therefore that attention is key to the formation of memory (R.A. Cohen, 1993b; Sohlberg & Mateer, 1989a) and, subsequently, has an impact on cognitive functioning. Theoretical foundations and models for

1

attention and executive function and their proposed neurological substrates are presented next.

ATTENTION AND
EXECUTIVE CONTROL

Attention is not unitary; rather, it is a nebulous and complex construct (Mirsky, Fantie, & Tatman, 1995). Zubin (1975) suggested that attention could be conceptualized as having multiple components or elements. Psychiatry (e.g., D. Siegel, 2000) views attention as the process that controls the flow of information processing in the brain, making it a fundamental, key element of all cognitive tasks. Among patients with psychiatric disorders, three components of attention are used clinically to describe attentional defects: selectivity, capacity, and sustained concentration. Ward Halstead (1947), an early pioneer of clinical neuropsychology, included attention and the related concept of vigilance in his theory of the biological basis of intelligence. Neuropsychologists, at the most basic level, conceptualize attention as involving selective processing and awareness of stimuli (Mesulam, 1985a, 1985b). In particular, the term "attention" may be used to refer to the following: (1) initiation or focusing of attention; (2) sustaining attention or vigilance; (3) inhibiting responses to irrelevant stimuli or selective attention; and (4) shifting of attention (Denckla, 1996; Mirsky, 1989; Mirsky, Anthony, Duncan, Ahearn, & Kellam, 1991; Sohlberg & Mateer, 1989a; Zubin, 1975). Others have included encoding, rehearsal, and retrieval as components of attentional functions (Mirsky, 1989; Mirsky et al., 1991). In addition, the construct of attention has been conceptualized in terms of sensory attention as well as motor intention (Heilman, Watson, & Valenstein, 1985). Table 1.1 provides a list of components of attention that are commonly addressed.

Broadbent (1953, 1957) viewed attention from the perspective of the perceptual system and information processing. He proposed that the capacity to take in information is limited; therefore, information that is not relevant needs to be filtered out. The likelihood that information would be filtered out or in was viewed as dependent on characteristics of the stimulus (i.e., intensity, importance, novelty). Notably, some of these same stimulus characteristics, as well as others, have a demonstrated impact on attention as measured by the CPT and are discussed in more depth in Chapter 2.

A second early theory of attention focused on arousal (Hebb, 1958; Moruzzi & Magoun, 1949; Samuels, 1959). Based on the arousal theory, optimal levels of arousal (or alertness) are necessary for effortful, organized function, and sensory stimulation provides an impetus for arousal.

Table 1.1
Components of Attention*

Arousal/alertness
  Motor intention/initiation

Selective attention
  Focusing of attention
    Inhibiting/filtering attention
  Divided attention
  Encoding, rehearsal, and retrieval

Sustaining attention/concentration

Shifting of attention

* Based on Mirsky et al. (1991); Stankov (1988);
van Zomeran and Brouwer (1994).

Pribram and McGuinness (1975) described arousal as a short-lived response to a stimulus. In the clinical arena, assessment of attention is perceived as entailing more than basic awareness and is concerned with more than arousal level. Related to but distinct from attention, arousal can be defined as the general state of the individual that allows for and affects attentional processes (Parasuraman, 1984a, 1984b).

In view of the complexity of attention and its component processes, Mirsky (1987) proposed restricting the myriad aspects of attention to the focusing of attention, sustaining of attention, and shifting of attention. Using these three components as organizers, selective attention, for example, becomes part of the process involved in focusing attention or, if deficient, in the level of distractibility. Selective or focused attention requires optimal arousal as well as information-processing capacity (Mirsky et al., 1991; Pribram & McGuinness, 1975). In contrast, sustained attention is the ability to maintain that focus over time (Mirsky et al., 1991). It has been argued that sustained attention as well as focused attention involve selective attention, attentional capacity, and response selection over time (R.A. Cohen & O'Donnell, 1993b). The shifting of attention is considered to reflect the need for flexibility and adaptation of various elements of attention as well as involving the capacity to inhibit the previously initiated attentional response (Mirsky, 1987; Mirsky et al., 1991).

Similarly, and more consistent with the importance of arousal to other components of attention, van Zomeran and Brouwer (1994) included arousal as one of two components of their model of attention, with the ability to sustain attention incorporated as a function of arousal. The second component of their model is selective attention, which is composed of focused attention and divided attention. Thus, the van Zomeran and

Brouwer model of attention incorporates the element of arousal as well as the information-processing components of attention included in Mirsky's (1987) model.

Based on a factor analytic study, Stankov (1988) suggested three components of attention: concentration or sustained attention, attentional flexibility or the ability to shift attention, and perceptual or processing speed. All three components were found to be strongly associated with measures of fluid ability (i.e., novel problem solving). Others have organized attentional processes by virtue of their information-processing demands (i.e., the extent to which flexibility is required) and the extent to which the attentional process is automatic or controlled (Posner, 1978; Shiffrin & Schneider, 1977). Controlled attentional processes are those that require effort, are serial, and are subject to interference. The controlled processes are believed to be slower and to have a more limited processing capacity as compared to the processing that is effortless and without subjective awareness, or automatic processing (Posner, 1978).

Attention is one of many processes incorporated into the larger construct of executive function. Executive function is a more general construct that includes such abilities as sustaining attention and maintaining a response set, shifting of set, problem solving, planning and follow-through (R.A. Cohen, 1993d). Executive control is that aspect of executive function that is involved in self-regulation, self-direction, goal directedness, and response inhibition as well as the actual capacity to inhibit the response (Barkley, 1997a, 1997b; R.A. Cohen, 1993d). These components of executive control are identified in Table 1.2.

Executive control is closely intertwined with attentional processes due to the need for attentional shifts and attentional flexibility in the regulatory and inhibition processes (R.A. Cohen, 1993d). Both executive control and attention are also necessary for initiation or generation of the response to a specific stimulus, for maintenance of the response or shifting of the response, and for flexibility of responding to meet changing demands (R.A. Cohen, 1993d; Whyte, 1992).

Table 1.2
Components of Executive Control

Self-direction
Goal directedness
Self-regulation
Response selection
Response inhibition

NEUROPSYCHOLOGICAL MODELS OF ATTENTION

The multifaceted nature of attention and executive control makes it difficult to map the behaviors of interest directly onto neurological components. J. Swanson, Cantwell, Lerner, McBurnett, and Hanna (1991) have argued, for example, that attentional deficits cannot be linked directly to cognitive operations nor to specific neural systems. When the arousal theory was the primary model of attention, the focus was on those neural structures associated with physiological arousal (e.g., Lindsley, Bowden, & Magoun, 1949; Moruzzi & Magoun, 1949). Specifically, there was a focus on the two pathways for sensory projections onto the cortex: the pathway through the thalamus and the pathway through the reticular activating system (RAS). Damage or dysfunction of the RAS is believed to have an impact on arousal and activation levels (R.A. Cohen et al., 1999). Over time, multiple models of attentional processes of increasing complexity have been posited (e.g., Goldman-Rakic, 1988; Heilman et al., 1985; Luria, 1966; Mesulam, 1981, 1985a, 1985b; Petersen, Fox, Posner, Mintur, & Raichle, 1989; Posner, 1988; Posner & Petersen, 1990; Pribram & McGuinness, 1975; Stuss & Benson, 1984, 1986).

With increasing frequency, models of attention and executive control involve a number of cortical structures and systems (van Zomeran & Brouwer, 1994). Functional system models of attentional processes include both peripheral autonomic and central nervous system (CNS) correlates of attention (R.A. Cohen & O'Donnell, 1993b). At the same time, current functional system models include cortical and subcortical structures as well as connecting pathways and projections, including those identified with the arousal theory. The major models are reviewed briefly to provide a backdrop against which to evaluate the clinical uses of the CPT. It is important to note that whereas earlier models tended to emphasize the RAS, there is increasing emphasis on the frontal lobes (van Zomeran & Brouwer, 1994). The major components of the various systems (e.g., RAS, frontal lobe, basal ganglia) are depicted in Figure 1.1.

Executive functions, including attentional processes and executive control, are thought to be mediated predominantly by the frontal system and the pathways connecting the frontal lobes with other cortical and subcortical areas (Fuster, 1980; Milner, 1963, 1964). The frontal lobes have been found to constitute a complex neurological and functional system (Luria, 1966; Welsh & Pennington, 1988). Within the frontal lobes, the prefrontal cortex is believed to integrate and regulate the behaviors needed to execute a planned and coordinated sequence (Fuster, 1989; Ingvar, 1985; Luria, 1966; Norman & Shallice, 1985; Stuss & Benson, 1984). Among those behaviors that are believed to be tied into frontal lobe function are

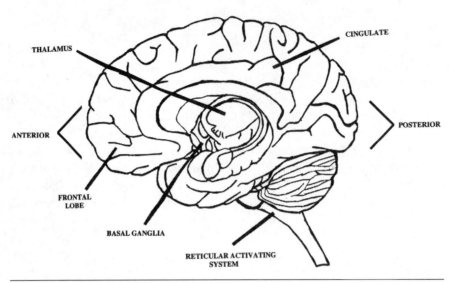

Figure 1.1 The Major Structures/Regions of the Brain Believed to Be Involved in Attention and Executive Control Based on Current Neuropsychological Models

the ability to (1) maintain a response set in a goal-directed fashion (Luria, 1966); (2) carry out a strategic plan in sequence (Luria, 1966); (3) plan and self-monitor one's own behavior (Flavell, 1971); (4) attend to and make use of environmental cues (Passler, Isaac, & Hynd, 1985); (5) focus attention (R.A. Cohen et al., 1999); and (6) form a mental representation of the task (Luria, 1966). The complexity and systemic nature of the frontal lobes are evident in the interconnections of the prefrontal cortex with the limbic system (thus incorporating motivation), the RAS (arousal), the posterior association cortex, and the motor regions within the frontal lobes themselves (Barbas & Mesulam, 1981; Johnson, Rosvold, & Mishkin, 1968; Porrino & Goldman-Rakic, 1982; Welsh & Pennington, 1988).

Mesulam (1981) was one of the first to offer a model of an integrated attentional system. His model was specific to understanding the phenomenon of those individuals who exhibited hemiattention or hemineglect as a result of brain damage and, as such, focused on spatial location. The model, however, continues to be viewed as a viable framework for understanding attentional processes. Mesulam posited that attentional processes involved the reticular system, the limbic system, the frontal cortex, and the posterior parietal cortex. Subcortical influences from the limbic system (including the cingulate), RAS, and hypothalamus are viewed as a systemic matrix that is necessary for the control of attention (Mesulam, 1985a, 1985b). The frontal lobes both are influenced by and have an influence on the reticular system via afferent and efferent pathways. In this model, the frontal lobes are involved in fixating or selective attention to the target as well as scanning, reaching, and so on. The contribution of the reticular system is preparedness or level of arousal as well as vigilance or maintenance of that level of arousal. Within the limbic system, Mesulam theorized that the cingulate gyrus in particular was involved in attentional processes due to its role in the individual's motivational state. Other researchers have found some indications that the anterior cingulate is involved in attentional processes as well (Petersen et al., 1989). Cingulate lesions are believed to have the greatest impact on motor intention as opposed to attentional control (R.A. Cohen et al., 1999).

The orbital prefrontal cortex is seen as modulating those impulses that originate in the limbic system and the hypothalamus (R.A. Cohen, 1993a, 1993c). Finally, the posterior parietal cortex is viewed as providing an internal sensory map. Neural systems of the parietal lobe are believed to be essential in selective attention. As such, sustained attention is the result of the interaction of the neural system of the frontal lobes, limbic structures, and subcortical structures and may be disrupted to varying degrees by compromise of virtually any structure within these systems (R.A. Cohen, 1993a, 1993c).

Luria (1966) posited that executive functions were of importance in the control of behavior with particular emphasis on the prefrontal cortex. The attentional system was central to his models of normal and abnormal brain function. Approaching attention from a combination of perspectives, including cognitive processing, Luria proposed two attentional systems: reflexive and nonreflexive. The reflexive system includes the orienting response (OR) and appears early in development. In contrast, the nonreflexive system develops at a slower rate, is the result of social learning, is associated with cognitive and linguistic mediation of behavior, and is necessary for sustained attention (R.A. Cohen & O'Donnell, 1993b, 1993d). Based on clinical evidence, Luria suggested that the limbic system and the frontal lobes mediated both attentional activation and inhibition. Clinical studies, for example, found that patients with damage to the limbic system were more likely to tire easily, be distractible, and be unable to sustain attention over time. Similarly, studies of patients with severe frontal damage consistently reported difficulty with sustaining attention and resisting distractions.

A second model, the frontal-diencephalic-brainstem system (FDB), was offered by Stuss and Benson (1984, 1986). As with Mesulam's model (1985a, 1985b), the reticular system is responsible for levels of alertness. While continuing to include the reticular system and the frontal lobes consistent with Mesulam's model, Stuss and Benson placed additional emphasis on the role of the frontal-thalamic gating system and the various projections associated with the thalamus. The frontal-thalamic gating system is seen as subserving selective attention, whereas the thalamic projections subserve the stability or variability in levels of alertness (van Zomeran & Brouwer, 1994). With damage to the thalamic projection system, for example, the individual's level of alertness is variable and results in distractibility and an inability to sustain attention (Stuss & Benson, 1984, 1986) as well as affecting response selection (R.A. Cohen et al., 1999). In contrast, damage to the frontal-thalamic gating system is associated with selective attention and self-monitoring as well as more complex behaviors (Stuss & Benson, 1984, 1986). Specific to CPT performance, the thalamic projections and the frontal-thalamic gating systems of the FDB model would be implicated by measures of consistency or variability and overall performance accuracy.

Heilman and colleagues (1985) offered another model of sensory attention or inattention. As with Mesulam's model (1985a, 1985b), Heilman et al.'s model is based on studies of neglect and hemiattention. The model posits that the normal attention system is dependent on arousal (reticular formation), sensory transmission (pathways), projections from sensory areas to association areas, projections to the thalamus, various portions of the cortex (frontal and parietal), and the limbic system. The involvement of the limbic and frontal areas is seen as resulting from their respective inputs into the association areas, which in turn impact on the inferior parietal lobes to inhibit or facilitate attentional response. The parietal lobe takes on increased importance with regard to visual and spatial information. As with Mesulam's model, the limbic system is involved with the motivational state of the individual. Thus, sensory inattention is viewed specifically as a dysfunction of the corticolimbic-reticular formation loop that impacts predominantly on the arousal-attention component.

The model proposed by Pribram and McGuinness (1975) involves the physiological systems associated with arousal, activation, and effort. As such, the neuroanatomical basis of attention processes involves the reticular system, the limbic system, and various subcortical structures that are involved in sensorimotor integration and control of attention. Similarly, Mirsky (1989) suggested that the reticular formation is important in the maintenance of arousal and, subsequent to this, attention; the thalamus is the relay station for projections between the reticular system and the cortical regions; the limbic system contributes to affective control and motivation; the prefrontal cortex is involved in decision making and executive function; and the parietal cortex is involved in selective and spatial attention. Mirsky also included the temporal lobes with an emphasis on integration of sensory information. In addition, Mirsky included the basal ganglia, with importance attached to its gating of information and control of motoric impulses. Notably, Mirsky's system was based on factor analytic studies of neuropsychological data.

Posner and Petersen (1990) posited an anterior-posterior and vigilance model of attention. The posterior network in this model subserves covert shifts in orientation of the visual system (Posner & Cohen, 1984). Based on animal studies, the structures involved in the posterior network include the posterior parietal lobe (as in Mesulam's model, 1985a, 1985b), the lateral pulvinar nucleus of the thalamus, and the superior colliculus (Petersen et al., 1989). Posner (1988) found that injuries in humans to any of these three areas reduced the ability to shift attention from one target to another. In contrast to previous models, the role of the parietal lobes is seen as specifically involved in covert shifts of attention and attentional disengagment. Consistent with Mesulam's model, Posner found that damage to the posterior parietal lobe affected the ability to shift from a target on the same side as the injury to a target located contralateral to the injury, resulting in hemineglect or hemiattention. Similarly, individuals with damage to the pulvinar nucleus of the thalamus had difficulty attending to targets located contralateral to the damage. Damage to the superior colliculus, on the other hand, appeared to be related to a slowed response or slowed attentional shifts as well as to saccadic eye movements (Posner, 1988). Thus, the posterior parietal system appears to be involved in engagement or disengagement of attention in general. Focus on specific features of the stimulus, however, may be related to posterior temporal regions.

The anterior network is connected to the posterior system via connections between the parietal lobe and the lateral and medial frontal lobes (Goldman-Rakic, 1988). The anterior network in this model is hypothesized to be related to voluntary control of attention and focusing of attention. Posner (1988) suggested a hierarchical model such that the anterior system can transfer attentional control to the posterior system as needed (van Zomeran & Brouwer, 1994). The anterior network component of this model is more theoretical and posited to include the anterior cingulate, the midline frontal areas, and the supplementary motor areas, based in part on studies by Corbetta, Miezin, Dobmeyer, Shulman, and Petersen (1991) and Corbetta, Miezin, Shulman, and Petersen (1993). The extent to which the frontal lobes are involved in task performance is believed to be directly related to the extent of attentional effort required by the task and inversely related to the amount of practice on the task. In attempts to segregate various cognitive processes that are highly related to attention (e.g., attention from memory), novel tasks are helpful. Posner and Petersen (1990) further postulated the involvement of the frontal lobe in working memory. Underscoring the relation between executive control and attention, they suggested that the frontal lobe is responsible for executive control and, as such, dictates the activation of the posterior attention system. In addition, it is believed that it is the neural traces left by attention that are likely the root of memory (R.A. Cohen, 1993b; Nussbaum & Bigler, 1990).

The third component to Posner and Petersen's (1990) model is specific to vigilance. Although theoretical, the proposed vigilance network is related to alertness and the ability to sustain attention. Based on their model, the norepinephrine system is implicated in vigilance; the locus ceruleus, frontal areas, and posterior areas of the brain are believed to be involved in vigilance as well. It is further believed that norepinephrine works via the posterior attention system. This component of Posner and Petersen's model is the least researched and developed; much more study has been done on the anterior-posterior gradient and attention.

Probably the most complex model offered with regard to attentional processes is based on the work of Goldman-Rakic (1988) and focuses on the corticostriatothalamic (CST) neural circuits and structures. In this model, the basal ganglia, specifically the striatum (caudate and putamen), are believed to subserve attentional processes in conjunction with the frontal and parietal areas (Damasio, Damasio, & Chang Chui, 1980). Basal ganglia involvement is believed to be related to selective attention in perception and reception of stimuli in addition to motor control (van Zomeran & Brouwer, 1994). The striatum is seen as having a gating function, with relays to the cortex via the thalamus resulting in selective attention (Hassler, 1978), and has emerged as a hub of influence over the thalamus and motor structures due to the number of crossing pathways that lead to and from the cortex (Selemon & Goldman-Rakic, 1990). Research has implicated the basal ganglia in sensorimotor integration, with unilateral damage to the basal ganglia resulting in hemiattention as well as motor intention problems (R.A. Cohen et al., 1999); as such, damage to the basal ganglia can be associated with increased response latency or decreased reaction time on tasks requiring information processing and response selection, as on the CPT.

The CST model includes not only the frontal lobes, basal ganglia, and the thalamus, but also the ascending pathways (responsible for arousal) and descending pathways (inhibition of behavior) that connect these structures and activate or inhibit other regions of the brain at the cortical or subcortical level. These pathways provide the means for transmission of the various neurotransmitters involved in arousal (e.g., dopamine, norepinephrine). The CST model and the level of complexity it offers, integrating both neuroanatomical and neurochemical influences, provide a plausible explanation for the multitude of manifestations of deficits in attention and executive control across other disorders as well. Thus, it is hypothesized that interference at any level of the system would lead to a cluster of clinically similar and yet potentially different behaviors. In applying the CST model to the study of ADHD, Voeller (1991; Heilman,

Voeller, & Nadeau, 1991) found this model to be most consistent with the myriad attentional problems found in children with ADHD. However, because compromise to any of these pathways or their origins may lead to attentional deficits or disturbances, the specificity of attention problems as a diagnostic consideration is suspect. Many disorders, as already noted, of widely disparate etiology and treatment regimens will include attentional problems in their spectre.

NEUROCHEMICAL BASIS OF ATTENTION

Not all models of attention focus on structures of the brain; some have focused on the impact of various neurotransmitters and neuromodulators, with an emphasis on the catecholamines (dopamine, norepinephrine). In his discussion of attentional disorders, Levy (1991) suggested that the underlying dysfunction rested in the dopaminergic circuits between the prefrontal and striatal centers. In conjunction with the dopaminergic models, it has been suggested that the frontal lobes are the locus of the attentional system, whereas the parietal lobes are involved in covert shifting of visual attention such that both work together to regulate attentional processes (Posner, Inhoff, & Fredrich, 1987). A reduction in dopamine in the prefrontal cortex has been implicated in the attentional problems associated with schizophrenia as well (J.D. Cohen & Servan-Schreiber, 1992), but this also may be part of the problem in at least some cases of ADHD.

Others have focused on the noradrenergic system. For example, animal studies have suggested that attention deficits may be associated with norepinephrine depletion (Lordon, Rickert, Dawson, & Pellymounter, 1980; Maas & Lockman, 1983; Mason & Fibiger, 1978). In fact, it has been suggested that there are actually two neural systems involved. The first is the activation system, modulated by norepinephrine (D. Tucker, 1986; D. Tucker & Williamson, 1984); the second is the dopaminergic system, involved in sustaining and shifting attention (D. Tucker, 1986). The involvement of dopamine and norepinephrine in the control of attention is linked directly with the use of stimulant medications for the treatment of ADHD and cannot be ignored.

In addition to dopamine and norepinephrine, of the other neurotransmitters, serotonin also has been implicated. Serotonin depletion in animals has been associated with observations of increased activity, and low levels of serotonin have been found in some, but not all, children with ADHD (Zametkin & Rapoport, 1987). Although most children with ADHD respond to stimulant medication that disproportionately supports dopamine and norepinephrine, many respond to serotonin facilitators such as Prozac and Zoloft (selective serotonin reuptake inhibitors or

SSRIs) and to buproprion, which acts on both sets of neurotransmitter systems. Links with levels of monamine oxidase inhibitors (MAOIs) also have been considered. In their review, Zametkin and Rapoport (1987) concluded that it is unlikely, given the interactions of neurotransmitters, that a single neurotransmitter is responsible; rather, it would seem that multiple neurotransmitters are involved, particularly dopamine.

ASYMMETRY OF ATTENTION

As already stated, attentional control is believed to involve two separate neural systems (D. Tucker, 1986; D. Tucker & Williamson, 1984). The first of these, the activation system, is believed to be centered in the left hemisphere and to be involved with sequential and analytic operations. The second system, arousal, is believed to be centered in the right hemisphere and responsible for holistic and parallel processing as well as the maintenance of attention. It has been suggested, therefore, that the attentional capacity of an individual is dependent on the functional integrity of both hemispheres (Colby, 1991), with some indications of involvement of interhemispheric regulation (Hynd, Hern, et al., 1991).

At the same time, however, there is some evidence of greater impact on attentional processes with damage to the right hemisphere. Although the vigilance network posited by Posner and Petersen (1990) has not yet been mapped onto brain structures, their model hypothesizes that the right hemisphere subserves the initiation and maintenance of arousal. This asymmetry is supported by evidence that hemineglect is more frequent and intensive after damage to the right hemisphere (Heilman et al., 1985; Mesulam, 1985a). Further, although the right hemisphere appears able to compensate when there is damage to the left hemisphere, the reverse is not true. Based on these findings, it has been hypothesized that there is asymmetry in the neurological substrates of attention, with greater involvement of the right hemisphere (e.g., Heilman et al., 1985; Heilman & van den Abell, 1979). Right hemisphere involvement has been substantiated further in simple reaction time studies where individuals with right hemisphere damage have been found to have longer response times as compared to those with left hemisphere damage (DeRenzi & Faglioni, 1965; Howes & Boller, 1975; Tartaglione, Bino, Manzino, Spadevecchia, & Favale, 1986). The idea of greater right hemisphere involvement is not only evident in Posner and Petersen's model but also is key to other theories specific to right hemisphere dysfunction (e.g., Rourke, 1989). There remains the possibility that the organizational responsibilities of the right frontotemporal systems are impaired in such damage cases, adding a greater appearance of attentional deficits when an interaction is actually at the root of the apparent increased attention problems. It is difficult to parse such problems succinctly, and the latent neural systems are likely not orthogonal.

In contrast to findings of simple reaction time tasks and theoretical models that posit greater right hemisphere involvement in attention, studies with more complex, choice reaction time tasks have found that individuals with left hemisphere damage demonstrated greater impairment on both speed and accuracy as compared to individuals with right hemisphere damage (Benton & Joynt, 1958; Dee & van Allen, 1973). This may be due to the difference in the extent of information processing, and so language processing, that is required in simple versus choice reaction time tasks. At the level of the reticular system, damage to the left (language-dominant) hemisphere is hypothesized to have a greater impact on arousal than would be evident with similar damage to the right hemisphere (Salazar et al., 1986). This is consistent with Luria's (1973) premise that most psychological processes are related to language processes and rely on left hemisphere processing (van Zomeran & Brouwer, 1994).

NEUROPSYCHOLOGICAL MODELS OF EXECUTIVE CONTROL

Shifting away from attention, within the construct of executive control is the ability for response inhibition as well as self-control. Neural inhibition (as opposed to behavioral inhibition) is the manner in which one neural structure/system brings about the cessation of activity of another neural structure/system (Brunton, 1983). Four types of neural inhibition have been posited: reciprocal, antagonistic, unidirectional, and lateral (R.A. Cohen, 1993d). Reciprocal inhibition is said to occur when the same system is involved in both the initiation and cessation of the activity; antagonistic inhibition involves incompatible responses (as in reciprocal), but with the responses controlled by differing structures, with one exerting influence on the other. In unidirectional inhibition, one system is seen as impacting another through direct pathways and generally is believed to involve both cortical (frontal) and subcortical processes including the hypothalamus; unidirectional inhibition is critical to system control of behavior. Finally, lateral inhibition is said to occur when adjacent neurons influence each other to bring about a modulated response (R.A. Cohen, 1993d).

Neuropsychological models for inhibition and disinhibition are less well developed. It is generally agreed that neurological influences on inhibition include the limbic system, medial temporal lobe, cingulate, frontal lobes, and the related pathways similar to those involved more generally in executive control. Based on Luria's (1973) model, the caudate and hippocampus are both involved in the elimination or inhibition of responses to irrelevant stimuli, with damage to either of these areas likely to result in impaired selective attention. R.A. Cohen and O'Donnell (1993c) further indicate that the frontal and limbic systems as well as the hypothalamus are involved in the inhibition process.

Specific to the inhibition process, Gorenstein and Newman (1980) focused on the orbitofrontal cortex in concert with the medial septum and hippocampus. Frontal involvement in disinhibition is evident from neuropsychological studies of children with ADHD. For example, Lou, Henrikson, and Bruhn (1984), observing regional cerebral blood flow (rCBF), found hypoperfusion in the frontal lobes of all children with ADHD ($n = 11$) relative to normal controls. Their results also implicated the caudate nucleus and the basal ganglia in hyperactivity. Dysfunction in the caudate had been indicated in a previous study (Lou, Henrikson, Bruhn, Borner, & Nielsen, 1989) and has been supported more recently with children with ADHD (Hynd, Hern, et al., 1991).

DEVELOPMENTAL ISSUES

Because attention and executive control are interconnected and dependent on complex cortical and subcortical structures and systems, the developmental trajectory of the central nervous system is critical. Neurodevelopment follows an ontogenetic course, with primary cortical areas generally mature by birth (Luria, 1980). Secondary and tertiary areas continue to develop postnatally. These include the functional systems involved in learning, memory, emotion, cognition, and language, as well as attention. It has been suggested that not only is there continued development of secondary and tertiary areas, but the pathways that connect structures within these areas and the primary areas also are likely to change over time (Merola & Leiderman, 1985; Rutter, 1981; Vygotsky, 1980). Consistent with this train of thought, Mattes (1980) suggested that one explanation for hyperactivity may be a developmental delay in the myelination of the prefrontal area. To some extent, the developmental sequence for the formation of neural pathways and myelination of locations related to specific behaviors has been identified, but these do not correspond directly to models of cognitive development (Spreen, Risser, & Edgell, 1995).

Directly related to the study of attention and executive control, Luria (1966) suggested that the frontal lobes become functional between the ages of 4 and 7 years. Consistent with Luria's hypothesis, research suggests that the greatest period of frontal lobe development occurs at the 6- and 8-year-old levels (Passler et al., 1985). Subsequent research, however, suggests that the development of frontal lobe functioning continues through at least age 12 (e.g., M.G. Becker, Isaac, & Hynd, 1987; Chelune & Baer, 1986; H. Levin et al., 1991; Welsh, Pennington, & Grossier, 1991).

Knowledge of typical neurodevelopmental progress has increased in the past two decades. The bulk of this knowledge, however, is grounded on observations and informal assessment of individuals with identified brain damage (Reynolds, 1997). Extensive research regarding typical neurodevelopmental trends, particularly in conjunction with higher-order cognitive skills, continues to be needed. As a result, the changing organization of functional systems of the brain in children is only beginning to be understood (Hynd & Willis, 1988). Research to determine the extent of additional development beyond age 12 is necessary. Although research has advanced the understanding of specific disorders (e.g., Alzheimer's), there is even less known regarding the sequence that occurs in the geriatric population and the extent to which typical structural changes in the older adult years can be associated with specific behaviors directly.

SUMMARY

Not only are attention and executive control multifaceted, but both appear to be subserved by a number of brain structures. The multifaceted and systemic nature of attention in particular suggests that attention can be disrupted by damage to myriad components of the CNS. As such, it is not surprising that attentional problems are the most frequent type of cognitive impairment resulting from neurological disorders or dysfunction (R.A. Cohen et al., 1999; Mapou, 1999). When considering constructs as complex as attention and executive control, a one-to-one correspondence between behaviors and brain structure or system is not viable. Taken together, the various models of attention and executive control consistently suggest the interaction of cortical structures (frontal, prefrontal, parietal) with subcortical structures (limbic system, RAS, basal ganglia) as well as the pathways/projections among the basal ganglia, thalamus, and frontal lobes to form a complex functional system. Similarly, both cortical and subcortical structures and the related descending pathways are posited to be involved with inhibition of responses (R.A. Cohen, 1993a, 1993c; R.A. Cohen & O'Donnell, 1993c, 1993d; Luria, 1973). Neurotransmitters, particularly dopamine, are implicated as well. The manner in which a neurological disorder or dysfunction manifests as attentional impairment depends not only on the location of the damage or dysfunction, but also on the extent of that damage or dysfunction.

Barkley (1997a, 1997b) has suggested that there are differences in the ways attentional and executive control deficits manifest in differing subtypes of ADHD, with different neurological substrates implicated. At the same time, the complexity of the constructs suggests that no single measure of the behaviors will provide information that is sufficiently comprehensive to address all facets of attention and executive control. It has been suggested that when one component of attentional processes is disrupted, it is more likely that other components of attention as well as executive control will be affected due to the interconnectedness of these components (Chelune & Baer, 1986; R.A. Cohen, 1993e). Assessment of attention and executive control must be multifaceted, paralleling the complexity of the functional systems involved. The best any single measure, including the CPT, can provide is data on specific aspects of attention and executive control that, in conjunction with other measures, can be considered in diagnostic hypothesis generation and in the monitoring of the treatment and rehabilitation process. Those components of attention and executive control identified in Tables 1.1 and 1.2 that are involved in the performance of a CPT and how they are measured are discussed in Chapter 2.

CHAPTER 2

Continuous Performance Test Paradigms and What They Do

CONCERNS WITH ATTENTION and executive control occur with high frequency regardless of the type of practice or setting or the age of the client. As discussed in Chapter 1, with the complex neurological systems involved, inattention, distractibility, hyperactivity, disinhibition, and related behaviors are associated with a number of disorders across the life span. The very nature of attentional and executive control functional systems makes it a formidable task to assess adequately and accurately the integrity of these systems. Given the association between attention and memory, comprehensive neuropsychological assessment should include measures of attention. For example, the Halstead-Reitan Neuropsychological Test Battery (HRNB: Reitan & Wolfson, 1985), a well-known, widely used and researched battery, includes numerous measures of various forms and aspects of attention, including auditory (linguistic and nonlinguistic) and visual stimuli. Although none are pure measures of attention, the Trail Making Test, Speech Sounds Perception Test, and the Seashore Rhythm Test are heavily laden with attentional demands, reflecting Halstead's (1947) early clinical concerns with attention and vigilance. Similarly, given the importance of assessing frontal lobe functioning, neuropsychological batteries routinely include some measure(s) of executive control.

Mapou (1995; Mateer & Mapou, 1996) provided one possible framework for the assessment of attention that includes components of arousal, focused attention, sustained attention, selective attention, and divided attention. A number of tests have been developed for the purpose of measuring these many facets of attention (R.A. Cohen, 1993a, 1993d). To rule out other confounds (e.g., cognitive ability), the task demands of measures of attention need to involve limited cognitive processing and thus be relatively simple. To eliminate confounds with memory limitations, the memory load must be minimal as well. Where sustained attention is the construct to be measured, repetition and duration of the task are key features. Where focus or selective attention is of interest, the characteristics of the relevant and nonrelevant stimuli become more important. Parameters of task complexity, memory load, temporal demands, processing speed requirements, and task or target salience also need to be considered in the assessment of attention (R.A. Cohen et al., 1999). Similar constraints apply to the measurement of executive control.

The CPT is one group of paradigms for the evaluation of attention and, to a lesser degree, the response inhibition (or disinhibition) component of executive control. CPTs are frequently used to obtain quantitative information regarding an individual's ability to sustain attention over time. The CPT is the most frequently used measure of vigilance (DuPaul, Anastopoulos, Shelton, Guevremont, & Metevia, 1992). It has been found to be sensitive to changes in the CNS in a number of studies (see Reynolds, Lowe, Moore, & Riccio, 1998, for a review; also see Chapters 5, 6, 7 of this volume). The basic paradigm for the CPT involves selective attention or vigilance for an infrequently occurring target or relevant stimulus; the CPT paradigm is generally characterized by rapid presentation of continuously changing stimuli with a designated target stimulus or target pattern. The duration of the task varies but is intended to be sufficient to measure sustained attention. For purposes of this text, and specific to the continuous change required in the above-stated definition, tasks that involved responding only when some aspect of a stimulus (e.g., clown's nose, star on the wing of a plane) changed color or lit up (e.g., J. Goldberg & Konstanareas, 1979; Kirchner, 1976) were excluded.

THE ORIGINAL CPT PARADIGM

Of those components of attention and executive control that were identified in Chapter 1, CPTs may be considered a measure of selective attention, inhibition or filtering of attention, focusing of attention, sustained attention, and response selection and control (R.A. Cohen et al., 1999). The extent to which any specific CPT addresses these components as well as the components of divided attention or response inhibition varies depending on the CPT used and the scores derived. The initial CPT was developed by Rosvold, Mirsky, Sarason, Bransome, and Beck in 1956 to study vigilance. In the original task, letters were presented visually one at a time, at a fixed rate or interstimulus interval (ISI) of 920 ms. The subject was required to respond by pressing a lever whenever the letter X, designated as the target stimulus, appeared. At the same time, the subject was to inhibit responding when any other letter appeared (X-type CPT). A variation of this task in which the target was the letter X only if the X was immediately preceded by the letter A (AX-type CPT), was used as well. Rosvold and colleagues found the X-type CPT correctly classified 84.2% to 89.5% of younger subjects with identified brain damage. Group differences were found between subjects with brain damage and controls on the X-type CPT; the magnitude of the between-group differences was larger with the increased difficulty level of the AX-type CPT.

MODIFICATIONS OF THE ORIGINAL PARADIGM

Since 1956, the CPT has continued to be used in the study of attention as well as impulsivity, with multiple variations in the components of the task. Greenberg and Waldman (1993) suggested there are over 100 different versions of the CPT in use; Halperin (1991) commented that there are as many versions of the CPT available as there are clinicians who used them. One difference across versions of the CPT is the choice of target and nontarget stimuli. For example, the target stimulus in the CPT may be the letter X, as in the original version, or a number (e.g., Gordon, 1983), a picture of an object or person (e.g., V. Anderson, Siegel, Fisch, & Wirt, 1969), a word (e.g., Earle-Boyer, Serper, Davidson, & Harvey, 1991), and so on. The task may be the simpler X-type CPT, an AX-type CPT, or a further modification of the AX such that the target must be preceded by itself (XX-type; e.g., Fitzpatrick, Klorman, Brumaghim, & Borgstedt, 1992). Color and letter are critical features in some CPTs (e.g., orange T followed by a blue S; Garfinkel & Klee, 1983); in others, the target is two digits in a number series (or letters in a letter string) in two consecutive stimulus sets (identical pairs or IP-type CPT; Cornblatt, Lenzenweger, & Erlenmeyer-Kimling, 1989; Cornblatt, Winters, & Erlenmeyer-Kimling, 1989). Another modification involves a change in the directions to respond *except* when the target is presented (not-X type) as in the Conners' CPT (Conners, 1992, 1995). These and other variations are presented in Table 2.1.

Still another variation involves changing the modality such that presentation may be visual, as in the initial version, auditory (e.g., Earle-Boyer et al., 1991; Keith, 1994), or vary from auditory to visual within the same task (e.g., Sandford & Turner, 1994–1999). To increase the difficulty level of the task, thus avoiding ceiling effects with adult subjects, the quality of the stimulus has been degraded or "blurred" (e.g., Buchanan, Strauss, Breier, Kirkpatrick, & Carpenter, 1997; Buchsbaum et al., 1990; Ernst et al., 1997; Hazlett, Dawson, Buchsbaum, & Nuechterlein, 1993; Mansour, Haier, & Buchsbaum, 1996). As can be seen in Table 2.1, target type, modality, and criteria for responding are not the only variations among CPTs. Studies have varied the frequency of the target (however defined) to provide a higher or lower frequency (e.g., Beale, Matthew, Oliver, & Corballis, 1987), or the duration of stimulus presentation has

Table 2.1
Variations in the CPT Paradigm

Study	CPT Type	Stimulus Type	ISI	Modality	Other	Score Types
Arcia & Gualtieri, 1994	X	Letter	1000	Visual	—	Omission and commission errors; reaction time
Bedi et al., 1994	X	Color and form	2500	Visual	—	Omission and commission errors
	X	Number	2000	Auditory	With distractor	Omission and commission errors
Benedict et al., 1994	X	Number	1000	Visual	Degraded; with distraction	Sensitivity (d'); sensitivity decrement over time; correct hits; false alarms
Bock, 1982	X	Letter	1000	Visual	—	Absolute correct; relative correct
Brandt, 1984	X	Number	1200	Auditory	With or without directed attention	Correct hits
Bremer, 1989	X	Letter	1000	Visual	—	Omission and commission errors; reaction time, reaction time standard deviation, reaction time distribution; adjusted percent correct score; anticipatory errors
Buchsbaum & Hazlett, 1989	X	Number	2000	Visual	Degraded	Sensitivity (d'); response bias (Beta)

Study		Stimulus	ISI	Modality	Condition	Measures
Buchsbaum et al., 1988	X	Number	2000	Visual	Degraded	Correct hits; omission and commission errors
Burland, 1985	X	Number	1200	Visual	—	Omission and commission errors; reaction time; variability over time
C. Carter et al., 1995	X	Position of square	2000	Visual	—	Omission and commission errors; reaction time; variability of performance
Chappell et al., 1995	X	Letter	NR	Visual	—	Omission and commission errors
Chee et al., 1989	X	Letter	1000, 2000, 4000	Visual	Also varied stimulus duration	Correct hits; false alarms; reaction time
R.M. Cohen et al., 1987	X	Tone	2000	Auditory	—	Correct hits; false alarms
R.M. Cohen et al., 1988	X	Tone	2000	Auditory	—	Correct hits; false alarms
Craig, 1983	X	Letter	1000	Visual	With and without distractors	Arcsin transformation of omission and late errors; number incorrect responses; reaction time and variability of reaction time
Dainer et al., 1981	X	Letter	1000	Visual	—	Omission and commission errors
Das et al., 1992	X	Fruit	1000	Auditory	—	Omission and commission errors
	X	Fruit and male voice	1000	Auditory	—	Omission and commission errors

(continued)

Table 2.1 Continued

Study	CPT Type	Stimulus Type	ISI	Modality	Other	Score Types
Dupuy, 1995	X	Form	2000	Visual	—	Omission and commission errors; reaction time and reaction time variability
Earle-Boyer et al., 1991	X	Word	1000	Visual	—	Omission and commission errors
	X	Word	1000	Auditory	—	Omission and commission errors
	X	Nonword	1000	Visual	—	Omission and commission errors
	X	Nonword	1000	Auditory	—	Omission and commission errors
Edley & Knopf, 1987	X	Letter	1000	Visual	—	Used ratio scales (relative correct)
Estrin et al., 1988	X	Letter	1000	Visual	—	Omission and commission errors; reaction time
C. Evans, 1988	X	Number	1400	Visual	Degraded; with and without feedback	Correct hits; commission errors
Fitzpatrick et al., 1992	X	Letter	1000–1800	Visual	—	Omission and commission errors; reaction time
Fleming, 1991	X	Number	NR	Visual	Degraded	Correct hits; sensitivity (d'); commission errors; variability of performance across time (vigilance decrement)

Study		Stimulus	Duration	Modality	Condition	Measures
Friedman et al., 1978	X	Number	1500	Visual	—	Reaction time
Friedman et al., 1981	X	Number	1000	Visual	—	Reaction time
Friedman, Erlenmeyer-Kimling, et al., 1985	X	Tone	1000	Auditory	—	Percentage correct hits; percentage errors; reaction time
Garretson et al., 1990	X	Picture of object	3000	Visual	Tangible reinforcers	Correct hits; vigilance decrement; multiple pressing; sensitivity (d'); commission errors
	X	Picture of object	1000	Visual	Tangible reinforcers	Correct hits; vigilance decrement; multiple pressing; sensitivity (d'); commission errors
Gilbert, 1995	X	Letter	975	Visual	Degraded	Sensitivity (d')
Greenberg, 1998	X	Position of square	2000	Visual	—	Omission and commission errors; reaction time; reaction time standard deviation; sensitivity (d')
Greenberg & Waldman, 1993	X	Position of square	2000	Visual	—	Omission and commission errors; anticipatory errors; reaction times; multiple responses; sensitivity (d')
Greenberg, 1996	X	Tone	2000	Auditory	—	Omission and commission errors; reaction time; reaction time standard deviation; sensitivity (d')

(continued)

Table 2.1 Continued

Study	CPT Type	Stimulus Type	ISI	Modality	Other	Score Types
Gribble, 1989	X	Number	1400	Visual	—	Correct hits; commission errors; reaction time
Guich et al., 1989	X	Number	2000	Visual	—	Sensitivity (d')
Harper & Ottinger, 1992	X	Letter	1500	Visual	—	Omission and commission errors
	X	Picture of animals	Varied	Visual	—	Omission and commission errors
Hazlett et al., 1993	X	Number	2000	Visual	Degraded	Sensitivity (d')
Hoffman et al., 1991	X	Number	NR	Visual	Degraded	Sensitivity (d')
Horn et al., 1989	X	Letter	1500	Visual	—	Omission and commission errors
Kaskey et al., 1980	X	Letter	950	Visual	—	Omission and commission errors; reaction time
J. Kaufmann, 1983	X	Letter	1000	Visual	Frequency of targets varied; 6 conditions	Correct hits; sensitivity (d'); vigilance decrement; reaction time; commission errors
Kerns & Rondeau, 1998	X	Animal, animal noises	1500	Visual and Auditory	—	Correct hits; commission errors
Klorman et al., 1983	X	Letter	1000–1500	Visual	—	Proportion omission and commission errors; reaction time
Leark et al., 1999	X	Position of square	2000	Visual	With standard and modified instructions	Omission and commission errors; reaction time; variability; sensitivity (d')

Reference		Modality	Duration	Stimulus	Condition	Measures
Levav, 1991	X	Visual	1000	Letter	With and without degraded stimuli	Reaction time; percent correct hits; percent errors
Levy & Hobbes, 1981	X	Visual	1500	Letter	—	Omission and commission errors; reaction time
Levy & Hobbes, 1988	X	Visual	1500	Letter	—	Omission and commission errors; reaction time
List, 1985	X	Visual	1300	Number	With and without auditory distractors	Omission and commission errors; reaction time
Llorente et al., 2000	X	Visual	2000	Letter	—	Errors of omission and commission; reaction time; reaction time variability
Loiselle et al., 1980	X	Auditory	NR	Tone	—	Reaction time; percentage correct; number of commission errors
Loken et al., 1995	X	Visual	2000–5000	Color and form	Warning stimulus	Omission and commission errors; reaction time
J.F. Lubar et al., 1985	X	Visual	2000	Position of square	—	Omission and commission errors; reaction time; reaction time standard deviation
Mansour et al., 1996	X	Visual	1500	Number	Degraded	Sensitivity (d')
Michael et al., 1981	X	Visual	800	Letter	—	Omission and commission errors
Michaels, 1996	X	Visual	2000	Position of square	—	Omission and commission errors; reaction time; variability

(continued)

Table 2.1 Continued

Study	CPT Type	Stimulus Type	ISI	Modality	Other	Score Types
J.M. Miller, 1996	X	Letter	750	Visual	—	Omission and commission errors
Mirsky & Van Buren, 1965	X	Letter	Varied	Visual	—	Omission and commission errors
	X	Letter	Varied	Auditory	—	Omission and commission errors
W.G. Mitchell et al., 1990	X	Color and form	NR	Visual	With and without distractors; also varied duration	Omission and commission errors
Nuechterlein, 1983	X	Number	1420	Visual	With and without visual distractors; also varied spatial location	Sensitivity (d') and response bias (Beta)
O'Dougherty et al., 1984	X	Number	1400	Visual	With and without degraded stimuli; with and without feedback	Omission and commission errors; sensitivity (d'); response bias (Beta)
O'Dougherty et al., 1988	X	Number	3000	Visual	—	Omission and commission errors; total errors; reaction time; sensitivity (d'); response bias (Beta)
Parasuraman et al., 1991	X	Number	1000	Visual	Standard and degraded	Sensitivity (d'); hit rate; false alarms
Reader et al., 1994	X	Position of square	2000	Visual	—	Omission and commission errors; reaction time; reaction time variability
Riccio et al., 1996	X	Word	1000	Auditory	—	Omission and commission errors; percentage correct; total errors

Study		Stimulus	ISI (ms)	Modality	Condition	Measures
Romans et al., 1997	X	Position of square	2000	Visual	—	Percent commission and omission errors; reaction time
Rosenberg, 1980	X	Letter	1100	Visual	With and without distractor	Correct hits; commission errors; reaction time
Rosvold et al., 1956	X	Letter	920	Visual	—	Total correct/number of responses
Rueckert & Grafman, 1996	X	Letter	800, 1800	Visual	—	Omission and commission errors; reaction time
Rueckert & Grafman, 1998	X	Letter	800, 1800	Visual	—	Omission and commission errors compared across time blocks
Sandford, 1994	X	Number	1000	Auditory and visual	—	Prudence; Consistency; Stamina; Vigilance; Focus; Speed; Response Control Quotient; Attention Quotient; Hyperactivity Scale
Sax, 1995	X	Number	1000	Visual	—	Sensitivity (d'); response bias (Beta)
Schachar et al., 1988b	X	Letter	1500	Visual	—	Omission and commission errors; reaction time
Seidel & Joschko, 1990	X	Letter	1500	Visual	—	Correct hits; commission errors; reaction time; variability of reaction time; sensitivity (d'); total time
Seidman et al., 1995	X	NR	NR	Auditory	—	Omission and commission errors

(continued)

Table 2.1 Continued

Study	CPT Type	Stimulus Type	ISI	Modality	Other	Score Types
Seidman, Biederman, Faraone, Weber, & Oeullette, 1997	X	NR	NR	Auditory	—	Omission and commission errors; late responses
Silverstein et al., 1999	X	Letter	900	Visual	Varied target frequency	Omission and commission errors; reaction time
J. Swartwood, 1994	X	Form and position	2000	Visual	—	Omission and commission errors; reaction time; variability
Sykes et al., 1971	X	Letter	1000, 1500	Visual	With and without distraction	Percent correct of total responses; commission errors
	X	Color and form	1000, 1500	Visual	With and without distraction	Percent correct of total responses; commission errors
Teicher et al., 1996	X	Position of square	2000	Visual	—	Percent correct; commission errors; reaction time; reaction time variability
Tupler, 1989	X	4-Letter noun that represents anything larger than a Volkswagon	1350	Visual	—	Correct hits; commission errors; reaction time
	X	4-Letter noun with "r"	1350	Visual	—	Correct hits; commission errors; reaction time
van den Broek et al., 1997	X	Number	1000	Visual and auditory	—	Prudence; Consistency; Stamina; Vigilance; Focus; Speed; Response Control Quotient; Attention Quotient

Study	Type	Stimulus	ISI	Modality	Condition	Measures
Verbaten et al., 1994	X	Letter	1600	Visual	—	Percent correct hits
A. Wagner, 1987	X	Letter	NR	Visual	—	Omission and commission errors
Werry & Aman, 1975	X	Letter	1000	Visual	—	Omission and commission errors
Wolgin, 1994	X	Position of square	2000	Visual	With and without distractors	Omission and commission errors; multiple responses; reaction time
Allen, 1993	AX	Letter	NR	Visual	—	Correct hits; omissions; commissions; Inconsistency Index (hits/false alarms per block); variability of performance across blocks
August & Garfinkel, 1989	AX	Color and letter	750	Visual	—	Omission and commission errors
Aylward et al., 1990	AX	Number	1000	Visual	—	Omission and commission errors
B.K. Baker, 1990	AX	Letter	1500	Visual	—	Sensitivity (d'); response bias (Beta); reaction time
D.B. Baker et al., 1995	AX	Number	1000	Visual	—	Omission and commission errors
	AX	Number	1000	Auditory	—	Omission and commission errors
Ballard, 1996a	AX	Letter	1000	Visual	Dual screen monitoring	Omission and commission errors

(continued)

29

Table 2.1 Continued

Study	CPT Type	Stimulus Type	ISI	Modality	Other	Score Types
Barkley et al., 1988	AX	Number	800	Visual	—	Omission and commission errors; vigilance correct; delay efficiency ratio
Bawden, 1985	AX	Letter	1300	Visual	—	Omission and commission errors
Beale et al., 1987	AX	Letter	500	Visual	Frequency of target varied	Sensitivity (d'); anticipatory errors (AO); total errors
Bedi et al., 1994	AX	Letter	NR	Visual	—	Omission and commission errors
Bock, 1982	AX	Letter	1000	Visual	—	Absolute correct; relative correct
Brumm, 1994	AX	Letter	1000 ±5%	Visual	—	Sensitivity (d'); response bias; mean ISI; Inconsistency Index; commission errors
Buchsbaum et al., 1985	AX	Letter	400 ±5%	Visual	—	Sensitivity (d')
Chappell et al., 1995	AX	Number	1000 ±5%	Visual	—	Sensitivity (d')
Coffey, 1993	AX	Letter	NR	Visual	—	Omission and commission errors
Dainer et al., 1981	AX	Number	1000	Visual	—	Percent correct; commission errors
Driscoll, 1994	AX	Letter	1000	Visual	—	Omission and commission errors
	AX	Letters	700	Visual	—	Number correct; commission errors

Study	Task	Stimulus	ISI	Modality	Conditions	Measures
Eliason & Richman, 1987	AX	Color and letter	600 ±5%	Visual	—	Omission and commission errors; reaction time
Ellis, 1991	AX	Form	NR	Visual	—	Total correct, omission and commission errors
Ernst et al., 1997	AX	Number	NR	Visual	With auditory distractor; degraded stimuli	Reaction time; correct hits; late responses; incorrect responses
Fallgatter et al., 1997	AX	Letter	1650	Visual	—	Omission and commission errors; reaction time
Gordon, 1983	AX	Number	800	Visual	—	Vigilance correct; omission and commission errors; response latency
	AX	Number	800	Visual	With distractor	Distractibility correct; omission and commission errors; response latency
Halperin et al., 1988	AX	Letter	1500	Visual	—	Errors by type—A not-X (AO), A-only, X-only, random; omission errors
Halperin, Sharma, et al., 1991	AX	Letter	1500	Visual	—	Correct hits; omission and commission errors; reaction time and reaction time variability; Inattention, Dyscontrol and Impulsivity Indices derived from error patterns

(continued)

Table 2.1 Continued

Study	CPT Type	Stimulus Type	ISI	Modality	Other	Score Types
Halperin, Wolf, et al., 1991	AX	Letter	1500	Visual	—	Total omission errors; reaction time; "fast guess" commission errors (AO); "X-only" (OX) errors; and random (NM) errors; Inattention, Dyscontrol and Impulsivity Indices derived from error patterns
Halperin et al., 1992	AX	Letter	1500	Visual	—	Inattention, Dyscontrol and Impulsivity Indices derived from error patterns
Harvey et al., 1990	AX	Number	1000	Visual	—	Omission errors; sensitivity (d')
Healy et al., 1993	AX	Letter	1500	Visual	—	Commission errors; correct hits; reaction time
Hooks et al., 1994	AX	Color and letter	900	Visual	—	Omission and commission errors
Kaskey et al., 1980	AX	Letter	950	Visual	—	Omission and commission errors; reaction time
Kaufmann, 1983	AX	Letter	1000	Visual	—	Correct hits; sensitivity (d'); reaction time
Keefe et al., 1997	AX	Number	1000	Visual	Degraded or standard	Omission and commission errors; sensitivity (d')
Klee & Garfinkel, 1983	AX	Letter	600	Visual	—	Omission and commission errors; total errors
Klorman et al., 1991	AX	Number	1500	Visual	Monetary reinforcement	Omission and commission errors
Koelega et al., 1989	AX	Letter	Varied	Visual	—	Correct hits; commission errors; sensitivity (d')

32

Study	Task	Stimulus	ISI	Modality		Measures
Koriath et al., 1985	AX	Letter	NR	Visual	—	Correct hits; commission errors
Kupietz, 1976	AX	Letter	NR	Visual	—	Omission errors
Kupietz, 1990	AX	Color and letter	800	Visual	—	Commission errors; correct hits; vigilance decrement
Kupietz & Balka, 1976	AX	Letter	1000	Auditory	—	Omission and commission errors
Kupietz & Richardson, 1978	AX	Letter	1000	Auditory	—	Omission and commission errors
	AX	Letter	1000	Visual	—	Omission and commission errors
Lam & Beale, 1991	AX	Letter	500	Visual	—	Sensitivity (d') and bias (Beta)
Lassiter et al., 1994	AX	Letter	800	Visual	—	Omission and commission errors; correct hits
Levav, 1991	AX	Letter	1000	Visual	—	Reaction time; percentage correct hits; percentage errors
Lewis, 1993	AX	Number	800	Visual	—	Vigilance correct; distractibility correct; response latency
	AX	Number	800	Auditory	—	Vigilance correct; distractibility correct; response latency
Loge et al., 1990	AX	Number	800	Visual	—	Vigilance correct; commission errors; distractibility correct; commission errors

(continued)

33

Table 2.1 Continued

Study	CPT Type	Stimulus Type	ISI	Modality	Other	Score Types
Lovejoy & Rasmussen, 1990	AX	Color and letter	NR	Visual	—	Vigilance correct
Luk et al., 1991	AX	Letter	NR	Visual	—	Correct responses; missed responses; unknown (multiple) responses
Matier et al., 1992	AX	Letter	1500	Visual	—	Inattention Index; Dyscontrol Index
McClure & Gordon, 1984	AX	Number	800	Visual	—	Efficiency ratio; total number of responses; number correct
McGrath, 1985	AX	Letter	NR	Visual	—	Omission and commission errors; reaction time
Michael et al., 1981	AX	Letter	800	Visual	—	Omission and commission errors
Milich et al., 1989	AX	Color and letter	900	Visual	—	Omission and commission errors
Mirsky & Van Buren, 1965	AX	Letter	Varied	Visual	—	Omission and commission errors
	AX	Letter	Varied	Auditory	—	Omission and commission errors
Newcorn et al., 1989	AX	Letter	1500	Visual	—	Inattention and Dyscontrol Indices
Newcorn et al., 1994	AX	Letter	1500	Visual	—	Omission and commission errors
Nigg et al., 1996	AX	Letter	1500	Visual	—	Halperin error patterns; Inattention Index; Dyscontrol Index

Study	Paradigm	Stimulus	ISI	Modality	Feedback	Measures
O'Brien et al., 1992	AX	Letter	1500	Visual	—	Omission and commission errors; reaction time; variability of reaction time
Ozolins & Anderson, 1980	AX or XA	Color	NR	Visual	With or without feedback	Correct hits; false alarms; total errors
Pelham et al., 1990	AX	Letter	300, 600, or 900	Visual	—	Percent omission; number of commission errors
Poley, 1995	AX	Number	800	Visual	—	Omission and commission errors
Ponsford & Kinsella, 1992	AX or XA	Color	2000	Visual	—	Correct hits; reaction time
Porrino et al., 1983	AX	Letter	500 ±5%	Visual	—	Omission and commission errors; mean ISI
Raggio, 1992	AX	Letter	800	Visual	—	Omission and commission errors; correct hits
Rapoport et al., 1980	AX	Number	Varied 5%	Visual	—	Omission and commission errors; mean ISI
Rapport et al., 1986	AX	Letter	1500	Visual	—	Omission and commission errors
Rapport et al., 1987	AX	Number	800	Visual	—	Omission errors
Rasile et al., 1995	AX	Number	800	Visual	—	Vigilance correct; distractibility correct; delay correct
Reichenbach et al., 1992	AX	Letter	1500	Visual	—	Inattention Index
Rezai et al., 1993	AX	Color and letter	700	Visual	—	Composite performance score

(continued)

Table 2.1 Continued

Study	CPT Type	Stimulus Type	ISI	Modality	Other	Score Types
Ringholz, 1989	AX	Letter	Varied ±5	Visual	—	Vigilance decrement; commission errors; omission errors; reaction time; mean ISI
Robins, 1992	AX	Number	800	Visual	—	Efficiency ratio: vigilance correct; vigilance commission errors; variability of commission errors
Rosvold et al., 1956	AX	Letter	920	Visual	—	Total correct/number of responses
Rumble, 1984	AX	Number	NR	Visual	—	Omission errors
Schachar et al., 1988a	AX	Number	2000	Visual	—	Omission and commission errors; reaction time
Schachar et al., 1988b	AX	Letter	1500	Visual	—	Omission and commission errors; reaction time
Seidel & Joschko, 1990	AX	Letter	1500	Visual	—	Correct hits; commission errors; reaction time; variability of reaction time; sensitivity (d'); total time
Serper, 1991	AX	Number	NR	Visual	—	Total errors
S. Shapiro & Herod, 1994	AX	Letter	1500	Visual	—	Omission and commission errors; reaction time
Sharma et al., 1991	AX	Form	1500	Visual	—	Inattention Index; Impulsivity Index; reaction time
Slicker, 1991	AX	Letter	700	Visual	—	Inconsistency index; Performance Index; Impulsivity Index

Study	Task	Stimulus	Duration	Modality		Measures
Sostek et al., 1980	AX	Number	800 ±5%	Visual	—	Sensitivity (d'); response bias (Beta)
Sprinkle, 1992	AX	Letter	700	Visual	—	Inconsistency index; omission and commission errors
Stamm et al., 1982	AX	Object	2000	Visual	—	Omission and commission errors; reaction time
H.L. Swanson, 1981	AX	Letter	1000	Visual	—	Correct hits; commission errors; sensitivity (d'); response bias (Beta); vigilance decrement
	AX	Letter	1000	Visual	—	Correct hits; commission errors; sensitivity (d'); response bias (Beta); vigilance decrement
H.L. Swanson, 1983	AX	Letter	1000	Visual	—	Percentage correct; percentage commission errors; sensitivity (d'); response bias (Beta)
	AX	Letter	1000	Auditory	—	Percentage correct; percentage commission errors; sensitivity (d'); response bias (Beta)
H.L. Swanson & Cooney, 1989	AX	Letter	1000	Visual	—	Omission and commission errors; hit rate; sensitivity (d'); response bias (Beta)
	AX	Letter	1000	Auditory	—	Omission and commission errors; hit rate; sensitivity (d'); response bias (Beta)

(continued)

Table 2.1 Continued

Study	CPT Type	Stimulus Type	ISI	Modality	Other	Score Types
Sykes et al., 1971	AX	Letter	1000, 1500	Visual	With and without distraction	Percent correct of total responses; commission errors
Tarnowski et al., 1986	AX	Number	1500	Visual	—	Sensitivity (d'); response bias (Beta)
Teixeira, 1993	AX	Letter	500	Auditory	—	Correct hits; commission errors
T.L. Thompson, 1988	AX	Symbol	400 ±5%	Visual	—	Sensitivity (d'); response bias (Beta); commission errors
R.W. Thompson & Nichols, 1992	AX	Color and letter	NR	Visual	—	Omission and commission errors
A. Wagner, 1987	AX	Letter	NR	Visual	—	Omission and commission errors
Weinstein, 1996	AX	Letter	1200	Visual	With and without distraction	Omission and commission errors
Yepes et al., 1977	AX	Letter	500–1500	Visual	—	Percent absolute correct; percent relative correct; omission and commission errors
Zentall, 1986	AX	Letter	1400	Visual	Varied stimulus to background contrast	Omission and commission scores
Zentall & Meyer, 1987	AX	Letter	1100	Auditory	With distractor	Omission and commission errors
Bergman et al., 1991	XX	Number	NR	Visual	—	Sensitivity (d'); response bias (Beta)

Reference		Stimulus	Duration (ms)	Modality	Condition	Measures
	XX	Form	NR	Visual	—	Sensitivity (d'); response bias (Beta)
Fitzpatrick et al., 1992	XX	Number	1500	Visual	—	Correct hits; reaction time
	XX	Letter	1000–1500	Visual	—	Omission and commission errors; reaction time
Friedman et al., 1981	XX	Number	1000	Visual	—	Reaction time
Friedman et al., 1978	XX	Number	1000	Visual	—	Reaction time
Luk et al., 1991	XX	Playing card	NR	Visual	—	Correct responses; incorrect responses; reaction time; standard deviation of the reaction time
Nuechterlein, 1983	XX	Playing card	1420	Visual	—	Sensitivity (d') and response bias (Beta)
Plomin & Foch, 1981	XX	Playing card	1000	Visual	With and without auditory distractors	Commission errors
Rutschmann et al., 1977	XX	Playing card	NR	Visual	—	Sensitivity (d'); likelihood ratio (L); correct hits
Schachar et al., 1988b	XX	Letter	1500	Visual	—	Omission and commission errors; reaction time
Taylor et al., 1987	XX	Playing card	1000	Visual	—	Correct hits
Valentino et al., 1993	XX	Letter	500	Auditory	—	Omission errors; vigilance decrement
Weiler, 1992	XX	Letter	500	Auditory	—	Omission errors; vigilance decrement

(continued)

Table 2.1 Continued

Study	CPT Type	Stimulus Type	ISI	Modality	Other	Score Types
Driscoll, 1994	2X	Color	700	Visual	—	Number correct; commission errors
	2X	Buzz	2400–3500	Auditory	—	Number correct; commission errors
	2X	Letters	700–900	Visual	—	Number correct; commission errors
Shekim et al., 1986	2X	Light	1000–3000	Visual	—	Omission and commission errors; correct hits
Keilp et al., 1997	Identical pairs	Number string	1000	Visual	—	Sensitivity (d')
	Identical pairs	Form string	1000	Visual	—	Sensitivity (d')
Holcomb et al., 1985	DTM	Symbols	2600	Visual	—	Omission and commission errors; reaction time
T.L. Thompson, 1988	ABCD	Tones	400 ±5%	Auditory	—	Sensitivity (d'); response bias (Beta); commission errors
C.A. Evans, 1988	Not X	Number	1400	Visual	—	Correct hits; commission errors
Cohan, 1995	Not X	Letter	1000, 2000, 4000	Visual	—	Correct hits; commission errors; ISI; reaction time; variability of reaction time
Conners, 1995	Not X	Letter	1000, 2000, 4000	Visual	—	Sensitivity (d') and response bias (Beta); omission and commission errors; correct hits; reaction time; reaction time standard error; reaction time in response to change in ISI; hit rate standard error by block

Study						Measures
Mahan, 1996	Not X	Letter	1000, 2000, 4000	Visual	—	Omission and commission errors; reaction time; reaction time standard error; variability of standard error; response bias (Beta); sensitivity (d')
Nuechterlein, 1983	Not X	Number	1420	Visual	—	Sensitivity (d') and response bias (Beta)
Parr, 1995	Not X	Letter	Varied	Visual	—	Correct hits; omission and commission errors; reaction time variability
Roy-Bryne et al., 1997	Not X	Letter	Varied	Visual	—	Correct hits; standard error of reaction time; standard error across varying ISI; CPT index

Notes: X = Respond when X appears; AX = Respond when X appears, but only if preceded by A; XX = Respond only when X appears on two consecutive trials; respond if two X's appear in string; DTM = Respond if three symbols are present in any order; ABCD = Respond if four-part pattern shows up; Identical pairs = Respond if the same pair shows up in consecutive target strings; Not X = Respond to all targets except X; ISI = Interstimulus Interval measured in milliseconds; NR = Not reported.

been varied (e.g., Chee, Logan, Schachar, Lindsay, & Wachsmuth, 1989). Still other studies have included distractor conditions (e.g., Crosby, 1972), provision of feedback conditions (e.g., O'Dougherty, Nuechterlein, & Drew, 1984), and provision of tangible reinforcers based on performance (e.g., Levy & Hobbes, 1988).

The time lapse between presentations of the stimuli, or ISI, has been varied in studies using a shorter, longer, or variable interval (e.g., Girardi et al., 1995; Rueckert & Grafman, 1996). Variable intervals may be preset such that for some blocks of trials the ISI is at one rate, and for other blocks the ISI is either longer or shorter and is test-generated (e.g., Conners, 1992, 1995). Another method involves an "adaptive" variable rate such that the computer program automatically increases or decreases the ISI by 5% based on the accuracy of the subject's prior response (e.g., Brumm, 1994; Girardi et al., 1995; Rapoport et al., 1980; Weingartner et al., 1980); in this way, the ISI is subject-driven.

EFFECTS OF DIFFERENCES
IN CPT PARAMETERS

As evident in Table 2.1, CPTs reported in the literature include variations in basic task or CPT type, the nature of the target, variations in the ISI, presence or absence of distractors, presence or absence of feedback following responses, modality of presentation, duration of the target presentation, duration of task, and so on. Clearly, the number of possible permutations of these variables is limited only by the imagination of those individuals developing them. Drawing from Broadbent (1953, 1957), it would be expected that the characteristics of the task and target (i.e., novelty, semantic content) could affect the likelihood that irrelevant (non-target) stimuli would be filtered out. The effects on performance of some of these possible variations and modifications to the basic CPT have been investigated (see Ballard, 1996b; Corkum & Siegel, 1993).

Which CPT version is used has been reported to have an effect on CPT scores (e.g., Friedman, Vaughan, & Erlenmeyer-Kimling, 1978, 1981; Schachar, Logan, Wachsmuth, & Chajczyk, 1988a, 1988b). A number of studies have compared performance on the X-CPT to performance on the AX-CPT. Generally, with the same type of target (i.e., letters or numbers), the findings suggested that the AX-CPT is the more difficult task, with some concerns for ceiling effects in adults with the X-CPT (e.g., D. Alexander, 1973; Goldstein, Rosenbaum, & Taylor, 1997; Rosvold et al., 1956). In comparisons of the X-CPT and the XX-CPT, and keeping type of target consistent, findings supported the premise that the X-CPT is the easier task (Friedman et al., 1978, 1981).

For example, Friedman and colleagues (1978) administered an X-CPT and an XX-CPT to six children, ranging in age from 10 to 15 years, who were considered at risk for schizophrenia. For both tasks the stimuli were numbers presented for the same amount of time (50 ms) with an ISI of 1500 ms. Results revealed that the children had longer response times with the XX-CPT as compared to the X-CPT. Friedman et al. (1981) found similar results when comparing an XX-CPT and an X-CPT with a shorter ISI (1000 ms). Unfortunately, the research designs did not include counterbalancing of task order, and all children were administered the XX-CPT first; therefore, the results may reflect practice effects.

In contrast, Schachar et al. (1988a) compared the performance of 114 clinic-referred males, ranging in age from 7 to 11 years, on an X-CPT, an XX-CPT, and an AX-CPT. For all CPT types, the stimulus display time was 500 ms and the ISI was 1500 ms. Unlike the Friedman et al. studies (1978, 1981), the order of administration for the three CPTs was counterbalanced. Results indicated that there was a larger deterioration of performance over time on the XX-CPT and the AX-CPT as compared to the X-CPT. Additional findings included faster reaction times for the AX-CPT and decreased correct hits with the AX-CPT and XX-CPT as compared to the X-CPT. Increased commission errors (false alarms) were evident on the XX-CPT, with more errors occurring with the initial presentation of the target X. Based on their findings, Schachar et al. concluded that the subjects showed a preparation effect evidenced by faster reaction times on the XX-CPT and AX-CPT versions and that there was a speed/accuracy trade-off effect associated with this preparation effect.

Studies have investigated the effect of differing ISIs (Chee et al., 1989; Sykes, Douglas, Weiss, & Minde, 1971) and duration of stimulus presentation (Chee et al., 1989) on performance. Related to ISI, yet discussed less frequently, is the stimulus onset asynchrony (SOA), which is the time between the onset of one stimulus and the onset of the next stimulus. The SOA is the sum of the duration of the stimulus presentation and the ISI, and, therefore, should be sensitive to the effects on differences in duration of presentation and differences in ISI. For example, Chee et al. administered the CPT with three different ISIs (1000 ms, 2000 ms, and 4000 ms) and systematically varied the duration of stimulus display at the same time. The effect of changing the stimulus display time thus resulted in varying SOAs as well. With children, Chee and colleagues found that correct hits decreased at the slowest and fastest ISIs and with decreasing display duration. Commission errors were also higher with the longer ISI and shorter display time. Finally, they found that a slower reaction time was associated with the longer ISI and longer display time. Chee and colleagues also found that stimulus display times impacted on performance, with the longer display time (800 ms) resulting in increased correct hits and reduced commission errors as compared to shorter display times (200 or 400 ms).

In addition to investigating effects of differences in duration of stimulus presentation, differences in target frequency have been studied (e.g., Silverstein, Weinstein, Turnbull, & Nader, 1999). Using the Vigil CPT (Vigil, 1996), Silverstein and colleagues compared CPT performance under three conditions of target frequency. The first of these conditions was referred to as an accelerating format (AF); here, the proportion of targets increased as the task progressed. In the second or high-frequency (HF) condition, the target frequency (90% of stimuli were targets) was consistent throughout the task. The third condition was the standard format, with a 30% target frequency maintained throughout the test. For all three conditions, an X-CPT with letters as stimuli were used. The stimulus duration was 85 ms, the ISI was 900 ms, and the task duration was 8 minutes across all conditions. Results indicated significant differences for all variables of interest. Omission and commission errors were lowest in the standard condition and highest in the HF condition. In contrast, reaction time was fastest in the HF condition and slowest in the standard version (Silverstein et al., 1999).

Modality differences have been compared as well, with corresponding differences found in CPT performance (e.g., D. Baker, Taylor, & Leyva, 1995; Draeger, Prior, & Sanson, 1986; Driscoll, 1994; Sandford, Fine, & Goldman, 1995a, 1995b; Sykes, Douglas, & Morganstern, 1972). D. Baker and colleagues administered both the Gordon Diagnostic System (GDS; Gordon, 1983) and the Comprehensive Auditory Visual Attention Assessment System (CAVAAS; L.E. Becker, 1993) to 82 college students ranging in age from 17 to 45 years. Using a counterbalanced design, the students completed four tasks (auditory vigilance, visual vigilance, auditory distractibility, visual distractibility). Based on comparison of omission and commission errors by tasks, D. Baker et al. found that college students performed better on visual than auditory tasks. Sandford and Turner (1995) reported similar findings, with children with ADHD making more commission errors when the stimuli were presented in the auditory format. These findings suggest that auditory vigilance tasks may be more sensitive and, hence, more useful in the identification of problems with sustained attention and executive control.

In another study, C. Evans (1988) compared performance on a standard X-CPT, an X-CPT with degraded or blurred stimuli, an X-CPT with feedback following each response, and a not-X-CPT. Findings suggested that the condition with degraded stimuli was the most difficult, and the standard X-CPT was the easiest. In other studies, the nature of the target (i.e., animal vs. letter; nonword vs. word) has been found to impact on CPT performance (e.g., Earle-Boyer et al., 1991; Harper & Ottinger, 1992). Blurring may, however, simply enhance the higher-level processing component and not necessarily the attentional demands, or at least not proportionately so, making it potentially a confound for assessing arousal and selective attention.

As noted in Table 2.1, the addition of extraneous noise or other distractors is another permutation of the CPT paradigm, with inclusion of distractors reported to influence performance (e.g., Crosby, 1972; Davies & Davies, 1975; Franke, Maier, Hardt, Hain, & Cornblatt, 1994; Golier et al., 1997; Hoy, Weiss, Minde, & Cohen, 1978; R. Parasuraman, 1984b). Sykes and colleagues (1971) investigated the impact of multiple permutations of the CPT. They assessed 40 children with hyperactivity and 19 control children ranging in age from 5 to 12 years on two versions of the X-CPT and an AX-CPT in two different noise conditions (minimal noise, intermittent white noise) with two ISIs (1000 ms and 1500 ms). Total correct hits and error scores were the dependent variables. Results indicated a main effect for ISI for total correct responses and error scores such that both groups of children performed better when the ISI was longer regardless of the noise condition. Crosby used a visual X-CPT and an AX-CPT with children under three conditions: no distractors, auditory distractors, and visual distractors. Results revealed deterioration in performance for all groups under the distractor conditions as compared to the no-distractor condition. Similarly, Franke et al., Golier et al., and Hoy et al., with different populations (i.e., clinical and control groups), consistently found a decline in performance for both the clinical and control groups under the distractor conditions. In the D. Baker et al. (1995) study described above, college students found the vigilance tasks to be less difficult in comparison to the distractibility tasks, as evidenced in increased errors on the distractibility tasks.

Another variable that differs across CPTs is the duration of the task itself. The condensed version of the MINI-CPT (Bremer, 1989) is probably one of the shortest available CPTs, with a duration of 3 minutes; in the standard form, the MINI-CPT is 6 minutes in length. On the other hand, the Test of Variables of Attention (TOVA; Greenberg, 1988–1999) is approximately 22 minutes long. At the extreme end, at least one CPT lasts over 30 minutes (Mansour et al., 1996). Obviously, the extent to which one can interpret the results as indicative of sustained attention is directly linked to the length of time (duration) the individual must sustain attention. On the other hand, tasks that are too long would not be practical for clinical use.

OTHER FACTORS KNOWN TO INFLUENCE CPT PERFORMANCE

Other experimenter-manipulated variables have been identified as potential factors influencing CPT performance (see Ballard, 1996b; Corkum & Siegel, 1993; Lowe, Reynolds, Riccio, & Moore, 2000). These factors include lighting or illumination (e.g., Campanelli, 1970) and time of day (e.g., A. Davies & Davies, 1975). For example, Davies and Davies assessed 40 older adults, ranging in age from 65 to 72 years, and 40 younger adults, ranging in age from 18 to 31 years, on the X-CPT. Independent variables of age (younger vs. older), noise (quiet vs. loud), and time of day (morning vs. afternoon) were of interest in their study. Main effects were found for time of day and age, with an interaction effect for age by time of day for correct hits. Regardless of the time of day, younger adults had a higher correct hit rate than older adults; regardless of group, individuals did better (more correct hits) in the afternoon. Finally, the improvement in correct hits in the afternoon as compared to the morning was greater for the older adults than for the younger group. In contrast, error rates increased in the morning and in the loud noise condition and were more likely to be delayed responses.

As pointed out in Ballard's (1996b) review, room temperature has been found to affect CPT performance (Enander, 1987; Hancock, 1984; Hancock & Warm, 1989). Deterioration of performance has been associated with colder room temperatures (e.g., Enander, 1987; Hancock, 1984), whereas sudden exposure to rooms with warmer temperatures has been associated with enhanced CPT performance (Hancock, 1984; Hancock & Warm, 1989). Clearly, as evidenced by the impact of distractors to the task itself, the room where the CPT is administered should be quiet, free from distraction (Conners, 1992, 1995), and of moderate temperature.

Another factor found to impact CPT performance is examiner presence or absence during the administration of the CPT (e.g., Draeger et al., 1986; Power, 1992). In the Draeger et al. study, using an auditory paradigm (target was "dog" presented to either ear), the performance of 16 children with ADHD and 16 control children was recorded under two conditions: examiner present and examiner absent. For children with ADHD as well as normal controls, a decline in performance was found to occur when the experimenter was absent, with the children with ADHD demonstrating greater deterioration. Results of the Power study support this finding, with some indications that the child's level of aggression was a factor in the deterioration of performance in the examiner-absent condition. Moreover, Power found that the performance decrement was greater when the examiner-absent condition occurred second as opposed to first in the sequence. Given these differences in performance based on examiner presence or absence, the applicability of CPT norms and the interpretation of CPT performance must take this factor into account (Lowe et al., 2000).

Related to examiner presence or absence, differences in the instructional set or directions given to the individual have been investigated (e.g., Sergeant & Scholten, 1985; Tupler, 1989). For example, Sergeant and Scholten administered the CPT under three different instructional set conditions. In one condition (speed), the instructions emphasized the need to respond as quickly as possible; in a second condition (accuracy), the instructions emphasized the need for accuracy; the third condition was the standard directions with both accuracy and speed emphasized. Results indicated that performance of control children was directly impacted by the instructional set, with decreased errors in the accuracy condition and increased errors in the speed condition. More recently, Leark, Dixon, Hoffman, and Huynh (1999) replicated these findings. They concluded that differences in performance could be elicited by changing the instructions given to the individuals taking the test. Manner of presentation of instructions (as opposed to content) has been investigated as well. Tupler evaluated adults with two instructional set conditions: graphemic and semantic. Adults in the semantic instruction condition were found to detect fewer signals, make more commission errors, and demonstrate longer latencies in responding as compared to adults in the graphemic instruction group.

Similarly, as noted in Corkum and Siegel's (1993) review, the provision of feedback (e.g., O'Dougherty et al., 1984; Ozolins & Anderson, 1980) and the provision of tangible reinforcers (e.g., Levy & Hobbes, 1988) have been found to impact the overall performance of individuals. O'Dougherty and colleagues used feedback and no-feedback conditions with children. The feedback consisted of a bell ringing each time the child correctly detected the target. Results indicated that all groups demonstrated a higher hit rate under the feedback as opposed to the no-feedback condition. Levy and Hobbes investigated the effects of feedback and contingency with the GDS using four conditions: reward, response cost, reward plus response cost, and no feedback or contingency. Children in the reward group were given a point each time they made a correct response; those in the response cost group lost a point from a starting total of 45 points each time they made an error. The combined reward plus response cost earned or lost points based on the accuracy of their responses. The no-feedback or contingency group did not earn or lose points during the task. The only difference that emerged was the finding that the response cost group made fewer errors of omission than the control (no-feedback or contingency) group. The ease of the task, rewarding nature of the task, and absence of immediate feedback were offered as explanations for the absence of more significant effects. However, in another study, it was found that the provision of incentives did not significantly impact CPT performance and that motivational issues did not account for the vigilance decrement evidenced (Corkum, Schachar, & Siegel, 1996).

Findings from these studies (e.g., Leark et al., 1999; Power, 1992) emphasize the importance of standardization procedures and adherence to these procedures in the administration of the CPT. Thus, modification of parameters of the task or the environmental constraints of the task, including the instructions given, can impact the overall results and, by implication, affect the interpretation. Many of the programs available allow for further manipulation of the variables by the clinician (e.g., Conners, 1992, 1995; Gordon, 1983). Given the number of CPTs in use for both research and clinical purposes, there is a paucity of studies that have explored the numerable differences across various population samples. As such, given the potential number of permutations, the impact of all these possible differences or combinations of differences on the clinical findings and conclusions reached is not known at this time.

SCORES REPORTED FOR THE CPT

When Rosvold and colleagues (1956) introduced the CPT, the focus was on correct hits (number or percent of correct responses to targets) as an indication of selective attention (e.g., Allen, 1993, Brumm, 1994; C. Carter, Krener, Chaderjian, Northcutt, & Wolf, 1995). Since that time, other variables have been used as measures of CPT performance. Examples of types of scores reported in the research literature are included in Table 2.1. Some of these, matched to components of attention and executive control identified in Chapter 1, are presented in Table 2.2. For example, both correct hits and omission errors (i.e., number of targets not responded to and, therefore, the inverse of correct hits) are interpreted as indicative of alertness (Gordon Systems, Inc., 1986) as well as the individual's ability (as measured by correct hits) or inability (as measured by omission errors) to selectively attend to (focus on) the target. The number of commission errors, or responses to stimuli other than the target, is frequently reported as a measure of response inhibition (or disinhibition), impulsivity, or response control. Additionally, relative accuracy, defined as the percent of correct responses of total responses (including incorrect responses), or total errors (combining omission and commission errors) may be reported (e.g., Bock, 1982).

CPTs also can be viewed as measures of cognitive efficiency. In addressing issues of cognitive efficiency and processing capability, reaction time is another measure frequently reported. Reaction time or latency is believed to reflect the speed of processing and decision to respond as well as the speed of motor responding. Reaction time may be reported directly as latency or reaction time or as a Speed Quotient (Sandford & Turner, 1995). For example, children with memory disorders may demonstrate increased omission errors and a slower rate of responding without an associated increase in commission errors; this type of pattern is believed to support the hypothesis of difficulty with allocation of processing resources (Eliason & Richman, 1987). Another method of ascertaining the information-processing capability of the

Table 2.2

Common Continuous Performance Test Indices and What They May Measure

Component of Attention/ Executive Control	CPT Variable
Alertness/arousal	Correct hits Omission errors Random errors Readiness Persistence
Selective or focused attention	Correct hits Omission errors Vigilance Perceptual sensitivity (d') Comprehension
Sustained attention	Perceptual sensitivity (d') Reaction time block change (slope) Stamina Focus Consistency or inconsistency Vigilance decrement Block comparison for accuracy (slope) Block comparison for errors (slope)
Consistency of responding	Consistency Reaction time standard deviation Reaction time standard error Standard deviation of standard error Inconsistency index
Response speed/information processing speed	Reaction time/latency Speed quotient Focus
Response inhibition or dyscontrol	Anticipatory errors Response bias (Beta) Commission errors Random errors False alarms Multiple responses Prudence quotient
Shifting/alternating attention	Speed Balance Readiness Consistency Focus

Notes: Variable names and what they are purported to measure are based on the differing CPTs available (i.e., no CPT will provide all the variable names listed here, and some of the indices listed are specific to one CPT type).

individual is the use of an adaptive rate ISI. In those studies that employ an adaptive rate ISI, the mean ISI is believed to reflect the response latency associated with accuracy in responding (e.g., Girardi et al., 1995; Rapoport et al., 1980; Weingartner et al., 1980).

Another variable of interest is the consistency or variability of the individual's performance over time. As such, some CPT programs also provide information on the standard deviation of the reaction time across blocks as a measure of consistency in responding and ability to sustain attention over time. Some researchers argue that the standard error of the reaction time (e.g., Cohan, 1995) is a better indicator of the variability of responding over time. Still others use the standard deviation of the standard error over time as an indication of consistency (E. Levin, Wilson, et al., 1996; Mahan, 1996). The use of variability of reaction time may be confounded to a large extent with IQ. Jensen's (e.g., 1982; Vernon, 1989) extensive work on chronometrics notes significant correlations between the standard deviation of reaction time and traditional IQ measures (e.g., the Wechsler scales). These values often exceed the correlation between reaction time and IQ, sometimes reaching values as high as .60 to .70 (Vernon, 1989). This variability statistic is nonetheless more sensitive to CNS trauma than an IQ score and deserves considerably more study at this juncture. Another method of looking at consistency involves looking at the change in reaction time as measured by the slope over the duration of the task as well as comparing block scores over time (Gordon Systems, Inc., 1986). Similarly, the Consistency Quotient generated on the Integrated (or Intermediate) Visual and Auditory Continuous Performance Test (IVA; Sandford & Turner, 1994–1999) is believed to reflect the consistency of responding as well as fluctuations in attention over time. When the CPT includes a systematic variation of the ISI (e.g., Conners, 1992, 1995), an additional indicator of variability is the change in reaction time as a function of the change in the ISI as well as the standard error of this change. Finally, the Focus Quotient (Sandford & Turner, 1994–1999; Turner & Sandford, 1995a, 1995b) is based on the number of responses that have reaction times that are inconsistent (outliers) with the remaining response reaction times.

Related to consistency or variability, on tasks of sustained attention, the vigilance decrement is also of concern (Parasuraman, 1984a, 1984b). The term "vigilance decrement" is used to refer to the decline in performance (i.e., the extent to which the individual's accuracy declines over the course of the task) and may or may not include consideration of the decreased speed (or increased latency) in responding over time. Rather than relying on differences in the reaction time as a measure of consistency over time, some clinicians focus on comparisons of correct and incorrect responses over differing blocks of time within the same administration to determine if there is a significant vigilance decrement (e.g., Fleming, 1991). Some programs provide comparative information from blocks at the beginning of the task and at the end of the task (e.g., Conners, 1992, 1995). Alternatively, the vigilance decrement may be reflected by derived quotients (e.g., Stamina Quotient of the IVA; Sandford & Turner, 1994–1999). There is also an Inconsistency Index that is based on the change in the number of hits and false alarms per block (e.g., Allen, 1993; Brumm, 1994; Slicker, 1991). In contrast, Levav (1991) computed a Sustain Factor based on correct responses over time to assess variability. Regardless of the label used, the vigilance decrement is considered an index of sustained attention (R.A. Cohen et al., 1999).

Within the more inclusive variable of commission errors, researchers have investigated the types of errors produced. One broad category of commission errors is referred to as target-related errors (e.g., Gordon Systems, Inc., 1986). For example, on the AX-CPT, a target-related error is when the individual responds to the occurrence of the letter A when it is not followed by an X or an AO sequence. A second target-related error is to respond to the X when it is not preceded by the A or an OX sequence. Thus, in target-related errors, at least one item in the sequence is relevant to the correct target. Halperin and colleagues (1988) offered additional subtypes of commission errors. Specifically, they identified a fast reaction-time response associated with impulsivity and hyperactivity and a slow reaction-time response or delayed response associated with inattention. In those studies that differentiate commission errors into false responses as opposed to delayed responses, the false responses are believed to reflect impulsivity, whereas delayed responses are believed to be a secondary indication of inattention (Halperin, Wolf, Greenblatt, & Young, 1991).

In contrast to target-related errors, random errors are those responses to a sequence that include neither the A nor the X or an NM sequence (e.g., Gordon Systems, Inc., 1986). Alternatively, commission errors subtyped as random errors are not associated directly with inattention, impulsivity, or hyperactivity (Halperin, Wolf, et al., 1991). It has been suggested that the random type of commission error may be reflective of dyscontrol (Halperin, Sharma, Greenblatt, & Schwartz, 1991). Alternatively, random errors may be associated with problems in the individual's overall level of arousal or a lack of motivation (Gordon Systems, Inc., 1986). The extent to which interpretation of the commission error subtypes (AO, OX, NM) is supported by electrophysiological data is discussed in Chapter 5.

Based on their findings, Halperin and colleagues (1988; Halperin, Sharma, et al., 1991; Halperin, Wolf, et al., 1991) used combinations of commission error types and omission errors and developed various indices, including an Inattention/Passivity Index, an Impulsivity Index, and a Dyscontrol Index. Two additional error response patterns also are considered in the literature. Anticipatory errors are those responses that occur within a very short (predetermined) period of time following the display of the stimulus (Bremer, 1989); these are most similar to Halperin's fast reaction-time response. Alternatively, some programs provide a measure of multiple responses to the same stimulus (i.e., the individual responds more than once to the same stimulus). Multiple responses are believed to reflect hyperresponsivity (Sandford & Turner, 1994–1999) and may be most consistent with motor disinhibition as compared to other types of error responses.

Direct performance scores are the most easily obtained; however, many clinicians incorporate signal detection theory (SDT) in generating performance indices (e.g., Keilp, Herrera, Stritzke, & Cornblatt, 1997; Klorman, Brumaghim, Fitzpatrik, & Borgstedt, 1991; Koelega, Brinkman, Hendriks, & Verbaten, 1989; Liu, Hwu, & Chen, 1997). SDT posits that the decision to respond is based on the subject's setting himself or herself a certain standard or criterion for responding. SDT procedures are based on signal to noise (or nonsignal) ratios, and calculations are based on the distributions of responses to both signal and noise (R.A. Cohen, 1993a). For example, sensitivity (d' or d-prime) is derived from the mean distribution of responses to both signal and noise such that d' is equivalent to the difference between the sum of the distributions for both signal and noise, and noise alone. Sensitivity (d') is believed to represent the likelihood that the individual will detect the signal or respond to the target when the target is presented or the ability to discriminate targets from nontargets. Sensitivity (d') is believed to be dependent on the intensity of the stimulus and the sensitivity of the individual; it reflects the individual's ability to discriminate among stimuli. Response bias (Beta or lnB) is the other index that is derived based on SDT. Also referred to as response style or response criterion, Beta is believed to reflect the extent to which the individual is being conservative or impulsive in responding. Response bias is presumed to relate to the strategy used in making the decision to respond or the individual's response style; it is interpreted as representing the individual's tendency toward risk taking as well. Bias also contributes to the likelihood that a correct response will be made. For example, individuals who tend to be cautious and conservative in responding are more likely to miss signals (increased omission errors) but to have fewer commission errors. On the other hand, if the response style is less cautious, the individual may have decreased omission errors but increased commission errors. Because of the manner in which d' and Beta are computed (see Swets, 1964, 1973, 1984), Beta is also dependent on sensitivity.

As noted, many researchers use the measures of sensitivity (d') and response bias (Beta) based on SDT in reporting CPT scores; however, concerns have been raised as to the applicability of SDT to CPT performance (e.g., Jerison, 1967; Parasuraman, 1979). Based on SDT, the sensitivity and bias indices may be more sensitive to differences in performance on the CPT than omission or commission errors (Lam & Beale, 1991). R.A. Cohen (1993d) argued that SDT procedures may be particularly useful in neuropsychological assessment. SDT allows for the determination of response characteristics based on the frequency of the targets and is easily converted into indices for assessing the vigilance decrement and response inconsistency (R.A. Cohen et al., 1999). At the same time, it has been argued that the CPT does not truly meet the suggested criterion for SDT application (Parasuraman & Davies, 1977). Specifically, Parasuraman and Davies stated that only those tasks that require successive discrimination would show the sensitivity decrement with SDT. For successive discrimination, the target is a change in some feature (i.e., color or size) of the standard stimulus presented on all trials (Parasuraman, 1984a, 1984b); this is not the case for the CPT paradigm. Parasuraman also argued that for changes in d' to occur, the task must be of sufficient duration (i.e., 30–45 minutes). Thus, the arguments against the application of SDT to the CPT are related to characteristics of the task itself. Alternatively, R.A. Cohen pointed out that for those CPTs that have an increased emphasis on reaction time and test-generated changes in the ISI, vigilance is likely to be more variable and the CPT should approximate the traditional SDT task more closely.

The preceding discussion of possible score types is not exhaustive, but demonstrates the myriad methods available for measuring CPT performance. The sheer number of possibilities raises the question of which method of measurement is "better" or which method or variables increase the usefulness of the results in clinical practice. Unfortunately, few studies have investigated how score type differences may impact the interpretation of CPT performance. Buchsbaum and Sostek (1980) examined test-retest reliability for multiple indices of CPT performance using a visual AX-CPT with an adaptive rate ISI with 400 volunteers 18 to 22 years of age. Results indicated that the mean ISI was the most reliable measure temporally for Block 1 ($r = .74$), followed by commission errors ($r = .59$), d' ($r = .58$), Beta ($r = .39$), and omission errors ($r = .20$). The mean ISI was found to be significantly and inversely associated with d' ($r = -.77$) and Beta ($r = -.38$). In comparing blocks of time on the same administration, Buchsbaum and Sostek found a decrement in performance as measured by d'; however, the extent of the decrement varied as a function of d' in Block 1. For those subjects with a low d' for Block 1, there was less decrement of performance in Block 2. Conversely, for those with a higher d' in Block 1, Beta increased in Block 2, suggesting that the behavior became more conservative.

SUMMARY

The basic paradigm for the CPT was initially designed almost 50 years ago for the assessment of attention and, to a lesser degree, response inhibition or dyscontrol. Today, there are numerous variations of the CPT used in clinical and research settings. As can be seen in Table 2.1, the potential combinations and permutations that could be used in the development of a CPT are probably infinite. At the same time, different CPTs and clinicians report numerous scores for use in interpretation. Notably, the effect of the permutations as well as the scores used in the interpretation process on the usefulness of the CPT has not been investigated thoroughly. Research studies that incorporate multiple CPT paradigms with the same populations and extensive scoring options are needed. Further, there is no comparative discussion of CPTs available for use in clinical and research settings.

CPTs used in clinical settings need to be held to the same standards of technical adequacy and psychometric properties as any other measures used. The number of CPTs in use and the number of differences across CPTs suggest that although CPTs may constitute a similar group of tasks with a common paradigm, they are also very distinct in what they measure (Conners, 1992, 1995); as such, CPTs are not substitutable for one another. To highlight further some of the differences as well as similarities, four of the commercially available CPTs are discussed in greater detail in Chapter 3; the extent to which these four CPTs address the issues of standardization and meet the rigors of technical adequacy also are presented.

CHAPTER 3

Major CPTs in Clinical Use: Configuration, Use, and Technical Adequacy

As NOTED IN Chapter 2, since the introduction of the early versions of the CPT (by Rosvold and colleagues in 1956 with specific parameters), a plethora of CPTs have been developed. However, only a few of the CPTs are commercially available; these are identified, with publisher information, in Table 3.1. From the commercially available CPTs, four have been selected for inclusion in this text based on the differences in CPT parameters among the four tasks. The four tasks are the Conners' CPT (Conners, 1992, 1995), the Gordon Diagnostic System (GDS; Gordon, 1983), the Integrated (or Intermediate) Visual and Auditory CPT (IVA; Sandford & Turner, 1994–1999), and the Test of Variables of Attention (TOVA; Greenberg, 1988–1999) and TOVA-Auditory (TOVA-A; Greenberg, 1996–1999). Some of these measures have been reviewed elsewhere (see Dumont, Tamborra, & Stone, 1995, 1999; Grooms, 1998). In addition to the basic description of the tasks themselves, given the potential effect of instructional set, examiner presence or absence, and other factors as discussed in Chapter 2, the extent to which the administration directions and standardization accounted for these factors is highlighted. Following a description of each of the task demands, several aspects that relate to technical adequacy (i.e., normative data, types of score formats, reliability, etc.) as provided in the individual test manuals will be presented. For easy reference, comparative information is listed in Table 3.2.

Table 3.1

Commercially Available Continuous Performance Tests (CPTs)

CPT	Publisher
Auditory Continuous Performance Test (ACPT: R. Keith, 1994)	The Psychological Corporation 555 Academic Court San Antonio, TX 78204 Attn: Clinical Sales 800-211-8378 www.psychcorp.com
Comprehensive Attention Battery CPT (CAB:CPT, Rodenbough, in press)	John Rodenburgh, PsyD Neuropsychworks, Inc. 411-C Parkway Street Greensboro, NC 27401 910-373-0094 cab@neuropsychworks.com www.neuropsychworks.com
Conners' CPT (Conners, 1992, 1995)	MultiHealth Systems, Inc. 908 Niagara Falls Boulevard North Tonawanda, NY 14120-2060 416-414-1700 or 800-456-3003 www.mhs.com (also distributed by The Psychological Corporation)
Gordon Diagnostic System (GDS: Gordon, 1983)	Gordon Systems, Inc. P.O. Box 746 DeWitt, NY 13214 800-550-2343 www.gsi-add.com
Integrated (or Intermediate) Visual and Auditory CPT (IVA: Sandford & Turner, 1995)	BrainTrain 727 Twin Ridge Lane Richmond, VA 23235 804-320-0105 braintrain@braintrain-online.com www.braintrain-online.com
MINI-CPT (Bremer, 1989)	David Bremer Central Oahu Community Mental Health Center Hawaii State Department of Health 860 4th Street Pearl City, Hawaii
Raggio Evaluation of Attention Deficit Disorder (READD: Raggio, 1991)	Donald J. Raggio, PhD Director of Developmental Psychology University of Mississippi Medical Center 2500 North State Street Jackson, MS 39216-4505
Test of Variables of Attention (TOVA: Greenberg, 1988–1999); Test of Variables of Attention—Auditory (TOVA-A: Greenberg, 1996–1999)	Universal Attention Disorders, Inc. 4281 Katella Avenue, Suite 215 Los Alamitas, CA 90720 800-729-2886 info@uad.com www.tovatest.com (also distributed by Western Psychological Services)
Vigil Continuous Performance Test (Vigil, 1996)	The Psychological Corporation 555 Academic Court San Antonio, TX 78204 Attn: Clinical Sales 800-211-8378 www.psychcorp.com

Table 3.2

Comparisons across Major Commercially Available Continuous Performance Tests

	Conners' CPT	GDS	IVA	TOVA/TOVA-A
Configuration				
CPT type(s)	Not-X	AX (children, adult) X (preschool)	X	X (TOVA/TOVA-A)
Modality	Visual	Visual	Visual and auditory (same task)	Visual (TOVA)/Auditory (TOVA-A)
Stimulus display time (ms)	250	200	167 (auditory) 500 (visual)	100 (TOVA/TOVA-A)
Interstimulus interval	Varied within each block: 1,000, 2,000, 4,000	1,000 (children, adult) 2,000 (preschool)	1,500	2,000
Target	Letter	Number	Number	Position (up/down) of square within square (TOVA)/Tone (TOVA-A)
Task duration	14 minutes	9 minutes (children) 6 minutes (adults, pre-school)	13 minutes	Clinical Version: 22 min-utes (TOVA/TOVA-A) Preschool and brief ver-sion: 11 minutes (TOVA)
One or more stimuli as nontargets	More than 1	More than 1	1	1 (TOVA/TOVA-A)
Distraction/no distraction	No distraction only	Vigilance: no distraction Distractibility: with dis-traction (No distractibility task for preschool)	No distraction only	No distraction only
Stimulus quality (standard or degraded)	Standard	Standard	Standard	Standard

(continued)

Table 3.2 Continued

	Conners' CPT	GDS	IVA	TOVA/TOVA-A
Feedback or reinforcement condition	None	None	None	None
Target frequency varied	No	No	Yes	Yes
Divided into blocks	Yes	Yes	Yes	Yes
Can task be customized	Yes	Yes	No	No
Administrative Features				
Standardized instructions	Yes, but manual is not specific on additional prompts	Yes	Yes, computer generated	Yes
Stipulation of examiner presence or absence	Absent (by implication)	Present	Present (by implication)	Present
Practice trials provided	Yes	Yes	Yes	Yes
Observation scale	No	Yes	Yes	Yes
Other components?	No	No	Self-report	Rating scales; interview; success form; diagnostic checklist
Technical Features				
Sampling plan for normative data collection	No	No	No	No
Dates of norming specified	No	No	No	No
Size of normative sample (nonreferred only)	520	1,019 children 247 preschool 80 adult 43 older adult	781	1,596 (TOVA) 2,551 (TOVA-A)

Age distribution (nonreferred)	4 to 70 years	6 to 16 years (children) 4–5 years (preschool) 18–49 years (adult) 50 and older (older adult)	5 to 90 years	4 to 80 years (Brief TOVA) 6 to 80 years (TOVA) 6 to 19 years (TOVA-A)
Gender distribution (nonreferred)	51.2% male	59.75% male (adults); not reported for preschool, children, older adults	46% males	45% males (TOVA) 50% males (TOVA-A)
Extent of ethnic group representation (nonreferred)	Not reported	58.75% African American (adults); not reported for preschool, children, older adults	Not reported	Not reported for TOVA; 99% Caucasian for TOVA-A
Geographic areas represented	FL, KS, PA, NC, CA, Ontario	Syracuse, NY (91%) and Charlottesville, VA (9%) for children/preschool; not reported for adult/older adult		Minneapolis, MN (TOVA/TOVA-A)
Community variables (i.e., size of community) identified	Not reported	Not reported	Not reported	Not reported
Socioeconomic status reported	Not reported	Not reported	Not reported	Not reported
Educational levels reported	Not reported	Not reported for children; frequency reported for adults and older adults	Not reported	Not reported
Evidence of internal consistency	Not reported	Children's vigilance: alternate forms comparison	Not reported	Within condition comparison for blocks

(continued)

Table 3.2 Continued

	Conners' CPT	GDS	IVA	TOVA/TOVA-A
Evidence of temporal reliability	Not reported	Test-retest: at 2–22 days range from .67–.85 on vigilance and distractibility (children); test-retest: at 1 year range of .68–.94 for vigilance (children); no test-retest reported for preschool or adult versions	Not reported	Test-retest: at 90 minutes range from .77 to .93 on TOVA; no test-retest for TOVA-A reported
Validity studies (convergent) included in the manual	Not reported	For specific age groups data provided for correlation with IQ, achievement, behavior rating scales, alternate laboratory measure of attention/executive control	Correlations not provided, but diagnostic decisions compared for GDS, TOVA, and two rating scales	TOVA/TOVA-A comparison
Validity studies (discriminant) included in the manual	Children with ADD/ADHD only, children with ADD/ADHD and some other disorder(s), and "other"; children with ADHD compared to general population (normative sample)	Children with ADHD, other disorders, and control group; children with hyperactivity and nonhyperactive children	Children with ADHD compared to control (normal)	Children with ADHD compared to general population; children with UADD, ADHD, conduct disorder, and normal (TOVA)
Use with special populations addressed in manual	Children with ADHD, ages 6 to 17 years	Children with ADHD; adults with Alzheimers	Children and adults with ADHD; adults and malingering	Children and adults with ADHD (TOVA); children with ADHD (TOVA-A)

Interpretive Features

Performance variables included	Correct hits; omission and commission errors; reaction time; d'; Beta; reaction time standard error; standard error of standard deviation of reaction time; slope of reaction time; slope of standard error; slope at ISI change; slope of standard error at ISI change; overall performance index	Correct hits; omission and commission errors; reaction time; slope; target-related error vs. random error	Response Control Quotient (Auditory; Visual; Full Scale); Attention Quotient (Auditory; Visual; Full Scale); separate auditory and visual scores for prudence; vigilance; consistency; stamina; focus; speed; balance; persistence; fine motor/hyperactivity; sensorimotor; readiness; comprehension	Omission and commission errors; reaction time; reaction time standard deviation; sensitivity (d'); multiple responses; post-commission error response time; anticipatory errors; ADHD scale
Possibility of error analysis?	No	Yes	From Comprehension and Hyperactivity Scales only	Yes
How scores presented	Raw scores; percentiles; and T-scores	Raw scores; percentiles; threshold levels	Raw scores; standard scores	Raw scores; standard deviations; standard scores
Confidence intervals provided	No	No	No	No
Age-level increments	2-year intervals from 4 to 17 years; adults (18+ years) as one group		10 age groups of increments of 2 years to 10 years	1-year increments through age 19 (TOVA/TOVA-A); 10-year increments for adults (TOVA)
Threshold or cut score recommended for clinical significance	T > 60; score > 90th percentile: abnormal	> 5th percentile: abnormal 6th to 25th percentile: borderline	None indicated	None indicated
Descriptive labels provided for score categories	Markedly atypical; mildly atypical; within average range	Abnormal; borderline; normal	None indicated	Within normal limits; not within normal limits

(continued)

61

Table 3.2 Continued

	Conners' CPT	GDS	IVA	TOVA/TOVA-A
Group statistics provided by age	None in manual; supposed to be programmed into software	Preschool, children: none; adults, older adults: means, SD	Can be accessed from "read only" file once software installed	Means and SD by age and gender
Performance compared to norm group or clinical group	Either or both	Normative	Normative	Normative (TOVA/TOVA-A); ADHD Scale compares to ADHD population (TOVA)
Interpretive section to manual or separate manual to guide interpretation	Yes, but very brief	Yes	Yes	Yes
Sample report or interpretive statements provided	Only briefly in case studies	Yes	No	Minimally in case studies
Case studies included in manual	Yes (2), both children	Yes	Yes (4), all children	Yes (7), some child and some adult; additional case studies using TOVA to monitor medication effects
Interpretive report generated	Printout includes results table, graph, and interpretive descriptors	No	Printout includes scores and graphs, but no interpretation	Yes (6–7 pages in length)
Recommendations for interventions generated or included in manual	No	No	No	Yes; also a school intervention plan that can be customized for the child based on TOVA results
Capability for time series comparisons	Data can be saved and referred to, but there is no indication of the capability for comparison	No	Yes, but limited to comparison of two administrations	Yes, no limit in number of comparisons specified

Set-Up

Computer system requirements	IBM/PC; no indication of compatibility with windows setups	None	IBM/PC with DOS 5.0 or higher; screen saver or other programs need to be shut down while running test	IBM/PC but not compatible with workstation/ windows setups (TOVA/TOVA-A); Macintosh (TOVA)
Initial product cost (not including shipping and handling, or tax)	$590	$1,595	Unlimited use: $1,595 Limited use: $598	TOVA and TOVA-A combined: $525
Additional cost per administration	None	None	With limited use, each 10 additional scorings is $89	Each additional scoring beyond initial set is $15 for either TOVA or TOVA-A

Notes: CPT = Continuous performance test; GDS = Gordon Diagnostic System; TOVA = Test of Variables of Attention; IVA = Integrated (or Intermediate) Visual and Auditory Continuous Performance Test; IP = Identical pairs. ADHD = Attention-Deficit/Hyperactivity Disorder; SD = Standard deviation.

TASK DEMANDS AND
DESCRIPTIVE INFORMATION

Ballard (1996b) recommended that developers and users of CPTs provide detailed descriptions of task parameters as well as conditions for standardizations. As noted in Chapter 2, some of the variations to the CPT paradigm include differences in what constitutes a target, the type of target, the modality of presentation, the interstimulus interval (ISI), duration of stimulus presentation, quality of the stimulus, the relative frequency of the target, duration of the task, distractor conditions, examiner presence or absence, instructional set, and so on. The four CPTs selected for discussion here differ on many of these factors as well as others. These differences are highlighted in the descriptions of the tasks.

THE CONNERS' CONTINUOUS PERFORMANCE
TEST (CONNERS, 1992, 1995)

The standard version of the Conners' is a 14-minute, not-X-type CPT, presented visually. The examinee is required to respond by pressing a key, such as a space bar or a mouse button, every time a letter appears on the computer screen, except when the letter X (i.e., the target) appears; when the letter X appears, the examinee is to inhibit the response. Conners (1992, 1995) asserted that this format ensured a greater number of responses and therefore decreased chance error. The Conners' standard paradigm consists of six blocks, with each block divided into three subblocks. Each subblock is composed of 20 trials in which nontargeted and, sometimes, targeted stimuli are presented (Conners, 1992, 1995; Dumont et al., 1995, 1999; Grooms, 1998). The targeted and nontargeted stimuli (letters) are randomly shown for 250 ms, with the ISI varying within each block as opposed to across blocks of the task. For the three subblocks within a block, the ISI may be 1000, 2000, or 4000 ms; the order of the three different ISI subblocks varies from block to block (Conners, 1992, 1995). There is no distractor condition on the Conners' and the stimuli (letters) are not blurred or degraded.

Two short practice tests are available to help the client become familiar with the paradigm (Conners, 1992, 1995). Instructions are standardized and presented on-screen. In the administration portion of the manual, it is not clear whether the examinee reads these on his or her own or if the directions are read to the examinee by the clinician. In the discussion of the procedures for the normative data collection, however, the examinee reads the directions on his or her own, and only then does the examiner restate the directions. Although examiner presence or absence also is not stated explicitly, the examinee is directed by a message on the screen to get the examiner when the task is over; this implies that the examiner is not present during the test administration. As already noted, minimal direction to the examiner is provided in the portion of the manual specific to administration; additional details regarding task administration when normative data were collected are provided in other portions of the manual. For example, the manual mentions that the administration of the CPT should occur in a room or area free from distractors. It is noted that the examiner provided an additional prompt to respond quickly and accurately between the practice test and actual test administration. Further, although use of the mouse rather than the space bar is an option, it is recommended that the space bar be used to maintain consistency with the administration during collection of normative data. Since these details are included in the technical portion of the manual as opposed to the section relating to test administration, it is conceivable that clinicians may not adhere to these details and may not even be aware of them.

The Conners' software can be used to develop customized CPT paradigms. For example, researchers can change the number of blocks, the number of targets per block, target frequency, stimulus display time, and number of trials. Customized paradigms may be created with up to 500 trials per block and up to 60 blocks per testing session. The number of targets per block may vary, with 500 targets per block being the upper limit. The display time for each stimulus can range from 100 ms to 1000 ms, and the ISI can range from 500 ms to 4000 ms. Although the directions would continue to be to respond *except* when the target is displayed, the target may be one letter (e.g., the letter X) or a two-letter combination (e.g., the letter A followed by the letter X). As a result, a large number of customized paradigms may be created. A major drawback of these customized paradigms is the lack of normative data to support interpretation. Such examiner-created paradigms are inappropriate for clinical decision making until normative, reliability, and validity data concerning scores collected in any such manner are reported. For use in research paradigms where control subjects are available, examiners may create any paradigm necessary to answer specific questions. This is clearly a strength of the flexibility of the Conners' software but can be abused by clinicians who modify the standardized paradigm and then attempt to make clinical interpretation of the scores obtained.

GORDON DIAGNOSTIC SYSTEM (GORDON, 1983)

Of the commercially available CPTs, the GDS has been available for the longest amount of time. Review of the CPT literature reveals that the GDS is probably the most frequently used CPT in research studies. The GDS is a microprocessor unit, as opposed to a computer software program, that generates 11 tasks. Of these tasks, there are three basic paradigms—the delay task, the distractibility task, and the vigilance task—of which the vigilance and distractibility tasks are CPTs. More than one version of the distractibility and vigilance tasks are available (Gordon, 1986a, 1986b; Gordon & Mettelman, 1988; Gordon Systems, Inc., 1991).

The prototype for the vigilance task is the original version of the AX-CPT in a visual format (Rosvold et al., 1956). However, in contrast to Rosvold et al.'s AX-CPT, the GDS uses numbers instead of letters as stimuli (Gordon & Mettelman, 1988; Gordon Systems, Inc., 1991). The children's standard version of the vigilance task, for ages 6 to 16 years, lasts nine minutes and requires the child to press a button every time a two-number target combination (a 1 followed by a 9) is presented. In a second version of the children's vigilance task, a 3/5 combination (a 3 followed by a 5) is used as the target stimulus. The numerals for the standard and alternate children's versions are displayed for 200 ms, with a 1000 ms ISI (Gordon, 1986b; Gordon & Mettelman, 1988; Gordon Systems, Inc., 1991).

Another version is available for use with adults. The adult vigilance task has the same configuration (i.e., stimulus duration, ISI), uses the 1/9 combination with 10 targets per block, and lasts for six minutes. Yet, another version is available for use with preschoolers (i.e., 4- and 5-year-old children). In the preschool version, the vigilance task is an X-CPT (as opposed to the AX-CPT) with the numerals displayed for the same 200 ms as on the other versions. However, the ISI for the preschool version is increased to 2000 ms. As with the adult vigilance task, the preschool task takes six minutes to complete instead of the nine minutes required for the children's version (Gordon Systems, Inc., 1991). Regardless of the version (i.e., children's standard and alternate versions, preschool version, adult version), the vigilance task is divided into two or three blocks so that a client's performance may be monitored every three minutes, thus providing insight into the vigilance decrement over time (Gordon & Mettelman, 1988; Gordon Systems, Inc., 1991). Although the primary demand placed on the individual for the vigilance task is that of sustaining attention, the vigilance task is believed to tap into cognitive skills, behavioral regulation, and motivation as well (Gordon Systems, Inc., 1986).

Another task on the GDS is the distractibility task. The distractibility task incorporates the AX-CPT of the vigilance task but simultaneously includes the display of digits on either side of the target stimulus (i.e., distractors) to assess the extent to which the individual can selectively attend to the target stimuli (Gordon Systems, Inc., 1991). Stimulus duration, target frequency, and ISI are the same on the distractibility task as on the vigilance task. For children, the distractibility task, as with the vigilance task, lasts nine minutes. The adult version of the distractibility task maintains the same configuration as the children's version but lasts only six minutes (Gordon Systems, Inc., 1991). There is no preschool version of the distractibility task.

In addition to the two CPT-type tasks (vigilance and distractibility), the GDS includes one other task. Although not a CPT paradigm, the delay task of the GDS is designed as a measure of impulse control. On this task the child can earn points by inhibiting a response. The delay task takes less than nine minutes; there is no separate adult version or preschool version. According to the manual for the GDS (Gordon Systems, Inc., 1991), the delay task is always the first task administered. As the first task, it may serve as a warm-up for the vigilance and distractibility tasks. Regardless of the task, all stimuli are of standard quality.

The manual for the GDS includes instructions for administration, tables (Gordon Systems, Inc., 1991), an interpretive guide (Gordon Systems, Inc., 1986), and a technical guide (Gordon Systems, Inc., 1987a). Special administration considerations are reported, including the specific order in which the GDS tasks are to be administered and the standard instructional set that is to be used (Gordon & Mettelman, 1988). Prior to actual administration of the tasks, practice trials are available for the vigilance and distractibility tasks. The practice trials are slower versions of the tasks and can be discontinued once it is clear that the individual understands the task. Notably, the directions for the GDS clearly state that the examiner will remain present during the administration (Gordon Systems, Inc., 1991). In addition to the tasks themselves, the GDS includes an observational rating scale that can be completed by the examiner following the administration of the test to aid in interpretation (Gordon Systems, Inc., 1991). There is no scoring of this scale; it is qualitative in nature.

INTEGRATED (OR INTERMEDIATE) VISUAL AND AUDITORY CONTINUOUS PERFORMANCE TEST (SANDFORD & TURNER, 1994–1999)

The IVA is a 13-minute X-CPT that uses both auditory and visual modalities within the same task. Of the four major CPTs discussed here, it is the only one that requires the individual to shift modalities within the same task. On the IVA, the individual is required to press a mouse button in response to a visual or auditory target stimulus (i.e., the number 1) and to refrain from pressing the mouse button when the nontarget stimulus (i.e., the number 2) is presented in either a visual or auditory format. Unlike the Conners', the use of the space bar is not an option. The target and nontarget stimuli are presented in a pseudorandom pattern, with a 1500 ms ISI, for 500 trials (Sandford & Turner, 1995). Because there is only a single nontarget stimulus, the discrimination task is simpler than that involved in the Conners' or GDS. The order of auditory or visual presentation of stimuli is fixed and remains the same across the two test conditions provided. Stimuli are not degraded at any point in the task.

Whereas the Conners' varies the ISI and the GDS provides a distractor condition, the IVA provides conditions of differing target frequency.

During the test, depending on the block, the IVA's target-to-nontarget ratio is altered by blocks to elicit omission and commission errors. Under the frequent target condition, a response set is created such that the dominant response is to press the mouse button; therefore, an individual who is impulsive is more likely to respond and to make commission errors. In contrast, the infrequent target condition requires vigilance and response inhibition. If vigilance is not maintained during this segment of the test, the probability of omission errors will increase. The individual's readiness to respond or arousal level may impact the number of omission errors as well. The target-to-nontarget ratios and visual and auditory stimuli are altered in a counterbalanced design to reduce fatigue and to control learning effects (Sandford & Turner, 1995).

The IVA manual (Sandford & Turner, 1995) includes sections on administration and interpretation. The use of the software and database is incorporated into the administration portion. In describing special conditions for administration of the IVA when normative data were collected, it is noted that the same type mouse, 14-inch screen, and headphones were used for all subjects. Although there is no indication of whether changes to any of these would impact the CPT results, the authors suggest, for example, that speakers (in lieu of headphones) are sufficient (we strongly doubt this assertion, as the headphones provide an additional physical stimulus and also are at least a partial sound screen). The manual also includes very specific directions with regard to examinee distance from the screen, center of the screen relative to examinee eye level, and so on. Directions are provided by computer following prompts and directions by the examiner. Although there is no specific statement relating to examiner presence or absence during the test, the examiner is instructed not to redirect the examinee verbally during the task, but to "reposition the index finger or hand on the mouse when necessary" (Sandford & Turner, 1995, p. IV-7); this would imply that the examiner remains in the room during the test administration. The manual includes a notation specific to the use of the IVA with clients who have limited English proficiency (LEP) or English as a second language (ESL). Consistent with professional standards, the need for directions to be provided in the individual's first language is emphasized; the use of the practice task to determine if the client understands the task and if the administration would be valid is noted as well. As a final cautionary note, for clients with LEP or ESL, it is suggested that the IVA results be used only to rule out attentional problems and that impaired performance not be attributed to an attentional problem (Sandford & Turner, 1995).

Warm-up and cool-down sessions are provided prior to the practice test and after the regular test, respectively. Simple reaction time tests are given during the warm-up and cool-down sessions. The warm-up session provides the opportunity to become familiar with the operation of the mouse button as well. Following the warm-up session, a practice test consisting of 32 items is administered prior to the start of the regular test (Sandford, Fine, & Goldman, 1995a, 1995b; Sandford & Turner, 1995; Seckler, Burns, Montgomery, & Sandford, 1995; Turner & Sandford, 1995a, 1995b). The IVA includes two additional components. As does the GDS, the IVA has a behavioral scale for the examiner to complete based on the observed behavior during the task, and there is a self-report form that can be completed by the examinee relative to his or her own perception of his or her behavior during the task. Information from both forms can be entered into the software program to be printed out as a narrative report.

TEST OF VARIABLES OF ATTENTION (GREENBERG, 1988–1999)

The TOVA is an X-CPT available in separate visual (TOVA) and auditory (TOVA-A; Greenberg, 1996–1999) versions (Cenedela, 1996; Greenberg & Kindschi, 1996; Greenberg, Kindschi, & Corman, 1999; Leark, Dupuy, Greenberg, Corman, & Kindschi, 1996). The TOVA includes both a clinical version and a briefer screening or preschool version. The TOVA and TOVA-A require an individual to press a microswitch every time the target stimulus is presented. For the TOVA, the target stimulus consists of a colored square with a smaller square contained within and adjacent to the top edge of the larger square; the nontarget stimulus has a smaller inscribed square adjacent to the bottom edge of the larger square. For the TOVA-A, two audible tones are used as stimuli, one as the target and one as the nontarget. Thus, for both the visual and auditory tasks, the stimuli are non-language based.

It has been argued that by virtue of being non-language-based tests, the TOVA and TOVA-A may serve as "purer" measures of inattentiveness and executive control as compared to the other CPT measures. In addition, it has been pointed out that the TOVA has no left-right discrimination requirement and minimal spatial (i.e., up-down) discrimination requirements (Dumont et al., 1995, 1999; Greenberg & Crosby, 1992a, 1992b; Greenberg & Waldman, 1993). The non-language base, as well as the lack of emphasis on spatial or left-right orientation of the TOVA and TOVA-A, are considered pluses, as many individuals with attention and impulse control problems have language-based learning problems and left-right discrimination difficulties that could confound interpretation of CPT performance (Greenberg & Waldman, 1993; Lambert & Sandoval, 1980). As with the IVA, there are only two stimuli (one target, one nontarget) presented; therefore, the level of discrimination (visual or auditory) required is minimal.

The clinical versions of the TOVA and TOVA-A are approximately 22 minutes in duration. The preschool version (for 4- and 5-year-olds) is 11 minutes in duration. For both the TOVA and TOVA-A, the target and non-target stimuli are presented randomly for 100 ms with an ISI of 2000 ms; stimuli are of standard quality rather than degraded. The clinical versions are composed of four intervals (the preschool version has two intervals, intervals 1 and 3). During the first half of the test (intervals 1 and 2), the target stimulus is randomly displayed on 22.5% of the trials. This condition is referred to as the stimulus-infrequent condition. As previously noted with the IVA, it is believed that the stimulus-infrequent condition creates a situation in which a client who is inattentive is less likely to respond and therefore will make omission errors. Thus, the stimulus-infrequent state is used to assess the client's attention. In the second half of the test (intervals 3 and 4), the target stimulus is shown on 77.5% of the trials. This condition, known as the stimulus-frequent condition, creates a strong response set in which a client who has impulse control problems is more likely to respond and make commission errors. Thus, as on the IVA, the stimulus-frequent condition is used to assess the client's impulsivity (Dumont et al., 1995, 1999; Greenberg & Crosby, 1992a; Greenberg & Waldman, 1993; Leark et al., 1996).

The manuals (Cenedela, 1996; Greenberg et al., 1999; Leark et al., 1996) include standardized instructions to be given to the examinee. As with the IVA, it is specified that the instructions be given in the client's native language (Leark et al., 1996). A three-minute practice test is administered prior to the beginning of the regular test (Leark et al., 1996). Based on the instructions as well as the conditions for collection of normative data, the examiner is to remain present during the administration of the task. Special administration considerations are included, such as testing individuals in the morning (Greenberg & Crosby, 1992b; Greenberg & Waldman, 1993; Leark et al., 1996). An additional feature of the TOVA and TOVA-A software is the capacity to save and compare repeated administrations of the tasks for a given individual over time (Cenedela, 1996). As with the GDS and IVA, the TOVA/TOVA-A manual includes an observation rating scale to be completed by the examiner. Notably, the TOVA form includes documentation relating to intake of caffeine, nicotine, alcohol, and other medications (Leark et al., 1996). The importance of documentation of these substances will be discussed in greater detail in Chapter 8.

In addition to the observation form, the TOVA also includes multiple other forms that can be used in conjunction with the CPTs themselves. For children, there is a rating scale, an interview form for the child and parent, and a success form to monitor treatment effects. For adults, there is a self-report scale, an interview form, and a success form. Adolescents are included on either the adult or child form depending on the component. Finally, there is a diagnostic checklist that can be used with all clients. Notably, these components are included across three manuals

(Cenedela, 1996; Greenberg et al., 1999; Leark et al., 1996) with no single manual containing all of them. Other information is repeated across the three manuals; this makes for some redundancy and at the same time a need to have and use all three manuals.

ADEQUACY OF NORMATIVE DATA

As can be seen from the descriptions of these four CPT programs, there are similarities as well as differences in the task demands available. As noted in Chapter 2, differences in administration such as examiner presence or absence have been found to affect CPT performance, yet there is no consistency with regard to examiner presence across tasks. Differences related to use of space bar versus mouse, shape of mouse, sensitivity and response times of various mouse devices, screen size, use of headphones as opposed to speakers, use of laptop versus standard PC, and so on have not been investigated. For these reasons, it is important for administration to be standardized consistent with the collection of normative data; this makes it imperative for manuals to clearly state the conditions for standardized administration. Given differences in task demands across CPTs, performance on any one of these CPTs can be interpreted based only on the normative data for those specific task parameters. Although the capacity to customize the task may be beneficial for research purposes, clinical use of customized versions of CPTs is hampered significantly by the lack of normative data. To some extent, the use of the standard versions may be hampered as well by the state of the normative data available. When evaluating the quality of a measure where a comparison between an individual's performance and the performance of a normative group is to be made, adequate norms are required (e.g., R.J. Cohen & Swerdlik, 1999).

The adequacy of the norms must be evaluated within the context of the population for whom the measure is intended and to whom the scores are to be generalized (e.g., Anastasi, 1988; Crocker & Algina, 1986; Lowe et al., 2000). Specific criteria have been proffered as related to the establishment of the adequacy of a normative sample. For example, the normative sample must be representative (i.e., represent a cross-section) of the population for whom the measure is designed (e.g., Anastasi, 1988). The sample should be of sufficient size (the larger, the better) to produce stable values and reduce possible sources of error (e.g., R.J. Cohen & Swerdlik, 1999). The normative sample should be described in detail and stratified across a number of demographic variables, which are related to performance on the measure. When the normative sample is insufficient, "parameter estimates will have systematic biases and the latent distribution will be systematically miscalculated" (Lowe et al., 2000, p. 5). Procedures for selecting the norming sample (i.e., the sampling plan), refusals or nonresponse rates, dates of norming, special conditions under which the measure was administered, and group statistics (i.e., the mean, standard deviation, and standard error of the mean) should be reported as well (e.g., Anastasi, 1988; R.J. Cohen & Swerdlik, 1999; Crocker & Algina, 1986). The normative samples used for the major commercially available CPTs will be discussed with respect to their adequacy, as adequate norms are essential for a quality measure (e.g., R.J. Cohen & Swerdlik, 1999).

In addition to the above-mentioned criteria, from a psychometric perspective, it is important to examine and to understand the relation between demographic variables and CPT performance. Some understanding of the association can be found with the normative sample of a measure if appropriate information is included about the normative sample. Demographic characteristics of the normative sample such as age, gender, education level, socioeconomic status (SES), race or ethnicity, and geographic region should be included (e.g., Crocker & Algina, 1986; Lowe et al., 2000). In the past, limited research has been conducted on the relation between demographic variables and neuropsychological test scores (e.g., Lowe & Reynolds, 1999; Lowe et al., 2000; Reynolds, 1997, in press). For example, a small number of CPT studies have been conducted with individuals from different racial or cultural backgrounds (e.g., Bauermeister, Berrios, Jimenez, Acevedo, & Gordon, 1990; Boivin et al., 1996; Dahl et al., 1996; Levy, 1980; Levy & Hobbes, 1979, 1981; Mataix-Cols et al., 1997; Zentall, 1986). Researchers and clinicians must understand the relation between demographic variables and test scores to report and interpret test results accurately (e.g., Lowe & Reynolds, 1999; Lowe et al., 2000; Reynolds, 1997). Due to the importance of understanding demographic impact on performance, the extent to which the demographics of the sample are detailed in the manuals for the four major CPTs is presented as part of this review.

CONNERS' CPT

The Conners' CPT manual (Conners, 1992, 1995) provides normative data for its standard paradigm. The data reported indicate that the database for the Conners' consisted of 1,190 subjects, of which 520 were nonreferred, presumed healthy, individuals. The remaining 670 were clinic-referred individuals (Conners, 1992, 1995; Dumont et al., 1995, 1999). The norms for the clinical sample, however, were reduced from 670 to 238 individuals. Careful reading of the manual suggests that the removal of these 432 subjects from the clinic-referred group was based on multiple causes. Specifically, some clinic-referred individuals were removed from the group to be part of a cross-validation study ($n = 130$); other individuals ($n = 56$) were dropped because they were on medication or because it was felt that their performance on the CPT represented outliers. Moreover, 246 individuals were eliminated from the sample because they were not identified as having Attention Deficit Disorder (ADD) or ADHD as a primary or comorbid diagnosis (Conners, 1992, 1995; Dumont et al., 1995, 1999).

Limited information is available on the geographic regions where the Conners' data were collected. The manual indicates that the normative data were collected from five states (Florida, Kansas, Pennsylvania, North Carolina, and California) and the Canadian province of Ontario. The nonreferred sample consisted of individuals from schools and a research center, whereas the referred individuals were from several independent researchers and Conners' research clinic (Conners, 1992, 1995). Pertinent information about the geographic regions is missing, for example, the size of the population of the cities or type of setting (i.e., rural, suburban, urban) where the data were collected. Similarly, other information about the normative sample is not addressed adequately in the manual. For example, the procedures for selecting the individuals to be included in the normative sample are not articulated clearly in the manual; refusal or nonresponse rates, exclusionary criteria, and dates of norming are not stipulated. In effect, the sampling process does not appear to be have been planned to ensure adequate representation, and the resulting normative group appears to be a sample of convenience.

The age range of the normative sample is 4 to 70 years; the age range for the referred sample is 4 to 61 years. The nonreferred and clinic-referred groups are divided into two-year age intervals for ages 4 to 17 years. Although the majority of adults (82.4%) in the nonreferred group are between the ages of 18 and 30, the adults are combined into one age group (18 years and older) for the referred as well as the nonreferred sample (Conners, 1992, 1995; Grooms, 1998), resulting in eight age groups derived for both samples. The distribution of individuals in each age group for the nonreferred sample varies from 30 to 82 individuals, with more than 55 individuals in each age group, except for the 4- to 5-year-old group. Thus, the individuals in the nonreferred (normative) sample are somewhat evenly distributed across the age groups derived. In contrast, the individuals in the clinic-referred sample are not as evenly distributed. The number of referred individuals in each age group ranges from a low of 16 for the 4- to 5-year-old group to a high of 162 individuals for the adult age group. However, if the 4- to 5-year-old group was to be excluded from the clinic-referred age group distribution, the number of individuals in each age group would be more evenly distributed and would consist of 52 or more subjects per age group (Conners, 1992, 1995; Grooms, 1998).

A breakdown by gender for both the normative (nonreferred) sample and the clinical sample is provided. Specifically, males make up 51.2% of the nonreferred group and 75.4% of the referred group (Conners, 1992, 1995; Dumont et al., 1995, 1999; Grooms, 1998). Although comparisons made by the program are with the "general population," results of analysis of covariance (ANCOVA) for age and gender reported in the manual indicate significant effects for gender on hit reaction time, percent commission errors, variability of standard error, sensitivity (d'), and response style (Beta). Given these differences, it is imperative that the standardization sample has equal numbers of males and females in each age group or there may be a need for separate norms or consideration of gender in the interpretation process. Unfortunately, a breakdown of the normative sample by age and gender to describe the sample in more detail is not provided in the manual. Information also is unavailable on the educational level, SES, and ethnic composition for the normative sample. Limitations of the Conners' normative sample affect the extent to which results can be generalized to populations of differing educational levels, SES, or ethnicity.

GDS

Normative data for the preschool and children's versions of the GDS can be found in the work of Gordon and Mettelman (1988) as well as in the manual (Gordon Systems, Inc., 1991); adult normative data are found in the manual. The normative sample for the GDS vigilance task (standard children's version) consists of 1,019 nonreferred children, ranging in age from 6 to 16 years; when the preschool sample of 4- and 5-year-olds is included, the normative sample increases to 1,266 children. Thus, the GDS normative sample for the children's version is relatively large in comparison to other CPTs. Gordon and Mettelman described the normative sample for the children's version (and preschool version) as being composed of well-functioning children; children with psychological, learning, neurological, attention, and impulse control problems were excluded, as were children who had been retained in school, were in special education, or were using psychotropic medication. Children participating in psychotherapy were excluded as well.

Children included in the normative database came from schools in the Syracuse, New York (91% of the sample) and Charlottesville, Virginia (9% of the sample) areas (Gordon Systems, Inc., 1987a). Thus, the geographic region of this normative sample is restricted. Children were randomly selected from class lists of schools that participated in the standardization process, and every socioeconomic level of the geographic regions is represented. Refusal rates are mentioned, with only four children under the age of 5 refusing to participate in the standardization process. The number of parents who did not complete consent forms or behavioral rating scales sent via mail is not provided. Information on the ethnic composition of the sample is not available.

The distribution of children evaluated on the vigilance and distractibility tasks was somewhat uniformly developed, and Gordon and Mettelman (1988) are to be commended for the number of individuals included in each age group. For the children's version, sample size by age ranges from 160 (10- to 11-year-olds) to 258 (6- to 7-year-olds) on the vigilance task, and from 74 (10- to 11-year-olds) to 107 (6- to 7-year-olds) on the distractibility task. Of the 247 preschoolers, 89 are 4-year-olds; this represents the smallest age group among the 4- to 16-year-olds.

For the adult vigilance and distractibility tasks, two sets of normative data are provided (Gordon Systems, Inc., 1991). All adult normative data were collected at a single site, but the geographic region represented is not specified. For adults between the ages of 18 and 49, the normative sample consisted of 80 nonreferred (healthy) adults with a mean age of 27.3 years ($SD = 6.9$ years). The second normative sample for the adult version was comprised of 43 older subjects (mean age of 65.7 years). Clinicians are cautioned to consider the older adult data as preliminary due to the small sample size. How subjects were recruited, refusal rate, exclusionary criteria, and dates of data collection were not specified.

For the adult sample, 41.25% were females and 58.75% were African American, with a mean educational level of 14.3 years. However, normative data by gender, educational level, or ethnic group are not provided separately; all normative data are presented in a single group. For older adults, the mean years of education is provided; however, the breakdown by gender, ethnic group, or geographic setting is not provided. Notably, individuals 17 years of age are not represented in either the children's or the adult versions of the vigilance or distractibility tasks. Finally, there are no normative data related to the observation scale and CPT performance.

In addition to the normative sample provided in the manual and obtained in the United States, a second normative sample has been obtained with children in Puerto Rico (Bauermeister, Berrios, Jimenez, Acevedo, & Gordon, 1990). Bauermeister et al. compared the Puerto Rican GDS norms to the GDS normative data (Gordon Systems, Inc., 1987a). The Bauermeister normative sample consisted of 433 children and adolescents, ranging in age from 6 to 16 years, in Puerto Rico. For purposes of comparison, the Puerto Rican children were then matched to randomly selected children from the U.S. normative sample on the basis of age and gender. The performance of the children from the two samples on the delay and vigilance tasks were compared; the distractibility task was not included.

Bauermeister and colleagues (1990) found statistically significant differences between the two samples across variables generated (i.e., correct hits, commission scores, efficiency ratios). In comparison to the Puerto Rican children, U.S. children had higher efficiency ratios and total correct scores and committed fewer commission errors. Further analyses by age groups revealed statistically significant cultural differences in the 6- to 9-year-old groups, with the U.S. children making more correct responses and committing fewer commission errors in comparison to the Puerto Rican children. Thus, if U.S. norms were to be applied to the Puerto Rican children, a larger proportion of the Puerto Rican children would be identified as having potential attention and impulse control problems; in other words, an increase of false positive diagnoses of ADHD among Puerto Rican children could occur (Bauermeister et al., 1990; Lowe et al., 2000). Thus, the use of the normative data (U.S.) with children from other cultures may be problematic. Further study of the differences in performance that may be attributable to cultural differences, with appropriate development of separate norms for different ethnic groups as necessary, seems warranted not only for the GDS but for all CPTs.

IVA

The normative sample for the IVA consists of 781 individuals, 358 males and 423 females (Dumont et al., 1995, 1999), ranging in age from 5 to 90 years. The sample is made up of volunteers with no known learning, psychological, neurological, attention, or impulse control problems (Dumont et al., 1995, 1999; Sandford & Turner, 1995; Turner & Sandford, 1995b). Information on the geographic region(s) where the normative data were collected is not provided in the manual (Sandford & Turner, 1995). Refusal rates and exclusionary criteria are not reported. Other demographic characteristics such as education level, SES, and ethnicity are missing from the manual as well. Norms do not appear to be stratified (Dumont et al., 1995, 1999), and the sample appears to be one of convenience. Thus, test results obtained with the IVA must be interpreted with caution, as generalizations across the aforementioned demographic variables are limited.

The number of males and females does not appear to be evenly distributed across the age range of the sample. In each of the 10 age groups, there are approximately 36 males and 42 females per group; however, the number ranges from 17 to 68 males and 15 to 75 females per age group. If there are no gender differences or age-by-gender interactions on various scores, this is not a problem. However, females do tend to perform better than males in general on most CPT paradigms. Thus, gender must be a proportional variable for normative purposes or separate norms must be provided. In the absence of good studies that explore gender differences, the assumption cannot be made that they do not exist.

Although the IVA includes a behavior rating scale for the examiner (test behavior) and a self-report scale, no normative data or studies using these scales are provided in the manual. This is particularly notable given that entry of the responses on these forms results in a printed narrative. With no empirical basis, these forms should be used with extreme caution.

TOVA AND TOVA-A

The normative sample for the TOVA is composed of two samples, the original sample and a second sample that was later added to the original. The original sample of the TOVA consisted of 775 individuals, 377 males and 398 females, ranging in age from 6 to 16 years. Children were excluded from the original sample if they were using psychotropic medication or were participating in a special education program. The subjects were from three suburban, public schools in Minneapolis, Minnesota. Children in randomly selected classrooms, based on grade level (i.e., grades 1, 3, 5, 7, and 9), were invited to participate in the standardization process (Dumont et al., 1995, 1999; Greenberg & Waldman, 1993; Leark et al., 1996). Parental refusal rate for children's participation was reported to be less than 1% (Greenberg & Waldman, 1993). Although the children lived in areas that were predominantly White and middle to upper-middle SES, individual participants' SES and race or ethnicity were not recorded (Dumont et al., 1995, 1999; Greenberg & Waldman, 1993).

The second TOVA sample was comprised of 821 nonreferred individuals, 335 males and 486 females, ranging in age from 4 to 20 years or older. Subjects between the ages of 4 and 19 years were excluded if they scored two standard deviations above the mean on a behavioral rating scale completed by school personnel, if they were using psychotropic medication, or if they were participating in a special education program. Adult subjects were excluded if they were using psychotropic medication or had a history of a CNS disorder or injury. Individuals from an early educational screening program were included, as were children and adolescents whose classes were randomly selected from a rural public elementary school and a high school in Minnesota. Parental refusal rate for children's and adolescents' participation was reported to be less than 3%. Adult subjects were volunteers from three colleges and six adult community settings in Minnesota (Dumont et al., 1995, 1999; Greenberg & Crosby, 1992b). Information on adult refusal or nonresponse rate, ethnicity, and SES was not available. As with the original sample, these individuals were from areas where the population was predominantly Caucasian and middle to upper-middle SES (Greenberg & Crosby, 1992b).

Taken together, the TOVA combined normative sample consists of 1,590 individuals, 712 males and 884 females, ranging in age from 4 to more than 80 years. The distribution of subjects and of males and females in each age group are not uniform. A larger number of individuals are found in the 6- to 18-year-old groups, reflecting the combined sampling process.

Moreover, the number of males in each age group drops dramatically after age 19 (Dumont et al., 1995, 1999; Greenberg & Crosby, 1992b). For example, in the 30- to 39-year-old group, scores for only four males are included (Greenberg & Crosby, 1992b; Greenberg et al., 1999). This skewed representation may produce unstable values and possible error. Further, some standard scores (e.g., omission error scores) for males in the older age groups (e.g., ages 40 to 49) are artificially inflated because the subjects did not make any errors and, therefore, variability in the scores was absent (Dumont et al., 1995, 1999). Although separate norms are available by gender, norms are not stratified based on other demographic characteristics of the normative sample; demographic breakdowns for SES and ethnicity are not provided. Thus, generalization across SES and ethnicity is limited and caution is needed in interpreting the performance of individuals who are members of minority groups or who are from various levels of SES (Greenberg & Crosby, 1992b).

The current normative sample for the TOVA-A is limited to children ages 6 to 19 years. The sample is composed of 2,551 children recruited from public schools in Minneapolis. Ethnic representation of the sample is reported as 99% Caucasian and 1% Other; SES and educational level are not reported. Exclusionary criteria for subject selection were consistent with those employed for the TOVA sample. Distribution of subjects and gender across one-year age levels is fairly even for ages 6 to 18 years, with approximately 190 subjects at each age level, approximately 50% of whom are male. For the 19-year-old sample, however, the sample size is considerably smaller ($n = 32$) and 69% of the sample are male (Greenberg et al., 1999; Leark et al., 1996).

As noted in the previous section, multiple rating forms are available for use with the TOVA and TOVA-A, as well as a diagnostic checklist. At this time, however, no normative data are provided in the manual to support the use of these forms in clinical decision making. For this reason, it is suggested that clinicians use these forms with caution until research is available to assist in their interpretation.

SUMMARY

Adequate normative data are a prerequisite to sound clinical interpretation of any measure. The extent to which the normative data for the major commercially available CPTs meet the criteria for technical adequacy varies, but normative data for none of the four described here are stellar. This is particularly disconcerting given that these are the most widely used CPTs and have the best normative data available. In the manuals, the procedures for selecting the normative sample are not adequately addressed and do not reflect careful planning to ensure representation; in fact, most CPT normative samples appear to be samples of convenience. As such, the normative data are not likely to include cross-sectional representation of the general population. Refusal or nonresponse rates and dates of norming are not reported consistently. Across CPTs, the description of the demographic characteristics of the normative samples is limited. The normative data lack appropriate stratification by common demographic variables. Thus, the task of identifying those demographic variables (e.g., age, gender, educational level, SES, and ethnicity) related to CPT performance and therefore warranting consideration as mediator variables in the interpretation of results, rests with the independent researcher and clinician (Lowe et al., 2000). These CPTs were developed principally by physicians with biological orientations. There is an inherent assumption in these various tests' manuals that measurement of biological or neuropsychological variables such as attention and self-regulation is unrelated to demographic characteristics being examined. Although it may or may not be true that such latent variables are not influenced by various demographic characteristics, it is entirely likely that the way we measure them is so influenced. It is a great weakness of CPTs generally that studies of demographic variables have not been done, although this is common among neuropsychological tests (Reynolds, 1997). Studies of ethnic and gender bias are sorely lacking for these tests, particularly with regard to specificity and sensitivity of CPT scores (see Reynolds, in press, for methods for such research) and are desperately needed, particularly given their widespread use.

CPT SCORE FORMATS AND TABLES

Another area of concern related to the technical adequacy of a measure relates to the variables used for measurement of the construct of interest. From the descriptions provided here as well as in Table 2.3, it is apparent that a number of different CPT indices are available to assess an individual's performance. The variables generated by the individual CPTs have an effect on the interpretation of the individual's performance based on what the variable is purported to measure. At the same time, the format or metric used in the interpretation and reporting process can affect the conclusions as well. Finally, the organization of normative data by appropriate age-level increments as well as other demographic variables can impact interpretation of the results.

Results of the performances measured by CPTs, as with any measure, may be presented in a variety of formats, including raw scores, percentages correct or incorrect, percentiles, and standard scores (e.g., quotients, T-scores, z-scores, and deviation-scaled scores). Although the easiest to calculate, raw scores or percentages correct or incorrect have no meaning attached to the scores, as the scores do not convey any information about their relative positions (Anastasi, 1988; R.J. Cohen & Swerdlik, 1999; Crocker & Algina, 1986). In contrast, percentiles provide a yardstick for relative position of scores and have been a popular means of organizing CPT data (e.g., Gordon Systems, Inc., 1991). Percentiles are readily understood by a majority of people, and their use can address some of the issues associated with nonnormal score distributions (Gordon Systems, Inc., 1991; Reynolds & Kamphaus, 1992). At the same time, the problem with using percentiles is that, with a skewed distribution of scores, real differences between scores may become distorted (Anastasi, 1988; R.J. Cohen & Swerdlik, 1999; Crocker & Algina, 1986). In a normal distribution, fewer scores are found in the extremes of the distribution and the majority of scores are located in the middle of the distribution. From a psychometric perspective, equal interval standard scores are the preferred means of reporting data, as standard scores are more interpretable (i.e., standard scores have a set mean and standard deviation). Using standard scores allows comparison of an individual's performance to a normative group; when a comparison is made, the client's score is meaningful (i.e., the score has a relative position or rank). Thus, it is recommended that when score distributions are relatively normal, CPT results be reported in standard score formats, as standard scores are more psychometrically grounded, meaningful, and interpretable. Standard scores are more usable with nonnormal distributions as well, but must be accompanied by percentile ranks, and linear transformations are preferred. Unfortunately, the poor normative data generally available for CPTs do not allow clear definition of the latent score distributions. Experience and related behavioral measures suggest strongly that most, if not all, scores yielded by CPTs are positively skewed (where high scores indicate pathology) and should be scaled using standard scores with linear transformation and accompanying percentile ranks. Careful reporting and descriptions of scaling methods are needed as well and are generally not provided for the CPTs.

The metric used is not the only consideration in how scores are reported. As noted previously, consideration needs to be given to age, gender, SES, and educational level as mediating factors in CPT performance. From a developmental perspective, the increments of score reporting by age groups are of importance in assessing the neurophysiology of attention (Lowe et al., 2000). As noted in Chapter 1, many of the structures involved in the functional systems that subsume attention and executive control (e.g., frontal lobes) are continuing to mature throughout childhood and adolescence and possibly even into early adulthood. For children, state regulation has been found to mature as a function of age, with associated changes evidenced in the degree of impulsivity (e.g., van der Meere & Stemerdink, 1999). Similar developmental differences have been found with other components of executive function (e.g., Parrila, Äystö, &

Das, 1994). Research suggests that there are changes in neurophysiology associated with these functional systems that occur throughout adulthood and particularly in later adulthood or associated with a disease process (e.g., Alzheimer's). Further, age as a variable has been found to be associated with CPT performance (e.g., Burland, 1985; Conners, 1995; C. Evans, 1988; Gordon & Mettelman, 1988; Greenberg & Crosby, 1992b; Greenberg & Waldman, 1993; Grodzinsky & Diamond, 1992; Halperin, Sharma, et al., 1991; Holcomb, Ackerman, & Dykman, 1985; Klorman et al., 1991; Kupietz, 1990; Levy, 1980; Levy & Hobbes, 1979; List, 1985; Marks, Himelstein, Newcorn, & Halperin, 1999; O'Dougherty et al., 1984; Parr, 1995; Romans, Roeltgen, Kushner, & Ross, 1997; Sandford & Turner, 1995; Turner & Sandford, 1995a, 1995b).

Developmental differences in children's performance on CPTs have been reported by a number of researchers using normative samples (e.g., Gordon & Mettelman, 1988; Greenberg & Waldman, 1993; Turner & Sandford, 1995a). Similar error patterns have emerged with clinical samples of children with ADD and learning problems (e.g., Raggio & Whitten, 1994). Raggio and Whitten found the same error patterns in their clinical sample of children with ADD and learning problems ranging in age from 5 to 9 years. Moreover, the clinic-age groups (i.e., children between 6 and 9 years) made approximately 2 to 5 times more errors than the same-age comparison groups of nonreferred individuals. For example, Turner and Sandford (1995b) examined the mean reaction time for correct responses by age using the IVA normative data and found a curvilinear relation between mean reaction time and age. Specifically, Turner and Sandford noted a reduction in mean reaction time (improvement) from ages 5 to 12 years, with the most rapid decrease occurring between the ages of 5 and 7 years and optimum performance obtained by the midteen years. Using TOVA normative data, Greenberg and Crosby (1992b) noted that error scores and reaction times were highest for the 4- to 5-year-old group. After age 5, error scores and reaction time scores decreased with age through early to middle adolescence, and then leveled off and remained relatively stable during the early adult years.

Across studies, results indicate that the effect of age on CPT performance is curvilinear (e.g., Greenberg & Crosby, 1992b; Turner & Sandford, 1995b). For example, Turner and Sandford found that optimum performance in mean reaction time was demonstrated during the midteen to young adult years and remained relatively stable during the middle adult years; after age 45, a slight decline in performance or increased reaction time occurred. Similarly, Greenberg and Crosby examined CPT scores by age using a portion of the TOVA normative data and found curvilinear relations between CPT performance (i.e., omission and commission errors, and mean reaction time and standard deviation reaction time) and age. As noted by Turner and Sanford, following a gradual improvement in performance as a function of age, in later adulthood mean reaction time scores and omission and commission errors increased with age. Similar findings of decrements in performance have been reported in other studies as well (Parasuraman & Giambra, 1991; Turner & Sanford, 1995b). In one study, Ernst, Zametkin, Phillips, and Cohen (1998) found that CPT performance (correct hits) improved with age for females between 18 and 56 years. On the IVA, a decline in performance was found after age 45 (Turner & Sanford, 1995b), but reaction time and error scores started to increase after ages 30 to 39 and again at ages 60 to 69. With a larger sample of older adults, Parr (1995) reported significant increases in omission and commission error scores on the Conners' with increasing age, such that 70- and 80-year-olds made more errors than 50-year-olds. Unlike the other studies reviewed here (e.g., Greenberg & Crosby, 1992b; Turner & Sanford, 1995b) and other evidence of psychomotor slowing associated with increased age (e.g., Keys & White, 2000), Parr found no main effect of age for reaction time (sample ranging in age from 50 to 89 years).

These findings clearly denote a consistent association between CPT scores and age. CPT scores follow different U-shaped curves across the life span depending on the variable of interest; differences in the curve also appear to be a function of task demands. These different U-shaped curves across age and type of task or CPT score indicate that different components of attention develop and mature at different rates (Turner & Sanford, 1995a). Thus, it is not only important that tables or results generated from the measure be interpretable from a psychometric perspective, it is also important that data be provided in such a way as to allow for the incorporation of developmental theory into the interpretation process. To address developmental issues, age-appropriate norms consisting of brief intervals of 4 to 6 months for children ages 5 or 6 to 14 or 15 years, one-year intervals for ages 15 to 20 years, and no more than five-year intervals for ages 20 years and above are recommended (Lowe et al., 2000). This would require considerably larger standardization samples than are customary with CPTs but are nevertheless needed.

Gender also has been suggested to be associated with differential test score performance on CPTs (e.g., Greenberg & Crosby, 1992b; Greenberg & Waldman, 1993; King, 1996; Mataix-Cols et al., 1997; W. Mitchell, Chavez, Baker, Guzman, & Azen, 1990; Turner & Sandford, 1995a, 1995b; A. Wagner, 1987; Zentall, 1986). However, as Lowe et al. (2000) pointed out, few, if any, substantial gender differences in CPT performance have been reported in the literature (e.g., Bauermeister et al., 1990; Breen, 1989; Cohler, Grunebaum, Weiss, Gamer, & Gallant, 1977; Driscoll, 1994; Goldstein et al., 1997; Levy, 1980; Levy & Hobbes, 1979; List, 1985; Mansour et al., 1996; Parr, 1995). For example, Levy administered the X-CPT to 120 males and

110 females from Sydney, Australia, ranging in age from 3 to 7 years and representing every social class in Sydney, according to Congalton's (1969) classification criteria. The X-CPT target and nontarget stimuli consisted of letters, with a stimulus display time of 2000 ms and an ISI of 1500 ms. Levy found no significant gender differences for omission errors, commission errors, or mean reaction time scores. The equivocal findings support the need for additional studies of gender differences on CPT performance by CPT type and score.

Gender differences in CPT performance have been researched among the adult population as well (e.g., Mansour et al., 1996; Parr, 1995). In Mansour et al.'s study, 26 males and 15 females, all nonreferred adults ranging in age from 18 to 45, were assessed on the X-CPT. The stimuli consisted of numbers presented in a visual format, with an ISI of 1500 ms. The stimuli were degraded, which made detection more difficult. For CPT variables, Mansour et al. found no gender differences even though some gender effects in glucose metabolism rates in specific regions of the brain were noted. Similarly, Parr found no gender differences between 222 nonreferred older adult males ($n = 74$) and females ($n = 148$) on the Conners' on either commission and omission errors or reaction time. In one study (Gordon & Mettelman, 1988), significant differences were found; however, the differences were not considered clinically meaningful. Based on the normative data for the GDS, Gordon and Mettelman found statistically significant but clinically trivial gender differences. Differences were found for the main effects of gender for commission errors on the vigilance and distractibility tasks; however, the relation between gender and CPT scores was relatively weak and accounted for approximately 2% of the variance. Based on these results, Gordon and Mettelman recommended combined rather than separate male and female norms, at least on the GDS. If the numbers of males and females in the sample are proportionate, this may well be appropriate. However, it is not enough to test mean differences. The variances also must be evaluated or estimation of the score distributions will be biased if the standard deviations are different across gender.

As indicated in Lowe et al.'s (2000) review, when gender differences have been found, the differences reported are usually in reaction time scores and commission errors, with males making more commission errors (e.g., Barkley, 1995; Greenberg & Crosby, 1992b; Sandford & Turner, 1995; Wagner, 1987) and having faster reaction time scores (e.g., Barkley, 1995; Greenberg & Crosby, 1992b; Mataix-Cols et al., 1997; Sandford & Turner, 1995; Seidel & Joschko, 1991). For example, Mataix-Cols et al. found reaction times quicker for males ($n = 18$) than for females ($n = 53$) on the Identical Pairs CPT. For the total sample, males were reported to have faster reaction times than females. Similarly, Greenberg and Crosby found faster reaction times for males than for females for a portion of the TOVA normative sample. In addition to reaction time differences, Greenberg and Crosby found that males committed more errors of commission than did females.

In another study, Wagner (1987) examined gender differences in CPT performance in a sample of 83 boys and 34 girls on the X-CPT and AX-CPT. The sample consisted of two groups: children with ADHD and controls; the average age of the children with ADHD was 8.86 years, and the average age of the controls was 9.28 years. Consistent with the findings of Greenberg and Crosby (1992b), results revealed that boys made more errors of commission than girls. Sandford and Turner (1995) found similar patterns of faster reaction time and more commission errors with the normative sample of the IVA. Thus, depending on the variable of interest, gender as well as age may have an impact on CPT performance. Based on their findings of age and gender differences on CPT performance, Sandford and Turner (1995) suggested the need for comparison of the individual's performance to appropriate gender- and age-normative groups.

Few studies have addressed the relation between CPT scores and education (Dahl et al., 1996; Parr, 1995) or SES (C. Evans, 1988; Gordon & Mettelman, 1988; Greene, 1982; Levy, 1980; Levy & Hobbes, 1979), with a few exceptions (Gordon & Mettelman, 1988; Levy, 1980; Levy & Hobbes, 1979; Parr, 1995). Generally, a relation between educational level and CPT scores has not been found (Parr, 1995). In Parr's study described above, the adults had varying occupational and educational backgrounds. A breakdown of the sample by educational level showed that 111 individuals (50% of the sample) had 0 to 12 years of schooling, 70 subjects (31.5%) had 13 to 15 years of education, and 41 adults (18.5%) had 16 or more years of schooling. Results of a 4 × 3 (age × education) multivariate analysis of variance (MANOVA), with omission errors, commission errors, and reaction time scores being the dependent variables, yielded no main effects of education or age × education interaction effects. Educational level has been viewed as a suitable substitute for SES; given Parr's (1995) findings, a relation between SES and CPT scores would not be expected among adults, or at least among the older adult population. However, no studies have examined the relation of SES and CPT performance in the older adult population.

For adults, Greene (1982) investigated the relation between CPT performance and SES among two clinical samples; 50 adults, 21 males and 4 females with schizophrenia and 16 males and 9 females with affective disorders, mainly bipolar disorders, ranging in age from 18 to 65, were assessed on a CPT. The CPT consisted of numbers presented in groups of two up to groups of seven, and the task of the subjects was to respond verbally as to whether the numbers were the same or different. The numbers were displayed for 400 ms with an ISI of 5000 ms. The eight-minute task consisted of a distractor and a no-distractor condition. In the distractor condition, an auditory stimulus (i.e., a woman reading a psychological textbook passage) was used. Greene found a significant inverse relation between social class and CPT scores in the no-distractor condition for both clinical groups. The use of clinical samples may have accounted for the results obtained in this study. Whether the same findings would be obtained with a nonreferred, presumably healthy adult sample is not known at the present time.

A larger number of studies have been conducted to assess the relation between CPT scores and SES in the child population; however, the findings are equivocal (C. Evans, 1988; Gordon & Mettelman, 1988; Levy, 1980; Levy & Hobbes, 1979; List, 1985). Levy found SES differences among nonreferred children representing all SES levels in Australia on the X-CPT. Levy found that the children's ability to complete the CPT was dependent on both child's age and parental SES. Specifically, all children from the upper class were able to complete the CPT by 4 years to 4 years, 5 months; the lower-class children were not able to complete the CPT until about age 4 years, 6 months or older. Similarly, Gordon and Mettelman investigated the relation between CPT scores and parental SES using the normative data for the GDS children's version. All SES levels were represented in the sample based on Hollingshead and Redlich's (1958) criteria. On the vigilance task, a significant relation between mother's SES and total correct scores was found, whereas on the distractibility task, father's SES was significantly related to commission error scores. Although the relations between CPT scores and parental SES were found to be significant, Gordon and Mettelman reported that these relations accounted for a small percentage of the variance and thus were deemed trivial.

In contrast, C. Evans (1988) assessed 180 children, 164 children on the SES variable, ranging in age from 6 to 14 years, on the X-CPT with numbers as target and nontarget stimuli. A modification of Hollingshead and Redlich's (1959) criteria was used to determine a global SES index for each family. When age effects were partialed out, a nonsignificant relation was reported between CPT performance and SES. Thus, with differing task demands, differing analyses, and differing samples, the extent to which SES may act as a mediator variable is unclear. C. Evans' study highlights the importance of holding variables (e.g., gender, ethnicity, age) constant when subjects are not randomly selected across all variables (Lowe et al., 2000). C. Evans' study represents a step in the right direction when assessing the relation between demographic variables of interest and CPT scores. However, the study falls short, as other variables should have been controlled (i.e., gender). When different ethnic groups are included in the sample, this variable should be controlled as well.

Thus, the format of tables (including the age-level increments), the metrics of score reporting, and the extent of data provided (by age, gender, SES) are important to the interpretation process. Although mean differences for age, gender, or SES may not be the real issue in normative decision making (Reynolds, in press), it is important for these data to be provided in the technical manuals by the test developers. The extent to which the major commercially available CPTs provide this information is presented next.

CONNERS' CPT

A total of 13 indices are generated from the Conners' CPT for use in interpretation. Variables include the more commonly reported correct hits, omission errors, commission errors, and mean reaction time. The Conners' CPT also provides the variables from SDT of sensitivity (d') and response bias (Beta). Several measures relate specifically to the consistency or variability of the individual's performance across blocks and subblocks. These include the reaction time standard error; the standard deviation of the standard error for each subblock; the change in response time during testing as measured by the slope; the change in response time standard errors during testing, as measured by the slope; the reaction time at the subblock changes for the 1000, 2000, and 4000 ms ISIs, as measured by the slope; and the standard error of the subblock changes over the 1000, 2000, and 4000 ms ISI across the six blocks as measured by the slope. Finally, the Conners' CPT provides an overall index for the individual's performance, which is a weighted score derived from all of the other indices.

The Conners' CPT indices are presented in raw score, percentile, and T-score formats. The mean T-score for the comparison (i.e., normative) group is 50 ($SD = 10$). Certain index scores, including correct hits, reaction times, d', and Beta, have been transformed so that higher T-scores suggest that attention problems exist. T-scores of 60 or above and percentiles of 90 or above on two or more indices indicate potential attention problems (Conners, 1992, 1995; Grooms, 1998). This interpretation by Conners makes certain assumptions about the base rates of the disorders underlying problematic CPT performance (i.e., they occur in 10% of the population). The norms are not stratified and group statistics (e.g., mean scores, standard deviations, and standard errors of the mean) are not provided in the manual (Conners, 1992, 1995; Dumont et al., 1995, 1999). Conners indicated that the distributions are skewed for many of the variables reported, which may impact on interpretation.

The norms are divided into eight age groups. For children, ages 4 through 17, norms are based on two-year increments. Given the research findings on the effects of age on CPT performance, two-year increments in childhood and adolescence would not seem to be sufficiently small for developmental trends to be evidenced. Smaller increments, particularly through age 12, seem warranted. Otherwise, sensitivity and specificity of

CPT scores will be adversely impacted not in a common or systematic way, but rather will vary across age within each two-year interval. All adults, regardless of age, are considered as a single group for interpretation of CPT performance. Given the preponderance of adults in the 18- to 30-year range, as well as what is known about normal developmental decline, this is not acceptable. Further, the consideration of adults as a single age group may impede the ability to differentiate normal decline from the manifestation of disease process. Separate normative data by gender or ethnicity are not available.

GDS

For both the vigilance and distractibility tasks, measures of performance include correct responses, omission and commission errors, and latency (reaction time) for each block as well as the average latency for the entire task. Although not programmed to separate commission errors by type (i.e., target-related vs. random errors), error-tracking data are available for clinicians who wish to do an error analysis. Instructions for computing the slope of the reaction time across blocks (block variability) to assess consistency are provided (Gordon Systems, Inc., 1991).

Scoring formats include raw score, percentile, and threshold tables. The threshold tables were derived based on the percentile information with scores divided into three different ranges: abnormal (5th percentile or lower), borderline (6th to 25th percentile), and normal (26th percentile and above). Tables are available for children and adults, including a separate geriatric table (Gordon & Mettelman, 1988; Gordon Systems, Inc., 1991).

The norms for the preschool version are in one-year age intervals for 4- and 5-year-olds. For the children's version, norms are divided into five age groups, with two-year age intervals for 6- to 11-year-olds, and a five-year age interval for 12- to 16-year-olds. As noted with the Conners', the age intervals need to be narrower so that the neurophysiological development of attention may be examined and more accurately portrayed across the child and adolescent life span. Gender-based norms are not included (i.e., the norms for males and females were combined), as gender effects were reported to account for only 2% of the variance (Gordon & Mettelman, 1988; Gordon Systems, Inc., 1987a).

Some group statistics (i.e., raw scores, percentiles) are provided for the normative samples, but means, standard deviations, and standard errors of the mean are not included for the preschool and children's versions. In addition to the raw scores and percentiles for the adult versions for the adult and older adult samples, means and standard scores are provided; information on the standard error is not provided for any age group (Gordon Systems, Inc., 1991).

IVA

The IVA has 11 raw score scales, 6 quotient scales, and 2 composite scores, all of which are provided separately for visual and auditory portions of the task (Dumont et al., 1995, 1999; Sandford & Turner, 1995; Sandford et al., 1995a, 1995b; Seckler et al., 1995; Turner & Sandford, 1995a, 1995b). The two composite scores (Response Control Quotient, Attention Quotient) are provided in a combination (Full Scale) score as well as separately for visual and auditory portions. Each of the composites incorporates three of the six quotient scores. The Response Control Quotient (RCQ) is made up of prudence (avoidance of commission errors), consistency (minimal variability in response time), and stamina (response time maintained across testing) quotients. The Attention Quotient is based on the vigilance (avoidance of omission errors), focus (number of response time outliers across testing), and speed quotients (Sandford et al., 1995a, 1995b; Seckler et al., 1995; Turner & Sandford, 1995a, 1995b). Fine motor/hyperactivity is another global scale and incorporates anticipatory responses or continued pressure on the mouse (i.e., failure to release). Variables of comprehension (a measure of random errors), persistence (decrement in performance related to motivation or arousal), and sensory/motor (slow reaction time that may impair performance) are grouped together as validity measures. Performance differences based on target frequency are reflected in the readiness score, and differences in performance based on modality are reflected in the balance score.

Results of the IVA are presented in raw scores (actual time to respond, percent) as well as in standard scores with a mean of 100 ($SD = 15$). The printout generated includes all results in numeric as well as graphic form (Sandford & Turner, 1995). The normative sample of the IVA is divided into 10 age groups with varying age intervals, ranging from two years for the 5- to 10-year-old groups to 10 years for the 25- to 90-year-old groups. As with the age increments on other CPTs, these age intervals are too wide. Smaller age intervals would provide greater and more detailed information on the changes in performance across age on the various CPT indices. The actual normative data are not in the manual itself, but can be accessed through the software after installation from a read-only file. As noted in the discussion of gender differences, Sandford and Turner argued for comparison to same gender norms, and separate normative data on the IVA are available for males and for females.

TOVA AND TOVA-A

The TOVA and TOVA-A provide multiple measures of performance including omission and commission errors, response time, the standard deviation of the response time, and sensitivity (d'). It is important to note that omission errors on the TOVA are not simply the number (or percent) of targets to which the individual did not respond. On the TOVA tasks, the omission error score is the ratio of correct responses to the difference between the number of targets (possible responses) minus the number of anticipatory errors (Greenberg et al., 1999; Leark et al., 1996). In other words, the omission error score is a measure of relative accuracy. The commission error score is generated similarly but based on the number of responses to non-targets relative to the total number of nontargets minus the number of anticipatory responses. For both omission and commission error calculations, anticipatory errors are defined as those responses made within 200 ms of the appearance of the stimulus regardless of whether the stimulus is a target or nontarget (Greenberg et al., 1999; Leark et al., 1996). For error analysis purposes, the program also provides the number of multiple responses, postcommission error response time (average response time for correct responses after committing a commission error), and the number of anticipatory errors (Cenedela, 1996; Dumont et al., 1995, 1999; Greenberg & Crosby, 1992b; Greenberg et al., 1999; Greenberg & Waldman, 1993; Leark et al., 1996). A final index, the ADHD scale, is provided as well; it is derived based on the comparison of the examinee's scores to persons matched to the examinee for gender and age in the database who had a diagnosis of ADHD (Cenedela, 1996).

Results are reported as raw scores, percentages, standard scores (mean of 100), and standard deviations. A printout of all responses by response type is provided as well. The norms for both the TOVA and TOVA-A are divided into one-year intervals through age 19. For the TOVA, the adult norms are divided into 10-year intervals for ages 20 to 79 years, and all adults over 80 years are considered as a single group (Greenberg et al, 1999; Leark et al., 1996). As noted with the other CPTs, the intervals for the different age groups need to be smaller, especially the intervals for the adults. Group statistics (means and standard deviations) are provided by the age-level breakdown for both the TOVA and TOVA-A in the manuals, with separate male and female norms provided for each age group (Greenberg et al., 1999; Leark et al., 1996).

INTERPRETIVE GUIDANCE

As noted previously, the variables generated for measuring the construct of interest, as well as the format used in presenting results, can affect the interpretation of results. Given the differing variables and terminology used (i.e., omission errors vs. Vigilance Quotient as a measure of how well the individual avoids omission errors), it is incumbent on the developer of a test to provide some assistance in the interpretation of scores generated. For this reason, it is helpful if the test developer provides appropriate descriptors and interpretive guidance either in a separate manual or a specific section of the manual, complete with case studies. With increasing emphasis on the need to link assessment with intervention (e.g., Huberty, 1996; Maruish, 1999; Meier, 1999), the extent to which the manual assists in interpretation that is geared to treatment planning also is of concern. The extent to which the major CPT manuals provide interpretive information and guidance is discussed next.

CONNERS' CPT

The Conners' manual includes a brief chapter on interpretation as well as an interpretive guide as part of the report generated. Although referred to as an interpretive guide (Conners, 1992, 1995), the chapter is limited to the provision of descriptive labels (e.g., markedly atypical, mildly atypical, and within average range) for each of the variables generated. The manual includes two case studies, one of a boy and one of a girl. Both cases are brief and detail the decision-making process used in reaching a diagnostic decision based on Conners' CPT data. Conners emphasizes that the Conners' CPT is only one piece of information to be integrated with other available data and direct observation in the diagnostic process. A sample write-up of the results (narrative form) in conjunction with other test results is not provided and suggestions for intervention are not addressed.

GDS

Of the four major CPTs discussed here, the GDS is the only one that is not computer-based and therefore the only one that does not generate some form of printed report of the results. Examiners complete the test form and compute the variability (block variances) themselves. For interpretation, the manual (Gordon Systems, Inc., 1987a; Gordon, McClure, & Aylward, 1996) includes case studies (child) and an interpretation of the results in narrative form. Within the case studies, as part of the interpretation process, different conclusions depending on what other information is available (or the integration of data for a single child) are provided. Sample reports and interpretive statements are provided as well.

IVA

The IVA manual includes a section on interpretation. In this section, there is a discussion of the theoretical model used to derive the various indices used in reporting the individual's performance on the CPT (Sandford & Turner, 1995). In conjunction with this, there is a lengthy and detailed description of each of the obtained scores (e.g., Prudence), how the score is derived, and what it is believed to measure. Since the printout uses numerous abbreviations, there is a listing of all the abbreviations and codes in this section as well. The interpretive process stresses the importance of taking into consideration the three validity scales (Persistence, Sensory/Motor, and Comprehension). Diagnostic considerations specific to ADHD, including a 21-step procedure for decision making, are provided to facilitate interpretation, but may overwhelm most clinicians. Responsive to current concerns in the field, the interpretive portion of the manual includes a specific section on ruling out ADHD in adults (Sandford & Turner, 1995).

Of note, in conjunction with the interpretation process, Sandford and Turner (1995) suggested that CPT performance of individuals be adjusted if they have a high (standard score over 120) or low (standard score below 80) Performance IQ (PIQ). The method of adjustment suggested is to compare the individual to the normative sample that is of comparable mental age (as measured by Performance IQ [PIQ] not Verbal IQ [VIQ]) by changing the age of the normative sample used (i.e., for someone with a high PIQ, use an older age range). This appears to be based on an assumption that "cerebral development is more mature, and thus may mask ADHD" when PIQ is high and the reverse when it is low (Sandford & Turner, 1995, p. XII-22). There is no evidence that this is an empirically sound manipulation or means of interpretation of CPT results, and this type of adjustment should be used with extreme caution. The calculation and use of mental age as suggested therein is problematic as well (e.g., see Reynolds, 1997).

The interpretation section of the manual includes a number of child cases, including separate cases with a diagnosis of ADHD Predominantly Inattentive Type, ADHD Combined Type, and Dysthymia, and one case with excessive random responding. Variables that support the respective diagnoses are highlighted in each case and the interpretive process emphasized. Sample reports in narrative form are not provided.

TOVA AND TOVA-A

Interpretation is addressed briefly in the professional manual (Leark et al., 1996), with an emphasis on determining if the profile obtained is valid based on variable values. The basic process recommended for interpretation of TOVA results is then outlined. A more thorough presentation of the interpretation process is provided in the clinical manual (Greenberg et al., 1999). The software program generates a six- or seven-page interpretative report that presents and graphs the data as well as recommendations for intervention by behavioral category (Cenedela, 1996). A school intervention plan also can be generated (Greenberg et al., 1999). In the clinical manual, each page of the printout is explained in detail. The test report includes not only numeric results and graphs, but also multiple cautions (i.e., one piece of information that should be used in conjunction with other information) and interpretive statements (i.e., results are within normal limits). Numerous case studies are provided (all for the TOVA) that highlight specific characteristics such as excessive commission errors or excessive omission errors. In addition to case studies that demonstrate the diagnostic process, numerous case studies are provided to demonstrate how the TOVA can be used to monitor the effectiveness of medication. Case studies are included for children as well as adults.

One case is specific to the need to make adjustments for high or low IQ. In contrast to the process suggested by Sandford and Turner (1995), the adjustment suggested is in the interpretation process as opposed to substituting the normative data used for comparison. Greenberg and colleagues (1999) suggested that clinicians examine the extent to which CPT performance is consistent with (or is discrepant from) the IQ obtained for the individual similar to the discrepancy method used to establish a learning disability. The need for this type of adjustment appears to be specific to reaction time and reaction time variability. As with the method advocated by Sandford and Turner, however, an empirical basis for the use of a discrepancy method does not exist.

RELIABILITY AND VALIDITY STUDIES

Besides adequate norms and interpretive guidance, the quality of a measure such as a CPT is evaluated based on whether the measure is reliable and valid (e.g., Anastasi, 1988; R.J. Cohen & Swerdlik, 1999; Crocker & Algina, 1986). Reliability of a measure refers to test score consistency (e.g., Anastasi, 1988). In a more technical sense, reliability is defined as an estimate of the proportion of total variance in test scores that is attributed to true score variance, as opposed to error variance (e.g., Anastasi, 1988; R.J. Cohen & Swerdlik, 1999; Crocker & Algina, 1986). More and more, it is incumbent on test developers to conduct reliability studies, as well as clinical validity studies, as part of the test development process and to include these studies in the manual(s) that accompany the test itself.

The number of different types of reliability measures possible is relatively large, as a number of conditions can affect test scores (e.g., instructions, lighting, room temperature) and contribute to the error variance found in these observed scores. When the proportion of total variance in test scores attributed to error variance is high, lower reliability estimates or reliability coefficients will result (e.g., Anastasi, 1988; R.J. Cohen & Swerdlik, 1999; Crocker & Algina, 1986). In actual practice, the number of different types of test reliability calculated are relatively few (Anastasi,

1988). There are basically three techniques for estimating the reliability of test scores: test-retest reliability, internal consistency reliability (e.g., split-half reliability, true alternate or parallel forms correlations, Kuder-Richardson formulas, and coefficient alpha), and interscorer or interrater reliability (e.g., Anastasi, 1988; R.J. Cohen & Swerdlik, 1999; Crocker & Algina, 1986). These three techniques relate to different types of reliability; one is not interchangeable with another. A limited number of reliability studies have been conducted on CPTs (e.g., Buchsbaum & Sostek, 1980; Cornblatt, Risch, Farris, Friedman, & Erlenmeyer-Kimling, 1988; Finkelstein, Cannon, Gur, Gur, & Moberg, 1997; Halperin, Sharma, et al., 1991; Harper & Ottinger, 1992; Llorente et al., 2000; Rosvold et al., 1956; Sandford, 1994; Seckler et al., 1995; Seidel & Joschko, 1991). Reliability coefficients across the types of reliability for the different versions of the CPT are presented in Table 3.3 and discussed by type of reliability next. Reliability studies for the four major CPTs are then discussed by CPT.

Interscorer or interrater reliability refers to the degree of agreement in ratings between two or more raters on the same individuals (e.g., R.J. Cohen & Swerdlik, 1999; Crocker & Algina, 1986). With most CPTs, interscorer reliability is not a major issue, as CPT scores are generated by computers or microprocessors, not the examiner (e.g., Gordon, 1983; Raggio & Whitten, 1994). The Auditory Continuous Performance Test (ACPT; R. Keith, 1994), however, is an exception, in that the score is based on direct observation by the examiner of examinee responses. Internal consistency refers to the degree of consistency and quality of the item sampling from the total item domain of a test (i.e., the set of items chosen; e.g., Anastasi, 1988; Crocker & Algina, 1986). Most commonly, a single administration of a test is given to a group of individuals to assess the homogeneity of the test (e.g., Anastasi, 1988; R.J. Cohen & Swerdlik, 1999; Crocker & Algina, 1986). For timed tasks such as CPTs, however, the more standard indices of internal consistency (e.g., split-half, Chronbach alpha) may not be the most appropriate (Anastasi, 1988). Alternative means of demonstrating consistency may include comparison of the same condition (e.g., ISI, target frequency) across different time blocks or comparison of conditions across individuals to determine the unifactorial nature of the CPT.

Based on the original CPT, Rosvold et al. (1956) found high internal consistency estimates for scores on the X-CPT, with coefficients ranging from .86 to .88. Other researchers have conducted internal consistency studies on other versions of the CPT (e.g., Ellis, 1991; Halperin, Sharma, et al., 1991). For example, Halperin, Sharma, et al. assessed 138 nonreferred males ranging in age from 7 to 11 years, with a mean age of 9.4 years ($SD = 1.4$ years), on an AX-CPT. The subjects were from four suburban public schools and one parochial school in the New York City area.

Table 3.3

Reliability Studies of Continuous Performance Tests

Study	Type of Reliability	CPT Type	CPT Index	Reliability Coefficients
Aman & Mayhew, 1980	Internal consistency	X-CPT	Omission errors	.29
		X-CPT	Reaction time	.84
		AX-CPT	Omission errors	.74
		AX-CPT	Reaction time	.96
Buchsbaum & Sostek, 1980	Internal consistency	AX-CPT	Sensitivity (d')	.42
		AX-CPT	Response bias (Beta)	.59
		AX-CPT	Omission errors	.20
		AX-CPT	Commission errors	.57
	Test-retest (2 weeks)	AX-CPT	Sensitivity (d')	.58
		AX-CPT	Response bias (Beta)	.39
Cornblatt et al., 1988	Test-retest (1.5 years)	CPT-IP	Sensitivity (d')	.56–.73
		CPT-IP	Response bias (Beta)	.39–.61
Ellis, 1991	Internal consistency	AX-CPT	Total correct hits	.86–.92
		AX-CPT	Commission errors	.68–.80
		AX-CPT	Omission errors	.16–.64
Gordon & Mettelman, 1988	Test-retest	AX-CPT (GDS vigilance)	Correct hits	.72
		AX-CPT (GDS vigilance)	Commission errors	.84
		AX-CPT (GDS distractibility)	Correct hits	.67
		AX-CPT (GDS distractibility)	Commission errors	.85
	Test-retest	AX-CPT (GDS vigilance)	Correct hits	.68
		AX-CPT (GDS vigilance)	Commission errors	.94
Halperin, Sharma, et al., 1991	Internal consistency	AX-CPT	Correct hits	.72
		AX-CPT	False alarms	.84
		AX-CPT	Omission errors	.71
		AX-CPT	Mean reaction time	.92
		AX-CPT	Reaction time variability	.67
		AX-CPT	Very late correct response	.31
Harper & Ottinger, 1992	Test-retest (≥ 1 week)	X-CPT (version 1)	Omission errors	.55
		X-CPT (version 1)	Commission errors	.75

Study	Reliability	Test	Measure	Coefficient
Leark et al., 1996	Internal consistency	X-CPT (version 1)	Reaction time	.16
		X-CPT (version 2)	Omission errors	.80
		X-CPT (version 2)	Commission errors	.06
		X-CPT (version 2)	Reaction time	.17
		X-CPT (TOVA)	Sensitivity (d')	.52–.72
		X-CPT (TOVA)	Reaction time	.93–.99
		X-CPT (TOVA)	Omission errors	.70–.99
		X-CPT (TOVA)	Commission errors	.79–.82
		X-CPT (TOVA)	Reaction time variability	.70–.99
		X-CPT (TOVA-A)	Sensitivity (d')	.63–.74
		X-CPT (TOVA-A)	Reaction time	.88–.91
		X-CPT (TOVA-A)	Omission errors	.81–.94
		X-CPT (TOVA-A)	Commission errors	.83–.87
		X-CPT (TOVA-A)	Reaction time variability	.75–.87
	Test-retest (90 minutes)	X-CPT (TOVA)	Reaction time	.77
		X-CPT (TOVA)	Reaction time variability	.93
Llorente et al., 2000	Internal consistency	X-CPT (TOVA)	Omission and commission errors	.93–.99
	Test-retest	X-CPT (TOVA)	Omission errors	.51–.61
		X-CPT (TOVA)	Commission errors	.58–.71
		X-CPT (TOVA)	Reaction time	.70–.82
		X-CPT (TOVA)	Reaction time variability	.66–.75
Rosvold et al., 1956	Internal consistency	X-CPT	Not specified	.86–.88
	Test-retest	X-CPT	Not specified	.74–.90
Seckler et al., 1995	Test-retest	X-CPT (IVA)	Auditory Attention Quotient	.66
		X-CPT (IVA)	Auditory Response Control Quotient	.39
		X-CPT (IVA)	Visual Attention Quotient	.75
		X-CPT (IVA)	Visual Response Control Quotient	.37
		X-CPT (IVA)	Full Scale Attention Quotient	.74
		X-CPT (IVA)	Full Scale Response Control Quotient	.41

Notes: CPT = Continuous performance test; GDS = Gordon Diagnostic System; TOVA = Test of Variables of Attention; TOVA-A = Test of Variables of Attention-Auditory; IVA = Integrated (or Intermediate)Visual and Auditory Continuous Performance Test; IP = Identical pairs.

Racial composition of the sample consisted of Whites (79%), Blacks (4%), Hispanics (10%), and Asians (7%). Halperin, Sharma, and colleagues reported split-half reliability estimates for correct hits, reaction time scores, reaction time standard deviations, false alarms (commission errors), and omission errors ranging from .67 to .92. Although these are all within the acceptable range, one split-half reliability estimate, that for very late correct responses, fell short of the standard at .38, possibly due to its infrequent occurrence.

In another study, Ellis (1991) reported split-half reliability estimates for scores on an AX-CPT with 25 children with attention problems (18 males and 7 females) and 29 controls (18 males and 11 females) in grades 3 through 5. Racial composition of the sample was Whites (38.9%), Blacks (57.4%), and Others (3.7%). The CPT stimuli were geometric shapes, with the target stimuli consisting of a black circle followed by a white square. The duration of the task was nine minutes. Internal consistency estimates over the three blocks for total correct hits and commission error scores ranged from .86 to .92 and .68 to .80, respectively. In contrast, adequate reliability was not demonstrated for the omission error scores, with reliability estimates ranging from .16 to .64 depending on blocks compared.

When parallel forms or alternate forms are available, alternate-forms reliability estimates are needed to evaluate the equivalence of the two versions of the CPT. Parallel-forms or alternate-forms reliability refers to the degree of test score consistency resulting from the administration of different but presumably equivalent versions of a test to the same group of individuals at the same or different points in time and are thus attempting to assess internal consistency or appropriateness of domain sampling (e.g., Anastasi, 1988; R.J. Cohen & Swerdlik, 1999; Crocker & Algina, 1986). The terms parallel-forms and alternate-forms reliability are often used interchangeably. However, unlike alternate-forms reliability, the means and variances of the observed scores and true scores (in theory) are equal on parallel forms but not necessarily equal on alternate forms of a test. With alternate-forms reliability, only the content and level of difficulty of the different versions of a test are assessed with regard to their equivalency (R.J. Cohen & Swerdlik, 1999). Equivalency of scores is not the same as equivalency of reliability.

Test-retest or temporal reliability refers to test score consistency across time for the same group of individuals on the same test (e.g., Anastasi, 1988; R.J. Cohen & Swerdlik, 1999; Crocker & Algina, 1986). Temporal reliability refers to the extent to which the test measures the construct of interest over time with consistency or the stability of the measurement over time (Anastasi, 1988). If a measure does not demonstrate stability over time, clinicians cannot be sure that the performance obtained at any given time is indicative of performance at other times (e.g., Lowe et al.,

2000; Raggio & Whitten, 1994; Seckler et al., 1995). For a state measure, this is of relatively less importance, but for a trait condition (e.g., ADHD) it is crucial. Rosvold and colleagues (1956) reported test-retest reliability estimates ranging from .74 to .90 on the original CPT.

Independent researchers have conducted studies on the temporal stability of different CPT paradigms (e.g., Buchsbaum & Sostek, 1980; Cornblatt et al., 1988; Finkelstein et al., 1997; Halperin, Sharma, et al., 1991; Harper & Ottinger, 1992; Rosvold et al., 1956). For example, Harper and Ottinger assessed 20 children with hyperactivity (17 boys and 3 girls) and 20 controls (17 boys and 3 girls) ranging in age from 4 to 6 years on two versions of the X-CPT. One version consisted of letter stimuli, with the target stimulus being the letter X. The stimulus display time was 200 ms, with an ISI of 1500 ms and duration of six minutes. The second version used pictures of objects, with the target stimulus being a bird sitting on a limb. The stimulus display time was increased to 500 ms and the duration of the task was increased to 14.5 minutes. The test-retest interval for both tasks was at least one week. Harper and Ottinger's study yielded test-retest reliability estimates of .55, .75, and .16 for omission error scores, commission error scores, and reaction times, respectively, for the first task, and .80, .06, and .17 for omission error scores, commission error scores, and reaction times, respectively, on the second task. The low reliability estimates for commission error scores on both tasks were attributed to the impulsive and sporadic behavior of the children with hyperactivity who were in the sample. Another possible explanation is the potential impact of age, as the authors' failed to control for the effects of age.

In the Halperin, Sharma, et al. (1991) study discussed previously, moderate test-retest reliabilities were reported on an AX-CPT with 34 nonreferred boys between the ages of 7 and 11 years who were part of the larger sample of 138 males from the New York City area. The subsample used for test-retest was reported to be ethnically and culturally diverse. The stimuli consisted of letters, with the A/X letter combination (i.e., the letter A followed by the letter X) serving as the target stimulus. The stimulus display time was 200 ms, with an ISI of 1500 ms and task duration of 12 minutes. The interval between test and retest was approximately 4.8 months ($SD = 1.4$ months). The test-retest reliability estimates for correct hits, reaction times, omission errors, inattention scores, and impulsivity scores ranged from .65 to .74, indicative of moderate temporal reliability. In contrast, the test-retest reliability estimate for total false alarms or commission errors was lower at .50 (Halperin, Sharma, et al., 1991).

Using still another variation of the CPT, Cornblatt et al. (1988) retested 23 families who were part of a larger study assessing normal attentional processing with the CPT-Identical Pairs (CPT-IP). The 23 families consisted of parents ranging in age from 36 to 59 years and their children, ranging in age from 12 to 22 years. The sample was predominately White and middle class and lived in the suburbs of the Northeast. The stimuli consisted of numbers and shapes with a stimulus display time of 50 ms and ISI of 1000 ms. Visual and auditory distractors were included in the study to assess performance in distractor and no-distractor conditions. The interval between test and retest ranged from 7 to 21 months (mean interval of 13.2 months, $SD = 4.09$ months). Test-retest reliability estimates for sensitivity (d') ranged from .56 to .73, and estimates for response style or bias (Beta) ranged from .39 to .61. A number of factors may have contributed to the magnitude of the reliability estimates, including time between testings, subject characteristics, task parameters, and scores or indices generated. All the potential differences may have influenced the magnitude of the reliability estimates and may account for or contribute to the differences in reliability estimates reported (Lowe et al., 2000).

Reliability is one consideration. Validity also is of concern when selecting various measures for use in a clinical battery, and test developers should include some initial study or studies specific to the convergent validity of the measure as well as the clinical or discriminant validity of the measure for populations of interest. For the purposes of this chapter, only the validity studies that were conducted in conjunction with test development and included in the test manuals are reviewed. More in-depth discussion of studies specific to construct validity (i.e., the extent of association of CPT performance to other measures of attention and executive control) as well as the extent of association of CPT performance to other variables (e.g., intelligence, achievement) is presented in Chapter 4. The issue of discriminant validity and the related issues of sensitivity and specificity are explored in more depth in Chapter 6 specific to children and ADHD, and in Chapter 7 specific to adults and adult disorders.

CONNERS' CPT

The manual for the Conners' CPT (Conners, 1992, 1995) does not include any studies that investigated temporal or internal consistency reliability. There is no indication that test-retest data were collected as part of the standardization process, nor are comparisons made across individuals for block performance on the differing ISIs.

Included in the manual, however, are clinical validity studies. In one study, the referred children with ADHD are compared to the general population (normative sample). For this study, Conners (1992, 1995) reported a 13.0% false negative rate and a 12.9% false positive rate. A second validity study investigated performance differences among the children in the referred sample (with ADHD as opposed to no ADHD or ADHD comorbid with other disorders). In addition to these two studies, the manual includes a bibliography of 35 studies that include CPT performance as a variable.

GDS

Temporal stability of the GDS children's standard version is provided in the technical manual (Gordon Systems, Inc., 1987a) and in Gordon and Mettelman (1988). The test-retest reliabilities are reported for a group of nonreferred ($n = 32$) and referred children ($n = 20$). The nonreferred children were retested between 2 and 22 days after the initial administration and completed both the vigilance and the distractibility tasks, whereas the referred children were retested one year after the initial administration on only the vigilance task. Test-retest reliability estimates for the nonreferred sample on the vigilance task were found to be .72 for total correct hits and .84 for commission error scores; reliability estimates for the scores on the distractibility task were .67 and .85, respectively. For the clinical sample, the test-retest reliability estimates at one year were .68 and .94 for total correct scores and commission error scores, respectively, for the vigilance task. These results indicate that the GDS demonstrates moderate to high test-retest reliability. One drawback of these studies is that a description of the clinic and nonreferred samples' demographic characteristics was not provided.

An alternate forms reliability study is included in the manual (Gordon Systems, Inc., 1987a) and in Gordon and Mettelman (1988). In this study, the scores of 174 children were compared on the two versions of the vigilance task (the 1/9 version and the 3/5 version). Each sample ($n_1 = 102$ and $n_2 = 72$) was selected randomly and matched for age. Gordon and Mettelman reported no significant differences between the two groups for total correct scores and commission error scores. Based on these findings, it was concluded that the two tasks were consistent and that "children perform similarly on both versions of the vigilance task" (p. 687). There are several major flaws associated with this statement if one views this experiment as an alternate-forms reliability study. First, different people were assessed on different versions of the vigilance task; when conducting an alternate-forms reliability study, the same people are required to take both versions of the test. Second, neither the reliability estimates nor the means and variances on the different indices were provided; thus, it remains unclear whether the 1/9 and 3/5 versions are equivalent forms of the vigilance task. In an alternate-forms reliability study, the correlation between the individuals' scores across forms must be reported. If random data with no reliability (i.e., $r_{ab} = 0$) are gathered by the two tests, the means and standard deviation will be equal. Comparison of means and standard deviations thus provide information only

on equivalence of aggregated data across tests and no information about the accuracy of the parameter estimation for the individual.

Although not specific to internal consistency and given that the addition of distraction changes the task demands, the degree of association between the vigilance and distractibility tasks is reported. Correlation coefficients were found to range from a small association ($r = -.22$) for vigilance correct and distractibility commission errors to a moderate association ($r = .57$) for vigilance commission errors and distractibility commission errors for children. The tasks are certainly not equivalent based on these values.

All of the studies reviewed above used the children's version of the GDS. Comparable data for the adult or preschool versions were not available. There were also no reliability data provided (i.e., interrater reliability) for the observation form (Gordon Systems, Inc., 1991). Thus, reliability of the adult and preschool versions and the observation form are unknown.

Validity studies are included in the technical section of the 1987 manual. These include convergent validity studies that document the correlation of GDS results with IQ, achievement, behavior rating scales, and scores from alternate measures of attention and executive control for samples at various age levels. Results reported indicate that age is most related to vigilance correct ($r = .53$) and distractibility correct ($r = .43$). For the standardization sample, minimal to no correlation was found with IQ. Two discriminant validity studies (see Gordon, 1986b) are included specific to children with ADHD, children with other disorders, and a control group, and children with hyperactivity as compared to children without hyperactivity. Results reported for these studies support the use of the GDS in the diagnosis of ADHD with approximately 70% agreement with parent and teacher ratings of children with ADHD depending on the age, the rater, and the scale. The manual also suggests the use of the GDS in the assessment of Alzheimer's disease in adults; however, a clinical validity study with this population is not provided (Gordon Systems, Inc., 1987a). These validity studies are not summarized or included in the 1996 manual.

IVA

A temporal reliability study (test-retest) with 70 volunteers, ages 5 to 70 years (mean age of 21.8 years), is reported by Seckler et al. (1995) and in the manual (Sandford & Turner, 1995). The test-retest interval ranged from one to four weeks. Depending on the variable, test-retest correlations across auditory and visual variables ranged from a low of .18 (Stamina Visual Reaction Time) to .88 (Mean Visual Reaction Time). For the composite quotients, test-retest correlations ranged from .37 (Visual Response Control Quotient) to .75 (Visual Attention Quotient). These findings suggest that the temporal stability of some variables is adequate, whereas the stability of other variables is below expected levels. As Lowe et al. (2000) commented in their review, the range and the low values of some of the reliability estimates dictate a need for additional studies before clinicians and researchers can be confident using the IVA scales for diagnostic purposes and for reflecting medication or treatment effects. There are no indications of internal consistency studies in the manual, and although auditory to visual performance differences are explored, the consistency of the degree of association of auditory to visual performance across individuals is not reported.

The manual includes clinical validity studies specific to discriminant validity of the IVA for 26 children diagnosed with ADHD compared to 31 normal children. Results suggested that IVA results were in agreement with group membership in 92% of the cases. Although the extent of association with other measures is not reported, the level of agreement with classification based on results of the GDS, the TOVA, and two rating scales is provided as well. Although the correlation of results on these other measures is not reported, Sandford and Turner (1995) suggested that the consistency of classification results across measures would be indicative of concurrent validity. No other validity studies are included in the manual.

TOVA AND TOVA-A

To evaluate the internal consistency for both versions of the TOVA, correlation coefficients were obtained across blocks for high- and low-frequency target conditions. Results suggest moderate reliability of the TOVA, with reliability coefficients ranging from a low of .52 for d' for the target-infrequent condition to a high of .99 for reaction time for the target-frequent condition. Similar results were found for the internal consistency of the TOVA-A. The lowest obtained reliability coefficient was .63 for d' for the target-infrequent condition; the highest coefficient ($r = .99$) was obtained for omission errors, reaction time, and reaction time variability in the target-frequent condition, and for omission errors on the target-infrequent condition (Leark et al., 1996).

In an independent study, Llorente et al. (2000) investigated the internal consistency of the TOVA with 52 boys and 11 girls identified with ADHD. The ethnic breakdown of the sample was 79% White, 16% Black, and 5% Hispanic; the mean age was 9.5 years. Children were administered the TOVA at baseline, two months, and four months. For internal consistency, only the third administration data were used. Each half of the test was compared to the other half as well as the whole test. Internal consistency coefficients were high, with a range of .93 (Half 1: Half 2) to .99 (Half 2: Total). These results suggest strong internal consistency for the TOVA.

Temporal stability of the TOVA was investigated with 24 normal children with a test-retest interval of 90 minutes. Correlation coefficients ranged from a low of .77 (variability) to a high of .93 (reaction time). Although the 90-minute interval was seen as useful for same-day testing to investigate medication effects (Leark et al., 1996), the extent to which results are stable over time and could therefore be useful in long-term monitoring of medication effects is not addressed with such a short interval.

In conjunction with the study described previously, Llorente et al. (2000) also investigated test-retest reliability of the TOVA. Performance on the TOVA at initial visit was compared to the performance at the second follow-up visit (four months later) and found to range in magnitude from .51 to .82. Llorente and colleagues concluded that of the performance variables on the TOVA, omission and commission errors were the least stable, and reaction time and reaction time variability were the most stable. No test-retest study with the TOVA-A was found.

The professional manual (Leark et al., 1996) also includes validity studies. To demonstrate construct validity, the authors provide results of a factor analysis of the variables generated. For the TOVA, the three factors and respective factor loadings are consistent with the premise that the task is measuring attention, disinhibition, and reaction time or processing speed. For the TOVA-A, however, five factors emerged: the reaction time/processing speed of the TOVA, and separate attention and disinhibition factors for the target-frequent and target-infrequent conditions. Between-test (TOVA/TOVA-A) comparisons indicated that children made twice as many omission errors on the auditory task but significantly more commission errors on the visual task, as well as evidencing a faster reaction time on the visual task. At the same time, children demonstrated greater variability in response time on the auditory task (Leark et al., 1996). These differences may contribute to the differences noted in the factor analysis.

Two clinical validity studies are provided with the TOVA. In the first, the performance of children with ADHD is compared to that of a presumably normal group of children. Depending on the cutoff used for predicted group membership, false positive rates of 80% and 90% were obtained, with sensitivity quotients ranging from .60 to .76 (Leark et al., 1996). The second study demonstrates the use of the TOVA with three clinical groups and a normal control group to study the effects of caffeine on CPT performance.

DISCUSSION AND CONCLUSION

Since Rosvold et al. (1956) introduced the original CPT over 40 years ago, a plethora of CPTs have been developed. Although a number of CPTs exist, only a handful are commercially available. In this chapter, reviews of four of the major commercially available CPTs have been provided. Clearly, these CPTs demonstrate some of the significant differences in task parameters and configurations possible in a CPT. As evidenced here, CPTs are not identical assessment tools. Different CPTs apparently measure different components of attention and executive control. Moreover, different CPTs may place different demands on an individual's attention, executive, and memory systems. When the possible numbers of differences are considered, it is clear that CPTs are not a unitary measure (Lowe et al., 2000) but a family of measures (Conners, 1992, 1995), with different parameters and scoring indices. The extent to which the differences in parameters and measures across these four CPTs affect diagnostic considerations is unknown. Notably, no study was found that compared a sample of subjects across all of these. Summary results of a study comparing the classification rates for the IVA, GDS, and TOVA were found (Sandford & Turner, 1995), but a fully detailed report of this study including correlational results by variables was not available.

Ethical and professional standards demand that psychologists use measures that are technically adequate. As pointed out by Lowe et al. (2000), CPT manuals and supporting research do not meet current professional standards of technical adequacy for testing. Existing CPT manuals lack technical data and are far from meeting the standards for test manuals set by Kaufman and Kaufman (1983) in the early 1980s. Results of the review found the normative data of the various commercially available CPTs to be limited in scope using samples of convenience. Moreover, test developers did not adequately address their procedures for selecting normative samples. Refusal or nonresponse rates and dates of norming are consistently omitted; exclusionary or selection criteria are not consistently provided.

The CPT normative samples should be of substantial size to allow for stratification across a number of different demographic dimensions. Test developers and researchers should provide detailed descriptions of their samples, as some demographic variables have been reported to be related to CPT scores. Description of demographic characteristics of the CPTs' normative samples was found to be inadequate. CPT norms lacked common stratification, and breakdowns by common demographic variables were not reported.

Research addressing the relations between demographic variables and CPT scores is still in its infancy; what is known from the research literature was reviewed. Progress has been made in this area; however, it has been slow due to a number of obstacles, including normative data that are limited in quantity and scope. Additional research is needed to investigate these relations. Further comment on the gender-based norms issue is needed. Lowe et al. (2000) reported that most CPT manuals do not indicate whether homogeneous or heterogeneous gender norms represent the correct normative base. If gender differences reflect true differences in CPT scores, combined gender norms should be used. Our interpretation of the CPT literature is that gender differences represent true differences, and thus combined gender norms should be used (see discussion in Reynolds, 1999a, and Reynolds & Kamphaus, 1992). Lowe and colleagues encouraged authors of CPT manuals to review their criteria for making decisions regarding which gender norms to publish. Perhaps the best solution at the present time, based on the current state of the CPT research, is to publish both separate and combined gender-based norms, as other authors (e.g., Reynolds & Kamphaus, 1992) have done on other behavioral measures in the past (Lowe et al., 2000).

On a final note regarding gender differences in CPT performance, as Lowe et al. (2000) pointed out in their review, computer experience has been reported to be a confound in gender studies with CPTs (e.g., Dahl et al., 1996). In the Dahl study, it was found that the boys outperformed the girls; however, when the authors controlled for computer experience or familiarity, the gender differences almost disappeared. Very few CPT studies have controlled for this variable. Thus, computer facility may be another factor to be considered and controlled in CPT studies and norms developed as a function of this variable if necessary (Lowe et al., 2000).

Only one study has addressed the issue of potential cultural bias of CPTs (Bauermeister et al., 1990), with indications that there may be a cultural confound to CPT performance. Whether similar findings would be found with other CPTs or other CPT indices or with individuals from different cultural or ethnic groups is not known at the present time. It remains unclear as to whether CPTs are culturally or ethnically biased. Not one study could be found that addressed the cultural test bias hypothesis with CPTs (Lowe et al., 2000). As pointed out by Lowe et al., Bauermeister et al.'s study highlights the potential pitfalls associated with cross-cultural testing. A translated test or a test administered in its original form to individuals from a different cultural or ethnic group who were not included in the normative sample may not be equivalent to or the same as the original test. A test may need to be renormed and rescaled (Reynolds, Lowe, & Saenz, 1999), as was discovered in the Bauermeister et al. study. For use with different ethnic or cultural groups, construction of new test items and modification in instructions and test stimuli may be needed as well (Lowe et al., 2000; Reynolds et al., 1999).

Another shortfall of the CPTs reviewed here is the limited extent to which reliability studies are provided in the manuals. Overall, moderate to high temporal stability and internal consistency were noted when reliability studies had been completed. However, there is a paucity of studies relating to reliability for the major commercially available CPTs. As different versions of the CPT may be conceptualized as separate measures, and these various CPT paradigms may not measure the exact same construct, reliability estimates from studies using one CPT task cannot be presumed to apply to other CPTs. Studies addressing the comparative reliability of CPT scores across demographic variables and diagnostic groupings are needed as well if CPT scores are to be used and interpreted (Lowe et al., 2000). The lack of evidence for temporal stability calls into question the use of the CPT in clinical contexts as well as research contexts. Without evidence of both internal consistency and temporal stability, any conclusions related to diagnostic considerations or treatment effectiveness become spurious. Additional reliability and validity studies are needed.

More extensive discussion of the concurrent and construct validity (relation with other variables) of the CPT, based on the expansive research base, is found in Chapter 4. CPT manuals included minimal studies related to discriminant validity, with an emphasis on ADHD, predominantly with children. The fact that the manuals suggest the use of CPTs in the diagnostic process specific to ADHD as well as other disorders (e.g., Alzheimer's disease, malingering) should not be interpreted as indicating high levels of sensitivity or specificity. Discriminant validity and issues of sensitivity and specificity with children and ADHD are discussed in more depth in Chapter 6. Similar issues of sensitivity and specificity in conjunction with adult disorders (e.g., ADHD, schizophrenia, and Alzheimer's) are discussed in Chapter 7.

Based on this review as well as other reviews (Ballard, 1996b; Corkum & Siegel, 1993; Dumont et al., 1995, 1999; Grooms, 1998; Lowe et al., 2000), a number of recommendations for clinicians, researchers, and test developers are offered. Test developers of the various CPTs should publish their norms and task parameters in technical or examiner's manuals, along with other pertinent measures. As recommended by Ballard (1996b), detailed descriptions of task parameters, tighter experimental controls to prevent potential confounds from influencing test results, and examination of interaction effects seem warranted in future CPT studies and replication of existing studies is needed. Standardized conditions of administration should be included in the CPT manuals in explicit detail with regard to all these variables. A number of experimenter-manipulated variables have been reported to influence CPT scores (see Chapter 2); still others (e.g., use of space bar vs. mouse, type of mouse, use of laptop vs. PC, size of screen) have yet to be investigated. Clinicians are advised to use standardized procedures when administering CPTs, as instructional set has been found to influence CPT performance (e.g., Sergeant & Scholten, 1985; Tupler, 1989).

As mentioned previously, the customized CPTs, including the customized versions of CPTs like the Conners' CPT and GDS, lack norms even though normative data may exist for another (i.e., standard) version.

A clinician who chooses to use a customized paradigm will not be able to make comparisons between an individual's performance and the performance of the normative group. Without information on the normative group's performance, a client's score will have little or no real meaning. (This problem is discussed in more detail for psychological measures in general in Reynolds, 1999.)

Clinicians need to be cautious in their interpretation of CPT results, as the CPT is only one measure and multiple measures and sources are needed to come to the conclusion that significant attention problems really do exist (Conners, 1992, 1995). Multiple sources of information and multiple measures should be used when assessing attention and impulse control problems to corroborate CPT findings. When interpreting CPT results, demographic and experimenter-manipulated variables should be taken into account. On a final note, based on the literature we have been able to locate and review, generalizations across CPT paradigms, indices, and task parameters cannot be made (Lowe et al., 2000).

CHAPTER 4

The Relationship of CPTs to Other Cognitive and Behavioral Measures

In conjunction with the review of four commercially available CPTs in Chapter 3, this chapter presents results of a review of research studies relating to the internal consistency and temporal reliability of CPTs. On a very superficial level, the chapter also explores the extent to which the four commercially available CPTs include evidence of validity. Validity, like reliability, is a means of evaluating the quality of a measure (e.g., Anastasi, 1988; R.J. Cohen & Swerdlik, 1999; Crocker & Algina, 1986). The term validity is used in association with the meaningfulness of test scores. Validity is a characteristic of the interpretations given to scores or performance on a test, not a test per se. Thus, the question "Are CPTs valid tests?" is essentially nonsensical. A better question would be, for example, "Are commission errors on this CPT measuring impulsivity?" Many factors influence proper, valid interpretation of performance on CPTs, just as they do with other tests. Since CPTs have a cognitive component, and all cognitive tasks appear to have a positive manifold (i.e., correlate positively to at least some, but obviously varying, degree with other cognitive tests), it is instructive to consider the correlations, or shared variance, between CPT performance and various other cognitive tasks.

In Chapter 2, the intended components of attention and executive control that CPTs are purported to measure were identified. Chapters 2 and 3 discussed the extent to which differences in CPT task demands (e.g., ISI), environmental factors, and demographic variables could affect results and, ultimately, the diagnostic interpretation of CPT performance. Sandford and Turner's (1995) discussion of the need to make adjustments for high or low IQ suggests that, in addition to age and other demographic variables,

IQ or cognitive ability may serve as a confound to CPT performance and interpretation specific to attention and executive control. Similarly, it was noted that computer exposure has an effect on CPT performance (Dahl et al., 1996); this finding suggests the possibility that individual achievement as well as educational level may be factors to consider in interpreting CPT data. The degree and pattern of association between CPTs and other measures need to be established to determine how other factors (e.g., cognition) might affect CPT performance. How a test relates to other tests informs clinicians and researchers about the inferences that may be made from test scores and the extent to which common variables may be at work (e.g., Anastasi, 1988; R.J. Cohen & Swerdlik, 1999).

The Standards for Educational and Psychological Testing (American Educational Research Association, 1999) indicate three principal categories for accumulating evidence of validity: construct validity, criterion-related validity, and content validity. These three categories of validity represent a convenient typology for thinking about and categorizing evidence related to test score interpretation and is somewhat artificial. All validity evidence is ultimately construct-relevant, but we review correlational and other data in this chapter in the traditional vein for ease of understanding.

Content validity refers to the examination of test items to determine whether the item content of a measure adequately samples the domain of the behavior or trait of interest (e.g., Anastasi, 1988; R.J. Cohen & Swerdlik, 1999). For the CPT paradigm, this evaluation is almost entirely inferential and is based on expert judgment by clinicians and researchers in the discipline and, to a lesser extent, correlations among various CPT paradigms. The increased use and plethora of CPTs available and the expansive CPT research base suggest that the basic CPT paradigm has been accepted by clinicians and researchers as measuring attention and executive control. Some version of the CPT, in fact, is the most frequently used laboratory measure of attention (DuPaul, Anastopoulos, Shelton, & Guevremont, 1992), and the CPT has been described as the gold standard for measuring sustained attention (Fleming, Goldberg, & Gold, 1994, p. 205). This suggests, informally at least, that CPTs have been accepted by the discipline as being relevant measures of attention and executive control mechanisms.

Criterion-related validity refers to the adequacy of test scores for making inferences about individuals' behavior on some performance criterion (e.g., R.J. Cohen & Swerdlik, 1999; Crocker & Algina, 1986) or other task. The criterion measure may be obtained at the same time as the test scores (concurrent validity) or at some future date (predictive validity) (e.g., Anastasi, 1988; R.J. Cohen & Swerdlik, 1999; Crocker & Algina, 1986). Concurrent validity addresses the issue of the degree of association with other measures and is the more frequently addressed type of criterion-related validity. Concurrent validity may be studied to determine the extent to which a test or method measures the same construct as other measures or to establish that the test or method measures something not already measured by other tests (i.e., measures some unique construct or trait). Construct validity refers to the extent to which the inference that performance on a test measures or reflects a particular theoretical construct or trait, such as the constructs of attention and executive control. Thus, one can see why all aspects of validation of influences from test scores are truly construct validity work. Construct validity relates most to the interpretive meaningfulness of the measure (Anastasi, 1988).

A synthesis of the CPT literature is needed to help clarify what CPTs actually do measure (Dumont et al., 1995, 1999; Lowe et al., 2000). CPTs seem to be simple in some paradigms, but cognitively complex in others. To clarify the meaning of performance on these tasks, this chapter reviews the correlates of CPT performance, especially in the intellectual and behavioral domains. In addition, studies that address the relationship of the CPT with other measures included in neuropsychological assessments (e.g., cognitive, achievement, personality, memory, language) are reviewed.

CONSTRUCT VALIDITY

One method of assessing construct validity is through the use of factor analytic methods. As noted in the discussion of the TOVA in Chapter 3, the results of the factor analysis of the TOVA variables were consistent with hypothesized constructs of attention, disinhibition, and processing speed (Leark et al., 1996). This is consistent with Luria's (1966) model of brain organization as well as the neurological basis of attention and executive control described in Chapter 1. Notably, however, the factor analytic results for the TOVA-A resulted in five factors, as opposed to three factors, suggesting that when the modality of the task is changed, the underlying constructs are affected as well (Leark et al., 1996).

Either through factor analysis with other measures or correlational study, a second method of establishing the validity of the interpretation of a test score is through studies of concurrent validity with other accepted measures of the same constructs, in this case, other measures of attention and executive control. In effect, if CPTs are to be interpreted properly as measures of attention or executive control, then CPT scores would be expected to correlate significantly with scores from other measures of attention and executive control; thus, one could derive (or support) their interpretive meaning from these relations (Lowe et al., 2000). At the same time, as previously pointed out, the constructs of attention and executive control are multifaceted, and, therefore, a one-to-one correspondence between CPT performance and other measures or methods would not be expected.

When factor analytic studies incorporate other measures, construct validity can be demonstrated either by the loading of CPT variables on factors by themselves or with other variables believed to assess similar behaviors. A number of factor analytic studies have been conducted to address the question of patterns of intercorrelations of the CPT paradigm and other tasks (e.g., Aylward, Gordon, & Verhulst, 1997; Boivin et al., 1996; J.W. Campbell, D'Amato, Raggio, & Stephens, 1991; Hoerig, D'Amato, Raggio, & Martin, 1998; Kardell, 1994; Lovejoy & Rasmussen, 1990; H.L. Swanson & Cooney, 1989). For example, Aylward et al. attempted to identify the commonalities between CPT results and intelligence, academic achievement, and memory variables in a sample of 1,005 males and 275 females, between 5 and 17 years, who had been referred for suspected learning disabilities and ADHD. The battery of tests administered to the children included some measure of cognitive ability, achievement, memory, and the GDS. Using pairwise principal axis factoring with varimax rotation, the factor analysis produced a four-factor solution that accounted for 43% of the variance. The results of the GDS were found to load on two of the four factors. The Delay Task scores from the GDS loaded on what was called the Delay Task Factor. The CPT scores (vigilance correct and commission errors) were the only scores that loaded on the CPT Factor. At the same time, the vigilance task's loadings on the other three factors were negligible (i.e., $-.30 <$ loading $< .30$).

Similarly, Lovejoy and Rasmussen's (1990) factor analytic study examined the relation between CPT scores and scores from a variety of measures with a sample of 73 boys and 27 girls who had been referred for attention and learning problems. The children ranged in age from 6 to 12 years. The AX-CPT stimuli consisted of colored letters, with an orange H followed by a blue T serving as the target stimulus. The duration of the CPT task was five to six minutes. Factor analysis via principal components with varimax rotation yielded a five-factor solution that accounted for 74.7% of the variance. Omission and commission error scores of the CPT loaded primarily on Factor IV and were the only scores that had primary loadings on this factor. Together with the results of Aylward and colleagues (1997), the findings obtained by Lovejoy and Rasmussen suggest that CPTs have some unique characteristics not shared with the other measures and, thus, may provide information not otherwise available from traditional cognitive tests.

A number of other studies have included direct and indirect measures of attention and executive control as well as some version of the CPT. Barkley (1998) argued that direct observation continues to be the optimal method for assessing attention. Further, Barkley (1991) indicated that measures strong in their representativeness of natural behavior, such as direct observations, have high ecological validity. Moderate to high, statistically significant correlations were reported in the majority of the studies addressing the relation between CPT scores and scores from direct behavioral observations (Barkley, 1991; Garretson, Fein, & Waterhouse, 1990; Gordon, DiNiro, Mettelman, & Tallmadge, 1989; Harper & Ottinger, 1992; Kupietz & Richardson, 1978). The correlations ranged from −.86 to +.81, with the majority of the correlations between ±.40; one-fourth of the correlations ranged between |.45|≤ r≤|.81| , suggesting moderate to strong concurrent relations between CPT scores and scores from direct behavioral observations (see Table 4.1). One study with a high coefficient was conducted by Arcia and Roberts (1993). They found the scores from the Attentiveness/Cooperativeness Scale of the Test Behavior Inventory (Kohn & Rosman, 1973) to be significantly correlated ($r = .67$) with the slope of the reaction time across trials (Arcia & Roberts, 1993). Significant validity coefficients were found for both the X-CPT (Garretson et al., 1990; Harper & Ottinger, 1992) and the AX-CPT (Barkley, 1991; Kupietz & Richardson, 1978). Higher validity coefficients were found among the studies that included clinical samples of children regardless of the diagnostic category (e.g., ADHD: Barkley, 1991; Harper & Ottinger, 1992; autism: Garretson et al., 1990; learning disabilities: Kupietz & Richardson, 1978). With nonclinical samples, the range of scores may be artificially restricted, there may be a threshold effect of attention and executive control problems prior to a comprehensive effect appearing, or both of these factors may be at work, resulting in the lower validity coefficients.

Although direct observation may be the most accurate and ecologically sound method of assessing attention, natural observations can be time consuming. In clinical practice, laboratory measures of attention and executive control are used in place of, or in addition to, natural observation. The research suggests that CPT performance is correlated with scores from laboratory measures assessing shifts in attention (Allen, 1993; Kardell, 1994; Robins, 1992; Slicker, 1991; Suslow & Arolt, 1997), focused attention (Bock, 1982; Burg, Burright, & Donovick, 1995; Das, Snyder, & Mishra, 1992), selective attention (Cohler et al., 1977; Das et al., 1992), and motor activity (Allen, 1993; Kardell, 1994; Robins, 1992; Trommer, Hoeppner, Lorber, & Armstrong, 1988), as well as impulsive behavior (Kardell, 1994; Robins, 1992; Slicker, 1991). Validity studies related to other laboratory measures of attention and executive control are presented in Table 4.2.

In Kardell's (1994) study using an AX-CPT, participants also were administered the Trail Making Test, Parts A and B (Reitan, 1958; Reitan & Wolfson, 1985) and the Wisconsin Card Sorting Test (WCST; Heaton, 1981). Both Trail Making A and B and the WCST are believed to measure attention and/or cognitive shifting (Trails B). When Kardell included the

Table 4.1

Validity Coefficients for CPTs and Direct Behavioral Observation of Children

Behavioral Observations	Study	CPT Type	Population	Correct Hits	Omission Errors	Commission Errors	Other Index
Communication/speech	Garretson et al., 1990	X-Visual	Autistic, control	-.36--.04			.10-.26 (FA)
							.24-.58 (Multiple)
Fidgets	Barkley, 1991	AX-Visual	Referred		.03-.26	.17-.24	
Looking away	Garretson et al., 1990	X-Visual	Autistic, control	-.86--.69			-.15-.69 (FA)
							.19-.42 (Multiple)
Plays with objects	Barkley, 1991	AX-Visual	Referred		.10-.12	.12-.26	
Off-task	Barkley, 1991	AX-Visual	Referred		.22-.32	.24-.41	
	Harper & Ottinger, 1992	X-Visual	ADHD, control		.33-.51	.78	
	Kupietz & Richardson, 1978	AX-Auditory	Reading problems		.31-.66	.03-.23	
		AX-Visual			.46-.56	.47-.63	
	Richman, 1986	AX-Visual	Control	-.73--.66			
Out of seat	Barkley, 1991	AX-Visual	Referred		.17-.34	.21-.44	
Vocalizes	Barkley, 1991	AX-Visual	Referred		.13-.15	.32-.39	
	Garretson et al., 1990	X-Visual	Autistic, control	-.57-.24			.19-.26 (FA)
Self-monitoring	Garretson et al., 1990	X-Visual	Autistic, control	-.63-.00			.41-.76 (FA)
							.57-.81 (Multiple)
Self-stimulation	Garretson et al., 1990	X-Visual	Autistic, control	-.34-.05			-.24-.13 (FA)
							-.11-.17 (Multiple)
Total observed behaviors	Gordon, DiNiro, et al., 1989	AX-Visual	Referred			.35	

Notes: CPT Type does not include additional modifications (e.g., degraded stimulus). CPT = Continuous performance test; ADHD = Attention-Deficit/Hyperactivity Disorder; FA = False alarms; Multiple = Multiple responses.

Table 4.2

Validity Coefficients for CPTs and Other Laboratory Measures of Attention and Executive Control

Measure	Study	CPT Type	Population	Correct Hits	Omission Errors	Commission Errors	Other Index
Actigraph	Reichenbach et al., 1992	AX-Visual	Children/control				-.01 (Inattention)
Activation task	M.B. Shapiro et al., 1999	AX-Visual	Children/control			-.02--.00	
AFAT	Bedi et al., 1994	AX-Visual	Children/control		-.11		-.04 (FA)
Ankle actometer	Barkley, 1991	AX-Visual	Children/referred		.13	.36	
Bakan task	Koelega et al., 1989	AX-Visual	Adults/control	.60			.62 (A')
Cancellation task	A. Davies & Davies, 1975	X-Visual	Adults/control				.66 (Speed)
	Laidlaw, 1993	AX-Visual	Adults/TBI, control	.16--.39	-.38--.17		-.26--.20 (FA)
Category test (errors)	Trommer et al., 1988	AX-Visual	Children/ADHD, control	.66	.39	-.54	
Cue Annulment Test	Slicker, 1991	AX-Visual	Children/referred				
MFFT errors	Barkley, 1991	AX-Visual	Children/referred		-.20--.01	-.20--.06	
	Klee & Garfinkel, 1983	AX-Visual	Children/referred	-.58	.31	.34	.28 (Total errors)
	Robins, 1992	AX-Visual	Children/ADHD, LD			.27	.11 (Comm. var.)
	Rasile et al., 1995	AX-Visual	Adults/control	-.26--.14			
	Slicker, 1991	AX-Visual	Children/referred	.38			.42 (Inconsistency) -.38 (Perform)
	Mahan, 1996	Not-X Visual	Children/ADHD			-.02--.13	-.06--.12 (d') -.25--.18 (Beta) -.09--.03 (RT) .11--.21 (RT SD) .14--.17 (Var. SE)
MFFT- first trial correct	Klee & Garfinkel, 1983	AX-Visual	Children/referred		-.28	-.35	-.36 (Total errors)
	Rasile et al., 1995	AX-Visual	Adults/control	.35			
	Rasile et al., 1995	AX-Visual	Adults/control	.29			
MFFT latency	Robins, 1992	AX-Visual	Children/ADHD, LD	.31		-.18	-.11 (Comm. var.)
	Slicker, 1991	AX-Visual	Children/referred	.29			
	Barkley, 1991	AX-Visual	Children/referred		.13--.33	.18--.34	
	Mahan, 1996	Not-X Visual	Children/ADHD			-.09	-.01 (d') .18 (Beta) -.05 (RT) -.12 (RT SD) -.01 (Var. SE)
MFFT total	Klee & Garfinkel, 1983	AX-Visual	Children/referred		-.09	-.33	-.26 (Total errors)

(continued)

Table 4.2 Continued

Measure	Study	CPT Type	Population	Correct Hits	Omission Errors	Commission Errors	Other Index
PASAT	Burg et al., 1995	AX-Visual	Adults/TBI, controls	.56			
	Laidlaw, 1993	AX-Visual	Adults/TBI, controls	-.52–-.07	.09–.52	.37	.01–.03 (FA)
PASAT task 4	Burg et al., 1995	AX-Visual	Adults/TBI, controls	.49	-.15		
Posner task: name match	Das et al., 1992	X-Auditory	Children/control		.39–.54	.18–.32	
Posner task: physical match	Das et al., 1992	X-Auditory	Children/control		.22–.36	.17–.24	
Posner Test: cost of invalid cue	Karper et al., 1996	AX-Visual	Adults/schizophrenic			-.14–-.18	
Prepulse inhibition: vigilance habituation	Karper et al., 1996	AX-Visual	Adults/schizophrenic			-.41	
Preschool checking task: omission	Floyd, 1999	Not X-Visual	Children/control		-.10	.05	
Preschool checking task: commission	Floyd, 1999	Not X-Visual	Children/control		.24	.25	
Stroop-color time	Allen, 1993	AX-Visual	Children/referred		-.24–-.10	-.48–-.10	
Stroop-color word time	Bock, 1982	X-Visual	Adults/referred				-.40 (Absolute) -.43 (Rel. accuracy)
	Allen, 1993	AX-Visual	Children/referred		-.28–-.03	-.33–-.19	-.51 (Absolute) -.65 (Rel. accuracy)
	Bock, 1982	AX-Visual	Adults/referred				
Stroop-errors	Das et al., 1992	X-Auditory	Children/control		.36–.52	.31–.38	
	Bock, 1982	X-Visual	Adults/referred				-.49 (Absolute) -.48 (Rel. accuracy)
	List, 1985	X-Visual	Children/control		.02		
	Bock, 1982	AX-Visual	Adults/referred			.16	-.25 (Absolute) -.36 (Rel. accuracy)
Stroop interference	C.S. Carter et al., 1995	X-Visual	Children/ADHD, controls		.05		
	Allen, 1993	AX-Visual	Children/referred		-.10–-.02	-.03–-.12	
	Kardell, 1994	AX-Visual	Children/referred	-.21	.17	.03	-.05 (Dyscontrol)
	Rasile et al., 1995	AX-Visual	Adults/control	-.30–-.13			
Stroop word	Allen, 1993	AX-Visual	Children/referred		-.16–-.06	-.31–-.00	
Stroop total	List, 1985	X-Visual	Children/control		.17	-.07–.18	
Stroop 2	Burg et al., 1995	AX-Visual	Adults/TBI, controls	-.52		.26	
Stroop 4	Burg et al., 1995	AX-Visual	Adults/TBI, controls	-.41		.36	
Stroop items completed	Kardell, 1994	AX-Visual	Children/referred		-.10	-.08	-.07 (Dyscontrol)
Time sharing-left	Allen, 1993	AX-Visual	Children/referred		-.25–-.06	-.21–-.02	
Time sharing-right	Allen, 1993	AX-Visual	Children/referred	.12	-.18–-.12	-.25–-.01	

Measure	Citation	CPT Type	Group				
Trails A	Kardell, 1994	AX-Visual	Children/referred	-.44	.41	.32-.36	.36 (Dyscontrol)
	Robins, 1992	AX-Visual	Children/ADHD, LD	-.51		.34	.09 (Comm. var.)
Trails B	Kardell, 1994	AX-Visual	Children/referred	-.49	.44	.22-.28	.30 (Dyscontrol)
Trails A & B total errors	List, 1985	X-Visual	Children/control		.04	-.28	
Trails A & B total time	List, 1985	X-Visual	Children/control		-.07	-.15	
	Kardell, 1994	AX-Visual	Children/referred	-.51	.46	.26-.32	.33 (Dyscontrol)
VFAT	Bedi et al., 1994	AX-Visual	Children/control		-.26		-.08 (FA)
Visual span total	Burg et al., 1995	AX-Visual	Adults/TBI, controls	.41	-.29		
WCST: categories obtained	Reader et al., 1994	X-Visual	Children/ADHD		.29	.38	.00 (RT); .35 (RT SD)
	Allen, 1993	AX-Visual	Children/referred	.34	-.31--.18	-.32--.06	-.21 (Dyscontrol)
	Kardell, 1994	AX-Visual	Children/referred		-.30	-.17--.05	-.29 (Inconsistency)
	Slicker, 1991	AX-CPT	Children/referred		-.33		-.40 (Perform); -.45 (Impulse)
WCST: correct responses	Green et al., 1992	X-Visual	Adults/psychiatric	.25			-.22-.05 (A')
	Kardell, 1994	AX-Visual	Children/referred		-.14	.00-.08	-.07 (Dyscontrol)
WCST: errors	Allen. 1993	AX-Visual	Children/referred		-.42--.11	-.29-.12	
	Allen. 1993	AX-Visual	Children/referred		.07-.43	-.10-.29	
WCST: failure to maintain set	Kardell, 1994	AX-Visual	Children/referred	-.36	.34	.08-.23	.27 (Dyscontrol)
WCST: learning to learn	Kardell, 1994	AX-Visual	Children/referred	.20	.04	-.12-.08	.08 (Dyscontrol)
WCST: nonperseverative errors	Kardell, 1994	AX-Visual	Children/referred	-.51	-.16	-.08-.32	-.14 (Dyscontrol)
	Slicker, 1991	AX-Visual	Children/referred		.44		.29 (Impulse); -.29 (Perform)
WCST: perseverative errors	Reader et al., 1994	X-Visual	Children/ADHD		.05	.09	.10 (RT); .04 (RT SD)
WCST: set breaks	Reader et al., 1994	X-Visual	Children/ADHD		.13	-.04	.01 (RT); -.22 (RT SD)
WCST modified version	Suslow & Arolt, 1997	X-Visual	Adults/schizophrenic, control		.08		
Wrist actometer	Barkley, 1991	AX-Visual	Children/referred			.21	.54 (d')

Notes: CPT Type does not include any modifications (e.g., degraded stimuli); for correct hits, omission errors, and commission errors, this may be the number, percentage, or mean. ADHD = Attention-Deficit/Hyperactivity Disorder; A' = Variation of sensitivity; AFAT = Auditory Focused Attention Test; CPT = Continuous performance test; Comm. var. = Commission error variability; CPT = Continuous performance test; d' = Sensitivity; FA = False alarms; LD = Learning disability; MFFT = Matching Familiar Figures Test; Multiple = Multiple responses; PASAT = Paced Auditory Serial Addition Test; Perform = Performance index; Rel. accuracy = Relative accuracy; RT = Reaction time; SD = Standard deviation; TBI = Traumatic brain injury; Var. = Variability of the standard error; VFAT = Visual Focused Attention Test; WCST = Wisconsin Card Sorting Test.

CPT, Trail Making A and B, and the WCST in factor analysis, the mean number of CPT correct response scores, the total time to complete Trails A and B, and the total errors score for the WCST had primary loadings on the same factor (Factor I). Further, the time scores on Trail Making A and the sum of time on Trails A and B were found to be moderately associated with CPT omission errors ($r = .41 - .46$) and commission errors ($r = .26 - .32$) in Kardell's study. Two other studies included the Trail Making Test and CPT performance. Robins' (1992) study, also using an AX-CPT, revealed similar results for correct hits ($r = -.51$) and commission errors ($r = .34$), but not for the consistency index ($r = .09$). In contrast, with an X-CPT, List's (1985) study yielded much lower correlations ($-.30 \leq r \leq .30$) between CPT performance and Trails tasks.

Specific to the WCST, Kardell (1994) reported CPT omission errors to be most related to WCST total errors ($r = .34$) and total categories ($r = -.30$). Similarly, Slicker (1991) and Allen (1993) found validity coefficients for WCST categories and omission errors to be $-.33$ and $-.31$, respectively. Further, depending on the age group, Allen found that the relation between CPT omission errors and WCST total errors ranged from .07 to .43, with similar age-dependent range in degree of association for CPT omission errors and WCST percentage correct responses. In contrast, the WCST variable of Failure to Maintain Set, which is believed to be associated with sustained attention (Heaton, 1981), was considered in only one study (Kardell, 1994). Notably, regardless of the CPT performance variable (omission errors, commission errors, dyscontrol scores), correlations with Failure to Maintain Set were relatively low ($-.20 \leq r \leq .20$). Compared to studies using an AX-CPT (Allen, 1993; Kardell, 1994; Slicker, 1991), studies using the X-CPT paradigm (e.g., Reader, Harris, Schuerholz, & Denckla, 1994) tended to yield lower validity coefficients for the WCST and CPT variables.

Another task believed to measure attention as well as executive control, but not included in Kardell's (1994) factor analysis, is the Stroop task (Golden, 1975). A number of studies investigated the relation between omission and commission errors as well as other CPT indices and Stroop variables (Allen, 1993; Bock, 1982; Burg et al., 1995; C.S. Carter, et al., 1995; Das et al., 1992; Kardell, 1994; List, 1985; Rasile, Burg, Burright, & Donovick, 1995). Validity coefficients differed across studies depending on a number of factors. For example, Burg et al. administered both the GDS and the Stroop to 30 adults with traumatic brain injury (TBI). For the TBI population, the highest correlations were found between vigilance total correct ($r = -.52$) and distractibility total correct ($r = .57$) and the Stroop 2. It was noted, however, that the correlations were somewhat lower for the 25 adults in the control group in the same study with the Stroop 4. Das and colleagues (1992) used both an auditory and a visual version of the X-CPT and the Stroop with 49 presumably healthy children. Validity coefficients for omission and commission errors of the auditory CPT and commission errors on the visual CPT were consistently between .31 and .38. The level of association of omission errors on the visual CPT with the Stroop was much higher at .52 (Das et al., 1992). In contrast, C.S. Carter et al.'s study used the Stroop and the TOVA with 19 children with ADHD (mean age of 10.58 years) and 19 control children (mean age of 10.63 years). Results indicated only a negligible correlation ($r = .05$) between the Stroop and omission errors on the CPT. Thus, although there is a somewhat consistent pattern of association, the pattern is not without exception based on differences in the parameters of the CPT and the sample characteristics.

The degree of association between CPT variables and a number of other measures believed to tap attention and executive control also have been studied (see Table 4.2). Across measures, the highest correlations ($r \geq \pm.50$) were found to be for the cognitive tasks (i.e., requiring the individual to recognize odd but unequal digits) with CPT correct hits, and modified perceptual selectivity (A') scores (Koelega et al., 1989), errors on the Category Test (Reitan & Wolfson, 1985) with CPT correct hits and commission error scores (Trommer et al., 1988), and the Paced Auditory Serial Addition Test (PASAT; Gronwall, 1977) scores with CPT correct hits (Burg et al., 1995; Laidlaw, 1993). Unfortunately, for most of the measures of attention and executive control, only one or two studies were found that examined the concurrent validity with CPT performance, and these studies included different CPT paradigms and different populations. As such, replication of these findings is needed.

Although the above-mentioned studies lend support to the construct validity of the CPT, there are exceptions. For example, H. Swanson and Cooney's (1989) factor analysis revealed that CPT results loaded on the same factor as measures not related directly to attention or executive control, in this case, cognitive ability. Specifically, using an auditory format CPT, H. Swanson and Cooney found that VIQ of the Wechsler Intelligence Scale for Children-Revised (WISC-R) loaded with commission errors on the CPT. The differing results of their factor analysis are consistent with the differences found for the TOVA and TOVA-A (Leark et al., 1996) and support the notion that differences in CPT modality may impact the underlying factor structure that results. In another study, using the Conners' CPT, Hoerig et al. (1998) found that correct hits and omission errors loaded separately; however, commission errors were found to load with memory measures. Since the Conners' has a visual format, the modality would not seem to be a factor in these results.

In still another study, CPT scores loaded exclusively on the Academic Achievement Factor (J. Campbell et al., 1991). J. Campbell et al. examined the construct specificity of the CPT paradigm with cognitive, achievement, and behavioral measures. The CPT used was an AX-CPT with letters presented every 800 ms; the duration of the CPT was eight minutes. Omission and commission error scores were recorded. The sample consisted of 33 males and 21 females with learning disabilities, ranging in age from 6 to 15 years. Results of the factor analysis produced a four-factor varimax solution that accounted for 79% of the variance. CPT scores in this study loaded with the scores from achievement measures. Based on their findings, J. Campbell and colleagues concluded that CPTs may measure attention or response strategies associated with information processing that are required for achievement as well.

Lovejoy and Rasmussen's (1990) factor analytic study also included a number of measures purported to reflect attention and executive control. These included the Children's Checking Task (CCT; Margolis, 1972) and the Matching Familiar Figures Test (MFFT; Kagan, Rosman, Day, Albert, & Phillips, 1964). When CPT scores were included in the factor analysis, they did not load on the same factor as the CCT or the MFFT. Other studies have yielded correlations of CPT and MFFT variables ranging from ±.01 to ±.36 depending on the variables of interest and the population (Barkley, 1991; Klee & Garfinkel, 1983). These studies (J. Campbell et al., 1991; Lovejoy & Rasmussen, 1990) are consistent with findings of lower validity coefficients in other studies (e.g., List, 1985). The fact that the CPT variables loaded with variables representing constructs other than attention or disinhibition across studies demonstrates the need to examine the extent to which CPT performance may be related to other behavioral domains.

Taken together, the studies reviewed thus far generally support the notion that the CPT paradigm is measuring some aspect(s) of attention or executive control. The consistency of moderate and significant validity coefficients, particularly with direct behavioral observations, supports the construct validity. Given that various measures may be more specific to the assessment of different components involved in attention and executive function, it is not surprising that there is a range of degree of association between CPT performance and other measures. At the same time, the magnitude of the range (ignoring the direction of the relation) appears to be larger than would be expected. As noted, however, specific differences in CPT parameters (e.g., auditory vs. visual modality, AX-CPT vs. X-CPT), as well as differences in the populations sampled (e.g., clinical sample vs. presumably healthy sample, differing clinical samples) and the age of the individuals in the sample may contribute to the lack of consistency in the validity coefficients. Alternatively, the findings of shared factor loadings across measures purported to measure different traits raise the question of the degree of association between CPT constructs and other constructs. The relationship of CPT performance to scores on other measures is discussed in more detail next.

RELATIONS WITH OTHER MEASURES

Cognitive Measures

A review of the CPT literature produced multiple studies in which scores from different cognitive measures were correlated with scores from CPT paradigms (Allen, 1993; Assemany & McIntosh, 1999; Aylward et al., 1997; Bedi, Halperin, & Sharma, 1994; Bock, 1982; Boivin et al., 1996; Burg et al., 1995; J. Campbell et al., 1991; J.D. Carter, 1992; Chae, 1999; A. Davies & Davies, 1975; Edley & Knopf, 1987; Flansburg, 1986; Garretson et al., 1990; Gordon & Mettelman, 1988; Gordon, Thomason, & Cooper, 1990; Grant, Ilai, Nussbaum, & Bigler, 1990; Halperin, Sharma, et al., 1991; Hoerig et al., 1998; Kardell, 1994; King, 1996; Klee & Garfinkel, 1983; List, 1985; Lovejoy & Rasmussen, 1990; Mayes, Calhoun, & Crowell, 1998; Pascualvaca et al., 1997; Raggio, 1992; Rasile et al., 1995; Reichenbach, Halperin, Sharma, & Newcorn, 1992; Robins, 1992; Rosenberg, 1980; Seidel, 1989; M. Shapiro, Morris, Morris, Flowers, & Jones, 1999; Slicker, 1991; Strauss, Buchanan, & Hale, 1993; H. Swanson & Cooney, 1989; Trommer et al., 1988; Tupler, 1989; van den Broek, Mattis, & Golden, 1997; Wherry et al., 1993). Validity coefficients are presented in Table 4.3. An examination of the magnitudes of the validity coefficients indicates a wide range, −.66 to .67, with the majority of the validity coefficients between ±.30.

The majority of the coefficients reported are low and support results of factor analytic studies (e.g., Aylward et al., 1997). In Aylward et al.'s factor analytic study of 1,280 referred children described above, children were or had been previously assessed on either the WISC-R (Wechsler, 1974), Wechsler Intelligence Scale for Children-Third Edition (WISC-III; Wechsler, 1991), or the Wechsler Preschool and Primary Scale of Intelligence-Revised (WPPSI-R; Wechsler, 1989) in conjunction with the GDS as well as measures of achievement and memory. The VIQ scores, PIQ scores, memory scores, and mathematics achievement scores had primary loadings on the Cognitive/IQ factor, and the CPT results loaded on a separate factor.

Similarly, Hoerig et al.'s (1998) factor analysis of scores obtained on 80 children with learning disabilities on the Conners' CPT, the WISC-III, and the Test of Memory and Learning (TOMAL; Reynolds & Bigler, 1994) produced a seven-factor structure via principal components analysis with varimax rotation in which scores on the intelligence and CPT measure loaded on different factors. The results of Hoerig et al. as well as Aylward et al. (1997) are in agreement with other factor analytic studies (e.g., Boivin et al., 1996; J. Campbell et al., 1991; Lovejoy & Rasmussen, 1990). In only one study (H. Swanson & Cooney, 1989) did the factor analysis result in CPT scores loading on the same factor as the VIQ or PIQ scores of the WISC-R. However, the loadings in that study may reflect the auditory format of the CPT used as well as the scores used to reflect CPT performance. Only one other study suggested a significant

Table 4.3

Validity Coefficients for CPTs and Cognitive/Language Measures

Measure	Study	CPT Type	Population	Correct Hits	Omission Errors	Commission Errors	Other Index
K-ABC MPC	Gordon et al., 1990	AX-Visual	Children/referred	.44		-.37	
	Slicker, 1991	AX-Visual	Children/referred				-.24 (Inconsistency) / .26 (Multiple)
K-ABC sequential	Gordon et al., 1990	AX-Visual	Children/referred	.49		-.38	
K-ABC simultaneous	Gordon et al., 1990	AX-Visual	Children/referred	.29		-.24	
K-BIT matrices	M.B. Shapiro et al., 1999	AX-Visual	Children/control				-.24--.19 (RT)
K-BIT vocabulary	M.B. Shapiro et al., 1999	AX-Visual	Children/control				-.23--.21 (RT)
Mill Hill Vocabulary Test	A.D.M. Davies & Davies, 1975	X-Visual	Adults/control				.53 (Accuracy)
PPVT	Garretson et al., 1990	X-Visual	Children/autistic, control	.30-.64			-.37--.11 (FA) / -.34--.31 (Multiple)
PPVT-R	Edley & Knopf, 1987	X-Visual	Children/control				.39 (CDR)
	Pascualvaca et al., 1997	X-Visual	Children/control		-.31--.11	-.26--.14	-.20--.07 (RT)
Ravens	Halperin, Sharma, et al., 1991	AX-Visual	Children/control				-.28 (Dyscontrol)
	Grant et al., 1990	AX-Visual	Children/ADHD	.30	-.23	.08	
Slosson	Gordon & Mettelman, 1988	AX-Visual	Children/control	.00-.17			
SB:FE verbal	J.D. Carter, 1992	AX-Visual	Children/at-risk, control				.09-.29 (RT)
SB:FE abstract/visual	J.D. Carter, 1992	AX-Visual	Children/at-risk, control				.03-.38 (RT)
SB:FE quantitative	J.D. Carter, 1992	AX-Visual	Children/at-risk, control				.00-.26 (RT)
SB:FE memory	J.D. Carter, 1992	AX-Visual	Children/at-risk, control				.00-.32 (RT)
SB:FE Test composite	J.D. Carter, 1992	AX-Visual	Children/at-risk, control				.04-.31 (RT)
Wechsler Scales VIQ	Aylward et al., 1997	AX-CPT	Children/referred	.17-.26		.01-.18	
WISC-R VIQ	Bedi et al., 1994	AX-Auditory	Children/control				.23 (Distractibility)
		AX-Visual					-.10 (Distractibility)
	H.L. Swanson & Cooney, 1989	AX-Visual	Children/control				.29-.53 (d') / -.40--.30 (Beta) / -.53--.35 (FA) / .35-.36 (RT)
		AX-Auditory					.28-.54 (d') / -.40--.26 (Beta) / -.26-.43 (FA) / .31 (RT)

Measure	Study	Task	Sample				
WISC-III VIQ	Grant et al., 1990	AX-Visual	Children/ADHD	.33		.11	-.15 (Inattention)
	Reichenbach et al., 1992	AX-Visual	Children/control				
WPPSI-R VIQ	Chae, 1999	Not described	Children/ADHD	-.04			.01 (Composite)
	J.D. Carter, 1992	X-Visual	Children/ADHD				.01–.42 (RT)
Wechsler Scales PIQ	Aylward et al., 1997	AX-Visual	Children/at-risk, control	.21–.22		.13–.14	
WISC-R PIQ	Bedi et al., 1994	AX-Visual	Children/referred				.35 (Distractibility)
		AX-Auditory	Children/control				-.01 (Distractibility)
	Grant et al., 1990	AX-Visual	Children/ADHD	.33		.23	-.32 (Inattention)
	Reichenbach et al., 1992	AX-Visual	Children/control				
	H.L. Swanson & Cooney, 1989	AX-Auditory	Children/control				.31–.33 (d')
							-.33–-.25 (Beta)
							-.42 (RT)
		AX-Visual					-.31 (FA)
							.27 (RT)
WISC-III PIQ	Assemany & McIntosh, 1999	Not described	Children/ADHD	-.09			.12 (Composite)
WPPSI-R PIQ	Chae, 1999	X-Visual	Children/control				
Wechsler Scales FSIQ	J.D. Carter, 1992	AX-Visual	Children/at-risk, control	.23–.25		.11–.19	.13–.49 (RT)
WISC-R FSIQ	Aylward et al., 1997	AX-Visual	Children/referred	.00–-.01	.03		
	Gordon & Mettelman, 1988	AX-Visual	Children/control	-.05			
	Reichenbach et al., 1992	AX-Visual	Children/control				-.27 (Inattention)
WISC-III FSIQ	Assemany & McIntosh, 1999	Not described	Children/ADHD				-.07 (Distractibility)
	Chae, 1999	X-Visual	Children/control				.13 (Composite)
WPPSI-R FSIQ	Mayes et al., 1998	AX-Visual	Children/ADHD, control				.22–.34 (Composite)
	J.D. Carter, 1992	AX-Visual	Children/at-risk, control				.21–.24 (d')
							-.10–-.00 (Beta)
							.0–-.39 (RT)
							.20 (FA)
WISC-III VC Factor	Raggio, 1992	AX-Visual	Children/ADHD	.00	-.53	-.44	
WISC-III PO Factor	Assemany & McIntosh, 1999	Not described	Children/ADHD	.05			
WISC-R FFD Factor	Assemany & McIntosh, 1999	Not described	Children/ADHD	.28			
	Grant et al., 1990	AX-Visual	Children/ADHD			.16	

(continued)

Table 4.3 Continued

Measure	Study	CPT Type	Population	Correct Hits	Omission Errors	Commission Errors	Other Index
WISC-III FFD Factor	Lovejoy & Rasmussen, 1990	AX-Visual	Children/referred	.04	−.46	.02	
	Assemany & McIntosh, 1999	Not described	Children/ADHD				
	Chae, 1999	X-Visual	Children/ADHD				.11 (Composite)
	Kardell, 1994	AX-Visual	Children/referred	.21		.17	−.17 (RT)
							.04 (RT SD)
							.23 (Impulse)
							−.13 (Inattention)
							.11 (Dyscontrol)
WISC-III PS Factor	Kardell, 1994	AX-Visual	Children/referred	.14		−.17	−.08 (RT)
							−.19 (RT SD)
							−.12 (Impulse)
							−.12 (Inattention)
							−.19 (Dyscontrol)
							.06 (Composite)
WAIS-R arithmetic	Chae, 1999	X-Visual	Children/ADHD				
	Burg et al., 1995	AX-Visual	Adults/TBI, controls	.27–.42		−.57––.28	−.29––.28 (BV)
	Rasile et al., 1995	AX-Visual	Adults/control			−.09	
WISC-R arithmetic	Flansburg, 1986	AX-Visual	Children/ADD, clinical	−.03–.39	−.39––.02	−.36––.05	
	Klee & Garfinkel, 1983	X-Visual	Children/referred		−.37	−.12	.05 (Total errors)
	Trommer et al., 1988	AX-Visual	Children/ADHD, control	.66		−.31	
WAIS-R digit span	Rasile et al., 1995	AX-Visual	Adults/control			.16	
WISC-R digit span	Flansburg, 1986	AX-Visual	Children/ADD, clinical	.01–.34	−.34––.04	.03–.05	
	Robins, 1992	AX-Visual	Children/ADHD, LD	.00		−.08	.00 (Comm. var.)
WISC-R coding	Flansburg, 1986	AX-Visual	Children/ADD, clinical	.13–.44	−.43––.17	−.04–.17	
	Klee & Garfinkel, 1983	X-Visual	Children/referred		−.32	−.25	−.31 (Total errors)
	Robins, 1992	AX-Visual	Children/ADHD, LD	.00		−.08	−.09 (Comm. var.)
WISC-III coding	M.B. Shapiro et al., 1999	AX-Visual	Children/control				−.35––.32 (RT)
WAIS-R digit symbol	Burg et al., 1995	AX-Visual	Adults/TBI, controls	.21		−.39	−.39 (BV)
	Rasile et al., 1995	AX-Visual	Adults/control			−.06	
WISC-R mazes	Robins, 1992	AX-Visual	Children/ADHD, LD	.00		.46	.06 (Comm. var.)
WISC-R block design	Trommer et al., 1988	AX-Visual	Children/ADHD, control	.59		−.09	
WISC-R object assembly	Trommer et al., 1988	AX-Visual	Children/ADHD, control	.67		−.02	
WISC-R similarities	Trommer et al., 1988	AX-Visual	Children/ADHD, control	.60		−.66	

Test	Reference	CPT Type	Group		
WAIS-R PA & PC	Strauss et al., 1993	AX-Visual	Adults/schizophrenic, schizoaffective		.14 (d')
WAIS-R vocabulary	Tupler, 1989	X-Visual	Adults/control	.03–.42	-.58–-.11 (FA) -.46–-.29 (RT)
WAIS-R vocabulary and comprehension	Strauss et al., 1993	AX-Visual	Adults/schizophrenic, schizoaffective		.30 (d')
WISC-R subtests	Grant et al., 1990	AX-Visual	Children/ADHD	.35	.14

Notes: CPT Type does not include any modifications (e.g., degraded stimuli); for correct hits, omission errors, and commission errors, this may be the number, percentage, or mean. ADHD = Attention-Deficit/Hyperactivity Disorder; Comm. var. = Commission error variability; CPT = Continuous performance test; BV = Block variance; Comp. = Comprehension; CDR = Correct detection ratio; d' = Sensitivity; FA = False alarm; FFD = Freedom from distractibility; FSIQ = Full Scale IQ; K-ABC = Kaufman Assessment Battery for Children; K-BIT = Kaufman Brief Intelligence Test; LD = Learning disability; Multiple = Multiple responses; PA = Picture arrangement; PC = Picture completion; PIQ = Performance IQ; PPVT = Peabody Picture Vocabulary Test; PS = Processing speed; RT = Reaction time; SD = Standard deviation; TBI = Traumatic brain injury; VIQ = Verbal IQ; Vocab. = Vocabulary; WAIS-R = Wechsler Adult Intelligence Scale-Revised; WISC-R = Wechsler Intelligence Scale for Children-Revised; WISC-III = Wechsler Intelligence Scale for Children, 3rd ed.; WPPSI-R = Wechsler Preschool and Primary Scale of Intelligence-Revised; SB:FE = Stanford Binet, 4th ed.

relationship between cognition and CPT performance. Chae (1999) examined the relation between cognitive ability as measured by the WISC-III and the TOVA. Overall, TOVA performance was not found to be significantly correlated with VIQ, PIQ, or Full Scale IQ (FSIQ); however, PIQ and FSIQ scores were found to be moderately and significantly associated with the TOVA Inattention Scale ($r = .46$ and $.44$, respectively). Notably, Chae's study included only a clinical sample of children with ADHD (mean age of 10.3 years); this may account for the difference in the findings.

Taken together, the results across studies generally suggest a potentially statistically significant but small, clinically meaningless relation between CPT scores and general cognitive ability (g), at least as measured by traditional intelligence tests. Other than the H. Swanson and Cooney (1989) study and the Chae (1999) study, the only other indications from factor analytic or correlational studies that suggest a significant association between measures of cognition and CPT performance come from research that focused on the shared abilities across subtests or individual subtests as opposed to g. For example, Kardell's (1994) and H. Swanson and Cooney's factor analytic studies produced solutions in which CPT scores and subtest scores from cognitive measures had primary loadings on the same factor. Kardell examined the relation between CPT scores and the subtest scores purported to be associated with attention (i.e., Arithmetic and Digit Span) and processing speed (i.e., Symbol Search and Coding) from the Wechsler scales. Results of the factor analysis revealed that the Arithmetic and Digit Span subtest scores loaded on the same factor as the CPT commission error and mean reaction time scores (Kardell, 1994).

Some of the more significant validity coefficients also reflect similarities with specific subtest scores (Burg et al., 1995; Flansburg, 1986; Trommer et al., 1988; Tupler, 1989). Burg et al. and Tupler correlated several of the Wechsler Adult Intelligence Scale-Revised (WAIS-R; Wechsler, 1981) subtest scores with CPT scores in samples of adults, and Trommer et al. (1988) correlated several of the WISC-R subtests scores with CPT scores in a group of children. Arithmetic subtest scores were included in the Burg et al., Flansburg, and Trommer et al. studies. Flansburg examined the relation between Arithmetic, Digit Span, and Coding subtests on the WISC-R and performance on the GDS Vigilance task in two clinical groups of children ($n = 60$). Results suggested moderate correlations with vigilance correct scores and vigilance omission errors for all three WISC-R subtests included. In contrast, only the subtest scores on Arithmetic were significantly correlated with vigilance commission errors (Flansburg, 1986). However, inferences that these results are supportive of the use of the Arithmetic and Digit Span Index scores from the WISC-III or Wechsler Adult Intelligence Scale-Third Edition (WAIS-III; Wechsler, 1997) as a measure of attention or executive control should not be made. The intercorrelation indicated by the factor analytic results could be attributed to other shared abilities of these two subtests, such as sequencing ability, facility with numbers, and working memory (Kaufman, 1994). Also, the magnitude of the correlations and factor pattern coefficients are simply too small to support such conclusions.

Using the factor/index scores from the WISC-III, Chae (1999) examined the relations between the third factor (Freedom from Distractibility) and the fourth factor (Processing Speed) and overall performance on the TOVA. Based on the evaluations of 40 children with a mean age of 10.3 years, results indicated that there are minimal relations between the third and fourth factors of the WISC-III and overall performance on the TOVA. Individual TOVA subscales were not examined in conjunction with the factor scores. However, association of TOVA subscales with subtests from the performance portion was examined. Results indicated that scores on the Picture Arrangement and Object Assembly subtests were significantly correlated ($r = -.50$ and $-.54$, respectively) with the TOVA Inattention subscale scores. No other correlations were significant.

Less research is available on adult populations. Moderate and statistically significant correlations were found between false alarm index scores (a measure of impulsivity) and the WAIS-R vocabulary subtest scores (Tupler, 1989). In another study, Rasile et al. (1995) examined the degree of association between results of the GDS and scores on the WAIS-R subtests of Digit Span, Digit Symbol, and Arithmetic. The sample included 29 female and 40 male undergraduate students at a state university. Validity coefficients yielded ranged from $-.09$ to $.16$ for vigilance correct and from $.02$ to $.04$ for distractibility correct. Thus, any association demonstrated with subtests of the Wechsler scales and CPT performance in a clinical sample of children is not demonstrated in a presumably normal adult population.

Although few in number, moderate and statistically significant correlations were found between cognitive scores and CPT scores in studies with referred samples (Burg et al., 1995; Garretson et al., 1990; Raggio, 1992; Trommer et al., 1988) and younger children (Garretson et al., 1990; Raggio, 1992). Significant validity coefficients were reported in studies that included adults with TBI (Burg et al., 1995), children with autism (Garretson et al., 1990), children with ADD (Trommer et al., 1988), and children with neurological impairment (Raggio, 1992). Significant validity coefficients across behavioral domains for clinical populations may be directly related to the clinical status and the underlying neurological basis of the disorder in question and the potential of a threshold effect, as noted earlier. In particular, the high correlations among measures that presumably reflect functional levels across domains may be due to more diffuse neurological impairment as opposed to reflecting a flaw in the assessment process itself.

In addition to clinical status, the age of the sample was found to be a factor. Samples with younger children (Garretson et al., 1990; Raggio, 1992) yielded moderate and statistically significant validity coefficients. These findings are most consistent with the research reviewed in Chapter 3 that suggests a developmental trend in CPT performance. From a developmental perspective, it may be more difficult at younger ages to obtain a more explicit delineation of attention or executive control as relatively distinct from cognition or general level of development. This happens with other functions as well. For example, prior to age 5, it is nearly impossible to assess math skills or abilities separate from language skills in a normally developing youngster; yet, with age, the two constructs clearly differentiate. Finally, as discussed in Chapter 3, other demographic characteristics of the samples may have some bearing on the validity coefficients reported.

Overall, the results of the studies reviewed with regard to g and CPT performance suggest that cognitive ability is not likely, in and of itself, to be a confound in CPT performance, at least with IQs above 70. This is consistent with findings related to vigilance performance in general (Berch & Kanter, 1984). Based on their review, Berch and Kanter concluded that there is not a significant relationship between vigilance (however measured) and general intellectual ability after age 7. They pointed out, however, that in younger children, there is evidence of an association between overall intellect and attentional capacity. Thus, developmental differences need to be considered in the interpretation of CPT performance, as well as performance on a traditional IQ test, in younger children.

At the same time, as noted in Chapter 3, Sandford and Turner (1995) recommend that clinicians may want to use the normative data consistent with the individual's IQ (e.g., estimated mental age) instead of chronological age when IQ is significantly above or below normal. No specific studies addressed this issue (i.e., looked at norms based on mental age as opposed to chronological age); however, the existing data do not suggest that IQ would be a factor except to the extent that a very low IQ is likely to reflect diffuse neurological impairment which would be expected to impact attention and executive control as well. For example, with an individual with mental retardation, the use of the individual's mental age might well result in a conclusion of nonimpaired attention or executive control when, in fact, deficits in attention and dyscontrol are manifestations of the mental retardation and need to be addressed as part of the overall treatment program. However, if the question is one of deficits relative to intellectual development as opposed to absolute deficits, then mental age may be a more appropriate referent. Sandford and Turner further suggest that the need for adjustment is specific to the PIQ rather than VIQ. The results of the H. Swanson and Cooney (1989) study, however, suggest that with an auditory CPT, the VIQ is more directly involved in CPT performance.

Achievement

Eighteen different validity studies have been conducted in which the scores from 12 different academic achievement tests have been correlated with scores on CPT paradigms (Aylward et al., 1997; Bedi et al., 1994; Edley & Knopf, 1987; Gordon et al., 1990; Grant et al., 1990; Halperin, Sharma, et al., 1991; J. Kaufmann, 1983; Kirchner & Knopf, 1974; Kupietz & Richardson, 1978; Lam & Beale, 1991; Lassiter, D'Amato, Raggio, Whitten, & Bardos, 1994; List, 1985; Raggio, 1992; Reichenbach et al., 1992; Seabrook, 1995; Slicker, 1991; H. Swanson & Cooney, 1989). Validity coefficients ranged from −.81 to .77, with the majority between ±.30 (Lowe et al., 2000). These studies are presented in Table 4.4.

As noted previously, J. Campbell et al.'s (1991) factor analysis produced a four-factor varimax solution that accounted for 79% of the variance. Achievement tests used included the Wide Range Achievement Test-Revised (WRAT-R; Jastak & Wilkinson, 1984), and the Peabody Individual Achievement Test (PIAT; Dunn & Markwardt, 1970). Commission and omission errors of the AX-CPT were found to load on the same factor as the results of the achievement measures, suggesting shared variance. Moreover, results suggest that the CPT may serve as a predictor of academic achievement (J. Campbell et al., 1991).

In contrast, Aylward et al.'s (1997) factor analytic study also included achievement testing. Achievement tests administered included the Wechsler Individual Achievement Test (WIAT; Psychological Corporation, 1992), Kaufman Test of Educational Achievement (KTEA; Kaufman & Kaufman, 1985), WRAT-R, or PIAT-Revised (Markwardt, 1989) in conjunction with the GDS. In their factor analysis, achievement was not found to load with the results of the CPT.

Lowe et al. (2000) found the correlations to be higher between achievement composite scores and those CPT indices that focused on correct responses (e.g., relative percent correct and total correct scores) as compared to other combinations. For example, Gordon et al. (1990) found the Achievement Scale of the Kaufman Assessment Battery for Children (K-ABC; Kaufman & Kaufman, 1983) to be directly related to vigilance correct scores on the GDS ($r = .42$) and inversely related to vigilance commission errors ($r = −.27$). The composite scores on the Metropolitan Readiness Test (Nurss & McGauvran, 1976) were moderately related to the distractibility index scores used by Edley and Knopf (1987). Further, Kirchner and Knopf's (1974) study yielded the highest validity coefficient for the Stanford Achievement Test scores and correct hits.

Some patterns emerged with regard to specific academic areas as well. Correlations between reading scores and reaction time scores were found to be higher than the correlations between reading scores and other CPT

Table 4.4

Validity Coefficients for CPTs and Achievement Measures

Measure	Study	CPT Type	Population	Correct Hits	Omission Errors	Commission Errors	Other Index
K-ABC: achievement	Gordon et al., 1990	AX-Visual	Children/referred	.42		-.27	
	Slicker, 1991	AX-Visual	Children/referred				-.24 (Inconsistency)
							.26 (Performance)
Metropolitan Readiness Test	Edley & Knopf, 1987	X-Visual	Children/control				.59 (CRR)
PIAT: reading comprehension	Kupietz & Richardson, 1978	AX-Auditory	Children/reading problems		-.02	-.37	
		AX-Visual			-.32	-.33	
PIAT: word recognition	Kupietz & Richardson, 1978	AX-Auditory	Children/reading problems		-.24	-.31	
		AX-Visual			-.36	-.31	
PIAT-R: total	Lassiter et al., 1994	AX-Visual	Children/referred	-.05	.03		
PAT: reading comprehension	Lam & Beale, 1991	AX-Visual	Children/ADHD		.07		.24 (d')
							.27 (Beta)
PAT: vocabulary	Lam & Beale, 1991	AX-Visual	Children/ADHD				.36 (d')
							.25 (Beta)
Roswall-Chall Achievement Test	Kupietz & Richardson, 1978	AX-Auditory	Children/reading problems		-.29	-.44	
		AX-Visual			.07	-.55	
SFAT: language	H.L. Swanson & Cooney, 1989	AX-Auditory	Children/control	.44-.58			.38-.57 (d')
							-.79--.57 (Beta)
							-.27 (FA)
		AX-Visual		.33-.42			-.27-.66 (d')
							-.45 (FA)
SFAT: mathematics	H.L. Swanson & Cooney, 1989	AX-Auditory	Children/control	.36			.38-.40 (d')
							-.57--.50 (Beta)
							-.71-.25 (FA)
		AX-Visual		.26-.28			.47 (d')
							-.33 (FA)
SFAT: reading	H.L. Swanson & Cooney, 1989	AX-Auditory	Children/control				.31 (d')
							-.36 (FA)
		AX-Visual					.26 (d')
							-.29--.25 (Beta)
							-.38-.29 (FA)

Measure	Study	CPT Type	Group				
WRAT-R: reading	Halperin, Sharma, et al., 1991	AX-Visual	Children/control				-.25 (Dyscontrol); -.23 (FA); -.23 (Inattention); -.31 (RT SD); -.43-.54 (Slope corr.); -.16-.81 (Slope d'); -.64-.08 (Slope FA); .24 (d'); -.31 (Slope RT SD)
	Kaufmann, 1983	X-Visual	Children/control	.19			
		AX-Visual					
	Lassiter et al., 1994	AX-Visual	Children/referred	.03	.05	-.06	
	Raggio, 1992	AX-Visual	Children/ADHD		-.38	-.29	
	Reichenbach et al., 1992	AX-Visual	Children/control				-.12 (FA)
WRAT-R: spelling	Grant et al., 1990	AX-Visual	Children/control	.11		.06	
	Lassiter et al., 1994	AX-Visual	Children/referred	-.02	.10	.05	
	Raggio, 1992	AX-Visual	Children/ADHD		-.55	-.51	
WRAT-R: arithmetic	Bedi et al., 1994	AX-Auditory	Children/control				.11 (Distractibility)
		AX-Visual					-.14 (Distractibility)
	Lassiter et al., 1994	AX-Visual	Children/referred	.03	-.02	.03	
	Raggio, 1992	AX-Visual	Children/ADHD		-.47	-.34	
	Reichenbach et al., 1992	AX-Visual	Children/control				-.16 (FA)
Generic achievement tests	List, 1985	X-Visual	Children/control		.32		
Reading (Combination)	Aylward et al., 1997	AX-Visual	Children/referred	.15-.19		.12	
Spelling (Combination)	Aylward et al., 1997	AX-Visual	Children/referred	.18-.20		.13-.15	
Math (Combination)	Aylward et al., 1997	AX-Visual	Children/referred	.19	.14		

Notes: CPT Type does not include additional modifications (e.g., degraded stimulus); for correct hits, omission errors, and commission errors, this may be the number, percentage, or mean. ADHD = Attention-Deficit/Hyperactivity Disorder; CPT = Continuous performance test; CRR = Correct response ratio; d' = Sensitivity; FA = False alarms; K-ABC = Kaufman Assessment Battery for Children; PIAT = Peabody Individual Achievement Test; PAT = Progressive Achievement Test; RT = Reaction time; SD = Standard deviation; SFAT = Scott Foresman Achievement Test; Slope comm. = Slope commission; Slope corr. = Slope correction; WRAT-R = Wide Range Achievement Test-Revised.

index scores. Notably, the use of a visual CPT was associated with higher correlation coefficients between commission error scores and reading scores (e.g., Kupietz & Richardson, 1978). In contrast, the correlations between math scores and perceptual sensitivity (d'), response bias (Beta), and commission error scores tended to be higher than the correlations between math scores and other CPT index scores (e.g., H. Swanson & Cooney, 1989). As with the correlations with reading and language, the degree of association was found to depend on the modality of the CPT used as well as the CPT index.

As with the significant correlation of VIQ and CPT performance being evident only in a study using an auditory CPT, the significant correlations between achievement and CPT performance were evidenced in the one study with auditory presentation of stimuli (H. Swanson & Cooney, 1989). With an auditory CPT, H. Swanson and Cooney found higher validity coefficients between reaction time, response style (bias), and sensitivity (d') scores with language scores as opposed to reading scores. Thus, the findings suggest that CPT sensory modality (auditory vs. visual) and CPT index used may influence the magnitude of the validity coefficients with achievement as well as cognition.

Other differences in the CPT administered, in addition to modality, may affect the magnitude of the validity coefficients. For example, correlations between achievement scores and X-CPT performance are slightly higher than correlations between achievement scores and AX-CPT performance (see Friedman et al., 1978, 1981; Schachar et al., 1988b). Although not a significant difference, it may reflect the difference in information-processing demands for the X- and AX-CPT (Friedman et al., 1978, 1981). Other differences (e.g., the addition of distractors) have been found to impact the degree of association as well. Grant et al. (1990) evaluated 119 boys with ADHD or ADHD with learning disabilities who ranged in age between 6 and 12 years on the GDS vigilance, distractibility, and delay tasks as well as on the WRAT-R. A relation between the GDS correct response scores and WRAT-R Spelling scores may have been task-dependent. Grant and colleagues found Spelling scores to be significantly correlated with the distractibility task correct response scores ($r = .33$), but not with the vigilance task correct response scores ($r = .11$). Thus, the presence of distractors affected the degree of association between CPT performance and the results of a spelling test.

Along with the academic area assessed, the achievement measure used may influence the magnitude of the validity coefficients. For example, validity coefficients with the WRAT-R for math, reading, and spelling (e.g., Grant et al., 1990; Lassiter et al., 1994) were consistently lower than those obtained with other achievement tests. At the same time, overall higher validity coefficients were reported in the single study that used the Scott

Foresman Achievement Test with coefficients ranging from −.79 to .58 (H. Swanson & Cooney, 1989).

The youngest group of children sampled on both a CPT and an achievement measure was the study by Raggio (1992). The study included high-risk 5- and 6-year-old children ($n = 43$), who were administered the WRAT-R and an AX-CPT as part of an evaluation battery. In contrast to other studies that included the WRAT-R, the correlation coefficients yielded with these young children were consistently −.29 and −.55 for omission and commission errors, respectively. Given the age of the children, these correlations may be the result of the constricted range of performance on the WRAT-R or developmental issues in general.

Based on these results, CPT paradigm, CPT index, CPT task, sensory modality, academic area assessed, and achievement measure administered may influence the magnitude of the validity coefficients. Across studies, however, the validity coefficients reported were generally low and would not support the conclusion of J. Campbell et al. (1991) that CPT results may be predictive of achievement. The generally low to moderate correlations with achievement, along with the low to moderate correlations with cognition, suggest that CPTs may tap some construct or trait (i.e., attention or executive control, persistence) that is salient in most cognitive and academic tasks. At the same time, however, CPTs also appear to measure unique abilities or traits that are not tapped by traditional cognitive or academic tasks.

Memory and Learning

As noted in Chapter 1, one of the reasons so much emphasis is placed on attention is the belief that attention is the precursor to memory (e.g., R.A. Cohen, 1993b; Sohlberg & Mateer, 1989b). At the same time, in designing tasks to measure attention, it is important to decrease the memory load such that memory is not a confounding factor. Because of the association between memory and attention, the degree of association between CPT performance and measures of memory is particularly important, and yet, there is a paucity of research available in this area (see Table 4.5).

Aylward et al.'s (1997) factor analytic study included the Wide Range Assessment of Memory and Learning (WRAML; Sheslow & Adams, 1990) in conjunction with measures of achievement and intelligence as well as the GDS. As noted above, memory scores had primary loadings on what was termed the Cognitive Factor along with the VIQ, PIQ, and mathematics achievement scores, as opposed to loading with the CPT scores.

In Hoerig et al.'s (1998) factor analysis with the Conners' CPT and the TOMAL, it was found that commission errors and verbal memory subtest scores had primary loadings on Factor III, suggesting possible overlap or

Table 4.5

Validity Coefficients for CPTs and Memory and Learning Tasks

Measure	Study	CPT Type	Population	Correct Hits	Omission Errors	Commission Errors	Other Index
BVRT-Revised	Grant et al., 1990	AX-Visual	Children/ADHD	.20		.02	
K-ABC hand movements	Allen, 1993	AX-Visual	Children/referred		−.21−−.20	−.21−−.00	
K-ABC word order	Mann, 1997	X-Visual	Children/referred, control				.26 (Composite)
Recognition Memory Test	Mann, 1997	X-Visual	Children/referred, control				.21 (Composite)
	Tupler, 1989	X-Visual	Adults/control	.43			.46 (RT)
RAVLT	Robins, 1992	AX-Visual	Children/ADHD, LD	.34		−.06	−.08 (Comm. var.)
TOMAL: delayed recall	Allen, 1993	AX-Visual	Children/referred		−.36	−.38	
TOMAL: nonverbal memory	Allen, 1993	AX-Visual	Children/referred		−.44	−.42	
TOMAL: verbal memory	Allen, 1993	AX-Visual	Children/referred		−.65	−.46	
VADS: aural-input	Oppenheimer, 1986	AX-Auditory	Children/control, referred	.44		−.24	
		AX-Visual		.42		−.41	
VADS: aural-oral	Oppenheimer, 1986	AX-Auditory	Children/control, referred	.38		−.11	
		AX-Visual		.35		−.29	
VADS: aural-written	Oppenheimer, 1986	AX-Auditory	Children/control, referred	.43		−.33	
		AX-Visual		.45		−.45	
VADS: oral expression	Oppenheimer, 1986	AX-Auditory	Children/control, referred	.46		−.23	
		AX-CPT		.49		−.39	
VADS: written expression	Oppenheimer, 1986	AX-Auditory	Children/control, referred	.52		−.35	
		AX-Visual		.57		−.54	
VADS: visual input	Oppenheimer, 1986	AX-Auditory	Children/control, referred	.52		−.33	
		AX-Visual		.62		−.51	
VADS: visual oral	Oppenheimer, 1986	AX-Auditory	Children/control, referred	.45		−.28	
		AX-Visual		.54		−.41	
VADS: visual written	Oppenheimer, 1986	AX-Auditory	Children/control, referred	.52		−.33	
		AX-Visual		.61		−.35	
VADS: total	Oppenheimer, 1986	AX-Auditory	Children/control, referred	.51		−.31	
		AX-Visual		.57			
WMS-R: visual span	Rasile et al., 1995	AX-Visual	Adults/control	−.02−−.08		−.49	

WRAML factor I	Aylward et al., 1997	X-Visual	Children/referred		.20
WRAML factor II	Aylward et al., 1997	X-Visual	Children/referred		.11
WRAML factor III	Aylward et al., 1997	X-Visual	Children/referred		.10
WRAML design memory	Aylward et al., 1997	X-Visual	Children/referred		.12
WRAML finger windows	Aylward et al., 1997	X-Visual	Children/referred	.12	.21
WRAML number/letter	Aylward et al., 1997	X-Visual	Children/referred		.13
WRAML picture memory	Aylward et al., 1997	X-Visual	Children/referred		.17
WRAML sound/symbol	Aylward et al., 1997	X-Visual	Children/referred		.15
WRAML verbal learning	Aylward et al., 1997	X-Visual	Children/referred		.09

Notes: CPT Type does not include additional modifications (e.g., degraded stimulus); unless designated as -A for Auditory format or -A/V for combined Auditory and Visual format, the presentation of the CPT was Visual. For correct hits, omission errors, and commission errors, this may be the number, percentage, or mean. ADHD = Attention-Deficit/Hyperactivity Disorder; CPT = Continuous performance test; BVRT = Benton Visual Retention Test; K-ABC = Kaufman Assessment Battery for Children; LD = Learning disability; RAVLT = Rey Auditory Verbal Learning Test; TOMAL = Test of Memory and Learning; VADS = Visual Aural Digit Span Test; WMS-R = Wechsler Memory Scale-Revised; WRAML = Wide Range Assessment of Memory and Learning; RT = Reaction time; Comm. var. = Commission error variability.

interaction between verbal memory and commission errors. As noted previously, CPT correct hits and omission errors loaded together on a separate factor, suggesting that memory was not as intricately linked to these variables (Hoerig et al., 1998). Also with the TOMAL, Allen's (1993) study yielded significant validity coefficients for all combinations of omission and commission errors on an AX-CPT. For omission errors, validity coefficients ranged from −.36 (Delayed Recall) to −.65 (Verbal Memory); for commission errors, validity coefficients ranged from −.38 (Delayed Recall) to −.46 (Verbal Memory). However, the most consistent moderate correlations were found with the Visual Aural Digit Span (VADS; Koppitz, 1970, 1977) in a study by Oppenheimer (1986) using both an auditory and visual AX-CPT. Across scales and modalities, validity coefficients ranged from .35 to .62 for correct hits. Validity coefficients were somewhat lower for commission errors, ranging from −.11 to −.54.

Even fewer studies have included measures of memory with adult populations, and the results of these studies are equivocal. Stronger relations appear to be associated with recognition tasks and correct hits as well as reaction time (Tupler, 1989), and list learning with correct hits (Robins, 1992). Notably, in view of the developmental trajectory for memory across the life span and memory loss associated with dementia, no study was found with adults that included both CPT scores and a memory battery.

Behavior Rating Scales

Another alternative to direct observation for obtaining information about the behavior of children and youth is the use of behavior rating scales. Behavior rating scales may focus on a specific symptom cluster (i.e., behaviors associated with depression) or provide a more global view (e.g., omnibus scales). The rating scale method is used most frequently with children and youth as opposed to adults, and depending on the scale, the respondent may be the child's parent, the child's teacher, or the child. If the CPT paradigm is measuring attention and executive control, it would be expected that correlations of CPT performance and scales or subscales on behavior rating instruments that also are believed to reflect inattention or executive control would be strong. At the same time, given the potential for inattention, for example, to be manifest secondary to other emotional or behavioral problems (e.g., anxiety, depression), it is important to identify the extent of association between CPT performance and scales or subscales reflecting these problems.

A number of studies have examined the relationship between CPT performance and behavior rating scales (Allen, 1993; Arcia & Roberts, 1993; Atkins, Stoff, Osborne, & Brown, 1993; Barkley, 1991; Bedi et al., 1994; Das et al., 1992; Driscoll, 1994; DuPaul et al., 1992; Edley & Knopf, 1987; Ellis,

1991; Flansburg, 1986; Forbes, 1998; Garretson et al., 1990; Gordon, DiNiro, Mettelman, & Tallmadge, 1989; Halperin et al., 1988; Halperin, Wolf, et al., 1991; Harper & Ottinger, 1992; Kardell, 1994; Klee & Garfinkel, 1983; Kupietz & Richardson, 1978; Lam & Beale, 1991; Lassiter et al., 1994; List, 1985; Mahan, 1996; Mayes et al., 1998; McClure & Gordon, 1984; T. Mitchell & Quittner, 1996; Oppenheimer, 1986; Prinz, Meyers, Holden, Tarnowski, & Roberts, 1983; Raggio, Whitten, & Shine, 1994; Reichenbach et al., 1992; Rosenberg, 1980; Sandford, Fine, & Goldman, 1995b; Schachar et al., 1988b; Seabrook, 1995; Seidel, 1989; Slicker, 1991; Sprinkle, 1992; Teicher, Ito, Glod, & Barber, 1996; R. Thompson & Nichols, 1992; Wherry et al., 1993). As can be seen in Table 4.6, across studies, validity coefficients ranged from −.86 to +.81 (Lowe et al., 2000).

Lovejoy and Rasmussen's (1990) factor analytic study included the Child Behavior Checklist (CBCL; Achenbach & Edelbrock, 1986a), Conners Parent Rating Scale (CPRS; Goyette, Conners, & Ulrich, 1978), Conners Teacher Rating Scale (CTRS; Goyette et al., 1978), and the Iowa Conners (Loney & Milich, 1982). Notably, scores from these scales did not load on factors with the variables from the AX-CPT, but on other factors. At the same time, although behavioral measures in the J. Campbell et al. (1991) study included the CPRS, commission and omission errors of the AX-CPT were not found to load on the same factor as the results of the CPRS. Similarly, Gridley, Hinds, and Hall (2000) found that teacher ratings did not load with TOVA scores.

Studies that included correlations with subscales of inattention or distractibility obtained validity coefficients generally in the ±.45 range. For those studies that included a scale specific to impulsivity or dyscontrol, the coefficients tended to be lower and in the ±.16 range. Unfortunately, for many of the rating scales, the subscales are combinations of behaviors (i.e., inattention/passivity, inattention/overactivity). Notably, validity coefficients increased for combination scales of inattention/overactivity and impulsive/hyperactive. For example, the correlations of commission error scores, impulse index scores, inconsistency index scores, and performance index scores from an AX-CPT with the impulsive/hyperactivity scale scores of the CPRS were consistently greater than |.25| (Slicker, 1991). Similarly, for Slicker's sample, the inattention/overactivity scale scores of the Iowa Conners correlated with CPT variables at a magnitude greater than |.27|. With an X-CPT, Teicher et al. (1996) found the inattention/overactivity scale scores to correlate moderately with CPT variability as measured by the standard deviation of the mean reaction time scores.

The degree to which hyperactivity scales or subscales was associated with CPT performance tended to be stronger than attention (or inattention) or impulsivity. There was a substantial degree of association between commission errors and the scores on hyperactivity scales from the

Table 4.6

Validity Coefficients: CPT Scores and Scores on Behavioral Rating Scales and Personality Measures with Children

Measure	Study	CPT Type	Population	Correct Hits	Omission Errors	Commission Errors	Other Index
ACTeRS: attention	Forbes, 1998	X-Visual	ADHD		-.25	-.16	-.32 (Multiple), -.15 (RT), -.30 (Variability)
	Lassiter et al., 1994	AX-Visual	Referred	.02–.09	-.08–-.02	-.07–.01	
	Oppenheimer, 1986	AX-Auditory	Control, referred	-.15		-.27	
		AX-Visual		.08		-.20	
	Kardell, 1994	AX-Visual	Referred	.10		-.23	-.21 (Dyscontrol), -.22 (Impulse), -.14 (Inattention), .07 (RT), -.02 (SD)
ACTeRS: hyperactivity	Forbes, 1998	X-Visual	ADHD		-.37	-.30	-.25 (Multiple), -.14 (RT), -.33 (Variability)
	Lassiter et al., 1994	AX-Visual	Referred	.09–.12	-.11–-.09	-.11–-.09	
	Oppenheimer, 1986	AX-Auditory	Control, referred	.15		.29	
		AX-Visual		-.06		.25	
	Kardell, 1994	AX-Visual	Referred	.04		.16	.16 (Dyscontrol), .17 (Impulse), -.05 (Inattention), -.03 (RT), .03 (SD)
ACTeRS: oppositional	Forbes, 1998	X-Visual	ADHD		-.38	-.25	-.07 (Multiple), .16 (RT), -.03 (Variability)
	Lassiter et al., 1994	AX-Visual	Referred	.08–.10	-.05–.03	-.18–-.15	
	Oppenheimer, 1986	AX-Auditory	Control, referred	.21		.26	
		AX-Visual		-.02		.22	
ACTeRS: social skills	Raggio et al., 1994	AX-Visual	ADHD			-.27	
	Forbes, 1998	X-Visual	ADHD		-.27	-.17	-.08 (Multiple), .06 (RT), -.07 (Variability)

Measure	Study	CPT	Group				
ADDES (Teacher): hyperactivity	Lassiter et al., 1994	AX-Visual	Referred	-.14--.09	.10-.14	-.13--.10	
	Oppenheimer, 1986	AX-Auditory	Control, referred	-.04		-.26	
	Driscoll, 1994	AX-Visual	Control	.16		-.25	-.16--.27 (Attention); -.06--.15 (Impulse)
		AX-Auditory	Control				-.16 (Attention); -.03 (Impulse)
ADDES (Teacher): impulsivity	Driscoll, 1994	AX-Visual	Control				-.02--.12 (Attention); .00--.15 (Impulse)
		AX-Auditory	Control				-.15 (Attention); -.05 (Impulse)
ADDES (Teacher): inattention	Driscoll, 1994	AX-Visual	Control				-.09--.17 (Attention); .02--.08 (Impulse)
		AX-Auditory	Control				-.25 (Attention); -.21 (Impulse)
ADHD Rating Scale: impulsive	DuPaul, Anastopoulos, et al., 1992	AX-Visual	ADHD	-.09		-.10	
ADHD Rating Scale: inattention	DuPaul, Anastopoulos, et al., 1992	AX-Visual	ADHD	-.15		.08	
ADHD Rating Scale: total	Barkley, 1991	AX-Visual	Referred		.01-.27	.05-.40	
	DuPaul, Anastopoulos, et al., 1992	AX-Visual	ADHD	-.14		.07	
Attention checklist	Wherry et al., 1993	AX-Visual	ADHD, control	-.46	.46	.22	
BASC PRS: aggression	Das et al., 1992	X-CPT-Auditory	Control		-.14--.12	-.21-.37	
	Floyd, 1999	Not-X Visual	Control		.53	.09	
BASC PRS: anxiety	Sprinkle, 1992	Not-X Visual	Referred		.00	.15	
	Floyd, 1999	Not-X Visual	Control		.40	.29	
BASC PRS: attention problems	Floyd, 1999	Not-X Visual	Control		.49	.41	
BASC PRS: depression	Sprinkle, 1992	AX-Visual	Referred		-.07	-.02	
BASC PRS: hyperactivity	Floyd, 1999	Not-X Visual	Control		.42	.19	
	Floyd, 1999	Not-X Visual	Control		.73	.25	
BASC PRS: withdrawal	Floyd, 1999	Not-X Visual	Control		.03	.24	

(continued)

Table 4.6 Continued

Measure	Study	CPT Type	Population	Correct Hits	Omission Errors	Commission Errors	Other Index
BASC TRS: aggression	Floyd, 1999	Not-X Visual	Control		.25	.38	
BASC TRS: anxiety	Floyd, 1999	Not-X Visual	Control		.22	.40	
BASC TRS: attention problems	Floyd, 1999	Not-X Visual	Control		.38	.41	
BASC TRS: depression	Floyd, 1999	Not-X CPT	Control		.30	.55	
BASC TRS: hyperactivity	Floyd, 1999	Not-X CPT	Control		.18	.44	
BASC TRS: withdrawal	Floyd, 1999	Not-X CPT	Control		.25	.44	
BASC SRP: social stress	Sprinkle, 1992	AX-Visual	Referred		.01	.07	
Child Attention Problems Scale: inattention	Barkley, 1991	AX-Visual	Referred		.26	.25	
Child Attention Problems Scale: overactivity	Barkley, 1991	AX-Visual	Referred		.30	.37	
CBCL: aggression	Oppenheimer, 1986	AX-Auditory	Control, referred	-.06		.22	
		AX-Visual		-.21		.23	
CBCL: externalizing	DuPaul, Anastopoulos, et al., 1992	AX-Visual	ADHD	.01		.02	
	T.V. Mitchell & Quittner, 1996	AX-Visual	HI, control	-.06			-.30 (d') .52 (FA)
CBCL: hyperactivity	Barkley, 1991	AX-Visual	Referred		.19-.29	.22-.36	
	DuPaul, Anastopoulos, et al., 1992	AX-Visual	ADHD	-.07		-.02	
	Oppenheimer, 1986	AX-Auditory	Control, referred	-.04		.14	
		AX-Visual		-.22		.22	
	T.V. Mitchell & Quittner, 1996	AX-Visual	HI, control	-.13			-.40(d') .65 (FA)
CBCL: total	T.V. Mitchell & Quittner, 1996	AX-Visual	HI, control	-.24			-.32 (d') .32 (FA)
	Mahan, 1996	Not-X Visual	ADHD			.18	.16 (d') .09 (Beta) .20 (RT)
TRF: aggression	R.W. Thompson & Nichols, 1992	AX-Visual	Referred	-.15	.28	.09	
	Oppenheimer, 1986	AX-Auditory	Control, referred	.08		.24	
		AX-Visual				.27	
TRF: externalizing	DuPaul, Anastopoulos, et al., 1992	AX-Visual	ADHD	-.22		-.07	

Measure	Study	Task	Group				
TRF: inattention	T.V. Mitchell & Quittner, 1996	AX-Visual	HI, control	−.24			−.48 (d') .46 (FA)
	DuPaul, Anastopoulos, et al., 1992	AX-Visual	ADHD	−.08		−.18	
	Oppenheimer, 1986	AX-Auditory	Control, referred	.12		.20	
		AX-Visual		−.09		.18	
	T.V. Mitchell & Quittner, 1996	AX-Visual	HI, control	−.45			−.55 (d') .31 (FA)
TRF: nervous/overactive	Oppenheimer, 1986	AX-Auditory	Control, referred	.20		.33	
		AX-Visual		−.10		.29	
TRF: overactive	DuPaul, Anastopoulos, et al., 1992	AX-Visual	ADHD	.06		−.10	
TRF: total	Gordon, DiNiro, et al., 1989	AX-Visual	Children/referred			.37	.35 (Inattention)
	McClure & Gordon, 1984	AX-Visual	ADHD, control	−.21			
	T.V. Mitchell & Quittner, 1996	AX-Visual	HI, control	−.20			−.38 (d') .50 (FA)
Children's Attention Scale	Sandford et al. (1995b)	X-Auditory/Visual	ADHD, control				1.00 (% Agreement)
CADS: communication	Stein et al., 1994	X-Visual	Referred		.04	−.08	
CADS: lability	Stein et al., 1994	X-Visual	Referred		.05	.21	
CADS: social relatedness	Stein et al., 1994	X-Visual	Referred		.04	.09	
CADS: preoccupation	Stein et al., 1994	X-Visual	Referred		−.04	−.09	
CADS: total	Stein et al., 1994	X-Visual	Referred		.09	.15	
Children's Depression Inventory	Sprinkle, 1992	AX-Visual	Referred		.00	.06	
CPQ: anxiety	Reichenbach et al., 1992	AX-Visual	Control				.03 (Inattention)
CPQ: conduct	Reichenbach et al., 1992	AX-Visual	Control				.11 (Inattention)
CPQ: hyperkinesis index	Reichenbach et al., 1992	AX-Visual	Control				.20 (Inattention)
CPQ: impulsive/hyper	Reichenbach et al., 1992	AX-Visual	Control				.20 (Inattention)
CPQ: learning	Reichenbach et al., 1992	AX-Visual	Control				.14 (Inattention)
CPQ: psychosomatic	Reichenbach et al., 1992	AX-Visual	Control				−.12 (Inattention)
CPRS: hyperactivity index	Flansburg, 1986	AX-Visual	ADD, clinical	.00–−.05	−.18–−.00	−.59–−.11	.30 (Inconsistency) .41 (Impulse) −.39 (Performance)
	Slicker, 1991	AX-Visual	Referred		.33	.35	

(continued)

Table 4.6 Continued

Measure	Study	CPT Type	Population	Correct Hits	Omission Errors	Commission Errors	Other Index
CPRS: impulsive/hyper	Allen, 1993	AX-Visual	Referred		.05	.21	
	Raggio et al., 1994	AX-Visual	ADHD			-.32	
	Allen, 1993	AX-Visual	Referred		.04	.16	
	Slicker, 1991	AX-Visual	Referred		.37	.26	.38 (Impulse) / .29 (Inconsistency) / -.39 (Performance)
CPRS: learning problems	Slicker, 1991	AX-Visual	Referred			.30	.29 (Impulse) / .25 (Inconsistency) / -.28 (Performance)
CPRS: total	Lassiter et al., 1994	AX-Visual	Children/referred		.14-.20	.17--.11	-.26--.20 (d')
	Sandford et al. (1995b)	X-Auditory/Visual	ADHD, control				.92 (% Agreement)
CPRS-R: hyperactivity	Barkley, 1991	AX-Visual	Referred		.15-.34	.25-.34	
	Flansburg, 1986	AX-Visual	ADD, clinical		-.18-.00	-.59-.01	
CTQ: conduct problems	Halperin et al., 1988	AX-Visual	Control	.00-.05	-.03	.32 (A-Not-X) / .17 (X only) / .09 (A only) / .15 (Random)	
CTQ: hyperactivity	Halperin et al., 1988	AX-Visual	Control		.14	.37 (A-Not-X) / .16 (X only) / .17 (A only) / .19 (Random)	
CTQ: inattention/passivity	Halperin, Sharma, et al., 1991	AX-Visual	Control				.22 (Dyscontrol)
	Halperin et al., 1988	AX-Visual	Control		.25	.19 (A-Not-X) / .25 (X only) / .17 (A only) / .18 (Random)	
	Halperin, Sharma, et al., 1991	AX-Visual	Control				.38 (Dyscontrol) / .32 (FA)
CTRS: aggression	Kupietz & Richardson, 1978	AX-Auditory	Reading problems		.12-.19	.24-.27	
		AX-Visual			-.06-.00	.48-.49	
CTRS: anxious	Klee & Garfinkel, 1983	AX-Visual	Referred		-.10	-.01	-.04 (Total Errors)
CTRS: conduct	Klee & Garfinkel, 1983	AX-Visual	Referred		-.05	-.03	-.04 (Total Errors)

Scale	Study	CPT	Sample				
CTRS: hyperactivity	Lam & Beale, 1991	AX-Visual	ADHD				-.10 (d'), -.07 (Beta)
	McClure & Gordon, 1984	AX-Visual	ADHD, control	-.20	.18–.33	.36–.42	
	Kupietz & Richardson, 1978	AX-Auditory	Reading problems		-.18–.06	.57–.61	
	Klee & Garfinkel, 1983	AX-Visual	Referred		.36	.34	.35 (Total errors)
	Lam & Beale, 1991	AX-Visual	ADHD				.03 (d'), .04 (Beta)
CTRS: hyperactivity index	McClure & Gordon, 1984	AX-Visual	ADHD, control	.08			.38 (Impulse), -.33 (Performance)
	Slicker, 1991	AX-Visual	Referred	.25	.33		.33 (Impulse), -.28 (Performance)
CTRS: inattention	Slicker, 1991	AX-Visual	Referred		.27	.30	
	Kupietz & Richardson, 1978	AX-Auditory	Reading problems		.20–.24	.19–.23	
	Klee & Garfinkel, 1983	AX-Visual	Referred		.31–.34	.33–.36	.33 (Total errors)
	Lam & Beale, 1991	AX-Visual	ADHD		.31	.33	-.20 (d'), -.09 (Beta)
CTRS: social	McClure & Gordon, 1984	AX-Visual	ADHD, control	-.21	.21	.05	
CTRS: tension	Klee & Garfinkel, 1983	AX-Visual	Referred				.12 (Total errors)
	Lam & Beale, 1991	AX-Visual	ADHD				-.10 (d'), .11 (Beta)
CTRS: total	Klee & Garfinkel, 1983	AX-Visual	Referred		.32	.36	.38 (Total errors)
	List, 1985	X-Visual	Control		.37		.56 (RT SD)
CTRS (abbreviated)	Teicher et al., 1996	X-Visual	ADHD, control				.24 (Resp. var.)
CTRS-R: conduct problems	Rosenberg, 1980	X-Visual	LD, control		.06		.51 (FA)
	Forbes, 1998	X-Visual	ADHD			.10	.14 (Multiple)
CTRS-R: hyperactivity	Allen, 1993	AX-Visual	Referred		.11	.04	-.05 (RT)
	Barkley, 1991	AX-Visual	Referred		.27	.41	.15 (Variability)

(continued)

Table 4.6 Continued

Measure	Study	CPT Type	Population	Correct Hits	Omission Errors	Commission Errors	Other Index
	Forbes, 1998	X-Visual	ADHD		.07	.01	.00 (Multiple) .04 (RT) .07 (Variability)
CTRS-R: hyperactivity index	Allen, 1993	AX-Visual	Referred		.13	.06	
	Flansburg, 1986	AX-Visual	ADD, clinical	-.16-.07	-.14-.07	-.21-.01	
CTRS-R: hyperkinesis index	Forbes, 1998	X-Visual	ADHD		.09	-.03	-.01 (Multiple) .09 (RT) .10 (Variability)
CTRS-R: inattention	Barkley, 1991	AX-Visual	Referred		.28	.22	
	Allen, 1993	AX-Visual	Referred		.07	.02	
CTRS-R: inattention/passivity	Forbes, 1998	X-Visual	ADHD		.17	.06	.05 (Multiple) .20 (RT) .10 (Variability)
CTRS-R: passivity	Das et al., 1992	X-Auditory	Control		.07-.18	-.37-.16	
DSM III Scale: hyperactivity	Halperin et al., 1988	AX-Visual	Control		.06	.43 (A-Not-X only) .20 (A-only) .07 (X-only) .17 (Random)	
DSM III Scale: impulsivity	Halperin et al., 1988	AX-Visual	Control		.03	.39 (A-Not-X) .08 (X only) .15 (A only) .12 (Random)	
DSM III Scale: inattention	Halperin et al., 1988	AX-Visual	Control		.25	.20 (A-Not-X) .11 (X only) .14 (A only) .19 (Random)	
HSQ: number	DuPaul, Anastopoulos, et al., 1992	AX-Visual	ADHD	.11		-.24	
HSQ: severity	DuPaul, Anastopoulos, et al., 1992	AX-Visual	ADHD	-.01		.00	
Hostile aggressive responses	Atkins et al., 1993	AX-Visual	Referred			.51	

IOWA Conners: aggression	Bedi et al., 1994	AX-Auditory	Control				.06 (Distractibility)
		AX-Visual	Control				-.21 (Distractibility)
	Reichenbach et al., 1992	AX-Visual	Control				.09 (Inattention)
	Teicher et al., 1996	X-Visual	ADHD, control				
	Allen, 1993	AX-Visual	Referred		.22	.23	.61 (RT SD)
IOWA Conners: inattention/overactivity	Bedi et al., 1994	AX-Auditory	Control				-.08 (Distractibility)
		AX-Visual	Control				-.25 (Distractibility)
	Reichenbach et al., 1992	AX-Visual	Control				.32 (Inattention)
	Slicker, 1991	AX-Visual	Referred		.27	.29	.35 (Impulse); .27 (Performance); .40 (RT SD); .27 (Impulse)
IOWA Conners: total	Teicher et al., 1996	X-Visual	ADHD, control			.31	
	Slicker, 1991	AX-Visual	Referred			-.15	
Jr. EPQ: extroversion	Matosich, 1988	AX-Visual	ADDH	-.02–.06		-.01–.02	
Jr. EPQ: neuroticism	Matosich, 1988	AX-Visual	ADDH	.33–.41		.05–.07	
Jr. EPQ: psychoticism	Matosich, 1988	AX-Visual	ADDH	-.13–-.11		.13–.14	
Jr. EPQ: lie scale	Matosich, 1988	AX-Visual	ADDH	-.35–-.34			
PSI: child distractibility/hyperactivity	Oppenheimer et al., 1986	AX-Auditory	Control, referred	-.04		.17	
RCMAS: total score	Pliszka, 1992	AX-Visual	ADHD	-.17		.27	
	Sprinkle, 1992	Not X-Visual	Referred			-.34	
RCMAS: physiological	Sprinkle, 1992	AX-Visual	Referred		-.13	.13	
RCMAS: social concerns/concentration	Sprinkle, 1992	AX-Visual	Referred	.00	-.07	.09	
RCMAS: worry/oversensitivity	Sprinkle, 1992	AX-Visual	Referred		-.18	.07	
SSQ: number	DuPaul, Anastopoulos, et al., 1992	AX-Visual	ADHD	.09		.02	
SSQ: severity	DuPaul, Anastopoulos, et al., 1992	AX-Visual	ADHD	-.12		.01	

(continued)

Table 4.6 Continued

Measure	Study	CPT Type	Population	Correct Hits	Omission Errors	Commission Errors	Other Index
SNAP: attention	Kardell, 1994	AX-Visual	Referred	-.07		.19	.16 (Dyscontrol) .22 (Impulse) .09 (Inattention) -.01 (SD total) -.19 (RT)
SNAP: hyperactivity	Kardell, 1994	AX-Visual	Referred	.00		.11	.20 (Dyscontrol) .16 (Impulse) .00 (Inattention) .09 (SD total) -.07 (RT)
SNAP: impulsivity	Kardell, 1994	AX-Visual	Referred	.05		.19	.09 (Dyscontrol) .16 (Impulse) -.09 (Inattention) -.08 (SD total) -.16 (RT)
SCRS	McClure & Gordon, 1984	AX-Visual	ADHD, control	.08			
TBI: attentiveness/ cooperativeness	Arcia & Roberts, 1993	X-Visual	OME				-.67--.63 (RT Slope)
TRAD	Edley & Knopf, 1987	X-Visual	Control				.41 (CRR)

Notes: CPT Type does not include additional modifications (e.g., degraded stimulus); unless designated as -A for Auditory format or -A/V for combined Auditory and Visual format, the presentation of the CPT was Visual. For correct hits, omission errors, and commission errors, this may be the number, percentage, or mean. ACTeRS = ADDH Comprehensive Teachers Rating Scale; ADDES = Attention Deficit Disorder Evaluation Scale; ADHD = Attention-Deficit/Hyperactivity Disorder; BASC = Behavior Assessment System for Children; CADS = Children's Atypical Development Scale; CBCL = Child Behavior Checklist; Comm. var. = Commission error variability; CPT = Continuous performance test; CPQ = Conners Parent Questionnaire; CPRS = Conners Parent Rating Scale; CTQ = Conners Teacher Questionnaire; CTRS = Conners Teacher Rating Scale; CRR = Correct response ratio; d' = Sensitivity; DSM = Diagnostic and Statistical Manual of Mental Disorders; FA = False alarm; HI = Hearing impaired; HSQ = Home Situation Questionnaire, Jr. EPQ = Junior Eysenck Personality Questionnaire; Multiple = Multiple responses; OME = History of otitis media with effusion; PRS = Parent Rating Scale; PSI = Parent Stress Index; -R = Revised; RCMAS = Revised Children's Manifest Anxiety Scale; RT = Reaction time; SCRS = Self-Control Rating Scale; SD = Standard deviation; SRP = Self-report; SSQ = School Situation Questionnaire; TBI = Test Behavior Inventory; TRF = Teacher Report Form; TRAD = Teachers Rating of Academic Development; TRS = Teacher Rating Scale.

teacher ratings (Barkley, 1991; Halperin et al., 1988; Kupietz & Richardson, 1978). For example, in the Kupietz and Richardson study, commission errors for both the auditory and visual formats of the AX-CPT were significantly correlated with teacher ratings of hyperactivity. Notably, the relation between hyperactivity scores on the CTRS and commission errors was found to be stronger with the visual CPT format (.57 to .61) as compared to the auditory format (.36 to .42). At the same time, Flansburg (1986) found the strongest association between the CPRS and the GDS vigilance task to occur with the fathers' hyperactivity index scores and vigilance commission errors ($r = -.59$).

Using the Behavior Assessment System for Children (BASC; Reynolds & Kamphaus, 1992), Floyd (1999) found that the Parent Rating Scale (PRS) subscale scores of Hyperactivity and Attention Problems were significantly and substantially correlated with omission errors ($r = .73$ and .49, respectively) on the Kiddie Continuous Performance Test (Conners, 1999). Scores on the Attention Problems scale also moderately correlated with commission errors ($r = .41$). In contrast, neither the Hyperactivity nor Attention Problems subscale coefficients were significant for the Teacher Rating Scale (TRS). Although nonsignificant, coefficients were moderate for Hyperactivity ($r = .44$) and Attention Problems ($r = .41$) with commission errors. At the same time, significant coefficients resulted from the combinations of PRS Aggression and omission errors, PRS Depression and omission errors, and TRS Depression and commission errors. Although nonsignificant, coefficients were in the moderate range (+.30) for PRS Anxiety and omission errors, TRS Aggression and commission errors, TRS Withdrawal and commission errors, and TRS Anxiety and commission errors (Floyd, 1999). Using the Children's Atypical Development Scale (CADS; Barkley, 1990) and an X-CPT with 474 children, Stein et al. (1994) found that commission errors loaded on Factor II of the CADS; that is, commission errors correlated significantly, but at a relatively low level ($r = .21$) with emotional lability scores.

Although correlations with attention, impulsivity, and hyperactivity may appear, at first glance, to be lower than expected, it is likely that the scales themselves sample behaviors that represent multiple components of attention and executive control as well as other behaviors that may be tapped by a given CPT. At the same time, it is important to note that the correlations with other scales also are low. For example, comparable or lower correlations were found for CPT performance with oppositional behavior (e.g., Forbes, 1998; Lassiter et al., 1994; Raggio et al., 1994), social skills (e.g., Forbes, 1998; Klee & Garfinkel, 1983; Oppenheimer, 1986), anxiety/depression (Slicker, 1991), and conduct problems (Forbes, 1998). Thus, the relation between CPT performance and behavioral clusters seems to vary depending on the rater as well as the CPT variable and the behaviors included in a scale or subscale of the behavior rating instrument.

In some studies (e.g., Cicerone, 1997; Melnyk & Das, 1992), other measures of attention were found to be more consistent with teacher ratings or diagnostic classification. For example, Posner (Posner & Boies, 1971) tasks that include physical and name-identity tasks were more accurate than a CPT task in discriminating good versus poor attenders (Melnyk & Das, 1992). The Posner tasks are measures of selective attention, and according to Melnyk and Das, selective attention requires individuals to be selective in what they attend to and to inhibit responding to nonselected or external stimuli (i.e., distractors). For students to be good attenders, they must inhibit responding to distractors in the classroom. Thus, teacher ratings are more likely to be sensitive to the "resistance to distractor" component in selective and sustained attention tasks. Melnyk and Das speculated that if the strength of the distractors is increased in CPT tasks, the false detection rate would increase and reflect the individual's inability to inhibit responding to the distractors and thus discriminate good and poor attenders. Melnyk and Das suggest that future research with CPTs should focus on examining the relation between teacher ratings and CPT false detection scores as a function of distractor strength.

Personality and Symptom Presentation in Adults

There is a fine line between behavioral rating scales and measures of personality, and it could be argued that in some cases, the scales are in fact measuring the same behavioral tendencies but from different perspectives (Kamphaus & Frick, 1994). In the child literature, the majority of studies using CPTs included behavior rating scales of some type; these were discussed above. In the adult literature, many studies have included various personality measures or measures that are specific to traits or symptom clusters with a self-report format (e.g., Benedict et al., 1994; Finkelstein et al., 1997; Franke et al., 1994; Lenzenweger, Cornblatt, & Putnick, 1991; Liu et al., 1997; Nuechterlein, Edell, Norris, & Dawson, 1986; Roitman, Keefe, Harvey, Siever, & Mohs, 1997; Serper, 1991). A wide range of personality measures was used in these investigations, including objective personality measures and projective measures (see Table 4.7). In some cases, measures included in the adult studies have been specific to those behavioral symptoms associated with a disorder (i.e., the negative and positive symptoms associated with schizophrenia) or the measures may have been more global in nature. Due to the nature of adult measures, there are few, if any, scales that directly and solely tap attention and executive control. As a result, it would be expected that the correlations with CPT performance would vary considerably depending on the behaviors included in a given scale. Across studies, the validity coefficients ranged from −.66 to .67, with the majority of the validity coefficients between

Table 4.7

Validity Coefficients for CPTs and Measures of Personality and Symptom Presentation in Adults

Measure	Study	CPT Type	Population	Correct Hits	Omission Errors	Commission Errors	Other Index
Abbreviated Anhedonia Scale	Franke et al., 1994	IP-Visual	Control, schizophrenic				-.05–.07 (d') -.11–.12 (Beta)
Abbreviated Perceptual Aberration Scale	Franke et al., 1994	IP-Visual	Control, schizophrenic				-.43–-.32 (d') .04–.26 (Beta)
Assessment of negative symptoms	Benedict et al., 1994	X-Visual	Schizophrenic				.28 (d')
AIPSS: receiving skills	Addington et al., 1998	AX-Auditory	Schizophrenic				.22 (Attention)
AIPSS: processing skills	Addington et al., 1998	AX-Auditory	Schizophrenic				.61 (Attention)
AIPSS: sending skills	Addington et al., 1998	AX-Auditory	Schizophrenic				.50 (Attention)
Boredom coping	J.A. Hamilton et al., 1984	AX-Visual	Control			-.36	-.43 (ISI)
Boredom susceptibility	J.A. Hamilton et al., 1984	AX-Visual	Control			-.09	-.25 (ISI)
BPRS: negative symptoms	Strauss et al., 1993	X-Visual	Schizophrenic, schizoaffective				-.18 (d')
	Karper et al., 1996	AX-Visual	Schizophrenic				-.25 (Index)
	Roitman et al., 1997	AX-Visual	Control, clinical		.67	.36	.63 (d') .08 (Beta)
BPRS: positive symptoms	Strauss et al., 1993	X-Visual	Schizophrenic, schizoaffective				.13 (d')
	Karper et al., 1996	AX-Visual	Schizophrenic				.12 (Index)
	Roitman et al., 1997	AX-Visual	Control, clinical		.07	.02	-.10 (d') .25 (Beta)
BPRS: total scale	Karper et al., 1996	AX-Visual	Schizophrenic				-.06 (Index)
	Roitman et al., 1997	AX-Visual	Control, clinical		.22	.05	-.23 (d') .07 (Beta)
BPRS: anergia factor	Serper, 1991	AX-Visual	Schizophrenic				-.34–-.49 (Attention)
	Nuechterlein et al., 1986	AX-Visual	Schizophrenic				-.44–-.36 (d')
BPRS: anhedonia	Nuechterlein et al., 1986	AX-Visual	Schizophrenic				-.05–.05 (d')
BPRS: anxious-depressed	Nuechterlein et al., 1986	AX-Visual	Schizophrenic				-.30–-.08 (d')
BPRS: hostile-suspicious	Nuechterlein et al., 1986	AX-Visual	Schizophrenic				-.36–-.11 (d')

(continued)

Table 4.7 Continued

Measure	Study	CPT Type	Population	Correct Hits	Omission Errors	Commission Errors	Other Index
BPRS: thought disturbance	Nuechterlein et al., 1986	AX-Visual	Schizophrenic				-.08--.03 (d')
BPRS: blunted affect	Nuechterlein et al., 1986	AX-Visual	Schizophrenic				-.33--.13 (d')
BPRS: dissociation	Nuechterlein et al., 1986	AX-Visual	Schizophrenic				-.41--.19 (d')
BPRS: emotional withdrawal	Nuechterlein et al., 1986	AX-Visual	Schizophrenic				-.50--.15 (d')
BPRS: motor retardation	Nuechterlein et al., 1986	AX-Visual	Schizophrenic				-.45--.27 (d')
Conflict Tactics Scale	Prinz et al., 1983	AX-Visual / AX-Auditory	Parents of child with ADDH	-.19--.09		.06-.34	
EPQ: extroversion	Matosich, 1988	AX-Visual	Parents of child with ADDH	-.03--.01		-.06-.06	
EPQ: neuroticism	Matosich, 1988	AX-Visual	Parents of child with ADDH	-.14--.10		.07-.10	
EPQ: psychoticism	Matosich, 1988	AX-Visual	Parents of child with ADDH	-.19--.17		-.21-.14	
EPQ: Lie Scale	Matosich, 1988	AX-Visual	Parents of child with ADDH	-.15--.18		-.13-.18	
Global Assessment Scale	Sax et al., 1995	X-Visual	Psychiatric				.39-.94 (d'); .11-.36 (Beta)
Global Improvement Scale	Spohn et al., 1977	X-Visual	Schizophrenic		.24		
Global Severity Scale	Spohn et al., 1977	X-Visual	Schizophrenic		.45		
Heron Scale	A.D.M. Davies & Davies, 1975	X-Visual	Control				-.42 (Efficiency)
Intrinsic enjoyment	J.A. Hamilton et al., 1984	AX-Visual	Control			-.01	.06 (ISI)
O'Leary-Porter Scale	Prinz et al., 1983	AX-Visual / AX-Auditory	Parents of child with ADDH	-.17		.37	
PANSS: negative scale	Liu et al., 1997	AX-Visual	Schizophrenic				-.29 (d')
PANSS: positive scale	Cornblatt et al., 1997	IP-Visual	Schizophrenic				-.01--.09(d')
	Liu et al., 1997	AX-Visual	Schizophrenic				.30 (Beta)
	Cornblatt et al., 1997	IP-Visual	Schizophrenic				-.13-.05 (d')
PANSS: blunted affect	Liu et al., 1997	AX-Visual	Schizophrenic				-.25--.22 (d')
PANSS: delusion	Liu et al., 1997	AX-Visual	Schizophrenic				.28 (Beta)
PANSS: hallucination	Liu et al., 1997	AX-Visual	Schizophrenic				.26 (Beta)
PANSS: hostility	Liu et al., 1997	AX-Visual	Schizophrenic				.26 (Beta)
Rorschach: associated disorganization	Nuechterlein et al., 1986	AX-Visual	Schizophrenic				-.30--.25 (d')
Rorschach: confound thinking	Nuechterlein et al., 1986	AX-Visual	Schizophrenic				-.28 (d')
Rorschach: fluid thinking	Nuechterlein et al., 1986	AX-Visual	Schizophrenic				-.34 (d')

Measure	Citation	CPT Type	Group				
Rorschach: total thought disorder index	Nuechterlein et al., 1986	AX-Visual	Schizophrenic				-.34 (d')
SDI: total	Addington et al., 1998	AX-Auditory	Schizophrenic				-.07 (Attention)
SAS-II: work adjustment	Addington et al., 1998	AX-Auditory	Schizophrenic				.42 (Attention)
SAS-II: general adjustment	Addington et al., 1998	AX-Auditory	Schizophrenic				.19 (Attention)
SANS: affective flattening	Suslow et al., 1998	X-Visual	Schizophrenic, control				.38–.42 (d')
SANS: avolition/apathy	Suslow et al., 1998	X-Visual	Schizophrenic, control				-.42 (d')
SADS: negative scale	Keefe et al., 1997	AX-Visual	Schizophrenic		.22	.30	
SADS: positive scale	Keefe et al., 1997	AX-Visual	Schizophrenic		.44	.32	
SMAT	Prinz et al., 1983	AX-Visual AX-Auditory	Parents of child with ADDH	.07		-.13	
STAI	Ballard, 1996a	AX-Visual	Control		.27–.31		.17–.21 (FA)
TAT	Greene, 1982	IP-Visual	Schizophrenic, affective				.03–.14 (Attention)
TLC Scale	Strauss et al., 1993	X-Visual	Schizophrenic, schizoaffective				-.35 (d')

Notes: CPT Type does not include additional modifications (e.g., degraded stimulus). For correct hits, omission errors, and commission errors, this may be the number, percentage, or mean. ADHD = Attention-Deficit/Hyperactivity Disorder; AIPSS = Assessment of Interpersonal Problem-Solving Skills; Comm. var. = Commission error variability; CPT = Continuous performance test; d' = Sensitivity; FA = False alarm; EPQ = Eysenck Personality Questionnaire; Multiple = Multiple responses; -R = Revised; RT = Reaction time; SD = Standard deviation; BPRS = PANSS = Positive and Negative Syndrome Scale; SAS-II = Social Adjustment Scale-II; SANS = Scale for the Assessment of Negative Symptoms; SADS = Schedule of Affective Disorders and Schizophrenia; SDI = Social Dysfunction Index; SMAT = Short Marital Adjustment Test; STAI = State Trait Anxiety Inventory; TAT = Thematic Apperception Test; TLC = Thought, Language, and Communication Scale; IP = Identical pairs; ISI = Interstimulus interval.

±.25 (Lowe et al., 2000). The majority of these validity coefficients are low and suggest that CPTs and personality instruments measure different constructs or traits.

Although few in number, some moderate and statistically significant correlations between scores from personality measures and CPT scores were reported (A. Davies & Davies, 1975; Franke et al., 1994; Keefe et al., 1997; Nelson, Sax, & Strakowski, 1998; Nuechterlein et al., 1986; Roitman et al., 1997; Spohn, Lacoursiere, Thompson, & Coyne, 1977; Suslow, Junghanns, Weitzch, & Arolt, 1998). For example, Wilson (1995) examined the relation between schizophrenic-related deficits in perceptual sensitivity and interpersonal factors using path analysis. Although Wilson's sample did not consist of individuals diagnosed with schizophrenia, the 191 out of 703 undergraduates selected exhibited schizophrenic- or anhedonic-like characteristics based on scores from a schizotypy scale. The undergraduates who participated in the study consisted of 90 males and 101 females with a mean age of 19.3 years. Besides a schizotypy scale, the subjects completed an attachment and a causality orientation questionnaire and were administered a CPT under one of three motivational conditions: standard condition, intrinsic motivation condition, or low autonomy condition.

Wilson's (1995) path analysis produced a number of interesting findings regarding the relations among perceptual sensitivity (d'), interpersonal factors, and motivational states. Intrinsic motivation was found to attenuate decrements in perceptual sensitivity across time. In other words, high intrinsic motivation was associated with the maintenance of higher levels of perceptual sensitivity (d') or attention over time. Moreover, Wilson reported that intrinsic motivation, positive emotion, and persistence predicted perceptual sensitivity, and that these effects were independent of and could compensate for the effects of schizotypy. These findings suggest that motivation and schizotypy are independent factors in predicting performance on measures of attention. Thus, according to Wilson, attentional performance results from the additive combination of these factors (intrinsic motivation, positive emotion, persistence, schizotypy), along with other unidentified factors. The inverse relationship between motivation and persistence with CPT performance is a logical one and argues for the close observation of the individual (child or adult) during the administration, as well as consideration of any suggested methods of assessing validity (e.g., the extent of random responses or multiple responses) in the interpretation of CPT performance. Similarly, the Type-A personality (i.e., highly competitive) has been found to be associated with better performance on the CPT (Perry & Laurie, 1993).

In addition, Wilson (1995) found schizophrenic- and anhedonic-like tendencies to be poor predictors of the rate of decline in perceptual sensitivity (d') over time, as the pattern of schizophrenic-related attentional deficits was reported to be depressed across CPT blocks. A similar pattern has been reported by other researchers and clinicians (e.g., Cornblatt, Winters, et al., 1989; Nuechterlein, 1991). Other findings reported were nonsignificant relations between mood disorders and perceptual sensitivity (d'), as well as between response bias (Beta) and schizotypy or anhedonia (Wilson, 1995). In a related study, Wilson and Costanzo (1996) found a decline in attentional performance with heightened levels of positive and negative schizotypy. Taken together, these two studies (Wilson, 1995; Wilson & Costanzo, 1996) are significant, with results indicating that poor performance on CPTs may be due to factors other than deficits in attention or executive control per se (e.g., poor motivation, schizotypy, or both). Results further suggest that a relation between CPT scores and scores from personality measures may exist.

Although the research with children tended to focus on ADHD, the most frequent clinical population and the studies reporting the highest validity coefficients tended to include samples of adults with schizophrenia (Nelson et al., 1998; Nuechterlein et al., 1986; Roitman et al., 1997; Spohn et al., 1977). Notably, both positive and negative symptom scale scores of schizophrenic-like or schizotypic characteristics correlated with CPT scores at moderate levels (Keefe et al., 1997; Nelson et al., 1998; Roitman et al., 1997; Suslow et al., 1998). It is interesting to note that the Brief Psychiatric Rating Scale (BPRS; Overall & Gorham, 1972) was used in several of the studies (Nuechterlein et al., 1986; Roitman et al., 1997) in which moderate and statistically significant correlation coefficients were reported; this would suggest that this scale may be more consistent with the behavioral manifestations associated with deficits in attention and executive control as measured by the CPT relative to other measures.

Overall, the review of the literature yielded fewer studies investigating personality characteristics and behavioral symptomatology in adult populations relative to the literature available specific to rating scales and children. At the same time, whereas the child literature tended to focus on scales used in the identification of ADHD, adult measures were more likely to focus on symptom clusters associated with schizophrenia. As noted previously, the demarcation between behavior and personality measures is a fine one, and the research accumulated to date does not allow for any generalizations across the developmental trajectory from childhood to adulthood. Although there are some indications of positive relationships between personality factors and CPT performance, only a minimal number of studies have been conducted. Given that attention problems are reported across a number of psychiatric disorders, it is not surprising that there is some overlap of constructs when behavioral symptoms of psychiatric disorders are considered. Additional studies with more global measures, as well as replication of existing studies, are needed to address whether a relation really does exist between CPT scores and various scales or symptom clusters derived from personality measures.

Other Measures

In conjunction with neuropsychological assessment, a number of other measures or methods may be used to evaluate the integrity of the CNS. In a neuropsychological battery, functional domains not addressed directly by measures already discussed (e.g., global cognitive function, achievement, memory, attention and executive control, behavior/personality) include domains of sensory function (e.g., tactile sensitivity), motor function (e.g., coordination, motor speed), visual-spatial organization, and visual-motor integration. Studies with tasks used to assess the integrity of the domains not otherwise addressed thus far, as well as other miscellaneous tasks, are presented in Table 4.8.

When a standard battery is used, the overall global functioning score may be considered most important, or the scores on individual tasks within the standard battery may be considered separately. These domains may be assessed as part of a standard neuropsychological battery such as the HRNB or as part of an examiner-generated battery. In one study, for example, only the correlation for the full HRNB with CPT performance was reported (Raggio, 1992). Using an AX-CPT, Raggio found that an overall index of HRNB performance correlated better with omission errors ($r = .33$) as compared to commission errors ($r = .19$). Other studies have incorporated only specific subtests of the HRNB, Luria-Nebraska Neuropsychological Battery (LNNB; Golden, 1988), or other standard battery.

In the area of sensory function, Boivin et al. (1996) conducted a factor analysis that included scores from the Tactual Performance Test (TPT) of the Reitan-Indiana Neuropsychological Test Battery for Children (Reitan, 1969, 1974) in addition to the scores generated from the TOVA. The TPT is believed to measure tactile, motor, spatial, and memory functioning by determining the child's ability to complete a six-piece form board with each hand individually as well as both hands together. The individual is then asked to draw from memory the shapes in their appropriate location on the form board (Nussbaum & Bigler, 1997). Results indicated that the omission and commission scores (percentage/ratio scores) from the TOVA loaded on Factor II of the four-factor solution produced by principal components analysis with varimax rotation (Boivin et al., 1996). Scores from the TPT had a primary loading on a different factor; however, Boivin and colleagues found high secondary loadings ($r = -.51$) for the memory-location scores of the TPT on this same factor. At the same time, the learning effect scores from the TPT had primary loadings on Factor III

Table 4.8

Validity Coefficients for CPTs and Other Neuropsychological Measures

Measure	Study	CPT Type	Population	Correct Hits	Omission Errors	Commission Errors	Other Index
APT	Grant et al., 1990	AX-Visual	Children/ADHD	.21		.02	
BOTMP: bilateral coordination	E. Walker & Green, 1982	AX-Visual	Adult/psychiatric		−.66–.32	−.35–−.06	−.49–−.22 (RT)
BOTMP: response speed	E. Walker & Green, 1982	AX-Visual	Adult/psychiatric		−.49–−.29	−.18–−.08	−.57–−.31 (RT)
BOTMP: upper limb coordination	E. Walker & Green, 1982	AX-Visual	Adult/psychiatric		−.47–.05	−.48–−.29	−.54–−.29 (RT)
BOTMP: visual-motor control	E. Walker & Green, 1982	AX-Visual	Adult/psychiatric		−.78–−.46	−.39–.14	−.76–.03 (RT)
BOTMP: upper limb speed/dexterity	E. Walker & Green, 1982	AX-Visual	Adult/psychiatric		−.58–−.38	−.52–−.05	−.54–.14 (RT)
DTVMI	Grant et al., 1990	AX-Visual	Children/ADHD	.20		.02	
	Robins, 1992	AX-Visual	Children/ADHD, LD	.14		.03	
Draw-a-line time	Levy, 1980	X-Visual	Children/control		−.22	−.17	.02 (RT)
Draw-a-line fast	Levy, 1980	X-Visual	Children/control		−.08	−.10	.12 (RT)
Draw-a-line slowly	Levy, 1980	X-Visual	Children/control		−.38	−.30	−.27 (RT)
EFT time	Cohler et al., 1977	X-Visual	Adults, children/referred, control		.36–.49	.30–.57	
EFT failures	Cohler et al., 1977	X-Visual	Adults, children/referred, control		.45–.55	.47–.59	
ET: large saccades	Keefe et al., 1997	AX-Visual	Adults/schizophrenic		.11–.15	.24–.44	
ET: small saccades	Keefe et al., 1997	AX-Visual	Adults/schizophrenic		−.03–.41	−.08–.23	
ET: performance	Roitman et al., 1997	AX-Visual	Adults/control, clinical		.39		
ET: qualitative rating	Keefe et al., 1997	AX-Visual	Adults/schizophrenic		−.13–.45	.07–.33	
ET: smooth pursuit gain	Keefe et al., 1997	AX-Visual	Adults/schizophrenic		−.21–−.09	−.42–−.07	
ET:SPEM best cycle	van den Bosch, 1984	AX-Visual	Adults/psychiatric, control				.38–.44 (NOS)
ET: total	van den Bosch, 1984	AX-Visual	Adults/psychiatric, control				.25–.31 (NOS)
Finger oscillation	Grant et al., 1990	AX-Visual	Children/ADHD	.23		.24	
Finger recognition	Grant et al., 1990	AX-Visual	Children/ADHD	.32		.07	
Finger tapping-left	Allen, 1993	AX-Visual	Children/referred		−.38–.07	−.20–.03	
Finger tapping-right	Allen, 1993	AX-Visual	Children/referred		−.37–.26	−.22–.05	
Finger tip writing	Grant et al., 1990	AX-Visual	Children/ADHD	.10		−.02	
HRNB	Raggio, 1992	AX-Visual	Children/ADHD			.19	
Head movement	Teicher et al., 1996	X-Visual	Children/ADHD, control		.33		−.51 (RTSD)
Impaired insight	Mangone et al., 1991	AX-Visual	Adults/Alzheimer's				−.76 (NOS)
LNNB: associated movement	Allen, 1993	AX-Visual	Children/referred		.05–.40	−.12–.21	
LNNB: echopraxia	Allen, 1993	AX-Visual	Children/referred		.03–.28	−.12–.12	

(continued)

Table 4.8 Continued

Measure	Study	CPT Type	Population	Correct Hits	Omission Errors	Commission Errors	Other Index
LNNB: failure to cross midline	Allen, 1993	AX-Visual	Children/referred		-.06--12	-.14--14	
LNNB: motor scale T-Score	Allen, 1993	AX-Visual	Children/referred		.05--40	-.12--21	
ROCF: organization score	Reader et al., 1994	X-Visual	Children/ADHD		.38	.24	.02 (RT) .30 (RT SD)
Soft signs	Vitiello et al., 1990	AX-Visual	Children/BD, control				.05--38 (TE)
SAT	Maier et al., 1992	X-Visual	Adults/schizophrenic, control				.11--46 (d')
SAT	Strauss et al., 1993	X-Visual	Adults/schizophrenic, schizoaffective				.36 (d')
Tactile perception	Grant et al., 1990	AX-Visual	Children/ADHD	-.09		-.15	
TPT: memory	Grant et al., 1990	AX-Visual	Children/ADHD	.02		-.02	
TPT: total time	Grant et al., 1990	AX-Visual	Children/ADHD	.16		.12	
Time estimation task	Burg et al., 1995	AX-Visual	Adults/TBI, controls	-.32		.39	.22 (Block variance)
Verbal Fluency: letters	Reader et al., 1994	X-Visual	Children/ADHD		.50	.38	.15 (RT) .22 (RT SD)
Verbal Fluency: category	Reader et al., 1994	X-Visual	Children/ADHD		.39	.16	.28 (RT) .19 (RT SD)

Notes: CPT Type does not include additional modifications (e.g., degraded stimulus). For correct hits, omission errors, and commission errors, this may be the number, percentage, or mean. ADHD = Attention-Deficit/Hyperactivity Disorder; Comm. var. = Commission error variability; CPT = Continuous performance test; d' = Sensitivity; FA = False alarm; Multiple = Multiple responses; -R = Revised; RT = Reaction time; SD = Standard deviation; APT = Auditory Perception Test; DTVMI = Developmental Test of Visual Motor Integration; BOTMP = Bruininks-Oseretsky Test of Motor Proficiency; TPT = Tactual Performance Test; RT = Reaction time; EFT = Embedded Figures Test; ET = Eye tracking; SPEM = Smooth pursuit eye movement; NOS = Index not specified; RTSD = Reaction time; TE = Total errors; ROCF = Rey Osterreith Complex Figure; SAT = Span of Apprehension Test; LNNB = Luria Nebraska Neuropsychological Battery; HRNB = Halstead Reitan Neuropsychological Battery; TBI = Traumatic brain injury; LD = Learning disability.

along with the TOVA reaction time variability scores. Also in sensory areas, Grant et al. (1990) found minimal levels of association between auditory perception scores and correct hits ($r = .21$) and commission errors ($r = .02$) on a visual AX-CPT. Given the higher validity coefficients between verbal and language skills with performance on an auditory CPT, the low coefficients found by Grant and colleagues would likely be much higher on a comparable auditory CPT task.

Relation of CPT performance to visual-spatial and visual-motor integration has been investigated minimally as well. J. Campbell et al.'s (1991) factor analysis produced a four-factor varimax solution that accounted for 79% of the variance. In addition to cognitive, achievement, and behavioral measures, results of the Bender Visual Motor Gestalt Test (Bender, L. Bender, 1938) were included in the factor analysis. Bender and CPT scores did not have primary loadings on the same factor. Similarly, studies using the Developmental Test of Visual-Motor Integration (DTVMI; Beery, 1982) yielded coefficients below .20 regardless of the study or variable in question (Grant et al., 1990; Robins, 1992). Notably, the CPTs used in these studies did not include "position" or geometric form as a component of the CPT stimulus target.

Regardless of the CPT parameters, performance on the CPT requires some type of motor response. In an attempt to decrease the confound of motor ability, the motor response required is relatively simple (i.e., press the space bar, click on the mouse, raise the thumb, etc.) but is nonetheless a motor response. For this reason, it is important to assess the extent to which motor function can impact on CPT performance to ensure that poor motor control is not interpreted as evidence of deficits in attention or executive control. Studies that have investigated the degree of shared variance across measures of motor ability and CPT performance suggest that motor coordination and speed may, in fact, be confounds to CPT performance. For example, E. Walker and Green (1982) found strong correlations for most of the scales of the Bruininks-Oseretsky Test of Motor Proficiency (Bruininks, 1978) and omission and commission errors. Validity coefficients with eye movements, finger tapping, or finger oscillation (Allen, 1993; Grant et al., 1990), however, were found to be somewhat lower. Notably, none of the studies that included motor speed or coordination included reaction time or reaction time variability as a CPT outcome variable.

SUMMARY

In synthesizing the available research on the relations between CPT scores and scores on other measures, this chapter has reviewed the evidence of validity for the general CPT paradigm. Less emphasis was placed on content or face validity; the acceptance and widespread use of some version of the

CPT in clinical practice and research as a measure of attention and executive control are taken as evidence of face validity. From a more formal and statistical perspective, however, the construct and criterion-related validity of CPT performance was investigated across multiple studies.

Based on both factor analytic and correlational studies, the overarching conclusion is that the CPT tends to measure something unique from other standard components (e.g., cognition, achievement) of an assessment battery; therefore, the addition of the CPT to a battery potentially will increase the data available relative to brain function. At the same time, and consistent with the perspective of complex and interconnected functional systems (Luria, 1966), the CPT measures contribute to the variance of performance to some degree or measure some of the same underlying constructs or traits as other measures routinely included in assessment.

The CPT is intended to measure components of attention and executive function. Consistent with this, the strongest associations were found with direct behavioral observations (e.g., Barkley, 1991; Garretson et al., 1990; Harper & Ottinger, 1992), other measures of attention and executive control (e.g., Burg et al., 1995; Koelega et al.,1989; Slicker, 1991; Trommer et al., 1988), and behavioral ratings of children (e.g., Klee & Garfinkel, 1983; Slicker, 1991). The strong relationship between CPT performance and direct observation suggests that CPTs have moderate to high ecological validity. Although these validity coefficients are lower than expected based on the presumption that CPTs measure attention and executive control, it could be argued that given the multifaceted nature of attention and executive control, these measures are collectively assessing different components of the constructs of interest. In addition to attention and executive control, moderate to strong levels of association were found with some of the motor tasks (e.g., Allen, 1993; E. Walker & Green, 1982), suggesting that motor difficulties may provide a significant confound to interpretation of the CPT. These results, however, warrant further study.

With few exceptions, the correlations between g and CPT variables were not found to be sufficiently high to warrant special procedures or adjustment when ability is within two standard deviations of the mean of IQ. At the same time, consideration of intra-individual differences across measures of cognition and the CPT should not be ignored. Correlational studies with achievement variables also revealed a low to moderate relationship between achievement and CPT performance; this further supports the need to control for educational level as a demographic factor. Although it is tempting to want to predict achievement from attention, the level of association between scores on achievement measures and CPT results is lower than would be expected if one wanted to predict achievement from CPT performance. Lower correlations were found between CPTs and measures of visual-spatial ability, visual-motor integration, and tactual sensitivity.

Although there is believed to be an interaction between memory and attention, few studies examined the relation between CPT performance and memory, and no studies included older adults. Results across studies varied, but generally supported a relationship between CPT performance and performance on memory tasks. Another area where minimal investigation has been made is that related to personality traits and CPT performance. Notably, the degree of association with personality measures ranges from very low to very high for the adult population. This is not surprising given that attention problems are reported on a frequent basis regardless of the psychiatric disorder in question. The majority of this research, however, has focused on adults with schizophrenia or presumably healthy adults. Additional research with adults and children with different psychiatric disorders is needed.

These are, of course, generalizations based on the most prevalent findings across studies, and there is inconsistency across studies regardless of the behavioral domain. The importance of age, and therefore developmental level, of the sample appears to be a key factor when considering the relationship of CPT performance to other measures. This supports the need for consideration of developmental factors in individual interpretation of CPT performance as well. Lovejoy and Rasmussen (1990) speculated that the difference in the findings reported across studies may be due to the composition of the samples used in different studies. Consistent with this, Lowe et al. (2000) found that studies that included referred or clinical samples were more likely to report moderate and statistically significant validity coefficients regardless of the domain as compared to those samples of presumably healthy participants. Given the presumed neurological basis of CPT performance as well as attention and executive function, it is not surprising that the integrity and the maturation of the CNS would impact not only the functional systems associated with attention and executive control, but also those systems associated with cognition, memory, and motor coordination. The relations between CPT performance and psychophysiological indices of brain function are discussed in Chapter 5.

The magnitude of the validity coefficients found appears to have been influenced by a variety of other factors as well, including the CPT paradigm or CPT index used. In particular, higher validity coefficients were found between CPT performance and both cognitive ability and achievement when the CPT stimuli were presented in an auditory format. Unfortunately, the number of studies that examined the relationship between CPT performance and other measures across behavioral domains is minimal, and none of the studies controlled for any combination of other differences (e.g., population status, developmental issues, CPT modality, CPT target type, etc.). The actual test used to measure the behavioral domain appears to be a factor as well. Different coefficients were found to occur in conjunction with behavior rating scales depending on who served as the rater (teacher, mother, or father). Therefore, the role of the rater (i.e., the context and settings in which the child is observed differs for teachers and parents) is an additional factor that may impact the validity coefficients (Flansburg, 1986). Similarly, the choice of achievement test or adult symptom scale also seemed to affect the magnitude of the validity coefficients.

For researchers and clinicians, this review clearly highlights the need to specify the paradigm, performance index used, task demands, modality, normative sample, and measure used in reporting CPT results. Caution also needs to be exercised in the generalization of the findings reported here to interpretation of the individual case study. Although it is tempting, if not seductive, to see significant correlations and infer a causal or predictive relationship (i.e., poor attention is causing low achievement), correlational data do not provide this type of evidence (see Reynolds, in press). From a clinical perspective, even when high correlations are evidenced across measures, the moderate and statistically significant correlations of CPTs with other measures should not be interpreted to infer that the CPT paradigm is the best task for assessing attention. Nor does correlational study infer that any given task is effective in differentiating clinical samples for diagnostic classification. The extent to which CPTs are useful in diagnostic classification is discussed in Chapters 6 and 7.

Moreover, CPT results or results from any laboratory measure should never be used in isolation to make diagnosis and treatment decisions concerning behavioral disorders and related psychopathologies. Barkley (1991) recommends that multiple sources (e.g., analogue measures, CPTs, and behavioral ratings) be included in an assessment battery when the reason for referral is to rule out ADHD to bolster the ecological validity of the test results when direct observations in natural settings are not feasible. Similar practices should be used whenever complaints of problems with attention or executive control are indicated. When CPT results conflict with other valid sources of information (e.g., clinical interviews, behavioral ratings, and direct observations) specific to deficits in attention or executive control, clinicians may need to consider the relationship between CPT results and other behavioral domains (e.g., motor ability, emotional lability, motivation, persistence) and interpret results based on consistencies across multiple measures across domains.

CHAPTER 5

Brain-Behavior
Correlates of CPT Scores

THE PREVIOUS CHAPTER explored the extent to which studies with the CPT demonstrated an association with other measures of attention and executive control, as well as other behavioral domains. What remains to be considered is the extent to which the CPT paradigm reflects the integrity of the CNS and the functional systems that are believed to subserve attention and executive control. There are obvious differences in the models described in Chapter 1 and elsewhere that are yet to be explored or demonstrated conclusively. Despite these differences, there is general agreement that the ability to direct and sustain attention to tasks is often compromised by both neurological and psychiatric problems. As noted earlier, the complex functional systems that involve neuroanatomical components as well as neurochemical systems are believed to be responsible for attention and executive control. Due to the complexity of these functional systems, R.A. Cohen and O'Donnell (1993b) proposed that differential impact on the attentional system occurs depending on the localization of the damage or dysfunction and that more diffuse damage would impact more structures and pathways, resulting in greater impairment to the attentional system. In fact, the two most frequent complaints following all types of brain injury are disturbance of attention/concentration and memory. The extent to which performance on the CPT reflects damage or dysfunction to the CNS has been reviewed elsewhere (Riccio, Moore, Lowe, & Reynolds, 1998; Riccio, Reynolds, Lowe, & Moore, in press) and will be summarized here.

Taking into consideration the components and neuropsychological models of attention and executive control (Chapter 1), as well as the variations in task demands of the available CPTs (Chapter 2), it may be helpful to relate the potential task demands and variables of the CPT to neuropsychological models and components at a very basic and theoretical level before reviewing the empirical research. Mapping neuropsychological models onto the behaviors required for CPTs, selective or focused attention is somewhat consistently believed to be most impaired following damage to the parietal lobes (R.A. Cohen & O'Donnell, 1993b), with less impairment evident with damage to the frontal lobes or RAS. Thus, impairment in the parietal lobes most likely would be reflected in CPT variables of correct hits, omission errors, or sensitivity (d'); the Inattention Index would reflect dysfunction in these areas as well. Damage to the frontal lobes or RAS would be expected to affect the same variables, but to a lesser degree than with parietal damage. Cognitive efficiency or processing speed, as determined through the use of an adaptive ISI, measured through actual reaction time data, or inferred by evaluation of error types, is posited to be most impacted by hypothalamic lesions, but also may be impacted by damage to the parietal lobes and RAS. Persistence or consistency of performance over time (i.e., the vigilance decrement) is believed to be impacted most by damage to the frontal lobes and hypothalamus, with mild impairment evident with lesions to the parietal lobe. The limbic system is seen as being important to persistence as well (R.A. Cohen & O'Donnell, 1993d); as such, damage to the limbic systems may affect the vigilance decrement. Frontal lobe involvement is believed to be the greatest with regard to response inhibition, and therefore, frontal lobe damage would be reflected in commission errors, response bias (Beta), or the dyscontrol index. As noted in Chapter 1, the neurochemical models of attention and executive control involve afferent and efferent pathways of the multiple structures identified here and, thus, could impact performance in a variety of ways as well.

SUPPORT FOR CPT PERFORMANCE AS REFLECTING CNS DYSFUNCTION

Having identified what theoretically would be the behavioral manifestations of neurological dysfunction on CPT performance, the research available to evaluate the extent to which these theoretically based manifestations are supported by CPT performance will be reviewed. These studies incorporate a number of different methodologies, including the effect of localized lesions for specific case studies and the use of electrophysiology and tomography. For example, it is assumed that physiological responses, whether measured by electroencephalography (EEG), positron emission tomography (PET), single photon emission computed tomography (SPECT), or other methods, can provide direct indications of the physiological mechanisms underlying the behavior, in this case, attention or inhibition as measured by CPT performance. With regard to attention, it has been argued that the physiological responsiveness provides some measure of the allocation of attentional resources (R.A. Cohen & O'Donnell,

1993d). Studies on the orienting response (OR) and changes in EEG to the orienting response provide a basis for assuming that attentional processing can result in changes in brain electrical activity (R.A. Cohen & O'Donnell, 1993d). Consistent with these findings and specific to the CPT, Mirsky and Van Buren (1965) administered the CPT to individuals with a seizure disorder while conducting an EEG. Results indicated that there was an association between correct responses and seizure-related "burst" activity such that correct responses declined immediately prior to and as the burst was evidenced, and then improved sharply as the burst ended and the normal EEG pattern returned.

An alternative to EEG measurements is the use of event-related potentials (ERPs). By using averaged ERPs, many of the problems with measuring EEG responses (e.g., time, signal-to-noise ratios) can be reduced, and it has been found that ERP components are highly reactive to attentional processes (R.A. Cohen & O'Donnell, 1993b). The most common paradigm for ERP study is the oddball paradigm, which is somewhat similar to the CPT task. In this paradigm, subjects are to attend to a rare target (e.g., count how many times they hear the higher tone) among more frequently occurring nontargets (e.g., lower tone), but no actual response is required; it is a passive task. For the oddball paradigm, P3 (or P300) does not appear to be modality-specific (i.e., it does not matter if the task is visual or auditory) and the peak amplitude is in the parietal area similar to what would be expected with a measure of attention based on existing models (R.A. Cohen & O'Donnell, 1993d). In addition, medial temporal lobe and frontal lobe structures may be involved on the oddball paradigm (Okada, Kaufman, & Williamson, 1983; Squires, Halgren, Wilson, & Crandall, 1983) and would be expected, therefore, to be involved in CPT responding. In addition to requiring an active response (e.g., pressing the space bar), most CPTs differ from the oddball paradigm in that the nontarget stimuli may be variable (e.g., multiple digits or letters may be the nontarget); the IVA, the TOVA, and TOVA-A, however, each has only a single nontarget stimuli (e.g., on the IVA, the number 2) and more closely approximates the oddball paradigm.

As noted earlier, there are multiple variations to the CPT that may also impact on results of the CPT as well as on the ERP evidenced. For example, ERP studies with other types of tasks suggest that selection by color (selective attention) may be subserved by different mechanisms, with greater activity evident in the left hemisphere as compared to selection by spatial location, which would result in greater activity to the right hemisphere (Harter, Aine, & Schroeder, 1982; Hillyard & Munte, 1984). Whereas EEG and ERP readings are limited to readings from the scalp surface, the use of tomographic and imaging methods, including PET scans, SPECT scans, magnetic resonance imaging (MRI), functional MRI (fMRI), and near infrared spectroscopy (NIRS), provide additional information with regard to actual brain structures involved with task performance, particularly with regard to subcortical structures.

EFFECTS OF DIFFUSE DAMAGE

Sensitivity to CNS damage or dysfunction is the most global level for evaluation. When Rosvold and colleagues (1956) initially developed the CPT and demonstrated its sensitivity to brain damage, their subjects involved a variety of clinical groups including those with mental retardation (unknown and known etiology) and those identified as "brain damaged." Since that time, others have replicated the sensitivity of CPTs with subjects with more general types of brain damage (e.g., D. Alexander, 1973; Schein, 1962). In addition, a number of studies have been completed with individuals with TBI, stroke, or seizure disorders using the CPT (see Table 5.1). As reported by Riccio et al. (1998; Riccio, Reynolds, et al., in press), across studies, the CPT performance of subjects with TBI, lesions, or infarcts was significantly below that of presumed normal control subjects, as evidenced by slower reaction times (e.g., Arcia & Gualtieri, 1994; Gribble, 1989; Ponsford & Kinsella, 1992; Rueckert & Grafman, 1996), omission errors (e.g., Cicerone, 1997; K. Katz et al., 1996; Laidlaw, 1993; Rueckert & Grafman, 1998; Wolfe, Linn, Babikian, Knoefel, & Albert, 1990), commission errors (e.g., Cicerone, 1997; K. Katz et al., 1996; Laidlaw, 1993; Parasuraman, Mutter, & Molloy, 1991), total errors (e.g., Cicerone, 1997), correct hits (e.g., Laidlaw, 1993; Parasuraman et al., 1991; Timmermans & Christensen, 1991), vigilance decrement (e.g., Rueckert & Grafman, 1996, 1998), and mean ISI (e.g., Ewing-Cobbs et al., 1998). Studies have included adults (e.g., Burg et al., 1995, Laidlaw, 1993) or children (e.g., Timmermans & Christensen, 1991) with similar results. The Timmermans and Christensen study, for example, included 38 children, age 5 to 16 years, who had experienced TBI. For the majority of the children in the study, CPT results were considered to be borderline to abnormal for correct hits on the GDS.

Across studies, regardless of age, more diffuse damage also has been found to be associated with greater impairment in CPT performance. For example, for subjects with generalized seizures, results indicated impaired performance (e.g., increased omission errors, increased reaction time) regardless of age (e.g., Brandt, 1984; Campanelli, 1970; Goldstein et al., 1997; Hara & Fukuyama, 1992; Lansdell & Mirsky, 1964; Miller, 1996; Mirsky, Primac, Marsan, Rosvold, & Stevens, 1960; Mirsky & Van Buren, 1965). In contrast, individuals with seizure disorders that are associated with more focal damage that is not specific to structures theoretically related to CPT performance (i.e., temporal lobe epilepsy or TLE) tended to perform comparably to controls (Brandt, 1984; Goldstein et al., 1997). All adult studies

Table 5.1

Evidence of Association between CPT Performance and Head Injury or Seizure Disorder

Study	CPT Type	N	Age (Years)	Groups	Results
Arcia & Gualtieri, 1994	X-Visual	26 35	27.1 ± 9.8 29.9 ± 11.0	Mild TBI Control	Adults with TBI demonstrated slower reaction times and impaired performance on the CPT.
B.K. Baker, 1990	AX-Visual	8	11.0 ± 2.7	TBI/ADHD	The mean number of months since injury was 2.73 (12.37); CPT results indicated impaired performance.
Brandt, 1984	X-Auditory	11 11 11 11	26.64 ± 9.2 34.55 ± 13.3 35.78 ± 8.7 35.45 ± 15.3	GSP TLE: left TLE: right Control	No main effect for group was found on bilateral presentation of the CPT for correct hits or commission errors. On dichotic presentation with directed attention, the GSP group was impaired on correct hits relative to all other groups.
Burg et al., 1995	AX-Visual	30 25	40 41	TBI Control	TBI group demonstrated mild to moderate deficits on both the vigilance and distractibility tasks.
Campanelli, 1970	X-Visual	20 20 20	10.1 ± 1.0 9.9 ± 1.3 9.9 ± 1.1	Focal Nonfocal Control	All lesion subjects had convulsive disorders. Controls performed consistently better (correct hits) than both focal and nonfocal lesion groups. No difference was found for focal versus nonfocal lesion groups except for the no-illumination condition. The nonfocal lesion group showed more marked decline in the no-illumination condition.
Chadwick et al., 1981	X-Visual	28 28	(Children) (Children)	TBI Control	At one-year post injury, no between group difference was found on CPT fast correct or commission errors.
Cicerone, 1997	X-Auditory AX-Auditory	50 40	34.6 ± 9.7 33.3 ± 12.4	TBI Controls	TBI group impaired on omission and commission errors, as well as total errors.
Crosby, 1972	X-Visual AX-Visual	24 24 24	15.4 ± 1.4 15.3 ± 1.4 14.8 ± 1.3	MR-BD MR- no BD EMR	MR group with identified brain damage (BD) differed from MR group without identified brain damage or lesions; MR with identified brain damage (BD) did better on AX- than X-CPT.

(continued)

163

Table 5.1 Continued

Study	CPT Type	N	Age (Years)	Groups	Results
Dennis et al., 1995	AX-Visual	83	11.0 ± 3.2	TBI	TBI group showed overall impaired performance with 64% of the children identified as abnormal or borderline.
Ewing-Cobbs et al., 1998	X-Visual	91	(Not reported)	TBI	All subjects were evaluated at 5 to 8 years postinjury. Significant age by mean ISI effect was found. Also, results indicated that severity of TBI (diffusion of damage) was a factor in the performance of older subjects but not of the younger subjects.
Goldstein et al., 1997	X-Visual AX-Visual	15 19 20	31.7 ± 11.7 35.3 ± 10.9 33.1 ± 12.2	GSP TLE Control	On X-CPT, GSP had significantly fewer hits than control or other clinical groups. On AX-CPT, GSP group had lower percentage correct scores. Scores of the TLE group were not significantly different from normal on either task for percentage correct. For both CPTs, both seizure group had slower reaction times than the control group; schizophrenic group had slower reaction time than control group only on AX-CPT.
Gribble, 1989	X-Visual	10 10 10	28.7 ± 6.5 30.3 ± 6.9 24.8 ± 4.0	Ataxic Nonataxic Control	Both TBI groups performed slower than controls. No difference based on ataxia was found for omission or commission errors.
Hara & Fukuyama, 1992	X-Visual	60 38	7.98 ± 1.0 7.93 ± 1.2	Seizure Control	Seizure group demonstrated impaired performance as compared to the control group.
M. Katz et al., 1996	AX-Visual	22 32 10 40	6.75 ± 0.4 6.64 ± 0.4 6.89 ± 0.6 6.78 ± 0.5	No lesion Mild lesion Severe lesion Control	Children in the lesion groups were all premature; mean differences among groups with lesions were not significant. Children with severe lesions made significantly more errors of omission and commission than controls. Children with mild lesions were poorer than controls on commission errors. The no lesion group also made more errors than controls.

Study	CPT	N	Age	Group	Findings
P.M. Kaufmann et al., 1993	X-Visual	11 13 12 36	12.40 ± 3.3 11.50 ± 2.5 9.6 ± 2.1 11.1 ± 2.8	Mild CHI Mod. CHI Severe CHI Control	Duration of impaired consciousness was found to be associated with CPT performance. Severe head injury associated with impaired CPT performance 6 months after injury.
Laidlaw, 1993	AX-Visual	21 21	27.85 24.32	CHI Controls	CHI group demonstrated impaired CPT performance as measured by correct hits, misses, and false alarms.
Lansdell & Mirsky, 1964	X-Visual AX-Visual	65 19	31.4 22.8	Focal epilepsy GSP	GSP group demonstrated greater impairment on X-CPT, but results were negatively skewed. Duration of seizure disorder was found to correlate significantly with performance on X-CPT (−.40) and AX-CPT (−.47).
H.S. Levin et al., 1986	X-Visual	16	(adults)	CHI	The shortest mean ISIs were associated with bilateral frontal, right frontotemporoparietal, and bilateral frontotemporal damage. The longest mean ISIs were associated with damage to the basal ganglia/midbrain (right and bilateral) and brainstem.
Loken et al., 1995	X-Visual	20 20	29.0 ± 11.6 29.1 ± 10.3	CHI Controls	Increased errors were associated with head injury. CHI group reaction times increased over course of task.
Miller, 1996	X-Visual	17 16 33	10.43 ± 3.16 10.60 ± 2.78 10.89 ± 2.61	GSP CPE Control	GSP group made significantly more omission errors suggesting impaired attention. No group differences were found for commission errors.
Mirsky et al., 1960	X-Visual	5 5	26.2 25.4	TLE Nonfocal	Nonfocal subjects tended to perform more poorly, but not at a level of statistical significance.
	AX-Visual	39 18 19 25	31.03 32.06 28.16 31.50	TLE Frontal Nonfocal Control	The nonfocal group had the poorest performance. Correlation between rating of focal abnormality and CPT performance was not significant.
Mirsky & Van Buren, 1965	X-Visual AX-Visual X-Auditory AX-Auditory	18	13–42	GSP	Results of all CPTs were combined. The GSP group was found to have greater omission and commission errors as compared to available data for other groups.

(continued)

Table 5.1 Continued

Study	CPT Type	N	Age (Years)	Groups	Results
R. Parasuraman et al., 1991	X-Visual	10 10 10	29.7 28.6 21.1	Mild CHI Control 1 Control 2	On a degraded CPT, the mild CHI group had lower sensitivity (d') scores as well as lower correct hits and a higher false alarm rate compared to both control groups.
Ponsford & Kinsella, 1992	AX-Visual	19 20	26.1 ± 8.0 25.6 ± 8.1	TBI Orthopedic	The TBI group had longer reaction time; no other differences noted.
Ringholz, 1989	AX-Visual	29 28 25	24.1 ± 3.5 26.3 ± 7.9 23.2 ± 3.1	CHI: dorso. CHI: orbital Control	Both CHI groups demonstrated impaired performance; the two CHI groups did not differ in performance.
Risser & Hamsher, 1990	AX-Visual	44	18–60	TBI	As a group, performance in the no distraction (vigilance) condition was within normal limits. In contrast, impairment was noted on the distractibility task with more diffuse brain injury associated with greater impairment.
Rueckert & Grafman, 1996	X-Visual	11 10 16	45.2 46.6 50.9	Left frontal Right frontal Control	The right frontal group had longer reaction times and missed more targets; the right frontal group also had the greatest vigilance decrement. Those with callosal involvement missed more targets over time, but callosal involvement was not related to commission errors or reaction time.
Rueckert & Grafman, 1998	X-Visual	4 6 6	48.2 47.3 NR	Left posterior Right posterior Control	Both posterior lesion groups had more omission errors and the difference increased with time on task. Impairment was increased when the ISI was decreased.
Schein, 1962	X-Visual AX-Visual	42 11 21 25	41.6 ± 12.2 39.9 ± 12.6 47.9 ± 11.0 31.5 ± 13.9	Cortical Subcortical Hospital controls Normal controls	Greater impairment in CPT performance was associated with more diffuse (cortical) damage.

166

Timmermans & Christensen, 1991	AX-Visual	38	10.7 ± 3.7	TBI	As a group, the TBI subjects tended to perform in the borderline to abnormal range on the vigilance task.
Wolfe et al., 1990	AX-Visual	11	64.6 ± 6.0	With Infarcts	Infarct group had impaired performance on CPT.
		11	63.0 ± 8.6	Control	

Notes: Studies may have included additional clinical groups; only those with documented brain damage or seizure disorder, and the results associated with those subjects are tabled here. ADHD = Attention-Deficit/Hyperactivity Disorder; BD = Brain damage; CHI = Closed head injury; CPE = Complex partial epilepsy; CPT = Continuous performance test; Dorso = Dorsolateral; EMR = Educable mental retardation; GSP = Generalized (centrencephalic) epilepsy; ISI = Interstimulus interval; Mod. = Moderate; MR = Mental retardation; TBI = Traumatic brain injury; TLE = Temporal lobe epilepsy.

and most child studies that compared subjects with generalized versus temporal lobe or complex partial seizures found that those individuals with the more diffuse damage associated with generalized seizures demonstrated a greater decline in performance with a higher frequency of omission errors.

Goldstein et al. (1997) administered an X- and AX-CPT to adults with generalized seizures ($n = 15$), TLE ($n = 19$), and schizophrenia ($n = 19$) as well as presumably normal controls ($n = 20$). Results revealed that the group with TLE performed comparably to the normal group for percentage correct and reaction time, whereas the group with generalized seizures performed well below both the TLE and control group on both CPTs. In another study, Miller (1996) compared children with generalized epilepsy, children with complex partial epilepsy, and normal control children. The children with generalized epilepsy made significantly more omission errors, than either of the other groups. In contrast, no significant group differences were found for commission errors, suggesting that response inhibition was intact (Miller, 1996). Lansdell and Mirsky (1964) found differences between group performance on an X-CPT for a group with focal seizures as compared to a group with generalized seizure disorder consistent with the results of Goldstein et al. (1997) and Miller (1996). In addition, the data from Lansdell and Mirsky revealed that the duration of seizure disorder (i.e., years since onset) was negatively correlated with CPT performance on both the X-CPT ($r = -.40$) and AX-CPT ($r = -.47$).

For those studies that included both a no-distractor and distractor condition (e.g., Burg et al., 1995; Risser & Hamsher, 1990), deficits were noted for both conditions, with increased deficits for the distractor condition when there was evidence of more diffuse brain injury. Consistently, deficits were greater in the presence of distractors, suggesting greater impairment in subjects' ability to filter or inhibit attention. For example, Risser and Hamsher administered the GDS vigilance and distractibility tasks to 44 adults between the ages of 18 and 60. All participants had sustained head injuries in conjunction with a motor vehicle accident. Notably, as a group, the participants obtained scores (correct hits, commission errors) within the normal range on the vigilance task. In contrast, group results on the distractibility task were below normal limits. The poorest performance on the distractibility task was found to be associated with the most diffuse brain injury.

Overall, based on studies with individuals with TBI as well as seizure disorders, research evidence suggests that CPTs are sensitive to CNS dysfunction, with more diffuse damage, and longer duration of the disorder in the case of seizures, associated with poorer overall performance. Although there are a number of studies that included participants with identifiable brain damage (e.g., TBI or stroke), in most of the studies, the location of the damage or lesion was not specified (e.g., Burg et al., 1995; Ewing-Cobbs et al., 1998; P.M. Kaufmann, Fletcher, Levin, & Miner, 1993; Parasuraman et al., 1991; Timmermans & Christensen, 1991). However, at the same time, some studies provided support more generally for the involvement of multiple structures as implicated in the neurological and neuropsychological models reviewed earlier. These studies are reviewed next, along with studies providing evidence of neurophysiological correlates of CPT performance (see Table 5.2).

ANTERIOR-POSTERIOR GRADIENT

Across studies that used EEG, it was found that CPT activation is associated with increased frontal, frontotemporal, and temporal beta in presumably normal adults with an associated decrease found in alpha and theta in the posterior portion of the brain (e.g., Valentino, Arruda, & Gold, 1993; Weiler, 1992). The increase in beta activity suggests increased alertness and attentiveness to the environment and would be consistent with decreases in alpha (associated with restfulness) and theta (associated with the transition from sleep to wakefulness). Further, it was found that better CPT performance was associated with a greater anterior-posterior gradient (Valentino et al., 1993). Similarly, in an ERP study with normal controls, an increased anterior-posterior gradient was found to be associated with better performance (Buchsbaum, Haier, et al., 1992). Thus, increased activation of the anterior portion of the brain (i.e., frontal lobes) relative to activation of the posterior portions of the brain has been found to be associated with better performance.

Notably, for both EEG and ERP studies, the anterior-posterior gradient found in the normal population was not evidenced in clinical populations (Buchsbaum & Hazlett, 1989; Buchsbaum, Haier, et al., 1992; Schröeder et al., 1994). For example, decreased alpha was associated with decreased sensitivity (d') in adults with schizophrenia (Hoffman et al., 1991). Buchsbaum, Haier, and colleagues administered an X-CPT to 18 adults with schizophrenia (mean age of 29.6 years) and 20 nonreferred adults (mean age of 27.1 years). Results of the PET scans revealed significantly reduced anterior-posterior ratios based on metabolic rates in the inferior and medial frontal regions and the occipital cortex, supporting the theory of hypofrontality (reduced anterior-posterior gradient or a lower ratio of anterior activation to posterior activation) in schizophrenia. Unlike the results of Hoffman and colleagues, Buchsbaum, Haier, et al. did not find the hypofrontality ratios to be significantly related to sensitivity (d').

Consistently across studies there is evidence of support for the involvement of the basal ganglia and posterior components of the functional system as theorized in neuropsychological models (e.g., Damasio et al., 1980;

Table 5.2

Neurophysiological Correlates of CPT Performance

Study	CPT Type	N	Age (Years)	Group	Results
Arruda, 1994	XX-Auditory	106	19.4 ± 1.4	Control	A greater increase in activation was found in the right hemisphere, but the difference between right and left hemisphere activation increase attenuated over time on task.
Buchsbaum et al., 1988	X-Visual	21 20	31.86 ± 9.88 39.3 ± 10.1	Control Affective	Using ERP, T_3, T_5, P_3 and C_4 for correctly detected targets had a larger amplitude for P100, N120, P20. Target stimuli elicited larger amplitudes than nontargets.
Buchsbaum et al., 1990	X-Visual	18	26.2 ± 8.1	Control	Using PET with normal controls, a significantly higher metabolic rate was found for the right frontal lobe for the task. Higher rates also were observed for the right posterior frontal cortex at the supraventricular level. A task-by-hemisphere-by-sector trend was associated with greater right posterior frontal and parietal temporal metabolic rate. No significant difference in metabolic rate was noted for the left hemisphere. Those with higher metabolic rates on the midventricular slice (midposterior sector) did better on the CPT as indicated by sensitivity (d').
Buchsbaum, Haier, et al., 1992	X-Visual	20	27.1 ± 6.4	Control	PET results indicated significantly reduced ratios of inferior and medial frontal regions in comparison to the occipital cortex with diminished metabolism in the basal ganglia. Reduced metabolism also was found for superior, middle, and inferior frontal gyri but not for the precentral gyrus.
Buchsbaum & Hazlett, 1989	X-Visual	13 18	28 ± 6.7 26.2 ± 8.1	Schizophrenic Control	Using PET, there was increased metabolic rate in the frontal regions in the control group. Hypofrontality was evident in the schizophrenic group, particularly at the infraventricular level. Across all three levels of scans, there was a main effect for anteroposterior activation by group.

Study	Task	N	Age	Group	Results
Buchsbaum, Potkin, et al., 1992	X-Visual	25	34.8 ± 8.7	Schizophrenic	Sensitivity (d') was associated inversely with activation, bilaterally, of the angular gyrus and left occipital lobe (Area 17); activation was directly correlated with the occipital lobe (Area 18) bilaterally.
R.M. Cohen et al., 1987	X-Auditory	27	32.9 ± 12.2	Control	On PET, metabolic rates correlated with performance for middle prefrontal cortex.
Coons et al., 1981: Study 1	X-Visual AX-Visual	13	23.84 ± 2.85	Control	Target-nontarget response differences were most pronounced at Pz. There were differences in P3 amplitude for targets versus nontargets on both CPTs. On the more difficult AX-CPT, further differentiation of the late positive component amplitude was found as a function of the salience of nontarget.
Study 2	X-Visual XX-Visual	23	19.68 ± 2.72	Control	Similar target to nontarget differences were noted as in the first study.
Coons et al., 1987a	XX-Visual	19	14.8	ADD	P3 had a posterior distribution with the greatest amplitude at Cz and Pz; P3 amplitude was larger for targets than for nontargets.
Costa et al., 1997	X-Auditory XX-Auditory	11 11	33.1 ± 5.8 32.7 ± 6.0	Control HIV+	Activation of the left hemisphere was greater for words than letters. Delta and beta differed depending on whether the X- or XX-CPT was used and whether the target was a word (semantic) or a letter.
Ernst et al., 1998	X-Auditory	56 39	28.6 ± 7.5 35.2 ± 9.9	Control ADHD	CPT correct hits and accuracy scores were not significantly correlated with global metabolic rate; no main effect on PET for diagnosis was found.
Estrin et al., 1988	X-Visual	6	27–35	Control	Results indicated a positive correlation between CPT reaction time and P3 amplitude.

(continued)

Table 5.2 Continued

Study	CPT Type	N	Age (Years)	Group	Results
Fallgatter et al., 1997	AX-Visual	10	29.1 ± 2.8	Control	ANOVAs revealed significant differences between target and nontarget stimuli with peak metabolic rates more anterior for nontargets. The nontarget P3 had a longer latency than the target P3.
Fallgatter & Strik, 1997	AX-Visual	10	30.0	Control	On near infrared spectroscopy (NIRS) study, execution of the CPT was associated with right frontal activation. Activation was greater in the left hemisphere, but did not differ significantly from baseline. Only activation of the right hemisphere differed significantly from baseline.
Fallgatter et al., 1998	AX-Visual	20 / 20	40.8 ± 11.1 / 44.1 ± 9.1	Control / Alcoholic	For both groups, the nontarget activation was more anterior. Target activation was more posterior for the control group with a shorter latency than for nontargets.
Fitzpatrick et al., 1992	XX-Visual	19	6.9 –11.5	Control	P3 had expected parietal maximum and larger amplitude for targets than nontargets.
Friedman et al., 1978	X-Visual / XX-Visual	6	13	At risk	Reaction time and latency were longer for the XX-CPT as compared to the X-CPT; P3 had was maximal at Pz.
Friedman et al., 1981	X-Visual / XX-Visual	30	14.4 ± 1.8	Control	Principal components analyses (varimax rotation) were performed separately on target and nontarget ERPs. Omission and commission errors were not used in the analyses due to the extent of artifact. N120, P150, N200 were similar for both tasks and target or nontarget anteriorly. For P240, the amplitude for the target was greater than for the nontarget, and it was frontocentral. P350 was maximum at Pz for both tasks to nontarget; inflection was noted on the XX-CPT for target that was not evident in X-CPT for target. P450 was most prominent with a parietal focus, and was larger for target than nontarget. Results indicated a lower amplitude to target on the XX-CPT than the X-CPT and a larger amplitude to nontargets on the XX-CPT than on the X-CPT.

Study	Paradigm	N	Age	Group	Findings
Friedman, Boltri, et al., 1985	X-Visual XX-Visual	72	12–17	Control	Age and gender were found to affect the amplitude of P3 and slow waves. The X-CPT resulted in a larger amplitude than the XX-CPT for targets, but the reverse was found for nontargets (XX-CPT was larger amplitude).
Friedman et al., 1986	X-Visual XX-Visual	72	14.5	Control	P2 was found to be frontocentral; P3, P4, and P5 were parietal. Slow wave activity was negative or zero at Fz, and positive at Pz. Similar differences for target versus nontarget were found as in previous studies.
Guich et al., 1989		9 15	27.8 ± 8.9 27.0 ± 6.4	Control Schizophrenic	The control group evidenced significant decrease in delta over the motor areas with a significant anterior-posterior gradient. For the schizophrenic group, a decrease in delta was found as well, but the decrease was in the right inferior frontal area; relative glucose metabolic hypofrontality with rightward asymmetry was evidenced.
Haier et al., 1995	X-Visual	10 7 10	28.4 ± 8.4 28.1 ± 6.6 26.4 ± 1.7	Mental Retardation Down Syndrome Control	The metabolic rate of the control group was significantly greater than that of both clinical groups in frontal, cingulate, and striatal areas during CPT administration.
Hoffman et al., 1991	X-Visual	9 13	34.6 33.7	Control Schizophrenic	The correlation between prefrontal alpha and d' was not significant for the control group, but it was significant for the schizophrenic group.
Holcomb et al., 1985	ABC-Visual	24 21 24 24	9–11 9–11 9–11 9–11	Control ADDWo ADDH RD	Significant differences were found for P3 amplitude to target versus nontarget in the control group. A difference was found in P3 latency for younger versus older subjects as well. Similar target and nontarget differences were found for clinical groups as well.
Kaskey et al., 1980	X-Visual AX-Visual	15	32.2–35.6	Bipolar	A similar pattern of target-nontarget differences was found with the bipolar group as with the controls in other studies, except on the AX-CPT when the stimulus followed the AN sequence.

(continued)

Table 5.2   Continued

Study	CPT Type	N	Age (Years)	Group	Results
M. Katz et al., 1996	X-Visual	22	28 ± 7 years	Control	A correlational difference by group was found. The frontal/thalamic correlation in the control group was positive, while the correlation in the schizophrenic group was negative (i.e., if the thalamus increased in activity, there was an associated decrease in the frontal area). In the schizophrenic group, thalamic activity was markedly different from that of controls suggesting dysfunction of the thalamicocortical pathways as a factor in the poor CPT performance for that group.
		18	30 ± 7 years	Schizophrenic	
Keilp et al., 1997	IP-Visual	7	28.3 ± 6.2	Control	With numbers as stimuli, left hemisphere activity increased in anterior subcortical region with SPECT incorporating cingulate, frontal white matter, and basal ganglia. Left hemisphere activation also increased in the posterior subcortical region including left thalamus. Relative perfusion to occipital regions, bilaterally, was more extensive with forms (shapes) than numbers. No significant correlations were found between task performance (numbers or shapes) and regional perfusion.
Klorman et al., 1979	X-Visual	17	9.60 ± 1.20	Control	Target-nontarget differences were significant and similar for both groups. The amplitude of the late positive component was smaller for the ADDH group.
		18	9.53 ± 1.38	ADDH	
Klorman et al., 1983	X-Visual	14	8.78	ADDH	Differences in P2 and P3 were found for X- and XX-CPT. For both tasks, P3 was maximal at Pz. The target-nontarget difference was also maximal at Pz.
	XX-Visual	14	9.00	ADDH: borderline	
Klorman et al., 1988	X-Visual	53	8.44 ± 1.52	Clinical sample	P3 was maximal at Pz with differences found between target and nontarget responses.
	AX-Visual				
Klorman et al., 1991	X-Visual	46	14.16 ± 1.7	ADD	P3 amplitude had a parietal maximum and was greater for targets than nontargets particularly at posterior sites and for older subjects. The amplitude of P3 decreased slightly in the second half of task.
	AX-Visual				

Study	Task	N	Age	Group	Findings
Kornetsky & Orzack, 1978		25	25 / 48	Control / Schizophrenic	On EEG, the schizophrenic group had significantly more beta 2 activity and less alpha activity than controls.
Leuthold & Sommer, 1993	X-Auditory	6	26.3	Control	P3 was evident at Pz. Amplitude of P3 was impacted by the ISI with longer ISIs associated with larger amplitude and increased latency of the P3.
Loiselle et al., 1980	X-Auditory	13	13.0	Control	Correct responses were significantly correlated with P3 amplitudes.
Mansour et al., 1996	X-Visual	41	18–45	Control	Some gender effects were found for specific regions (e.g., frontal) for glucose metabolic rate; no asymmetry of metabolic rate found.
Michael et al., 1981	X-Visual / AX-Visual	21 / 21	9.35 ± 1.94 / 9.31 ± 1.92	Control / ADDH	The late positive component (LPC) was maximal at parietal sites; the ADDH group had a smaller LPC amplitude.
Mirsky & Van Buren, 1965	X-Visual / XX-Visual / X-Auditory / XX-Auditory	18	13–42	Epilepsy	A significant drop in correct responses was noted in EEG pre-burst period, with a marked drop in performance once the burst was evident. Improvement in performance was associated with the end of the burst period.
Pass et al., 1980	X-Visual	16 / 17	29.06 ± 9.07 / 28.58 ± 7.64	Control / Schizophrenic	A larger late positive component was found to target than nontargets in controls; this difference was not changed by the introduction of auditory or visual distractors. The schizophrenic group was found to have a smaller late positive component and smaller amplitude.
Peloquin & Klorman, 1986	XX-Visual		11.39 ± 2.03	Control	P3 was maximal in the posterior area. P3 amplitude was greater for targets as opposed to nontargets but this difference was only significant at Pz and Cz.

(continued)

Table 5.2 Continued

Study	CPT Type	N	Age (Years)	Group	Results
Roberts et al., 1994	AX-Visual	21	33.4	Control	The location of the greatest amplitude of P3 was associated with the relevance of the nontargets, and target versus nontarget status, such that nontargets were more likely to have greatest amplitude frontally, while targets were more prominent centrally and parietally. Results indicated similar findings for P3 latency.
Schupp et al., 1994	AX-Visual	37	19–37	Control	The location of greater amplitude for P3 varied according to sequence (AX, OX, XO, NM). P3 had a parietal maximum for target sequences, but was more central or frontal for error sequences. A similar pattern of differences across the anterior-posterior gradient was found for P3 latency.
B.V. Siegel et al., 1995	X-Visual	20	25 ± 6	Control	Significant correlations were found between d' and relative glucose metabolic rate for right middle gyrus of the lateral frontal cortex, right inferior gyrus of the lateral temporal cortex, and right superior gyrus of the medial frontal cortex for the controls. Reduced metabolic rate was found for the medial frontal cortex, anterior cingulate, and right inferior temporal gyrus for the schizophrenic group. The autistic group evidenced decreased activity in the left medial thalamus.
		25	27 ± 7	Schizophrenic	
		15	24 ± 7	Autistic	
Simson et al., 1977a Study 1	XX-Visual XX-Auditory	8	21–45	Control	Differing patterns of activation were found for auditory and visual CPTs as well as for stimuli sequence (XX, OX, XO, NM).
Study 2	XX-Visual	14	20–24	Control	Findings were similar to the first study with P3 extending anteriorly into the midfrontal region for nontargets.
Stamm et al., 1982	AX-Visual	150	(Adults)	Control	Age differences in P3 were evident. Also, differences in P3 for targets versus nontargets were found; P3 for targets had a parietal maximum.
		25	9–10	Control	
		31	9–10	Inattentive	

Study	Task	N	Age	Group	Findings
Strandburg et al., 1990	XX-Visual	19 13	11.2 ± 1.3 11.2 ± 1.5	Control Schizophrenic	Rightward asymmetry was found for P1 and N1. P3 amplitude was maximal at Pz and greater for target sequences.
Strandburg et al., 1994	X-Visual XX-Visual	16 16	12.75 ± 1.67 12.5 ± 2.67	Control Schizophrenic	Rightward asymmetry for P1, N1, and amplitude of P3 was found. P3 was greater for the nontarget on the XX-CPT, but not for the target on the X-CPT. The schizophrenic group did not demonstrate the target-nontarget differences of the control group.
Teixeira, 1993	AX-Auditory	20	19.1 ± 1.46	Control	CPT performance was found to be associated with increased delta activity in frontal and frontal temporal regions as compared to resting state. Theta was also significant at frontal leads; alpha was significant at frontal temporal and temporal leads; beta 1 was significant at frontal, frontal temporal, and temporal leads; and beta 2 was significant at frontal and temporal leads.
Valentino et al., 1993	XX-Visual	54	(Adults)	Control	CPT performance was associated with increased beta in frontal, frontotemporal, and temporal leads. At the same time, there was also a significant association with decreased alpha and theta in posterior leads. Anterior slow waves increased in the frontotemporal areas. Better performance on the CPT was found to be associated with a greater anterior to posterior gradient.
Van Leeuwen et al., 1998	AX-Visual	11 9	10.9	ADD Control	For children with ADD, there was decreased activation on presentation of "A" relative to controls suggesting that the attentional deficit was a deficit in the orienting to cues.
Verbaten et al., 1994	X-Visual	12	11.2 ± 2.1	ADHD	P3 had a parietal maximum in the placebo condition.
M. Wagner et al., 1989	X-Visual	14 9	29 ± 5 25 ± 5	Control Schizophrenic	The variable ISI was found to be associated with P3 latency as well as reaction time. Clear differences were found for P3 to target and nontargets as well.

(continued)

Table 5.2 Continued

Study	CPT Type	N	Age (Years)	Group	Results
Weiler, 1992	XX-Auditory	102	(Adults)	Control	Frontal beta, frontal and right frontotemporal theta were significantly correlated with omission errors. Right frontotemporal, right temporo-occipital, right temporal theta, right occipital theta, and right occipital delta increased with CPT participation and all were correlated with the vigilance decrement. Frontal theta was found to increase over the course of the task. Using omission scores as the criterion variable, regression yielded two components: frontal and right frontotemporal components, but none of the components significantly accounted for the variance.

Notes: ADD = Attention Deficit Disorder; ADDWo = Attention Deficit Disorder without hyperactivity; ADHD = Attention-Deficit/Hyperactivity Disorder; ADDH = Attention Deficit Disorder with hyperactivity; ANOVA = Analysis of variance; CPT= Continuous performance test; EEG = Electroencephalogram; ERP = Event related potentials; ISI = Interstimulus interval; IP = Identical pairs; LPC = Late positive component; NIRS = Near infrared spectroscopy; PET = Positron emission tomography; RD = Reading disability; SPECT = Single photon emission computed tomography.

Mesulam, 1985a, 1985b; Posner & Petersen, 1990; van Zomeran & Brouwer, 1994). Across studies using ERP, P3 was maximal at Pz (parietal zone) for targets (e.g., Coons, Klorman, & Borgstedt, 1987a, 1987b; Coons et al., 1981; Friedman et al., 1978, 1981; Kaskey, Salzman, Ciccone, & Klorman, 1980; Klorman et al., 1991; Klorman, Brumaghim, Fitzpatrick, & Borgstedt, 1990; Leuthold & Sommer, 1993; Michael, Klorman, Salzman, Borgstedt, & Dainer, 1981; Stamm et al., 1982; Strandburg et al., 1990, 1994; Verbaten et al., 1994). For visual CPTs, there was a significant correlation between Area 18 (center occipital lobe) metabolic rate and CPT performance ($r = .70$; Buchsbaum, Potkin, et al., 1992). CPT performance also was correlated with activation of the angular gyrus bilaterally and Area 17 (occipital lobe) of the left hemisphere (Buchsbaum, Potkin, et al., 1992). Increased metabolic rate in the limbic system, basal ganglia, and thalamic areas have been found to be associated with CPT performance (Wu et al., 1991, 1992). Wu et al. (1991) studied the neural correlates of CPT performance in eight adult volunteers. Results indicated that poor performance on the CPT was associated with decrements in metabolic rate bilaterally for the amygdala ($r = .90$), thalamus ($r = .93$), caudate ($r = .83$), and putamen ($r = .90$). These findings would be consistent with theoretical models suggesting involvement of the basal ganglia as well as the limbic system in attentional processes. Similarly, Buchsbaum, Haier, et al. (1992) found diminished metabolic rate in the basal ganglia to be associated with poorer performance in the schizophrenic group. In contrast, Keilp et al. (1997) found no significant correlations between task performance and regional cerebral blood flow or perfusion. Appropriate levels of arousal are thus noted to be quite important to success on the CPT paradigm.

One study (H.S. Levin et al., 1986) used an adaptive rate ISI such that the initial ISI of 1000 was increased or decreased by 5% depending on the accuracy of the preceding response. H.S. Levin et al. included lesion location and mean ISI information by subject in reporting their results. It was noted by Riccio and colleagues (Riccio, Reynolds, et al., in press) that although all ISIs tended to be longer than the initial ISI of 1000, the three subjects with the longest ISIs ($X = 2829.17$ ms.) included the only two subjects with damage to the basal ganglia and midbrain (one right only, one bilateral) and the subject with damage to the brain stem. Although Wolfe et al. (1990) did not provide CPT results by subject, the majority of subjects in their study had infarcts to the basal ganglia. Wolfe and colleagues administered an AX-CPT to 22 older adults who had multiple and subcortical infarcts. Results revealed that the sample demonstrated significant omission errors. Taken together, the results from these two studies (H.S. Levin et al., 1986; Wolfe et al., 1990) suggest that on a CPT with a nonadaptive ISI of 1000 ms or less, omission errors may be related to functioning of the basal ganglia, midbrain, or brain stem and may reflect deficits in the arousal system or overall slowed processing as opposed to deficits in sustained attention or executive control.

The anterior component of the system is generally considered to be the frontal area. In studies using EEG, although increased beta was found to be associated with CPT activation, increased frontal and frontotemporal theta have been found to be associated with increased omission errors (Teixeira, 1993; Weiler, 1992). Multiple studies included subjects with frontal damage (H. Levin et al., 1986; Ringholz, 1989; Rueckert & Grafman, 1996, 1998). As discussed previously, the frontal lobes are believed to be involved in both attention and executive control, along with the limbic system, posterior parietal cortex, RAS, and hypothalamus (R.A. Cohen, 1993a, 1993c; Mesulam, 1985a, 1985b; Petersen et al., 1989; Posner & Petersen, 1990). The orbital prefrontal cortex has been implicated in particular in the modulation of impulses that originate in the hypothalamus and the limbic system (R.A. Cohen, 1993a, 1993c). Ringholz compared the performance of 29 adults with dorsolateral frontal injury to 28 adults with orbital frontal injury and 25 adult controls. Results of the AX-CPT revealed that both dorsolateral and orbital lesions impacted overall attention. No difference was found, however, between the two lesion groups, suggesting that both dorsolateral and orbital regions are involved in CPT performance.

Additional evidence of frontal involvement is found in other studies. On PET scans, normals have increased/higher metabolic rates in anterior-frontal, mesial frontal, and posterior frontal areas during CPT (e.g., Buchsbaum et al., 1990; R.M. Cohen, Semple, Gross, Holcomb, et al., 1988; R.M. Cohen, Semple, Gross, Nordahl, et al., 1988; Hazlett et al., 1993; Mansour et al, 1996; Rezai et al., 1993; Zemishlany et al., 1996). Based on their review of selected PET studies, Posner and Raichle (1994) concluded that the right frontal and right posterior parietal areas are involved in vigilance and that sustained attention as measured by CPT performance results from activation of the frontal system.

DIFFERENTIAL RESPONSE TO TARGET STIMULI

Differences between P3 to targets and nontargets provide additional information in terms of structures involved as well as latency and amplitude (e.g., Coons et al., 1981, 1987a; Klorman et al., 1983, 1991). For the X-CPT, there is a significant difference in P3 for target versus nontarget stimuli for both amplitude and latency with parietal maximum (Pz) for the target (e.g., Coons et al., 1981; Klorman et al., 1983, 1991). Effect sizes (ES) for target-nontarget differences for amplitude as reported by Riccio and colleagues (Riccio, Reynolds, et al., in press) support the notion that performance on the X-CPT is reflecting differential brain activity by stimulus with a mean *ES* of 1.46. Although less impressive, Riccio et al. revealed similar findings for AX-CPT and XX-CPT where all nontargets were combined (mean *ES* of .48 and 1.03, respectively) across studies.

Notably, for AX-CPT and XX-CPT, the *ES* suggest significant differences in P3 for target versus nontarget based on the type of nontarget (Riccio, Reynolds, et al., in press). For example, Roberts, Rau, Lutzenberger, and Birbaumer (1994) investigated the differing response to relevant versus irrelevant nontargets using an AX-CPT (letters, visual) with 21 normal adult males with a mean age of 33.4 years. A "relevant" nontarget sequence included one of the two required stimuli (A or X) but not the other. Thus, the two relevant nontarget conditions could be designated AN and NX. The "nonrelevant" stimulus sequences included neither A nor X and were designated NM. The difference in P3 amplitude and latency to AX-NX-AN-NM was significant ($p < .0001$). Of the nontargets, P3 was largest on NX and more frontal; for both NX and NM, P3 was larger on the left. Riccio, Reynolds, et al. (in press) found that the mean *ES* for target-nontarget amplitude differences based on saliency of the nontarget were fairly consistent across studies, with AX-NM comparisons yielding the largest *ES*. The mean *ES* of 1.45 ($SD = .67$) was comparable to the target-nontarget comparison of the X-CPT, probably reflecting the similar level of saliency between the targets and nontargets. Across studies, the P3 to NX (or AN, depending on the study) differed not only with the target but also with nontarget irrelevant stimuli (NM). For targets (XX or AX), P3 had a positive maximum at Pz and the amplitude of P3 was greater for the target than for all nontargets (AN, NX, NM). Of the nontargets, the smallest amplitude was found for the control nontarget (NM) or the nontarget with least relevancy. For relevant nontargets (NX or AN), P3 had a positive maximum at Cz but also greater amplitude at Fz as compared to the target (AX or XX) and the control nontarget (NM). In psychology generally, however, all of the *ES* are quite respectable. Target-nontarget differences from Klorman et al. (1991) are presented in Figure 5.1.

Latency of P3 was also related to nontarget type, with NX having the longest stimuli (Roberts et al., 1994). Paralleling the differences in amplitude, differences have been found for latency, with longer latency at Fz for relevant nontargets (NX or AN) and the shortest latency for control nontarget (NM) stimuli. The greatest differences between target and nontarget P3 were found at frontal and central sites for both latency and amplitude. Related to the findings of Schupp, Lutzenberger, Rau, and Birbaumer (1994), a longer latency in response to NX or XN as compared to the shorter latency of response to the target (AX or XX) was found at the anterior central sites (Gevins et al., 1989). This suggests initiation of widespread centrofrontal positivity in NX, XN, and reflect response inhibition of the

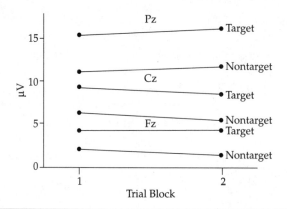

Figure 5.1   Target-Nontarget Differences of P3. P3 amplitude for each half of the session for electrodes at Pz, Cz, and Fz for target and nontarget stimuli. Figure provided by R. Klorman based on data from R. Klorman, J. T. Brumaghim, P. A. Fitzpatrick, and A. D. Borgstedt (1991), *Journal of Abnormal Child Psychology, 19*, 263–283. Copyright 1991 by Kluwer Academic/Plenum Publishers with permission and with permission of the author.

motor response and supports the idea of involvement of the prefrontal cortex in interruption of response activation (Gevins et al., 1989).

The increased frontal involvement (anterior) to nontargets suggests a greater role in inhibition of the response (executive control) by the frontal lobes, whereas the parietal lobes (posterior) appear to be more involved with attention and response to targets. Thus, the anterior-posterior gradient changes when nontargets as opposed to targets are considered. These differences of amplitude and latency in ERP components to relevant versus nonrelevant stimuli (i.e., targets vs. nontargets) provide physiological support to Halperin and colleagues' (e.g., Halperin, Wolf, et al., 1991) assertions that the types of errors may be as important as the number of errors made when interpreting CPT performance. Thus, the capacity of the CPT program used to identify error patterns as opposed to providing only total error scores so that error types can be considered as part of the interpretation process is an important consideration.

ASYMMETRY

As discussed previously, it has been hypothesized that the functional system that subserves attention is asymmetric, with the right hemisphere having greater involvement in the arousal and sustaining of attention. As noted earlier, Posner and Raichle (1994) concluded that the right frontal and right posterior parietal areas are key to sustained attention and vigilance. There is some evidence supporting this conclusion from CPT studies. In comparing left and right frontal lesion effects on CPT performance, Rueckert and Grafman (1996) found that the right frontal group had longer reaction times and more omissions and evidenced the greatest vigilance decrement as compared to the left frontal group and controls. Thus, at least one study suggests that the effect is greater if the damage is to the right frontal area.

Based on EEG studies (e.g., Valentino et al., 1993; Weiler, 1992), there is asymmetry of brain activation in the frontal areas with increased beta more evident in the right frontal and right frontotemporal than in the corresponding areas of the left hemisphere (R > L asymmetry). Attentional asymmetry has been addressed only minimally in ERP studies. Asymmetry (R > L) has been found for P1, N1, and P2 in presumably normal adults for relevant stimuli or targets. In contrast, P3 had leftward asymmetry (L > R) for nonrelevant stimuli or nontargets (Roberts et al., 1994; Strandburg et al., 1994). Arruda (1994) conducted a confirmatory factor analysis of quantified electroencephalography (QEEG) during CPT performance with 102 adults. One of the identified purposes of the study was to confirm right hemisphere involvement in attention. The XX-CPT task included in the study was 23 minutes long with letters as the stimuli and was presented in an auditory format to the participants. Consistent with other studies, results indicated that the increase in right hemisphere activation was greater than in left hemisphere activation (*p* < .05). However, Arruda also found that the rightward asymmetry became less pronounced (i.e., the activation became more symmetrical) over time. Thus, the length of the CPT task and the time when right-left activation patterns are compared may impact the findings.

Häger and colleagues (1998) used fMRI during XX-CPT performance with 12 adult volunteers (mean age of 27.9 + 6.4 years) and found rightward asymmetry of brain activation. With regard to specific structures involved, greater right hemisphere activation was evident in the anterior cingulum, dorsolateral prefrontal cortex, superior temporal gyrus, caudate nucleus, and thalamic nuclei. In reviewing their results, Häger and colleagues considered the emergence of the caudate nucleus activation as the most significant finding. Asymmetry of attention has been studied using NIRS. To examine the correlates of CPT performance, Fallgatter and Strik (1997) found that activation of the frontal areas occurred during CPT performance; although evident bilaterally, the increase in activation relative to baseline was significant only for the right frontal area. Also using PET, Buchsbaum and colleagues (Buchsbaum & Hazlett, 1989; Buchsbaum et al., 1990; Buchsbaum, Siegel, et al., 1992) also found rightward asymmetry of the frontal cortex in nonreferred adults. With 18 presumably healthy adults (mean age of 26.2 years), higher metabolic rate was found for the right frontal lobe, right posterior frontal cortex, and right midposterior sector; no significant differences were found for the left hemisphere (Buchsbaum et al., 1990). Further, Buchsbaum and colleagues found that higher metabolic rates for the midposterior sector were associated with better CPT performance (d').

Other studies also have demonstrated a relationship between rightward asymmetry of activation and CPT results. For example, B. Siegel, Nuechterlein, Abel, Wu, and Buchsbaum (1995) found that sensitivity (d') correlated with metabolic rate in the medial superior frontal gyrus and lateral inferior temporal gyrus. For the control group, d' correlated significantly with the right lateral frontal cortex ($r = .46$), the right lateral inferior gyrus ($r = .45$), and the right medial superior frontal gyrus ($r = .50$). In another PET study, R.M. Cohen and colleagues (Cohen, Semple, Gross, Holcomb, et al., 1988) found higher metabolic rates in areas of the right anterior frontal and right posterior frontal during CPT tasks for normal adults. Using MRI, Sax and colleagues (1999) investigated the association between volumetric measurements of specific brain structures and CPT performance. They found that prefrontal volume and hippocampal volume were significantly correlated with sensitivity ($r = .59$ and $.69$, respectively).

Mansour et al. (1996) found no hemispheric asymmetry but suggested that there may be gender differences on frontal activation. Two other studies, Hazlett et al. (1993) and Keilp et al. (1997), found asymmetry differences to depend on the nature of the stimuli, with numbers resulting in more leftward asymmetry as compared to activation in response to shapes. Using SPECT scans, there was an increase in anterior areas including the left cingulate, left frontal white matter, left basal ganglia, left thalamus, and the occipital lobes bilaterally (e.g., Herrera et al., 1991; Keilp et al., 1997). Rezai et al. (1993) administered an AX-CPT to 60 adult volunteers (mean age of 37.73 years) as well as other measures during PET scanning. In contrast to other studies, Rezai and colleagues found that the CPT activated the mesial frontal cortex bilaterally with leftward, as opposed to rightward, asymmetry. In addition to the left anterior frontal area, changes in blood flow were evidenced in the right lateral frontal areas as well.

NEURAL SUBSTRATES OF CPT PERFORMANCE AND PSYCHOPATHOLOGY

Neurophysiological evidence of brain-behavior correlates to CPT performance with presumably healthy individuals adds to our understanding of the neural substrates of attention and executive control. At the same time, use of neurophysiological methods during the CPT may provide a means for investigating the neural substrates of psychiatric disorders, thus increasing our understanding of these disorders. Unfortunately, fewer neurophysiological studies have been conducted with clinical populations (e.g., Ernst et al., 1998; M. Katz et al., 1996; Klorman et al., 1991; B. Siegel et al., 1995). For example, there is consensus across studies that there are differences in metabolic rate for schizophrenics during a CPT task (M. Katz et al., 1996; B. Siegel et al., 1995). In one study, the thalamic activation pattern of adults with schizophrenia was significantly different from that of controls, suggesting possible dysfunction of the thalamicocortical pathways (M. Katz et al., 1996). In another study, differences between adults with schizophrenia and controls were found in the medial frontal and right inferior temporal areas (B. Siegel et al., 1995). Generally, studies have consistently indicated hypofrontality and decreased anterior-posterior gradients in schizophrenia (C. Carter et al., 1998; Erkwoh et al., 1999; Spence, Hirsch, Brooks, & Grasby, 1998).

Only one study using neurophysiological methods included adults with autism (B. Siegel et al., 1995). Results indicated abnormalities in subcortical areas, particularly in thalamic and pallidal metabolism. In contrast, neither of two studies with adults with ADHD indicated any significant differences in activation or metabolism from controls. For example, Ernst et al. (1998) compared the metabolic rates for 39 adults with ADHD to 56 presumably normal adults. No main effect for group on metabolic rate during the CPT task was found. Similarly, Klorman et al. (1991) found that ERPs of adults with ADHD were similar to those of controls with a parietal maximum of P3 in the parietal area. Adults with ADHD also demonstrated differences in activation for targets versus nontargets similar to the control group's.

EFFECTS OF TASK VARIATIONS ON NEUROPHYSIOLOGICAL CORRELATES

In Chapter 2, the myriad possibilities for variations and permutations of the CPT paradigm were discussed. At the same time, some of the studies that administered CPTs with different task demands to the same population were reviewed in terms of CPT performance variables. Effects of task variations have been evidenced on neurophysiological measures as well. In addition, task variations that have been found to impact on P3 amplitude and latency include variations in target frequency (Sutton, Braren, Zubin, & John, 1965), personal relevance or semantic loading of the stimuli involved (Sutton et al., 1965), and length of ISI (K.B. Campbell, Courchesne, Picton, & Squires, 1979; Leuthold & Sommer, 1993; Näätänen, 1992; Polich, 1990; M. Wagner, Kurtz, & Engel, 1989). Although changing the ISI did not produce changes in P3 amplitude (Polich, 1990), changing the ISI produced changes in latency as well as changes in the distribution of the ERP components, with a significant correlation between the ISI of the CPT and P3 latency (Leuthold & Sommer, 1993; Näätänen, 1992). M. Wagner et al. found that the variable ISI correlated not only with P3 latency but also with CPT reaction time.

Reaction time has been linked to the amplitude and latency of ERPs (N2 and P3) such that it is believed that the vigilance decrement is analogous to a slowing (increased latency) of the reaction time and P3. This is evident in the significant correlation between CPT reaction time and P3 latency and amplitude (e.g., M. Wagner et al., 1989). It has also been found that changes in arousal are associated with faster reaction time and higher error rates on vigilance tasks (R.A. Cohen & O'Donnell, 1993d). As a result of these and other findings, it has been argued that reaction time on CPTs as well as other tasks may be interpreted as a direct measure of executive functioning of the brain (D. Davies & Parasuraman, 1977).

When task difficulty is manipulated (e.g., XX- or AX-CPT vs. X-CPT), only the reaction time and latency but not the amplitude of the P3 are impacted (Coons et al., 1981, 1987a, 1987b; Friedman et al., 1978, 1981; Friedman, Boltri, Vaughan, & Erlenmeyer-Kimling, 1985; Klorman et al., 1983; Strandburg et al., 1994). Friedman, Boltri and colleagues (1985) administered both the X- and XX-CPT with 74 presumably healthy adolescents grouped at one-year intervals. Results of the ERP study revealed significant differences between the X- and XX-CPT, with larger amplitudes for the target on the X-CPT but larger amplitudes for the nontarget or irrelevant stimuli on the XX-CPT at P450. At N150, similar effects were found, with larger amplitude for the target associated with the X-CPT. These differences in physiological responses to differences in task parameters replicated earlier studies by Friedman and colleagues (1978, 1981). In contrast, stimulus intensity and difficulty of discrimination have been found to be related to both P3 latency and amplitude (Papanicolaua, Loring, Raz, & Eisenberg, 1985; Walton, Halliday, Naylor, & Calloway, 1986), suggesting that a longer reaction time would be expected on CPTs with degraded stimuli.

Preliminary evidence from Benedict et al. (1998) suggests that the modality of the stimulus presentation (auditory vs. visual) may also impact on brain activation patterns. Modality differences in CPT tasks have been associated with different factor structures (Leark et al., 1996) as well as difference in the degree of association with verbal ability and achievement (see Chapter 4). Not surprisingly, psychophysiological correlates also differ based on the modality of input for the CPT (e.g., Simson et al., 1977a, 1977b). Across studies that used visual CPTs, there was a consistent pattern of posterior/parietal activation on both ERP and PET associated with CPT accuracy (e.g., Buchsbaum et al., 1990). In contrast, Benedict et al. found that with an auditory CPT, there was activation of the anterior cingulate gyrus and the right anterior/mesial frontal lobe. Only one study was found that compared auditory and visual CPT activation with the same methodology and same type of CPT and subjects (Simson et al., 1977b). Simson and colleagues administered two XX-CPTs to eight nonreferred adults in conjunction with ERP monitoring. One of the CPTs was auditory; the other was visual. For the auditory CPT, N1 was largest and anterior to the vertex, with a slight decrease in amplitude from the first X (X1) to the second X (X2) when the target pattern occurred. In contrast, for the visual CPT, N1 was almost entirely restricted to the primary and secondary visual areas. For both CPTs, P3 for X1 was found to have a parietal maximum with an extension into the parietotemporal area. The anterior prominent negative shift (CNV) for the auditory CPT was found to occur as P3 fell off, while the posterior CNV occurred more gradually. With the auditory CPT, CNV activation was found to be exclusive frontal negativity with posterior positivity at 500 ms. With the visual CPT, the CNV was anterior at 400 ms and posterior at 460 ms, with a central and parieto-occipital maximum. Consistent with this, Simson et al. (1977b) reported CNV correlations between auditory and visual versions to range from .77 (X2) to .96 (N in XN sequence). These results suggest that there are both similarities and differences in brain activation patterns depending on the modality of presentation.

ASSOCIATION WITH DEMOGRAPHIC VARIABLES

As noted earlier, demographic variables may have an association with CPT performance. With regard to age and neurophysiological response, developmental trends in glucose utilization at rest have been found to exist from infancy into adulthood (Chugani, 1999). Given that age can impact both the pattern of brain activation and CPT performance, developmental status is critical in the interpretation of results for both the CPT and the neurophysiological method used. Ernst and colleagues (1998) investigated both age and gender effects on cerebral glucose metabolism using PET with 56 presumably normal adults during administration of an auditory X-CPT. Adults spanned a large age range (19 to 56 years); however, no age-related differences were found for the normal population. In contrast, for the clinical group of 39 adults diagnosed with ADHD, results suggested that age affected metabolic rates during the CPT task. For the women with ADHD, significant correlations between global metabolism and age were found for 18 of the regions identified. For men with ADHD, only one area (left anterior frontal) yielded a significant correlation between global metabolism during the CPT task and age. Thus, increasing age was found to be a factor in the global metabolism during an auditory CPT predominantly for women with ADHD, but not for presumably normal adults of either gender or males with ADHD. These findings support the need for additional study of gender differences in CPT performance.

Using ERP with adolescents between the ages of 12 and 17 ($n = 74$), age and gender differences were noted (Friedman, Boltri, et al., 1985). In particular, on ERP recording during CPT administration, the amplitude of an early-onset negativity decreased as chronological age increased. Age effects were evidenced for P3 as well. Finally, gender effects were found for P5 and slow wave activity. Thus, not only is there evidence of age effects as well as possible gender effects on CPT performance, but there is also evidence of age and gender effects on brain activation during the CPT. These results underscore the importance of including consideration of age and gender whenever CPTs or ERPs are used in clinical practice or research studies.

SUMMARY

Attention as a construct is extremely complex, and theories that map this construct onto underlying neurological substrates are equally complex. Contemporary models of attention portray multiple, interactive functional systems that involve cortical (frontal, prefrontal, parietal) and subcortical (limbic system, basal ganglia) structures as well as descending and ascending pathways among the basal ganglia, the frontal lobes, and the thalamus. At the same time, models focusing on the anterior-posterior gradient and the attentional system have been suggested, as has an asymmetrical model of right hemisphere involvement in attention. The complexity of the construct of attention, as well as the multiple interactive components of the neurological system believed to underlie attention, provide a basis for understanding the heterogeneity of individuals who may demonstrate attentional deficits of some kind. This complexity most likely precludes the possibility of any single paradigm for the measurement of attention, or evaluation of function or dysfunction of all the underlying neurological components and interactions of attention. The available evidence suggests that a similarly complex functional system exists for executive control. This chapter has reviewed the available research related to the ability of the CPT to provide information relative to the integrity of the neurological systems associated with attention and executive function. Research specific to the extent to which the CPT reflects existing neuropsychological models of attention and executive control were reviewed as well. Based on the studies reviewed, areas of activation as well as identified lesions would suggest significant parallels with current models of attention and executive function.

Various components of the CPT tasks have been found to be associated with neural substrates believed to subserve attention and, at some level, with inhibition. Variations in CPT types (X-CPT vs. AX-CPT) may affect sensitivity as well. Similarly, the nature of the target (linguistic vs. non-linguistic) may impact sensitivity to damage/dysfunction in related areas of the brain and may impact findings of asymmetry. Similarly, variations in ISI also have been found to have differential effects, with shorter ISIs more likely to indicate dysfunction. ERP studies further suggest that the nature of the nontargets (similar or dissimilar to target) may affect results and that the error patterns (AN, NX, NM) of the individual as opposed to total errors may provide additional information. The differences in ERP components to similar or irrelevant nontargets support Halperin and colleagues' (Halperin, Sharma, et al., 1991; Halperin, Wolf, et al., 1991) contentions regarding the need to consider the types of errors made in the interpretation of CPT performance. Thus, the parameters of the CPT may affect the results and, therefore, the interpretation of those results in a clinical context.

Chapter 3 discussed the need to consider demographic variables in the development of CPT normative data and in the interpretation process. Notably, there is some evidence that developmental differences in CPT performance have parallel differences in brain activation. Similarly, some gender differences in brain activation during the CPT task would be consistent with indications of possible gender differences in CPT performance. Thus, once again, clinicians and researchers are reminded to account for demographic factors in the interpretive process. Additional research in these areas is needed.

Regardless of the version of CPT used, results clearly substantiate Rosvold et al.'s (1956) contention that CPTs are sensitive to brain damage or dysfunction. Studies reviewed suggest a direct relationship between impairment on the CPT and extent to which the damage/dysfunction is diffuse regardless of the etiology of that damage. Localized damage at a single point in the attentional system appears likely to result in less impaired performance as compared to diffuse damage. Given the various types and locations of brain dysfunction possible that could impact attention and executive control systems, impaired performance may best be interpreted as evidence of CNS dysfunction. The issues of sensitivity and specificity of the CPT paradigm are discussed in more detail in Chapters 6 and 7.

CHAPTER 6

Diagnostic Efficacy of CPTs for Disorders Usually First Evident in Childhood or Adolescence

MANY GROUPS HAVE been studied with regard to their performance on the various CPT paradigms we have reviewed. The producers of these various paradigms have asserted that these measures are useful in the process of diagnosis. Toward this end, over the past 40 years, considerable research has been conducted using CPTs with children and adults with ADHD (e.g., August & Garfinkel, 1989; Barkley, Grodzinsky, & DuPaul, 1992; Barkley, DuPaul, & McMurray, 1990; Chee et al., 1989; DuPaul et al., 1992; Halperin, O'Brien, et al., 1990; O'Brien et al., 1992; Werry, Elkind, & Reeves, 1987), schizophrenia (e.g., Asarnow & MacCrimmon, 1978; Buchanan et al., 1997; Cohler et al., 1997; Earle-Boyer et al., 1991), personality disorders (e.g., Weinstein, 1996), affective disorders (e.g., Cohler et al., 1977; Fleming, 1991; Michaels, 1996), TBI (e.g., Burg et al., 1995; Cicerone, 1997; Laidlaw, 1993; Rueckert & Grafman, 1996), and various other disorders. In fact, as of this writing, more than 400 studies have been published examining the CPT performance of a host of diagnostic groups, at multiple age levels. Our personal experience with third-party payors in recent years suggests that many such groups (e.g., Blue Cross/Blue Shield of Texas) think the CPT is a form of gold standard or, at least, a very powerful tool for determining the presence or absence of a disorder, ADHD in particular. Given that the most frequent symptoms associated with ADHD in childhood include inattention, hyperactivity, and impulse control problems, this suggestion may seem plausible on the surface. Unfortunately, most psychiatric and related behavioral syndromes are complex syndromes, that is, complex interactional systems of symptoms not easily defined by one or two dimensions or a single laboratory measure.

In this chapter, focused on children and adolescents, and the following chapter, focused on the adult years, we review evidence related to the sensitivity and specificity of CPTs to various disorders. Given the complexity of these syndromic disorders, it would not be surprising to find that CPTs are sensitive to the presence of many such disorders but lack sufficient specificity to allow them to be applied to diagnosis without other tests and clinical and historical data. First, however, the concepts of sensitivity and specificity require their own elucidation.

SENSITIVITY AND SPECIFICITY

Sensitivity refers to the ability of a diagnostic procedure to detect a disorder when it is present. Is it sensitive to the condition of interest? Sensitivity might be demonstrated, for example, when individuals with ADHD have high rates of commission errors on a CPT relative to individuals without ADHD. Sensitivity can be expressed mathematically as the probability that a particular method will detect (i.e., diagnose) a disorder when the subject undergoing examination in fact has the disorder.

Specificity, the natural complement of sensitivity, refers to the ability of a method (e.g., a CPT) to detect the absence of a disorder when it is not present. A high degree of specificity requires that a method be capable of differentiating among conditions, especially those with overlapping symptoms. There are many tests and methods in psychology with high levels of sensitivity, but few with high levels of specificity. If sensitivity levels are too high, overdiagnosis becomes a problem, but if too low, underdiagnosis will result. This problem is illustrated in part in Figure 6.1.

A clinician answering a diagnostic question is faced with four potential outcomes. The clinician can be (1) right about the presence of a disorder (a true positive); (2) wrong about the presence of a disorder (a false positive); (3) wrong about the absence of a disorder (a false negative); or (4) right about the absence of a disorder (a true negative). These are illustrated in Figure 6.1. Sensitivity can be viewed as the ratio of the value of square 1 to the sum of squares 1 and 3; specificity may be seen as the ratio of square 4 to the sum of squares 2 and 4.

Seldom is the diagnostic question as simple as whether the referred individual has a specific disorder (e.g., ADHD) or is normal. Since the majority of cases referred do indeed display sufficient abnormal behavior to warrant a diagnosis, the diagnostic question is usually more complex, for example, "Does this 15-year-old boy have ADHD, Bipolar II Disorder, Cyclothymia, an agitated form of Major Depressive Disorder, Intermittent Explosive Disorder, or perhaps Posttraumatic Stress Disorder (PTSD) or another type of anxiety disorder?" Comorbidity of behavioral disorders is also relatively frequent. For a test or assessment of behavior to be able

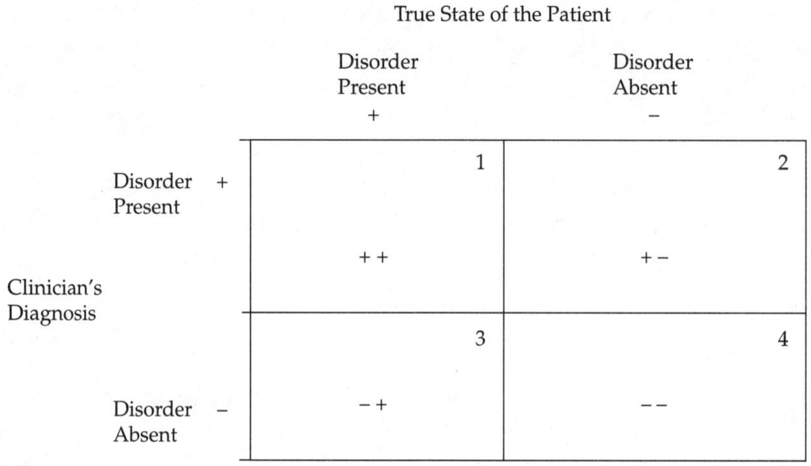

True State of the Patient

	Disorder Present +	Disorder Absent −
Clinician's Diagnosis — Disorder Present +	1 + +	2 + −
Disorder Absent −	3 − +	4 − −

Figure 6.1 Illustration of Possible Classification of Diagnostic Decision. 1 = True positives; 2 = False positives; 3 = False negatives; and 4 = True negatives

to pinpoint a specific disorder on the basis of a few scores reflecting broad symptoms such as attentional deficits and impulsivity would be unexpected.

Unfortunately, most of the research on the diagnostic efficacy of CPTs focuses on distinguishing a patient group from a nonpatient (or at least a nonpsychiatric) group. Although these studies cannot tell us directly how the CPT might differentiate among diagnostic groups, the various studies of CPT performance by diagnostic group do shed some light on the sensitivity and specificity of CPTs for some disorders. These studies also allow us to appraise the techniques of the CPT as producing a criterion for diagnosis.

DIFFERENTIAL GROUP PERFORMANCE

Our literature search revealed 162 research studies that provide group comparisons of some sort on CPT variables and that involve children and/or adolescents. These studies are listed, alphabetically by first author, and briefly annotated in Table 6.1 on pages 224 through 228. Additionally, the type of CPT variable and paradigm considered is listed (e.g., XX, not-X, AX, etc.), along with the sample size, age, and type. Sample type is taken as a grouping variable *uncritically* from the study cited. Without the original data, it would not be possible to regroup subjects with any hope of accuracy beyond what was presented in the original study group. A veritable cornucopia of diagnostic groups have been studied, with the most popular being some form of ADHD (93 of the 162 studies are of ADHD children or adolescents). Given that the predominant symptoms of ADHD are grouped under categories of inattention and hyperactive/impulsive, the abundance of CPT research with this group of children is not surprising. Other groups studied include children with sleep disordered breathing (e.g., Ali, Pitson, & Strading, 1996), phenylketonuria (V. Anderson et al., 1969), autism (Garretson et al., 1990), schizophrenia and children at high risk for schizophrenia (e.g., Rund, Zeiner, Sundet, Oie, & Bryhn, 1998; Rutschman, Cornblatt, & Erlenmeyer-Kimling, 1977), learning disabilities (e.g., Beale et al., 1987), Tourette's syndrome (e.g., Erickson, Yellin, Hopwood, Realmuto, & Greenberg, 1984), TBI (P. Kaufmann et al., 1993), fetal toxic exposure (including tobacco and alcohol; e.g., Fried, Watkinson, & Gray, 1992), low birth weight (Katz et al., 1996), Conduct Disorder (e.g., Chee et al., 1989), mental retardation (e.g., Kintslinger, 1987), neurofibromatosis (e.g., Eliason, 1988), Turner's syndrome (e.g., Romans et al., 1997), Renal Disease (e.g., Rasbury, Fennell, Eastman, Garin, & Richards, 1979), congenital heart defects (e.g., O'Dougherty, Berntson, Boysen, Wright, & Teske, 1988), seizure disorder (e.g., Levav, 1991), hearing impairment (T. Mitchell & Quittner, 1996), and general medical referrals (O'Dougherty et al., 1984), among others. Results for the most prevalent groups in these studies and some of the more interesting, for practical as well as theoretical reasons, are reviewed next.

CPTs AND ADHD

Of the studies reporting on CPT performance of children with ADHD, or ADD, as the syndrome was previously called, the majority reported to date unfortunately compare ADHD children only to presumably normal children. Most of these studies found significant differences between ADHD children and normal children, but not always. When variables such as age, SES, and verbal ability were controlled (e.g., Koriath et al., 1985; Werry, Elkind, & Reeves, 1987), the likelihood of finding differences across groups subsided somewhat. Nevertheless, a reasonably consistent set of findings occurred. Overall, normal and ADHD children differed in a majority of studies on all or nearly all CPT variables studied. However, the most effective discriminators were errors of omission and errors of commission. Errors of commission (reflecting impulsive responding) differentiated the normal and ADHD groups in twice as many studies as did omission errors (reflecting lapses in attention). At the same time, however, errors of omission distinguished the groups better than other variables of CPT performance (e.g., reaction time, sensitivity).

Few of the studies actually reported diagnostic classification rates based on actuarial determinations (i.e., hit rates for accurately identifying children as normal or ADHD based on CPT performance). Even those studies that do report such hit rates suffer from small sample sizes (e.g.,

Anastopoulos & Costabile, 1994, $n = 34$; Barkley & Grodzinsky, 1994, $n = 47$; Harper & Ottinger, 1992, $n = 40$), resulting in inflated estimates of diagnostic accuracy that are unlikely to withstand cross-validation (e.g., see Willson & Reynolds, 1982). Importantly, in nearly every study where data are reported, CPTs identify normal (non-ADHD) children far more accurately than they identify ADHD children. Moreover, CPT performance does not improve diagnostic accuracy over that of behavior rating scales (e.g., see Mann, 1997).

The inconsistency of findings across studies and variables may be due to a number of problems. The first of these has to do with the definition and criteria used for the diagnosis of ADHD. Many of the studies used the terminology consistent with the accepted diagnostic criteria at the time the study was completed; changes in the criteria over time may have affected the homogeneity of the population being studied. At the same time, methodological problems in the diagnosis of ADHD with different clinicians using different cutoff scores or behavior rating scales (see M.J. Cohen, Riccio, & Gonzalez, 1994) may have affected the results. Current as well as previous diagnostic criteria for ADHD include subtypes (APA, 1980, 1994). Based on the subtyping literature, the extent to which the symptoms of inattention and hyperactivity/impulsivity co-occur varies by subtype, with different neuropsychological profiles for each subtype (Clure et al., 1999; Dykman & Ackerman, 1993; Ebert, 1995; Marks et al., 1999; Marshall, Hynd, Handwerk, & Hall, 1997; Morgan, Hynd, Riccio, & Hall, 1996). In a number of the studies reviewed (e.g., August & Garfinkel, 1989; Bergman, Winters, & Cornblatt, 1991), no subtype information is provided, suggesting that the ADHD group likely includes some combination of subtypes. Use of a single group of ADHD without subtype information may have affected the consistency of results across studies as well.

The majority of studies that indicated subtype information focused only on the "with hyperactivity" subtype or what is currently considered the hyperactive/impulsive type or combined type (APA, 1994). Barkley's (1997b) theory asserts that the combined type differs from the predominantly inattentive type not only in that there is the presence of disinhibition, but that the types of attentional problems in the combined type differ from the attentional problems of the predominantly inattentive type. If Barkley's theory is correct and what are currently viewed as subtypes are significantly and qualitatively different, it would be expected that CPT performance would vary as a function of subtype. Notably, few studies (e.g., Barkley et al., 1990; Barkley & Grodzinsky, 1994; Forbes, 1998; García-Sánchez, Estévez-Gonzáles, Suárez-Romero, & Junqué, 1997; Holcomb, Ackerman, & Dykman, 1985; B. Johnson, 1993) compared the performance of children with ADHD by subtypes using either the subtype system of the

Diagnostic and Statistical Manual of Mental Disorders, third edition (*DSM-III;* APA, 1980) or the *DSM-IV* (APA, 1994).

Barkley and Grodzinsky (1994) compared children with ADD with hyperactivity (ADDH) to children with ADD without hyperactivity (ADDWo), children with learning disability (LD), and a control group. Using a visual AX-CPT, they concluded that although abnormal scores may be indicative of ADD, and the ADDH group made more commission errors than the ADDWo group, the subtypes could not be differentiated based on CPT performance. These findings did not support a previous study that suggested that commission errors could be used in subtyping children with ADHD (Barkley et al., 1990). Forbes (1998) compared ADHD subtypes as well. Using the TOVA, Forbes found that both ADHD groups had impaired performance relative to the other clinical group; however, CPT results did not discriminate between the subtypes. As with all studies with ADHD, the strict adherence to established criteria may be a factor in the conflicting results. Alternatively, it may be that subtype differences that might be more evident on the not-X-CPT, with the greater demand on inhibition of a preexisting response, or in the presence of distractors, were obscured on the AX-CPT.

One final note on the studies that included groups of children with ADHD in comparison to a control group. As can be seen from Table 6.1, the majority of these studies are with children with a mean age between 6 and 12 years. At this age range, Fischer, Newby, and Gordon (1995) reported a correct classification rate of 81% using a visual AX-CPT. In contrast, for the ages of 12 to 17 years, only 20% were classified correctly using the CPT. This suggests that the manifestation of ADHD as measured by the CPT may change with age. Thus, the extent to which the CPT paradigm continues to be sufficiently sensitive to ADHD for diagnostic purposes as children mature through adolescence is unknown, but classification accuracy compared to a normal control group decreases with increasing age.

ADHD-LD Comparisons

A minority of the studies reviewed contrasted children with ADHD with other diagnostic groups. The most common comparison among other diagnostic groups was with children with LD. The differentiation of ADHD from LD is complicated by the high level of co-occurrence of the two disorders (e.g., L. Baker & Cantwell, 1990; Dykman & Ackerman, 1991; Hynd et al., 1995; Riccio & Jemison, 1998). In general, differentiating children with ADHD from children with an LD problem on the basis of CPT performance proves very difficult. As an example, Aylward, Verhulst, and Bell (1990), in comparing ADHD groups with and without comorbid LD to each other and to a nondiagnosed sample, found the normal group consistently performed better. They also found that omission and commission errors were affected by the presence of ADHD, but did not vary by LD status. A series of studies by Barkley and his colleagues (Barkley, McMurray, Edelbrock, & Robbins, 1989; Barkley et al., 1990; Barkley et al., 1992; Barkley & Grodzinsky, 1994) show the complexity of the ADHD, LD, and CPT performance relationships. In some of these studies, the ADHD groups had significantly more omission and commission errors than the LD groups, whereas in others, the ADHD groups differed only from the normal groups and could not be distinguished from the LD groups. These studies all used the visual AX-CPT paradigm, so the inconsistent results cannot be attributed to the task. As such, the inconsistent results suggest heterogeneity in the population samples either in terms of subtypes, criteria used for diagnosis, or severity of symptom presentation for both ADHD and LD.

B. Johnson (1993) also compared children with ADHD with and without LD on a visual AX-CPT and found the presence or absence of the LD diagnosis to be irrelevant. Also using the AX-CPT, Robins (1992) compared groups of children with ADHD with and without comorbid LD to an LD group and found that impulsive responding (commission errors) differentiated both ADHD groups from the LD group. Oppenheimer (1986) found that the visual AX-CPT differentiated LD and emotionally disturbed (ED) children from hyperactive children with comorbid LD and ED and from a normal control group, but only for the variable of commission errors. Tarnowski, Prinz, and Nay (1986) compared 14 children with ADHD, 12 with LD, 12 with ADHD and LD, and 12 presumed normal children. They found a significant difference between their ADHD and LD groups using the visual AX paradigm, but only on the sensitivity (d') variable; no differences in response bias (Beta) were found.

In contrast, however, Richards, Samuels, Turnure, and Ysseldyke (1990) found no differences on omission errors, commission errors, correct responses, total responses, and reaction time between ADHD and LD students on the AX-CPT. When the students with comorbid ADHD were eliminated from the analyses, the children in the LD group had significantly slower reaction times than the normal controls. Similarly, using twice as large a sample, R. Tucker (1990) found no difference between ADHD ($n = 30$) and LD ($n = 30$) groups on any CPT performance variable, including errors of omission or commission, for the visual AX-CPT with or without distractors.

Other CPT paradigms have been used to compare ADHD and LD children. Chee et al. (1989) used a visual X-CPT paradigm and found their ADHD group performed less well overall on hit rate and had more false alarms than the LD group. Moreover, the ADHD group had a significantly faster reaction time than the LD or the normal control group. Riccio,

Cohen, Hynd, and Keith (1996) identified children with central auditory processing disorders (CAPD) and compared CAPD groups with and without ADHD on an auditory X-CPT paradigm. No significant differences were found between these two groups on omission errors, commission errors, total errors, or number correct. Schachar et al. (1988b) compared a number of clinical groups including children with ADHD and LD using X-, XX-, and AX-CPTs. Results indicated that the ADHD group differed significantly from other clinical groups on the CPTs.

Results thus far indicate a good deal of inconsistency in the differentiation of ADHD children from LD children on the basis of CPT performance. Methodological differences in the definition of learning disabilities as well as the level of severity may contribute to these inconsistencies. If ADHD and LD can be differentiated based on CPT performance, at this point, measures of impulsive responding (e.g., commission errors) are most promising, but clinical applications of these findings do not appear appropriate at this juncture.

ADHD-Conduct Disorder Comparisons

Another disorder that is frequently comorbid with ADHD is Conduct Disorder (CD) or, in younger children, Oppositional Defiant Disorder (ODD). Several studies have attempted to differentiate children with diagnoses of CD from ADHD groups; these have had more but not entirely consistent success than with LD. In the Chee et al. (1989) study discussed previously, the ADHD groups performed less well on the visual X-CPT than the CD group or the LD group. King (1996) obtained similar results on the visual X-CPT, with the ADHD group exhibiting a higher rate of commission errors. King, however, found no group differences on omission errors. Halperin and colleagues (Halperin, O'Brien, et al., 1990; Halperin et al., 1993, 1995) have found consistently that CD-only children perform better than ADHD children on the visual AX-CPT paradigm. Further, they found that they can achieve adequate group differentiation with the CPT. For example, Halperin et al. (1993) found that the ADHD group was significantly more impaired on attention, impulse control, and dyscontrol indices relative to the CD/ODD group. Halperin, O'Brien, et al. found that the CD group performed comparably to the control group, whereas the ADHD and ADHD with CD groups evidenced impairment. However, although differences were found, Halperin, O'Brien, et al. were not able to dissociate inattention and aggression based on CPT performance.

In contrast to other studies, Koriath et al. (1985), after controlling for age and SES, found no group differences between their ADHD and CD groups. O'Brien et al. (1992), also using the visual AX paradigm, found that children with CD made significantly fewer omission errors relative to ADHD children, but they saw no main effects by groups on any of the other CPT variables. These results are in large part due to the failure of CD children generally to perform any less well than nondiagnosed groups of children (i.e., normal children), whereas ADHD children are impaired consistently relative to normal samples.

ADHD and Other Group Comparisons

A few other group comparisons are of interest. When children with other psychopathologies that affect attention, executive control, and perception are contrasted with ADHD children, they sometimes perform worse than ADHD samples and sometimes equally as poorly, but seldom significantly better. Another disorder that includes executive control problems and tends to co-occur with ADHD is Tourette's syndrome (TS). Harris et al. (1995), using a visual X-CPT, found that children with TS and children with ADHD could not be differentiated reliably from each other on the basis of their CPT performance. In fact, both clinical groups performed poorly. Notably, the comorbid ADHD/TS group could be differentiated as having the poorest level of performance overall. This suggests an additive effect to having both ADHD and TS that was not evidenced with comorbid ADHD and LD or ADHD and CD.

Difficulty differentiating ADHD from other disorders has been evidenced as well. Studies have compared the inattention and perception problems associated with ADHD to schizophrenia. Erickson et al. (1984) using an X-CPT, found both adolescents with ADHD and adolescents with schizophrenia performed worse than normative data on CPTs. Moreover, the schizophrenic group had more omission errors than the ADHD group. O'Dougherty et al. (1984) found their ADHD group and a group of children with hypoxia both to have lower overall performance on the visual X-CPT paradigm than a normal control group, with the hypoxic group performing worse than the ADHD group on some variables and the ADHD group performing worse than the hypoxic group on others. In a later study, O'Dougherty et al. (1988) found children with congenital heart defects to perform more poorly than ADHD children on total error rate. Thus, although children with ADHD can be distinguished from normal (i.e., undiagnosed) children with reasonable consistency, especially using commission errors, on the basis of CPT performance it is far more difficult to differentiate them from many other diagnostic groups on a consistent, reliable basis.

CPTs AND LD

As noted above, in most but not all studies, LD and ADHD groups can be differentiated on the basis of CPT performance, but the discriminating variables are inconsistent. In most studies, comorbidity of ADHD and LD had no synergistic or compounding effects on CPT performance (e.g., Aylward et al., 1990; Chee et al., 1989; B. Johnson, 1993; Robins, 1992). Only August and Garfinkel (1989), using a visual AX-CPT, found their cormorbid ADHD/LD group to show significantly more errors of omission and commission than the mild ADHD, severe ADHD, and control groups.

There were 14 studies identified that included an LD group and a normal control group. Of these 14 studies, 8 reported significant differences between the LD group and the normal group on one or more CPT variables. There is very little consistency in the variable that differentiated the groups. When the LD versus ADHD comparisons are included, there exists a weak trend toward more omission errors by LD children as compared to normal control children and children with ADHD, whereas children with ADHD tend to make more commission errors. However, as was seen with ADHD children, the LD versus normal contrasts tended to be most accurate in the identification of the normal children, not the LD children.

The different pattern seen periodically for LD versus ADHD, wherein the LD groups tend to make proportionately more errors of omission as opposed to errors of commission, deserves more careful study. Much of this research is plagued by small samples and low power (i.e., difficulty detecting small effects). Age also appears to influence these outcomes; as children with LD get older, they tend to be distinguished somewhat more reliably from normal groups when age corrections are employed. The age and error type phenomena are by no means well established, but are of interest for practical, clinical reasons as well as theoretical reasons that relate to our phenomenological understanding of learning disabilities. At present, the use of CPTs to obtain information about attention and impulsivity of children with LD may be helpful; however, clinical uses of the CPT for the purpose of identifying children with LD are not justified by the extant literature.

Schizophrenia, High Risk for Schizophrenia, and CPTs

There were 10 studies located comparing children with a diagnosis of schizophrenia and/or children with a schizophrenic parent to normal controls or, in a few studies, to children with other psychopathologies. Most, but not all, of these studies show clear impairments on most CPT variables by children with schizophrenia and some show impairments in children of a schizophrenic parent.

Schizophrenia

Four studies were found examining children with a diagnosis of schizophrenia, and three of the four showed broad decrements in performance.

Erickson et al. (1984), using a visual X-CPT, compared children with a diagnosis of schizophrenia to children with diagnoses of conduct disorder, ADHD, and a combined group with diagnoses of anxiety and eating disorders. All of the groups in this study were impaired relative to normative data on reaction time, variability, and number of errors overall. However, the schizophrenic group could be distinguished on the basis of increased errors of omission relative to the other groups. Strandburg et al. (1990) compared children with schizophrenia to a group of normal controls using a visual XX-CPT paradigm. Significant differences were found, with the schizophrenia group performing more poorly on number correct and making more errors of commission. However, in contrast to Erickson et al.'s study, reaction time scores for the groups did not differ. A subsequent study by the same lead researcher (Strandburg et al., 1994) compared children with schizophrenia and control children on visual X- and XX-CPT paradigms and found broader effects. In this later study, the schizophrenic group demonstrated significantly slower reaction time, was significantly less accurate overall, and had more errors of commission on both tasks. In both Strandburg et al. (1990, 1994) studies, no other clinical group was included for comparison purposes.

Using a sample of adolescents, Rund et al. (1998) compared schizophrenic, ADHD, and a normal control group on a visual X-CPT task, with sample sizes of 20, 20, and 30, respectively. No differences were found among groups on any CPT variable, including number correct, commission errors, sensitivity (d'), response bias (Beta), or sensitivity decrement. This study seems anomalous. The reasons no differences appeared for the ADHD or the schizophrenic groups relative to the normal control group are unclear and confusing, especially because these are the two groups that are usually more impaired on the CPT. Thus, in three of the four studies, children and adolescents with schizophrenia were broadly impaired in their CPT performance, particularly with regard to commission errors. The single finding of no differences notwithstanding, our view of the results is that children with schizophrenia tend to be impaired on CPTs, with relatively greater impairment evident on measures of errors of commission. On a practical level, it is not likely that individual cases in a clinician's office could be differentiated reliably by their CPT performance if the primary question were schizophrenia versus ADHD. This is also not a likely question to arise in clinical practice.

Parental Schizophrenia

Even more studies have examined children of a parent with schizophrenia. These children have a four or five times greater risk for schizophrenia relative to offspring of nonschizophrenic parents. Of the six studies

examining these high-risk children, three reported no differences between children of a schizophrenic parent and control children on any CPT
variable. All three of these studies (see Table 6.1) used the X-CPT paradigm (Asarnow, Steffy, MacCrimmon, & Cleghorn, 1977; Cohler et al.,
1977; Grunebaum, Cohler, Kauffman, & Gallant, 1978).

Friedman, Cornblatt, Vaughan, and Erlenmeyer-Kimling (1986) used
both an X- and an XX-CPT and found that children whose parent had a
diagnosis of schizophrenia had significantly fewer correct hits than a control group or a group of children who had a parent with a diagnosis of an
affective disorder. Nuechterlein (1983) employed three visual CPT paradigms, X-, XX-, and not-X-CPT, in a complex design with multiple controls
and including ADHD and general psychiatric samples; 29% of the children of schizophrenic mothers had extremely low sensitivity (d') scores,
and the children with ADHD had generally very low response bias (Beta)
scores. The group of children at high-risk-for-schizophrenia also had
fewer overall correct hits. Erlenmeyer-Kimling and Cornblatt (1978),
using an XX-CPT paradigm, found their high-risk-for-schizophrenia
group to evidence significantly more errors of omission and errors of
commission than did the control group. No other differences were revealed. These latter studies, although finding some differences in CPT
performance, are not consistent as to which variables discriminate the
high-risk children from the controls. However, the studies reporting differences used more complex CPT paradigms than did the studies that
failed to find any CPT performance decrements by children of parents
with schizophrenia.

The latter information certainly makes this an area of interest.
Also, their studies do not differentiate predominant characteristics of
their schizophrenic samples along any dimension. There may be sub-
groups of schizophrenic presentations (e.g., predominantly positive
symptoms vs. predominantly negative symptoms) that produce these patterns, and this possibility is worth exploring. At present, we are left with
consistent findings that on the X-CPT paradigm, high risk for schizophrenia and normal control children do not differ. However, on more complex
CPT paradigms, they differ, but not consistently in the same manner. Future research should clarify this issue.

CPTs and CD

CD is another form of psychopathology that has attracted significant attention in the CPT literature. In eight studies located that included CD
groups, only two reported that children with CD performed more poorly
than controls. However, some of the studies report comparisons only
among pathological groups with no normal controls (e.g., Erickson et al.,

1984) and some used normative data as a control. The use of normative data as a control in this way is quite problematic from a research standpoint because a sample drawn for research will seldom match normative data for a test on many crucial variables. Given this problem, but also looking at the weight of studies so far in a more absolute sense, it appears that children with CD and no other comorbid disorder generally do not show deficits on CPT variables. The exception to this statement may be those children with CD who are physically aggressive and get into fights. Halperin et al. (1995) found, on their visual AX-CPT, that impulsivity scores correlated significantly with the frequency of fighting for ADHD, CD, and ODD groups. It appears that this finding is associated with the fighting variable, however, and is not associated with CD per se. As previously mentioned, Halperin, O'Brien, et al. (1990) also were not able to dissociate inattention and aggression with their sample based on CPT performance. Thus, level of aggression (or fighting) may confound the problem of syndrome differentiation.

CPTs AND TOURETTE'S SYNDROME

TS is a genetic, neuropsychiatric disorder consisting of chronic motor and vocal tics (Brown & Ivers, 1999). It has been suggested that TS involves pathology of the basal ganglia (e.g., Kurlan, 1994), and it represents a significant problem with disinhibition. There is strong support as well for the role of dopamine in this disorder, which is a neurotransmitter often implicated in ADHD as well (e.g., see Brown & Ivers, 1999). TS has a relatively high comorbidity rate with ADHD, with some studies finding as many as 60% of first-degree biological relatives of individuals with TS to have a diagnosis of ADHD. All of this makes the CPT performance of children with TS of special theoretical interest.

An extensive review of TS by Brown and Ivers (1999) makes no mention of CPT-related research with children diagnosed with TS. Regrettably, only two studies emerged from our search that included children with TS, although a third did use a group with generic motor tics. As previously mentioned, Harris et al. (1995) compared TS patients with ADHD and a comorbid TS/ADHD group using an X-CPT. All three groups performed poorly on all CPT variables assessed, with the TS and ADHD group being comparable and the comorbid TS/ADHD group performing the worst of all. Slowed reaction time was the most notable deficiency for all three groups. Shucard, Benedict, Tekok-Kilic, and Lichter (1997), using a visual AX-CPT paradigm, compared children with TS to a normal control group. As with the Harris et al. study, children with TS demonstrated significantly slower reaction time; no other differences in CPT performance were found. Van der Meere, Stemerdink, and Gunning (1995) compared a group of children with ADHD to a group with comorbid ADHD and generic tic disorder to a group of normal controls. The comorbid ADHD/tic disorder group had more difficulty with the short ISI presentations, and both ADHD groups had excessive errors of commission. Although admittedly scant, the CPT performance of children with TS, particularly with regard to reaction time, certainly appears to be abnormal. Considerably more research is necessary before the relationship of CPT variables to TS and its latent neurological substrates is understood. Its potential heuristic value, nevertheless, is great, and such research should be encouraged.

CPTs and Other Groups

A number of other child and adolescent groups have been studied, but not systematically, with regard to CPT performance. A good many of these groups show impairments on various types of CPT variables. Among the clinical groups, the most prominent is the group of children with TBI. Surprisingly, little has been published with regard to the CPT performance of children with TBI. As pointed out in Chapter 5, what little research has been done points clearly to performance decrements (e.g., Campanelli, 1970; Crosby, 1972). Mild TBI produces performance decrements (K.S. Katz et al., 1996), although they tend to resolve over six months post-TBI, whereas severe TBI produces long-lasting deficits (P.M. Kaufmann et al., 1993). Neurologic insult in general produces adverse effects on CPT performance, even if nontraumatic. Studies with children with seizure disorders, for example, show increases in errors of omissions (e.g., Miller, 1996). Levav (1991) found a group of adolescents with absence seizures to have slower reaction time, fewer correct hits, and more errors than sibling and parental control groups. Thus, as discussed in more detail in Chapter 5, direct CNS compromise results in impaired CPT performance.

Phenylketonuria (PKU) is an autosomal recessive metabolic disorder that, when untreated, causes severe mental retardation. With treatment, which is primarily dietary, PKU is associated with lesser neurological problems (see Waisbren, 1999, for a review). One prominent theory of why adverse neurological impact persists in PKU, despite dietary accommodations, relates to a reduction in the availability of dopamine. As noted earlier, dopamine is implicated in ADHD and in TS, and these groups show performance decrements on the most common CPT paradigms. Two studies in our review (V.E. Anderson et al., 1969; Brunner & Berry, 1987) included children with PKU. Although sample sizes were quite small, nevertheless, PKU children performed more poorly in both studies. V.E. Anderson et al. reported the interesting finding that the performance of children with PKU worsened as the task progressed (i.e., they demonstrated a vigilance decrement over time).

Table 6.1

Studies Using the CPT with Groups of Children

Study	CPT Type	N	Age Range or Mean (SD) in Years	Sample Types	Results
Ali et al., 1996	XX-Visual	12 11 10	7.5 7.4 7.6	Sleep disordered breathing Snoring Medical control	There were no significant differences in the groups prior to adenotonsillectomy. Following surgery, however, the sleep disordered breathing group and the snoring group demonstrated increased correct hits; no improvement was seen in the control group.
Anastopoulos & Costabile, 1994	Not-X-Visual	34	6–11	Clinic referrals	Classification accuracy ranged from 62% to 75% for ADHD depending on the variable used. Variability (standard error) of the reaction time yielded the highest accuracy (true positives) for ADHD at 75%. In contrast, omission error was the most accurate index for identification of subjects who were not ADHD (true negatives) at 100%.
V.E. Anderson et al., 1969	X-Visual AX-Visual	11 11	10.8 10.7	Phenylketonuria Normal control	Significant between-group differences (p < .001) were found for correct hits. Late responding (longer reaction time) was more frequent (p < .01) in the PKU group. The PKU group also showed a greater decrement in performance over time.
Asarnow et al., 1977	X-Visual	9 10 10	16.11 16.10 15.40	High risk: schizophrenia In foster care Community control	No significant differences found between adolescents with maternal history of schizophrenia (high risk), adolescents in foster placements, and presumably normal adolescents in the community.
August & Garfinkel, 1989	AX-Visual	16 23 11 43	11.5 11.0 10.9 11.0	Mild ADHD Severe ADHD ADHD/LD Control	The ADHD/LD group differed significantly from all other groups on omission and commission errors.
Aylward et al., 1990	AX-Visual	51 31 98 55	7.67 9.31 8.35 8.85	ADD/no LD No ADD or LD LD/ADD No ADD/LD	The no-ADD groups performed better on the delay task regardless of LD status. On the vigilance and distractibility tasks, omission and commission errors were affected by ADD status but not by LD status.

Study	Task	N	Age, M (SD)	Group	Results
Barkley et al., 1991	AX-Visual	84 77	14.1 (1.4) 14.3 (1.9)	ADHD Control	Significant ($p < .001$) between-group differences found for omission and commission errors on the vigilance task, but not on the distractibility task. ADHD group made more omission and commission errors than the normal controls.
Barkley et al., 1990	AX-Visual	42 48 16 34	8.3 (1.3) 9.0 (1.3) 9.3 (2.0) 8.8 (1.5)	ADDH ADDWo LD Control	The ADDH group had significantly more omission and commission errors than either the LD or normal control group ($p < .01$). The ADDWo group differed from the LD group only on commission errors.
Barkley & Grodzinsky, 1994	AX-Visual	12 12 11 12	9.2 (1.3) 9.1 (1.4) 9.9 (1.5) 9.1 (1.4)	ADDH ADDWo LD Control	Tests of positive predictive power (PPP) indicated only modest sensitivity for ADDH. This was slightly better for ADDWo for number correct (omission scores). The ADDH group had more subjects with abnormal scores for numbers correct than the normal group ($p < .10$), but did not differ from the ADDWo or LD groups. The number of abnormal scores for the ADDWo group differed significantly from the LD ($p < .04$) and normal ($p < .01$) for number correct. PPP was significantly greater for commission errors (100% PPP) but negative predictive power (NPP) was much lower at 40%.
Barkley et al., 1992	AX-Visual	12 12 11 12	9.2 (1.2) 9.1 (1.4) 9.9 (1.5) 9.1 (1.4)	ADDH ADDWo LD Control	Both ADD groups made more omission and commission errors than the LD or normal control groups, but the difference was significant only for omission errors.
Barkley et al., 1989	AX-Visual	37 37	8.5 (2.2) 8.0 (2.3)	ADHD aggressive ADHD nonaggressive	No significant between-group differences were found in baseline condition.
Beale et al., 1987	AX-Visual	11 11 11	12.50 12.35 9.08	LD Age matched control Reading level matched control	The LD group showed frequent anticipatory errors. Groups differed on sensitivity (d'). The LD group made more frequent errors (both AO/OX), but particularly AO type errors. The reading-matched group had a higher rate of errors than the age-matched group.

(continued)

Table 6.1 Continued

Study	CPT Type	N	Age Range or Mean (SD) in Years	Sample Types	Results
Bergman et al., 1991	XX-Visual	31 11 29	6–12	ADHD ADHD/RD Normal control	Pure ADHD subjects were more distractible and performed worse than normals on verbal and spatial conditions. The pure ADHD group did better on shapes than numbers. The ADHD/RD performed worse than normals on the verbal (numbers) task only.
Breen, 1989	AX-Visual	26 13	6–11	ADDH Control	The ADD group made significantly more omission errors than the control group on the vigilance task.
R.T. Brown et al., 1991	X-Visual	25 21 22	5.83 for combined groups	Exposed to alcohol in utero Not exposed to alcohol in utero Exposed only in first trimester	Results indicated a significant deterioration (vigilance decrement) for those children whose mothers had continued to drink throughout their pregnancy with increased omission errors in Block 3 of the task. Notably, when the current drinking pattern of the mother was used as a covariate, these differences disappeared. No differences in performance were noted for Block 1. Authors concluded that CPT performance may be impaired as a function of the caretaking environment.
Brunner & Berry, 1987	AX-Visual	22 12	16.4 (5.6) 13.4 (3.9)	PKU Control	Although the performance of children with PKU was poorer than the control group, the differences were not significant.
Burland, 1985	X-Visual	28 28	2nd–6th grade	Attention deficient Control	Performance of children identified as attention deficient based on rating scales was not uniformly depressed relative to control peers for omission errors or variability.
Campanelli, 1970	X-Visual	20 20 20	10.1 (1.0) 9.9 (1.3) 9.9 (1.1)	Focal lesions Nonfocal lesions Control	Controls performed consistently better (correct hits) than focal/nonfocal lesion groups for all three conditions of CPT administration. Differences between focal and nonfocal groups were found in the no-illumination condition with the nonfocal group demonstrating greater impairment in the challenge condition.
C.S. Carter et al., 1995	X-Visual	19 19	10.58 (1.26) 10.63 (1.21)	ADHD Controls	Significant between-group difference was found only for omission errors ($p < .025$).

Study	Task	N	Age (SD)	Group	Results
Chee et al., 1989	X-Visual	14 8 18 11 36	7.94 (1.38) 8.20 (1.69) 8.48 (1.38) 9.04 (1.42) 8.58 (3.25)	ADDH CD ADDH+CD LD Control	ADDH performed more poorly (lowest hit rate) than all others ($p < .01$). False alarms were higher for the ADDH group than the control group. Reaction time for the ADDH group was greater than the control group ($p < .01$) and all other groups ($p < .05$).
Cohan, 1995	Not-X-Visual	31	8.6 (1.5)	Clinic referred	For the combination of clinic-referred subjects, 41.9% were markedly atypical and 16.1% were mildly atypical on correct hits. When commission errors were used, 0% were markedly atypical and 6.5% were mildly atypical. Using reaction time, 0% were atypically fast, 22.6% were atypically slow, 3.2% were a little fast, and 22.6% were a little slow. For variability of reaction time standard error, 35.5% were markedly atypical and 16.1% were mildly atypical. It was concluded that classification differed depending on the variable(s) being considered.
Cohler et al., 1977	X-Visual	24 10 33	5.56 (0.63) 5.52 (0.56) 5.57 (0.56)	Maternal schizophrenia Maternal depression Well mother	No significant between-group differences found for omission or commission errors.
Crosby, 1972	X-Visual AX-Visual	24 24 24 24 24	15.38 (1.35) 15.28 (1.39) 14.82 (1.31) 9.03 (0.78) 14.82 (1.32)	MR with brain damage MR without brain damage EMR Mental age (MA) control Chronological age (CA) control	The CA control group performed significantly better than all others. A main effect for group was found, however, even when the CA group was excluded from the analyses. Results indicated that the MR-brain-injured group differed from the MR-non-brain-injured group with the brain-injured group demonstrating greater impairment. The control MA group (the youngest group) had the least adequate performance.
Dainer et al., 1981	X-Visual AX-Visual	19 19	11.2 (1.9) 11.3 (2.0)	LD Control	The LD group made more errors of commission and omission than normals, especially on the AX version.
Draeger et al., 1986	X-Auditory X-Visual	16 16	9-7 9-7	ADDH Control	The ADDH group was more affected by examiner present/absent condition. No between group differences in performance were noted in the examiner present condition. CPT correct hits were found to correlate moderately with motor activity for both groups.

Table 6.1 Continued

Study	CPT Type	N	Age Range or Mean (SD) in Years	Sample Types	Results
DuPaul, Anastopoulos, et al., 1992	AX-Visual	68	8.63 (1.55)	ADHD	Classification agreement with rating scales was not acceptable. Based on CPT correct, there was 22% agreement; CPT commission errors yielded 35.2% agreement. If CPT correct or commission errors was used, there was 44.1% agreement. If both CPT correct and commission errors were required, the classification agreement dropped to 13.2%.
Dupuy, 1995	X-Visual	54	13–15	At risk for dropping out	Based on results of the CPT, 30% of the sample would have been identified as ADD compared to 43% based on self-report and 24% based on teacher report.
Edwards, 1998	X-Auditory/ Visual	107 31	6–16	ADHD Non-ADHD	Of the ADHD group, 71% obtained an abnormal score for either the Response Control Quotient or the Attention Quotient. In contrast, only 36% of the non-ADHD group obtained an abnormal Response Control Quotient or Attention Quotient.
Eliason, 1988	AX-Visual	32 32	9.38 (2.57) 9.35 (2.43)	Neurofibromatosis LD	Both groups had slower reaction times relative to normative data. The LD children made significantly more omission errors than commission errors. The neurofibromatosis group was equally as likely to make omission or commission errors.
Eliason & Richman, 1987	AX-Visual	30 30	9.8 9.7	LD Not LD	The LD group had more omission errors and a slower rate of responding, but did not differ from controls on commission errors.
Eliason & Richman, 1988	AX-Visual	90	9.5 (1.9)	LD	Compared to the normative data for the CPT, 13% of the LD group obtained significantly abnormal scores for omission errors, 9% obtained abnormal scores for commission errors, and 21% obtained abnormal scores for reaction time. Mildly abnormal results were obtained for 36% on omission errors, 6% on commission errors, and 36% on reaction time.
Erickson et al., 1984	X-Visual	11 21 11 26	14.2 14.4 14.3 15.0	Schizophrenic CD ADD Anxiety/eating disorder	All groups demonstrated slowed reaction times, increased variability, and more errors relative to normative data. The schizophrenic group had more omission errors than any other group; no group effect was found for commission errors.

Study	Task	N	Age	Groups	Results
Erlenmeyer-Kimling & Cornblatt, 1978	XX-Visual	58	7–12	Children of schizophrenic parent control	The group of children for whom one parent had a diagnosis of schizophrenia (and considered at high risk) made more errors of omission and commission both with and without distraction. In contrast, no difference between groups with respect to reaction time was found with or without distraction.
Fischer et al., 1990	AX-Visual	100 60	12.9 (0.9)/ 16.5 (1.6) 13.2 (0.8)/ 15.4 (0.6)	ADDH Control	At both age ranges, the ADDH group had significantly more omission and commission errors on both the vigilance and distractibility tasks.
Fischer et al., 1995	AX-Visual	138	4–17	ADHD Control	The hit rate for classification based on the vigilance task differed depending on age ranges. For ages 4 to 11, 79% were classified correctly; for ages 6 to 11, 81% were classified correctly; for ages 12 to 17, 20% were classified correctly. Those who were misclassified tended to be from lower SES and older.
Flansburg, 1966	AX-Visual	30 30	8.95 (1.77) 9.37 (1.92)	ADD Non-ADD BD	The GDS was able to differentiate the ADD group from the non-ADD group based on the omission and commission errors of the vigilance task.
Forbes, 1998	X-Visual	63 13 18	6–12	ADDHD ADD Other	The ADDHD/ADD groups combined had significantly more omission errors, more multiple response, slower response time, and greater variability as compared to the other group. Using TOVA classification criteria, however, results did not differentiate the ADDHD and ADD groups.
Fried et al., 1992	AX-Visual	126	6	Exposure to alcohol, marijuana, smoking in utero	There was a main effect found for number of responses and efficiency ratio on the delay task as well as commission errors on vigilance. Those exposed to smoking performed poorly compared to others. When controlled for marijuana, total correct on vigilance was negatively correlated with use while omissions on vigilance were positively correlated with use. Results support

(continued)

Table 6.1 Continued

Study	CPT Type	N	Age Range or Mean (SD) in Years	Sample Types	Results
					association of maternal smoking and attentional and impulsivity problems of children. Results also support association of maternal marijuana use and aspects of attention. No attention impacts were found for low level alcohol use.
Friedman et al., 1986	X-Visual XX-Visual	74 34 26	14.5 (1.7) 15.1 (1.9) 15.3 (2.1)	Control Child with schizophrenic parent Child with parent with affective disorder	The children whose parent had a diagnosis of schizophrenia had lower levels of correct hits ($p < .05$) than either of the other two groups. There was no difference between the other two groups for omission errors. No group differences were found for errors or reaction time.
García-Sánchez et al., 1997	Not described	9 16 35	15.0 (0.5) 14.7 (0.5) 14.9 (0.7)	ADDWo ADDH Control	Results indicated that the groups could be discriminated (classified correctly) based on number correct and number of omission in the *without interference* condition.
Garretson et al., 1990	X-Visual	23 23 23	12.32 (3.92) 5.86 (1.79) 5.74 (1.95)	Autistic Control 1 Control 2	There was no significant group effect for correct hits, sensitivity (d'), response bias (Beta) or for multiple responses. The use of tangible reinforcers significantly countered the vigilance decrement for the autistic children. There was a group by reward interaction for correct hits. A vigilance decrement was noted for all groups. Changing the ISI had an effect on accuracy, sensitivity (d'), and Beta for all groups.
Girardi et al., 1995	AX-Visual	11 17	11 (1) 11 (1)	Control ADD	There was no difference between groups at baseline and both groups demonstrated a decline in performance over time.
Gordon et al., 1988	AX-Visual	180	6–12	ED, LD, and control	Subjects were classified as ADHD or not-ADHD based on parent and teacher rating scales. CPT classification accuracy was then compared with parent-teacher classification accuracy with results ranging from 48% (parent rating only) to 63% (combined parent and teacher rating).
Gordon, DiNiro, et al., 1989	AX-Visual	34 40	6–12	ED LD	Results of CPT (classification as normal or abnormal) were in agreement with teachers and parents for 70% of the cases.

Study	Task	N	Age	Groups	Results
Gordon et al., 1994	AX-Visual	89 93 85 115	9.1 (2.0) 8.9 (2.5) 9.4 (2.2) 8.5 (2.1)	Nonreferred, but retained Nonreferred, nonretained Referred and retained Referred, but nonretained	Children with a history of grade retention had significantly lower scores on measure of sustained attention than those who had never repeated a grade; this was most evident for those who were referred for assessment of ADHD and who had been retained.
Grassi, 1970	X-Auditory	25 25 25	13.20 13.00 13.40	Brain damaged BD Control	The subjects in the control group had more correct hits than either of the clinical groups; the brain-damaged group missed more targets than the behavior disordered group. The control group maintained vigilance at a higher level across the duration of the task as compared to both clinical groups.
Greenberg & Crosby, 1992a	X-Visual	73 775	6–13	ADHD Control	The ADHD group had significantly more omission and commission errors, longer response times, and greater variability in responding as compared to the control group. Discriminant analysis indicated better sensitivity at the .90 specificity level.
Griffiths et al., 1998	AX-Visual ABX-Visual	11 11	8.83 8.83	Phenylketonuria Control	There was no main effect for the group for correct hits, false alarms, or reaction time on either task. For the ABX-CPT, the PKU group was found to have a significant decrement in performance in Block 3, but recovered in Block 4.
Grodzinsky & Barkley, 1999	AX-Visual	66 64	6–11	ADHD Control	Based on CPT correct hits and commission errors, positive predictive power was 87% to 83% respectively; negative predictive power was closer to 60% and sensitivity was approximately 40%.
Grodzinsky & Diamond, 1992	AX-Visual	66 64	6–11	ADHD Control	Boys with ADHD demonstrated more difficulty with impulse control relative to the control group as evidenced by a higher rate of commission errors. Age effects were noted as well.
Grunebaum et al., 1978	X-Visual	10 12 22	6–12	Maternal schizophrenia Maternal affective Psychosis control	Children of depressed/psychotic mothers demonstrated the greatest number of errors; children of schizophrenic mothers did not differ significantly from control children.

(continued)

Table 6.1 Continued

Study	CPT Type	N	Age Range or Mean (SD) in Years	Sample Types	Results
Grunebaum et al., 1974	X-Visual	20 20 13 13	5 5 6 6	Index group Control Index group Control	The index group was made up of children whose mothers were schizophrenic, schizoaffective, or nonschizophrenic referred. The control group and the index group did not differ on omission errors. Mother child correlations were significant only for mother/son omission errors.
Halperin et al., 1992	AX-Visual	31 53 18	9.62 (1.91) 10.18 (1.76) 9.17 (1.78)	ADHD Non-ADHD, clinic referred Control	A high proportion of non-ADHD clinic referred children demonstrated poor performance (inattention) as did the children in the ADHD group. This suggests that children with other psychiatric disorders are at risk of being mislabeled based on CPT performance.
Halperin et al., 1995	AX-Visual	87 24	7–13 7–13	Psychiatric referrals: don't fight Psychiatric referrals: fight	Analysis revealed a significant main effect of CPT impulsivity with the frequency of fighting ($p < .002$) for ADHD, ODD and CD children. There was also a significant group effect for ADHD for impulsivity, that was not found for children with ODD or CD. A significant group effect was found for ADHD on CPT inattention such that those ADHD subjects who did not initiate fights accounted for most CPT inattention errors. For nonaggressive children, those with ADHD had more impulsive errors than the ODD/CD without ADHD group.
Halperin et al., 1993	AX-Visual	13 15 20 18	8.7 (1.5) 9.5 (1.7) 9.3 (1.6) 9.0 (1.8)	ADHD ODD/CD Anxiety Control	Using Halperin's indexes, between-group differences were found for attention, impulse control, and dyscontrol with the ADHD group significantly more impaired than all other groups.
Halperin, Newcorn, et al., 1990	AX-Visual	52	7.8	Nonreferred sample	Based on CPT performance, 47.4% of the group identified as ADHD by teacher ratings were found to be inattentive based on the CPT, while 13.6% of those not identified as ADHD by teacher ratings were found to be inattentive based on the CPT. The objectively identified inattention group based on CPT performance was found to have lower IQ scores and were rated as more aggressive based on teacher ratings.

Study	Task	N	Age	Groups	Findings
Halperin, O'Brien, et al., 1990	AX-Visual	85	1st–6th graders	CD ADHD ADHD/CD Control	The CD group did not differ from the control group on CPT performance. The ADHD group was more inattentive; the ADHD/CD group was more impulsive. Dissociation of inattention and aggression was not possible based on CPT performance.
Halperin, Wolf, et al., 1991	AX-Visual	54	9.25 (1.75)	Clinic referrals	With clinical referrals including ADHD, CD, major depression, and PDD four types of commission errors were identified and proposed as reflecting underlying psychological processes.
Harper & Ottinger, 1992	X-Visual	20 20	4–6 4–6	ADDH Control	Significant main effects for omission and commission on the X-CPT with letters and for omission with pictures. Using omission errors only, predictive discriminant analysis with the letters version resulted in correctly classifying 63.2% of the ADDH and 83.3% of the controls or 73.0% overall. With the picture version, 9.0% of the controls, 75% of the ADDH and 82.5% overall were correctly classified.
Harris et al., 1995	X-Visual	10 48 32	11.6 9.6 11.1	Tourette ADHD Tourette/ADHD	All groups demonstrated impaired performance with comorbid group having poorest performance. Deficiencies most notable in reaction time and excessive variability of reaction time in the course of the task.
Hickey et al., 1995	AX-Visual	12 12 12	9.7 (1.5) 10.1 (1.4) 9.7 (1.1)	Opiate exposure in utero Environmental drug exposure Drug free control	Both in utero exposure and environmental exposure to opiates resulted in decreased performance by boys in these groups on distractibility tasks compared to boys from drug-free homes. No between-group difference was found on the delay or the vigilance tasks.
Holcomb et al., 1985	ABX-Visual	21 24 24 24	8–11	ADDWo ADDH RD Control	A main effect for group was found with the control group having the fastest reaction time (646 ms) and the ADDWo group having the slowest (743 ms) reaction time. No significant differences for groups were found on commission or omission errors. On ERP, the control group had largest P3 amplitude and the ADDWo group had the smallest P3 amplitude; latency findings were consistent with reaction time findings with the shortest latency for the control group, and the longest latency for the ADDWo group.

(continued)

Table 6.1 Continued

Study	CPT Type	N	Age Range or Mean (SD) in Years	Sample Types	Results
Hooks et al., 1994	AX-Visual	40 52	7–12	ADHD Control	The performance of both groups was found to deteriorate over time on task. The ADHD group made significantly more omission errors and commission errors. Perceptual sensitivity (d') also differed significantly between groups. There was no significant between group difference for response bias (Beta).
Horn et al., 1989	X-Visual AX-Visual	54 31	8.1/8.2 8.2/7.9	ADHD Non-ADHD	Significant main effect by group found for omission and commission errors with the ADHD group found to be impaired.
Hoy et al., 1978	X-Auditory	15 15	14.73 (0.74) 14.70 (0.70)	ADDH Control	There was no significant difference between groups on the CPT for correct hits. A significant difference for total commission errors was found. Results indicated that both groups performed worse with distractors as evidenced by more commission errors in the distraction condition.
Kashden et al., 1993	AX-Visual	23 20 20	13–18	Suicidal Risk: in-patient Psychiatric: in-patient Control	Significant differences were found for commission errors on the vigilance task between the two in-patient groups and the control group, with the suicidal group demonstrating significantly greater impulsivity. No differences were found on omission errors.
K.S. Katz et al., 1996	AX-Visual	22 32 10 40	6.75 (0.44) 6.64 (0.41) 6.89 (0.59) 6.78 (0.47)	Premature/no lesion Premature/mild lesion Premature/severe lesion Control	The premature children with severe lesions made significantly more errors of omission and commission than controls. The performance of the mild lesion group was poorer than controls only on commission errors. Mean differences among the premature groups (no, mild, severe lesion) were not significant.
P.M. Kaufmann et al., 1993	X-Visual	11 13 12 36	12.4 (3.3) 11.5 (2.5) 9.6 (2.1) 11.1 (2.8)	Mild CHI Moderate CHI Severe CHI Control	Results indicated that severe head injury was associated with impaired CPT performance 6 months after injury.
Kaye-Swift, 1992	AX-Visual	19 38 24	3–5	Receptive language Expressive language Control	On the vigilance task, the receptive group had significantly more commission errors than either the expressive or control group. No other differences were significant.

Study	CPT Type	n	Age	Group	Findings
King, 1996	X-Visual	21 29 45 41 7 5 6	6–16.91	ADHD CD ADHD/CD ADHD/ODD ADDH ADDWo + CD ADDWo + ODD	There was no difference found between ADHD and CD on omission errors; there was a main effect for ADHD versus CD for commission errors. Also, the ADHD group improved on commission errors, reaction time, and variability with medication, but the CD group did not. The ADHD group also made more commission errors than the ADDWo. Discriminant analysis with variability, age, commission, and omission errors correctly classified 92% of the ADHD and CD groups, but this was in part a result of age.
Kintslinger, 1987	AX-Visual	20 20 20 20	9.30 (1.38) 9.4 (1.27) 9.35 (1.23) 9.30 (1.03)	LD MR BD Control	The BD group obtained the lowest number of correct hits and the highest number of commission errors; the controls obtained the highest number of correct hits, and the lowest number of commission errors. Differences, however, were not significant. Classification analysis using the CPT resulted in 47.5% classification accuracy with greater accuracy for the BD group (70% classified accurately) and the control group (95% classified accurately).
Klee & Garfinkel, 1983	AX-Visual	51	12.5	Psychiatric referral	Specificity (true negatives) for the CPT was found to be 75%; sensitivity (true positives) was found to be 47% using a combined ADD/CD portion of the sample as the subsample of interest.
Klorman et al., 1979	X-Visual	18 17	9.53 (1.38) 9.60 (1.20)	ADDH Control	ADDH performance was impaired relative to control, and the P3 for the ADHD group had a smaller amplitude.
Koriath et al., 1985	AX-Visual	32 31 19 12 22 11	8.59 8.59 10.45 9.49 8.61 9.91	Hyperactive-pervasive Hyperactive-single setting ED CD Hyperactive/CD Hyperactive/ED	Once age and socioeconomic status were controlled for, no group differences emerged on CPT variables of correct hits or commission errors.

(continued)

Table 6.1 Continued

Study	CPT Type	N	Age Range or Mean (SD) in Years	Sample Types	Results
Kupietz, 1976	AX-Auditory	16 16	9.28 (0.77) 9.89 (0.99)	Behavior problems Control	Children with behavior problems made more omission errors and demonstrated a greater vigilance decrement as compared to the control group.
Kupietz, 1990	AX-Visual	11 11 13	9.71 (1.65) 9.63 (2.46) 9.71 (1.55)	Control RD RD/ADDH	All groups showed decline in sustained attention over duration of task for correct hits, but this was most evident for the RD group. The type of commission error differentiated the RD group from the RD/ADDH group with the RD/ADDH group making more AO type errors, younger RD making more OX errors. In addition to RD or RD/ADDH, age was found to be a factor.
Leavell et al., 1999	Not-X-Visual	83	1.16 (2.89)	Clinic referred	For correct hits, group differences were significant with the attention-hyperactive-anxious (comorbid) group demonstrating the greatest impairment. For commission errors, however, no group differences were significant.
Leung & Luk, 1988	AX-Visual	7 8 12	8.33 (1.17)	ADDH reported ADDH reported and observed Medical control	Both ADDH groups demonstrated impaired performance as evidenced by greater commission errors; this was most evident with the ADDH reported and observed group. The reported and observed group also had fewer correct hits and more omission errors as compared to the other two groups. Data was reanalyzed based on presence or absence of CD and there was no significant difference between ADDH with CD versus ADHD without CD suggesting that CPT performance is attributable to ADDH and not CD.
Levav, 1991	X-Visual AX-Visual X-Auditory	14 16 15	10.6 (1.98) 39 (6.07) 12.13 (3.3)	Probands with absent seizure Parents Siblings	Probands had consistently lower scores for mean reaction time, percentage correct hits, and percentage of errors with a main effect of the group for the sustain factor.
Levy & Hobbes, 1981	X-Visual	30 166	5.99	ADDH Control	Using discriminant analysis and CPT results, 98.8% of the controls were classified correctly and 60% of the ADDH were classified correctly.

Study	Task type	N	Age	Group	Results
Levy & Hobbes, 1997	X-Visual	56 58	8.07 (1.85) 8.08 (1.87)	ADHD Control	Multivariate regression indicated that omission errors added little information, but commission errors added to the equation. Discriminant analysis using CPT variables resulted in accurately identifying 96.4% of the ADHD group as ADHD and 96.4% of the control group as normal.
Levy et al., 1987	X-Visual	39 40 34 25 20	7.73 (2.03) 8.36 (2.25) 8.50 (2.42) 8.75 (1.75) 9.18 (1.67)	Severe ADDH Moderate ADDH Mild ADDH CD Anxiety	When IQ, age, SES, and gender are controlled for, the severe ADDH group scored significantly worse only on commission errors as compared to other groups. No other between group differences were found.
Lewis, 1993	AX-Visual AX-Auditory	50 57	8.9 (0.78) 9.0 (0.82)	ADHD Control	Classification results varied by CPT with 31 (62%) of the ADHD group obtaining scores within normal limits on both CPTs. Differences occurred such that 8 of the ADHD group were abnormal on the auditory, but not the visual and 2 were abnormal on the visual, but not the auditory. The level of impairment for the ADHD group was greater on the auditory task.
Loge et al., 1990	AX-Visual	20 20	9.6 9.5	ADHD Control	The ADHD group had more commission errors on both the vigilance and distractibility tasks. The ADHD group also detected fewer targets on the distractibility task, but there was no difference on omission errors for the vigilance task.
Loiselle et al., 1980	X-Auditory	12 15	12.8 13.0	ADDH Control	The ADDH group demonstrated significant deficits in selective attention and vigilance as evidenced by percentage correct, number of commission errors, and reaction time relative to the control group.
Luk et al., 1991	AX-Visual XX-Visual	18 43	9.75 (1.78) 7.97 (1.61)	ADDH reported ADDH reported and observed	The reported and observed ADDH group demonstrated significantly poorer performance than the reported only group. When the subjects were redivided based on the presence or absence of CD, no significant between-group difference was found for presence versus absence of CD.

(continued)

Table 6.1 Continued

Study	CPT Type	N	Age Range or Mean (SD) in Years	Sample Types	Results
Mann, 1997	X-Visual	30 26	10.42 (2.33) 11.42 (1.79)	ADHD Control	CPT results (commission errors and variability) did not contribute to classification accuracy above and beyond parent and teacher rating scales.
Mariani & Barkley, 1997	AX-Visual	34 30	4–5	ADDH Control	The ADDH group made more commission errors relative to the control group.
Matier et al., 1992	AX-Visual	11 14 13	8.2 (1.0) 8.2 (1.2) 9.4 (1.3)	ADHD ADHD/aggressive Control	Using Halperin indexes, there were no main effects for the group on inattention or impulsivity at baseline; there was a main effect for the group, with both ADHD groups differing from the control group, for dyscontrol at baseline.
Matier-Sharma et al., 1995	AX-Visual	40 57 18	6.5–13	ADHD Non-ADHD Control	Discriminant analysis revealed a positive predictive power of 72.4% of the ADHD sample versus the control group and 66.2% of the ADHD sample versus the non-ADHD sample. The ADHD group was significantly more impaired on Halperin's Inattention and Impulsivity indexes as compared to the other two groups.
Mayes & Calhoun, 1999	AX-Visual	165	6–16	ADHD Clinic referred	Scores from the GDS were converted to standard scores and averaged; the difference between IQ and GDS average score was then computed. When the discrepancy score (IQ-GDS) exceeded 13 points, overall classification accuracy was 80%, sensitivity was 90%, specificity was 70%, positive predictive power was 91%, and negative predictive power was 67%.
McLaren, 1990	AX-Visual	12 12 14	10.5 10.6 10.3	ADHD ADHD/ODD Control	Significant differences emerged between the ADHD groups on omission errors and sensitivity (d').
Michael et al., 1981	X-Visual AX-Visual	21 21	9.31 (1.92) 9.35 (1.94)	ADDH Control	On placebo, ADDH made more omission and commission errors than the control group and displayed smaller late positive components on ERP.

Study	Task	Group	Age	N	Findings
Michaels, 1996	X-Visual	ADHD Affective disorder Anxiety disorder	6–16	18 18 18	Children with ADHD obtained significantly poorer first half omission scores than depressed or anxious groups. On discriminant analysis using CPT data, 52% of the cases were classified accurately.
Miller, 1996	X-Visual	Generalized epilepsy Complex partial epilepsy Control	10.43 (3.16) 10.60 (2.78) 10.89 (2.61)	17 16 33	There was a main effect for group for CPT omission errors with the generalized group showing greatest impairment. All groups made the most commission errors during the first block. There was no main effect for group on commission errors.
T.V. Mitchell & Quittner, 1996	AX-Visual	Hearing impaired/deaf Hearing	9.85 (2.67) 9.23 (2.67)	39 25	The subjects in the hearing-impaired group demonstrated difficulty with attention. A significantly greater proportion of the hearing-impaired group scored in the borderline or abnormal range relative to the hearing group on both the vigilance and distractibility tasks. For hierarchical regression of sensitivity (d') for vigilance, hearing status explained a substantial portion of the variance. Similarly, hearing status explained significant variance in d' on the distractibility task.
W.G. Mitchell et al., 1990	X-Visual	ADHD/no CD Control	10.22 (1.77) 9.08 (2.14)	49 152	The ADHD group had significantly slower reaction time and their reaction time was more variable; differences increased with use of the nondominant hand suggesting right hemisphere dysfunction. The CPT by itself did not provide adequate specificity.
Newcorn et al., 1989	AX-Visual	ADDH or ADHD (DSM III) ADHD by DSM III-R Control	8.63 (1.26) 8.07 (1.26) 9.23 (1.67)	10 6 68	The ADHD group diagnosed by DSM III-R criteria had significantly more commission errors than either of the other groups. Both ADHD groups made more AO type errors (anticipatory) than the control group.
Newcorn et al., 1994	AX-Visual	ADHD-hyperactive ADHD- (no hyperactivity) Control	8.83 (1.57) 8.55 (1.79) 9.87 (1.76)	12 7 47	The ADHD-hyperactive group missed more targets than the control group, but this was not true for the ADHD-no hyperactivity group. No significant between group difference found for commission errors.

(continued)

Table 6.1   Continued

Study	CPT Type	N	Age Range or Mean (SD) in Years	Sample Types	Results
Nigg et al., 1996	AX-Visual	23 15	8.63 (1.74) 9.28 (1.82)	ADHD Control	The boys with ADHD had slower mean reaction times and significantly poorer indexes of inattention and dyscontrol, but not impulsivity. These differences were more pronounced for those with high aggression than those for low aggression. It was concluded that the CPT has adequate sensitivity but poor specificity in identifying ADHD.
Nuechterlein, 1983	X-Visual XX-Visual Not-X-Visual	24 20 14 14 20 14	13.1 (1.8) 13.0 (1.5) 12.8 (1.5) 12.8 (1.5) 12.8 (1.5) 13.0 (1.9)	Maternal schizophrenia Maternal psychiatric ADDH Control for schizophrenia Control for psychiatric Control for ADDH	Twenty-nine percent of children of schizophrenic mothers obtained an extremely low sensitivity (d') scores as compared to 9% of the control group. Children of mothers with other psychiatric disorders did not differ from the control group on d' or response bias (Beta). Significantly more (29%) of the ADDH group had low Beta scores as compared to normals (7%–8%). Results also indicated a significantly higher false alarm rate and lower correct hit rate for children of schizophrenic mothers across conditions. No between group difference was found for the vigilance decrement.
O'Brien et al., 1992	AX-Visual	9 6 26	9.26 (2.19) 8.48 (1.19) 8.74 (1.80)	CD ADHD CD/ADHD	Children with CD made significantly less omission errors as compared to both ADHD groups. No main effect for group was found for reaction time or reaction time variability.
O'Dougherty et al., 1988	X-Visual	18 9 10	6–12	Congenital heart defect ADD Control	The performance of both the ADD and Congenital Heart groups was generally lower than that of normals; the difference was significant, however, only for total errors with the congenital heart group demonstrating the greatest total error rate.
O'Dougherty et al., 1984	X-Visual	30 30 47	8.5 (1.8) 9.0 (2.1) 8.8 (1.8)	ADDH Hypoxic Control	Significant differences were found on omission errors, sensitivity (d'), response style (Beta), and commission errors. Both the ADDH and hypoxic groups had lower performance relative to the control group. The hypoxic group demonstrated the steepest decline (vigilance decrement), while the ADDH group had the greatest number of commission errors and the most impaired

Study	Task	N	Age	Group	Findings
Oppenheimer, 1986	AX-Visual AX-Auditory	8 18 13 24 23 2	8.75 9.08 9.5 9.17 7.75 7.83	ED LD ED/hyperactive LD/hyperactive Control Hyperactive	The visual and auditory CPT commission error score were found to be useful in differentiating the groups identified as hyperactive from those identified as not hyperactive; this was evident to a greater degree with the visual format. The correct hits score was not found to add to the discriminant function on either the visual or auditory versions.
Oyler et al., 1998	X-Auditory	12 11	7–11	Non-ADHD ADHD	Using total errors, analyses revealed a positive predictive power of 83.3% for the non-ADHD group, but only 9.1% classification accuracy for the ADHD group. Similar results were found for the vigilance decrement.
Ozolins & Anderson, 1980	AX-Visual	20 20		Hyperactive Hypoactive	There was a main effect for group with the hyperactive group getting more correct hits with knowledge of errors. The hyperactive group had less correct hits with no feedback than with either feedback condition so they were able to benefit from feedback. The hypoactive group did better with feedback for correct hits than error feedback or no feedback.
Pantle et al., 1994	AX-Visual	55	14.09 (1.71)	Clinic referrals	Using the vigilance commission error score, classification accuracy for subjects with ADHD was not significant but had a 74.55% correct classification rate.
Pliszka, 1992	Not-X-Visual	34 58 12	6–12	ADHD/ANX ADHD/no ANX Control	The ADHD/no ANX group made significantly more commission errors (failure to inhibit responding) as compared to either of the other two groups. There was no significant difference between the control group and the ADHD/ANX group. No group differences were evidenced for omission errors.
Plomin & Foch, 1981	XX-Visual	18 198	7.6 (1.6)	ADDH Control	No group differences were found in either quiet or noise conditions but only commission errors were recorded.

Table 6.1   Continued

Study	CPT Type	N	Age Range or Mean (SD) in Years	Sample Types	Results
Pogge et al., 1992	AX-Visual	28 15 46	15.46 (1.20) 15.83 (0.99) 14.49 (1.41)	Alcoholic Other substance abuse Psychiatric control	There was a main effect of group that differentiated the alcoholic group from the other substance group for commission errors. No between-group differences were significant for errors of omission.
Porrino et al., 1983	AX-Visual	12 12	8.6 (2.1) 8.6 (1.9)	ADDH Control	The ADDH group made significantly more errors of commission and omission. The CPT omission error score added to the discriminant ability of activity level resulting in 87.5% accuracy rate. Of any single measure of attention, CPT commission errors had the highest discriminant ability with 75% classification accuracy. It was found that younger children were more likely to be misclassified than older children.
Raggio, 1993	AX-Visual	355 275	6–13	ADHD Control	There was a main effect of group at all age levels for omission and commission errors.
Rapoport et al., 1980	AX-Visual	15 14	9.44 (2.12) 10.10 (2.10)	ADDH Control	At baseline, the ADDH group differed significantly from the control group on commission errors and mean ISI.
Rasbury et al., 1979	X-Auditory	14 14	14.2 13.6	Renal disease Control	No significant between-group differences were found.
Reader et al., 1994	X-Visual	48	6.3–13.4	ADHD/RD ADHD/no RD	No significant between-group differences were found. Of the sample, 51.06% of ADHD were impaired (−1 SD) for omission, 4.42% for commission, 59.57% for reaction time, and 51.06% for variability.
Riccio et al., 1999	X-Auditory	15 15	11.20 (1.31) 10.55 (1.05)	CAPD CAPD/ADHD	No significant between-group differences were found on commission errors, omission errors, total errors, or percentage correct.
G. P. Richards et al., 1990	AX-Visual	30 20	11.5 11.5	LD Control	No significant differences were found for omission errors, commission errors, correct response, total responses, or reaction time. Results of students with ADHD and without ADHD, however, suggested that students with ADHD made more commission errors and had faster reaction times as compared to those who did not have ADHD. When students with ADHD were omitted from the sample, the LD group had significantly slower reaction times than the control group.

Study	Test type	N	Age	Group	Results
Robins, 1992	AX-Visual	18 25 25	7.99 (1.31) 9.38 (1.87) 8.40 (2.23)	ADHD LD ADHD/LD	Both ADHD groups evidenced greater impulsivity as compared to the LD only group. There was no between-group difference found for correct hits.
Romans et al., 1997	X-Visual	105 155	14.2 (1.2) 11.5 (2.6)	Turner syndrome Control	Significant between-group differences were found for percentage commission errors and response time suggesting higher than normal levels of impulsivity in girls with Turner syndrome.
Rosenberg, 1980	X-Visual	38 38	6–8	LD Control	The LD group had fewer correct hits, more false alarms, and a slower reaction time than the control group. Both groups had more difficulty with distracting visual stimuli especially in the proximal condition, and the LD group was no more impaired than controls in the distractor condition.
Rosvold et al., 1956	X-Visual AX-Visual	19 26	9.0 (3.0) 12.3 (2.9)	Brain damage Control	Individuals with identified brain damage performed more poorly on CPT. The X-CPT correctly classified 84.2% to 89.5% of those subjects with brain damage and 76.9% of those with no brain damage.
Rund et al., 1998	X-Visual	20 20 30	16.2 (1.1) 14.1 (1.5) 15.7 (1.6)	Schizophrenic ADHD Control	When the effects of age were controlled for, there was no significant effect for group found for any of the CPT variables of correct hits, commission errors, sensitivity (d'), response bias (Beta), or sensitivity decrement.
Rutschmann et al., 1977	XX-Visual	58 92	7–12 7–12	Parental schizophrenia Control	There was a main effect for group for correct hits as well as for sensitivity (d'). There was also a group by age interaction.
Sandford et al., 1995b	X-Visual/Auditory	26 31	7–12 7–15	ADHD Control	Use of the IVA resulted in 89% positive predictive power and 93% negative predictive power.
Schachar et al., 1988a	AX-Visual	33	8.6	ADHD Clinical control	The ADHD did not demonstrate deficits in sustained attention as compared to the clinical control group.

(continued)

Table 6.1   Continued

Study	CPT Type	N	Age Range or Mean (SD) in Years	Sample Types	Results
Schachar et al., 1988b	X-Visual XX-Visual AX-Visual	15 22 18 15 26 18	9.0 (1.29) 9.0 (1.14) 9.08 (1.33) 9.25 (1.79) 8.92 (1.36) 8.58 (1.65)	Control LD ED CD ADDH/ODD ADDH	All clinical groups differed from the control group, but the ADDH groups did not differ significantly from any other clinical groups.
Schechter & Timmons, 1985a	AX-CPT-Visual	75 15	6–12 6–12	Control Hyperactive	The hyperactive group was found to demonstrate more omission and commission errors and to have a longer reaction time as compared to the control group.
Seidel & Joschko, 1990	X-Visual AX-Visual	22 22	8.34 8.29	ADDH Control	The ADDH group demonstrated a greater vigilance decrement with a decreasing number of hits with time on task, but controls did not. The vigilance decrement was affected by age as well.
Seidel & Joschko, 1991	X-Visual AX-Visual	22 22	8.34 8.29	ADDH Control	For group comparisons, there was a main effect for group for correct hits; there was also a group by time and overall time effect for correct hits. There was a group effect for sensitivity (d'). Main effects were found for reaction time variability, false alarms, and response style (Beta) as well. There was no significant group difference for reaction time.
Seidman et al., 1995	X-Auditory	65 21 36 18 45	14.2 (3.3) 15.0 (3.0) 14.9 (3.5) 14.1 (2.2) 14.0 (3.4)	All ADHD ADHD with family history ADHD with comorbid condition ADHD/LD Control	The ADHD subjects (all) were significantly impaired on omission errors. The ADHD with family history group performed most poorly of all the ADHD subgroups on CPT omission errors.
Seidman et al., 1997	X-Auditory	43 36	11.4 11.9	ADHD Clinic control	Although the ADHD group performance was more impaired than the clinical control group, the difference was not significant.
Sergeant & Scholten, 1985	X-Visual	8 8 8	2nd–6th graders	Distractible/overactive Distractible Control	The distractible/overactive group performed more poorly and with longer response times as compared to control regardless of directions given. The distractible group did not differ from either group significantly.

Study	CPT Type	N	Age	Group	Results
S.K. Shapiro & Garfinkel, 1986	Not described	7 11 9	7–12.83	Inattentive/overactive Aggressive Inattentive/aggressive	The CPT did not differentiate the inattentive/overactive from the aggressive children.
S.K. Shapiro & Herod, 1994	AX-Visual X-Auditory	27 27	9.4 9.4	ADHD Control	The only significant between-group differences were found on commission errors for both the auditory and visual tasks. In the distractibility condition (visual), however, there was no significant difference on commission errors.
Sharma et al. 1991	AX-Visual	5 38 6	8.4 (0.58) 9.90 (0.28) 8.94 (0.61)	Overfocused Control Distractible	Significant group differences were found for reaction time with the distractible group having the longest reaction time.
Shucard et al., 1997	AX-Visual	22 22	11.6 (3.2) 11.1 (1.8)	Tourette syndrome Control	No group differences emerged for hit rate, commission errors, detection accuracy (d'), or response bias (Beta). No differences emerged for Halperin Indexes of Inattention or Impulsivity either. However, there was a main effect of group for reaction time with the Tourette group demonstrating a slower response time as compared to the control group.
Slicker, 1991	AX-Visual	68	9.28 (1.59)	ADHD referred Control	CPT results were able to differentiate the ADHD group from the control group.
Sostek et al., 1980	AX-Visual	15 14	9.4 10.1	ADDH Control	There was a main effect for group for sensitivity (d') but not for response style (Beta).
Steinhauer et al., 1997	X-Visual	54 47	8–18	Familial loading of alcoholism No family history of alcoholism	There was no main effect of group for variables of sensitivity (d'), response bias (Beta), sensitivity decrement, or reaction time. There were main effects of age and gender, however, depending on the variable of interest.
Strandburg et al., 1990	XX-Visual	13 19	11.2 (1.5) 11.2 (1.3)	Schizophrenic Control	Significant differences were found by group for mean percent correct hits and for commission errors. No group differences were found for vigilance decrement nor for reaction time.

(continued)

Table 6.1 Continued

Study	CPT Type	N	Age Range or Mean (SD) in Years	Sample Types	Results
Strandburg et al., 1994	X-Visual XX-Visual	16 16	12.50 (2.67) 12.75 (1.67)	Schizophrenic Control	Results indicated that the schizophrenic group had significantly lower response accuracy relative to the control group on both versions of the CPT. The schizophrenics produced more commission errors on both tasks as compared to the control group as well. Finally, the schizophrenic group was significantly slower than the control group in responding to the stimuli.
H.L. Swanson, 1983	AX-Auditory AX-Visual	36 36	8–15	LD Control	There was an age-by-group interaction with group differences emerging as children got older. The LD group had significantly more errors on the visual version as opposed to the auditory version; this difference was not evidenced in the control group.
H.L. Swanson, 1981	AX-Auditory AX-Visual	16 16	12.62 (6.8) 12.75 (6.45)	LD Control	There was a main effect for group on correct hits and sensitivity (d′) Both groups had more commission errors on the visual format.
J.N. Swartwood, 1994	X-Visual	23 23	9–11	ADHD Not ADHD	The ADHD group had significantly poorer performance on omission errors, reaction time, and variability.
Sykes et al., 1973	AX-Auditory AX-Visual	20 20	8.2 8.3	Hyperactive Control	Children in the hyperactive group made more commission and omission errors as compared to the control group. Both groups had greater omission errors on the auditory format as compared to the visual format.
Sykes et al., 1971	X-Visual AX-Visual	40 19	8.0 (1.9)	Hyperactive Control	Children in the hyperactive group detected significantly fewer targets and had a greater number of commission errors.
Tarnowski et al., 1986	AX-Visual	14 12 12 12	8.44 (1.09) 8.74 (0.93) 8.23 (1.02) 8.57 (0.81)	ADDH LD ADDH/LD Control	A significant group effect was found only for sensitivity (d′) and not for response style (Beta).
Teicher et al., 1996	X-Visual	18 11	9.3 (2.4) 8.6 (1.8)	ADHD Control	The ADHD group was significantly slower and more variable as compared to the control group. There were only marginal differences on commission and omission errors.

Study	Task	N	Mean (SD)	Group	Findings
T.L. Thompson, 1988	AX-Visual AX-Auditory	30 30	8.23 (1.74) 8.50 (1.93)	ADHD Control	For the visual format, the ADHD group performed significantly below controls for sensitivity (d'), response style (Beta), and false alarms. A similar pattern of impaired performance was found for the auditory format, however, group differences were only significant for sensitivity (d').
Trommer et al., 1988	AX-Visual	14 6	9.0 8.2	ADHD Control	For the ADHD group, 5 scored in the abnormal range, 5 in the borderline range, and 4 in the normal range. For the control group, 4 scored in the abnormal range, 1 in the borderline range, and 1 in the control range. It was concluded that the CPT may yield both false negatives and false positives.
R.L. Tucker, 1990	AX-Visual	30 30	9.55 (1.69) 8.99 (1.43)	ADHD Specific developmental disorders (LD)	There was no significant between-group difference found for vigilance correct, vigilance commission errors, distractibility correct, or distractibility commission errors.
van der Meere et al., 1995	X-Visual	24 26 24	9.5 9.75 9.58	ADHD ADHD/tic disorder Control	Both ADHD groups made more commission errors than the control group. The performance of the ADHD group without tics varied depending on the presentation rate (ISI) with normal performance on blocks with the longer ISI. In contrast, the ISI did not seem to effect the performance of the ADHD/Tic group with consistently more commission errors regardless of ISI.
A.E. Wagner, 1987	X-Visual AX-Visual	79 38	8.86 9.28	ADDH Control	There were main effects for both gender and diagnosis but there was no interaction effect for commission errors on the X-CPT. There was a main effect for diagnosis for omission errors on the X-CPT. For the AX-CPT, results were similar with main effects for gender and diagnosis for commission errors, and only a main effect for diagnosis for omission errors.
P.S. Walker, 1993	AX-Visual	15 13 15	10.2 (1.5) 10.7 (1.8) 10.5 (1.7)	Opiate exposure in utero Drug exposure in environment Control	There were no between-group differences on the distractibility task for the number of correct responses, however there was a main effect for group for commission errors with the opiate exposed group demonstrating significantly greater commission errors relative to the control group.

(continued)

Table 6.1 Continued

Study	CPT Type	N	Age Range or Mean (SD) in Years	Sample Types	Results
Werry et al., 1987	X-Visual	39 35 21 95	5–13	ADHD ADHD/CD-ODD Anxiety Control	Once age, gender, and verbal ability were controlled for, there were no significant between-group differences found.
Wherry et al., 1993	AX-Visual	29	8.83 (1.54)	Combined groups	The sample was divided into ADHD and control groups based on rating scale results. The CPT results failed to support discriminant validity of the CPT based on the group assignments.
Zentall, 1986	AX-Visual	66 80	8.49 (1.8) 8.54 (2.0)	Hyperactive Control	The hyperactive group made more omission and commission errors than the control group across conditions. When the stimulation level of the task was considered, it was found that the hyperactive group made more commission errors in the low-stimulation condition relative to their own performance in the high-stimulation condition; the significant between group difference was not evident in the medium- and high-stimulation conditions.
Zentall & Meyer, 1987	AX-Auditory	22 25	6–12	ADDH Control	In what was considered a high-stimulation condition, there was no significant between-group difference. In the low-stimulation condition, however, the ADDH performance was impaired relative to the control group.

Notes: CPT = Continuous performance test; ADD = Attention Deficit Disorder; ADDH = Attention Deficit Disorder with hyperactivity; ADDWo = Attention Deficit Disorder without hyperactivity; ADHD = Attention-Deficit/Hyperactivity Disorder; ADHD = ADHD combined type; ANX = Anxiety; BD = Behavior Disorder; CAPD = Central Auditory Processing Disorder; CD = Conduct Disorder; CHI = Closed head injury; DSM = Diagnostic and Statistical Manual of Mental Disorders; ED = Emotional disturbance; EMR = Educable mental retardation; ERP = Event related potential; GDS = Gordon Diagnostic System; ISI = Interstimulus interval; LD = Learning disability; MR = Mental retardation; ODD = Oppositional Defiant Disorder; PDD = Pervasive Developmental Disorder; RD = Reading disability; SES = Socioeconomic status; UADD = Undifferentiated Attention Deficit Disorder.

Other clinical groups are not well or consistently studied but are nonetheless interesting. Neurofibromatosis, another disorder that produces CNS compromise, also produces CPT decrements. Like TS, the compromise associated with neurofibromatosis is most evident in the form of slowed reaction time (Eliason, 1988). Turner's syndrome is another disorder with associated compromise, but it tends to produce more serious CNS problems. Relative to a control group, a large sample of affected girls produced more commission errors and exhibited a slower reaction time (Romans et al., 1997). Dealing with children with medical issues with a less direct CNS connection, Ali et al. (1996) investigated the CPT performance of children with sleep disordered breathing. They found that the CPT performance of these children improved following corrective surgery (adenotonsillectomy).

An area of contemporary interest is that of the effects of alcohol and other substances consumed by mothers during their pregnancy with this offspring. Research suggests that children whose mothers consumed alcohol throughout the term of pregnancy show CPT decrements (e.g., Brown et al., 1991). Effects on CPT performance of the children when there are lower levels of alcohol consumption by the mother are more controversial. Fried et al. (1992) found no effect for low levels of alcohol consumption by the mother; however, they did find CPT performance decrements associated with maternal marijuana and tobacco use. Studies such as these have numerous confounds, however (see Ramsey & Reynolds, 2000). Exposure to opiates in utero also tends to impair attention on CPT tasks (e.g., Hickey, Suess, Newlin, & Spurgeon, 1995). Finally, adolescents with a diagnosis of substance abuse performed more poorly on CPTs.

SUMMARY AND CONCLUSIONS

What have we learned from this narrative review of group differences on CPT performance, and how is it related to sensitivity and specificity of diagnosis with various CPT paradigms? Table 6.2 presents a summary listing of our gross impressions regarding impaired CPT performance across a host of child and adolescent diagnostic and study groupings.

It is apparent from this table, the studies reviewed above, and the exhaustive summary in Table 6.1, that virtually any disorder of childhood that disrupts or compromises CNS integrity or function is a strong candidate to produce decrements in CPT performance. In this age range (5 to 18 years), the CPT seems quite sensitive to CNS problems of many varieties. This does not grant the CPT high levels of sensitivity to a particular disorder if more than one potential psychopathology is present. If one were to use most CPTs to differentiate ADHD children from normal children, and no other diagnosis was possible, CPTs would perform quite well in most (but not all) cases, with high rates of sensitivity and even better specificity. However, similar results are obtained with most of the groups in the left-hand column of Table 6.2 as long as the comparison group is a normal control group. This is an artificial circumstance, however, created for research purposes.

Consider a far more common scenario. Instead of asking a clinician "Is my child ADHD or normal?" most parents or teachers who refer children for diagnostic evaluations know something is not normal and are asking "What is wrong with this child and what do we do about it?" This opens up the entire realm of *DSM-IV* diagnostic opportunities.

Kintslinger (1987) used CPT scores from a visual AX-CPT paradigm to classify children previously known to be either learning disabled,

Table 6.2
Diagnostic Groups of Children and Adolescents
Showing Impairment/Nonimpairment on CPTs

Impaired	Nonimpaired	Mixed Results
ADHD (all DSM-IV types)	Anxiety disorder	Chronic heart disorder
ADHD+	Conduct disorder	Learning disabilities
Autism	Diabetes	Oppositional defiant
CAPD	Hemophilia	disorder
Food allergies	Maternal depression	Parental schizophrenia
General medical clinic	Obsessive-compulsive	
General psychology	disorder	
clinic	Renal disease	
Hypothyroidism		
Hypoxic/anoxic injuries		
Intrauterine toxic		
exposure		
MDD with psychotic		
features		
Mental retardation		
Phenylketonuria		
Psychotic features		
(added to any		
diagnosis)		
Schizophrenia		
Seizure disorder		
Tourette's syndrome		
Traumatic brain injury		
Turner's syndrome		

Notes: CPT = Continuous performance test; ADHD = Attention Deficit/Hyperactivity Disorder; ADHD+ = ADHD with nearly any comorbid disorder; DSM IV = Diagnostic and Statistical Manual of Mental Disorders, 4th ed.; CAPD = Central Auditory Processing Disorder; MDD = Major Depressive Disorder.

mentally retarded, behaviorally disordered, or normal. Classification analysis resulted in only 47.5% overall accuracy in identifying members of these four groups. Half of all the correct classifications (38/80) were the correct identification of 19 of the 20 normal subjects. In other studies, where more than one psychopathology is potentially present, similar results are obtained. Using a general clinic referral sample, Halperin, Matier, Bedi, Sharma, and Newcorn (1992) report that the percentage of non-ADHD children demonstrating poor performance on a visual AX-CPT was as high as their ADHD sample. They concluded that children with a variety of psychiatric disorders are at risk of being misdiagnosed if CPT performance decrements are used as indicants of ADHD. We concur, as did Forbes (1998) in his review of this literature. Forbes, however, concluded that his empirical study demonstrated the ability of the TOVA paradigm to differentiate satisfactorily between an ADHD group and a non-ADHD clinical group. The non-ADHD clinical group in the study was composed of 12 children with ODD, 10 with LD, and 7 with a diagnosis of adjustment disorder or depression. We have discussed many of these groups above, and such a control group as this is seriously problematic. Even so, Forbes' TOVA performance variables would have misclassified 28% of the non-ADHD group as ADHD. Further, even though ADHD was the predominant diagnosis in the total sample, with 117 of his 146 referrals receiving a diagnosis of ADHD, based on TOVA variables 20% of the ADHD sample would not have been diagnosed.

CPT performance decrements are thus not disorder-specific. CPTs are, however, sensitive to the presence of impulsivity and, to a lesser extent, to attentional deficits associated with CNS dysfunction. They may certainly be useful in the objective documentation of these symptoms, but these symptoms are coincident with many disorders, not just ADHD, as they are so popularly applied. CPTs then lack sufficient sensitivity and specificity for differential diagnosis of child and adolescent psychopathologies but possess high degrees of specificity for symptoms of disorders that show decrements in self-regulation and moderate sensitivity. What this means most clearly is that CPTs are very good at detecting normality and in ruling out disorders that involve CNS compromise or dysfunction.

The following statements summarize our view of the state of the literature at this time with regard to the diagnostic use of CPTs:

- Most current CPT paradigms are sensitive to most types of CNS dysfunction.
- CPT performance may be adversely affected by most externalizing disorders and even some internalizing disorders (e.g., autism). All forms of schizophrenia adversely affect CPT performance.

- CPT performance is adversely affected by metabolic disorders with cognitive sequelae.
- CPTs tend not to be sensitive to disorders of mood or affect, except during manic episodes or in the presence of psychotic features.
- CPTs have high levels of sensitivity and specificity for all forms of ADHD, but only when ADHD or normal are the only two diagnostic possibilities.
- Normal levels of performance on CPTs are useful in ruling out ADHD and related disorders of self-regulation as the correct diagnosis.
- Reliance on CPTs as a primary diagnostic tool in determining the presence of ADHD will result in an unacceptably high number of false positive errors (i.e., overdiagnosis of ADHD).
- CPTs are useful tools for objective appraisal and documentation of the presence or absence of symptoms associated with disorders where problems of self-regulation may be evident, particularly impulsivity and attentional problems.

Once symptoms have been documented and a careful history obtained along with additional diagnostic tests (typically including direct observation, behavioral rating scales, and other psychometric tests as the referral question may dictate), the clinician can engage in differential diagnosis. The CPT provides useful data in this process but may not provide incremental validity beyond the data provided by good, psychometrically sound behavior rating scales and direct observation. However, CPTs do provide data directly from the child or adolescent and as such are not subject to rater bias or observer drift. In Chapter 7, the literature specific to adult clinical groups and the role of the CPT in diagnosis will be reviewed.

Diagnostic Efficacy of CPTs for Disorders in Adulthood

CPT STUDIES WITH adults have been even more varied than studies with children and adolescents. Our review located 91 studies of adults using clinical groups of one sort or another, including ADHD (e.g., Barkley, Murray, & Kwasnik, 1996; Downey, Stetson, Pomerleau, & Giordani, 1997; Epstein, Conners, Sitarenios, & Erhardt, 1998), Bipolar Disorder (e.g., Addington & Addington, 1998; Fleming, 1991), dementia (e.g., D. Alexander, 1973; Mendez, Cherrier, & Perryman, 1997), schizophrenia (e.g., Bergman, O'Brien, Osgood, & Cornblatt, 1995; Strauss, Novakovic, Tien, Bylsma, & Pearlson, 1991; Wolgin, 1994), TBI (e.g., Arcia & Gualtieri, 1994; Gribble, 1989), other medical conditions (e.g., L. Alexander, Hightower, Anderson, & Snow, 1980; Costa, Arruda, Stern, Somerville, & Valentino, 1997; Goldstein, Rosenbaum, & Taylor, 1997; Umans & Pliskin, 1998), and other psychiatric disorders (e.g., D. Byrne, 1976; Sax, 1995). This literature is summarized in Table 7.1 on pages 244 through 255.

Unlike studies of children and adolescents, studies of groups of adults with ADHD are in the distinct minority, and psychiatric groups with nondevelopmental disorders (e.g., schizophrenia) and groups of adults with dementia dominate the adult literature. Most of the groups studied are differentiated by their CPT performance, but, as we noted with children and adolescents, algorithms that correctly classify individuals from various pathological groups across the multiple groups studied are not available. Clinicians cannot, on the basis of this literature, take a set of CPT scores and say with confidence that the individual assessed has schizophrenia, dementia, Bipolar Disorder, TBI, ADHD, a history of toxic exposure, or seizure disorder, among the other potential diagnoses that have been studied. Despite this drawback, the CPT does remain useful in assessing and documenting symptoms associated with disturbances of the self-regulating systems of the brain throughout adulthood. The review that follows parallels to a great extent the format of Chapter 6. Even though ADHD is far less frequently studied with adults relative to children and adolescents, we will begin by reviewing the adult ADHD-CPT literature.

CPTs AND ADULT ADHD

The most frequent behavioral symptoms associated with ADHD in childhood include problems with inattention/concentration, hyperactivity, and impaired executive control, depending on subtype. The extent to which these same behaviors are manifest in adulthood has been researched, but to a lesser degree than in children. Similarly, whereas studies involving groups of children and adolescents with a diagnosis of ADHD dominate the youth literature on CPT performance (93 of 162 studies), we were able to locate only eight studies that included adults with ADHD. Roy-Byrne et al. (1997) compared three groups of adults (ADHD with CD, ADHD, and a non-ADHD clinic group) and found no difference in CPT performance using the visual not-X-CPT. This study represents an anomaly in the literature thus far. The remaining seven studies all found differences among the ADHD and control groups, typically on multiple CPT variables.

Using the same not-X-CPT paradigm as Roy-Byrne et al. (1997), two other studies found differences between adults with ADHD and presumably healthy adults (Barkley et al., 1996; Epstein et al., 1998). Barkley and colleagues compared the performance of adults with ADHD ($N = 25$) to a normal control group of adults ($N = 25$). Results indicated that their ADHD group made significantly more omission errors and commission errors than were made by the control group. Additionally, the ADHD group had greater variability of reaction time and a lower sensitivity (d') score relative to the control group. Epstein et al. compared 60 adults with ADHD to a control group of 72 individuals and reported similar findings. Consistent with the results of Barkley et al., the ADHD group committed more errors of omission and commission and displayed lowered sensitivity (d') relative to the control group. However, Epstein and colleagues did not find the increased variability of reaction time that Barkley et al. found with their sample (but did in another study; see discussion following).

Three studies used a visual AX-CPT paradigm. Garfinkel et al. (1986) and Klee, Garfinkel, and Beauchesne (1986) both reported higher rates of omission and commission errors by adults with ADHD relative to a control group. Epstein et al. (1997) used a variation of the AX-CPT paradigm to study reaction time. Although not finding significant differences with the not-X-CPT for reaction time in their later study (Epstein et al., 1998), using the modified AX-CPT Epstein and colleagues (1997) reported increased reaction time among their large group of adults with ADHD

($N = 143$). The authors also found that the reaction time of the ADHD groups increased as the ISI increased.

The two remaining studies of adults with ADHD used the visual X-CPT paradigm. Downey et al. (1997) found increased errors of omission and errors of commission based on the normative data for the TOVA; problems with comparisons to normative data were discussed in Chapter 6. Seidman et al. (1998) is the only study that included both a clinic control group (adults with schizophrenia) and a normal control group. Using both a standard and a degraded X-CPT, Seidman and colleagues reported that the ADHD group had more errors of omission and of commission than did the normal control group, but fewer errors than a group of chronic schizophrenic patients. Differences were such that although the schizophrenic group could be differentiated from the control group based on the CPT results, the ADHD group could not be differentiated from either the control group or the schizophrenic group.

Based on these studies, adults with ADHD seem to be more impaired on CPT performance than their child and adolescent counterparts. ADHD is a lifelong disorder for some but not others, and it may be that individuals with lifelong ADHD are more (or at least more consistently) impaired on most CPT paradigms. The most consistent finding for children and youth with ADHD was increased errors of commission. In contrast, for adults with ADHD, impairments on CPT tasks were almost consistently more pervasive and included errors of omission, errors of commission, and most likely decreased reaction time (especially at ISIs above 400 ms) as well as decreased sensitivity (d'). Notably, all of the studies used a visual format for stimulus presentation and only one study included a psychiatric comparison group. Further, none of the studies addressed subtype issues of ADHD, possibly reflecting disagreement in the existence of subtypes of ADHD in adulthood.

CPTs AND ADULT SCHIZOPHRENIA

Schizophrenia is by far the most often studied of the adult disorders via CPT performance. Of the 91 studies of adults with some form of psychopathology, 49 (54%) contained at least one group of individuals with a diagnosis of schizophrenia. That attentional problems are one facet of the cognitive impairments associated with schizophrenia and related disorders (e.g., schizotypal personality disorder) has been established for some time (Nuechterlein & Dawson, 1984). This is understandable given that the dopaminergic system is believed to be involved in the pathophysiology of schizophrenia (J.D. Cohen & Servan-Schreiber, 1993; Cornblatt & Keilp, 1994; Sadock & Sadock, 2000). On the basis of attentional impairment as a core deficit of schizophrenia, it has been suggested that attention, as measured by the CPT, may be a potential phenotypic marker for schizophrenia (Cornblatt & Keilp, 1994; Cornblatt, Winters, et al., 1989; Keefe, Silverman, & Cornblatt, 1992). This perception of the CPT as a gold standard for schizophrenia in adults is fraught with the same problems discussed with relation to ADHD in children and youth (see Chapter 6): CPT paradigms are sensitive to just too many disorders that involve disturbances of the self-regulatory mechanisms of the brain.

As with ADHD, schizophrenia and related disorders come in multiple forms. Few of the CPT studies made any attempt at subtyping the schizophrenia samples, but some did. Rarely did it seem to matter, however. Groups with a diagnosis of schizophrenia showed impairment on CPT performance in 46 of the 49 studies. Attention problems were the most pervasive set of deficits seen and occurred in most of the CPT paradigms employed. At the same time, increased errors of omission and commission were common as well. Some of the studies addressed potential confounds of age, medication status, remission status, and etiology (i.e., familial or sporadic). The more interesting of these studies are reviewed below.

AGE AND MEDICATION EFFECTS

Recency of diagnosis or length of illness appears to have little effect on CPT performance. Bergman et al. (1995) compared a group of young adults who had recently received a diagnosis of schizophrenia (mean age of 18) to a group of adults with chronic schizophrenia more than twice their age (mean age of 38) on an IP-CPT. Both groups showed significant impairment. Interestingly, the chronic group improved their CPT performance on medication, but the younger group did not.

Asarnow and MacCrimmon (1978) compared adults with active, chronic schizophrenia with adults with schizophrenia who were in remission and with a normal control group on an X-CPT. Both schizophrenia groups made more errors of omission and commission than did the control group. The interesting finding, however, was that the group designated as in remission performed more poorly (i.e., made more errors) than the active schizophrenia group in a distractor condition. Given that remission is usually accomplished after therapeutic levels of medication have been attained, one wonders if this could be a medication (i.e., sedation) effect.

Earle-Boyer et al. (1991) compared medicated and nonmedicated schizophrenics to each other and a control group on a visual X-CPT and an auditory X-CPT. Both groups of schizophrenics performed worse than the control group on all tasks. The medicated group outperformed the nonmedicated group on only one task. The nonmedicated group made more commission errors on nonlexical stimuli than the medicated group. Such an outcome is contrary to arguments that left hemisphere attentional deficits are more prominent in schizophrenia, especially in times of florid illness (see Strauss et al., 1991, for a brief review).

Several other studies have found no differences in CPT performance between groups of medicated and nonmedicated schizophrenics, although both groups consistently deviate from normal control groups. Harvey et al. (1990) and Serper, Bergman, and Harvey (1990), both using an AX-CPT paradigm, reported impaired performance in both groups relative to their control group. In neither study was there an indication of better performance by the medicated group. The potential confound of neuroleptic treatment on attention and executive control as measured by CPTs is discussed in more detail in Chapter 8.

FAMILIAL SCHIZOPHRENIA

As discussed in Chapter 6, a number of studies investigated the CPT performance of children of individuals with schizophrenia. Additional studies have been done with adult relatives of individuals with schizophrenia, with similar findings of decreased attentional ability (e.g., Chen, Hsiao, Hsiao, & Hwu, 1998). In addition, several studies have addressed the issue of CPT performance by familial versus nonfamilial or sporadic cases of schizophrenia. Roy, Flaum, Gupta, Jaramillo, and Andreasen (1994) studied 68 adults with familial schizophrenia and 62 with sporadic schizophrenia. Using an AX-CPT, Roy and colleagues found that both groups were equally impaired in their CPT performance. E. Walker and Shaye (1982), with a considerably smaller sample ($N = 12$ in each group), reported that adults with familial schizophrenia evidenced more overall errors on an AX-CPT than those with sporadic schizophrenia. Given only two such studies with clearly conflicting results, little else can be gleaned from this work. This is an area for future clarification with potential clinical heuristic payoffs.

ACTIVE SCHIZOPHRENIA AND CASES IN REMISSION

In the context of reviewing medication effects on the CPT performance of patients with schizophrenia, we touched on differences between active cases and cases of schizophrenia designated as in remission. Several studies have examined these groups (Asarnow & MacCrimmon, 1978; Wohlberg & Kornetsky, 1973) and found few disparities in their CPT performance when compared to each other. For example, Wohlberg and Kornetsky, using an AX-CPT, reported that their group of schizophrenics in remission made more errors of commission than a control group in standard and in distractor conditions; the schizophrenic group made more errors of omission only during the distractor condition. Thus, schizophrenia, whether active or in remission, results in impaired performance on the CPT relative to a normal control group, with few differences attributable to the status of the schizophrenia.

COMPARISON WITH OTHER GROUPS

Using AX- and X-CPT tasks, Strauss et al. (1991) compared the performance of adults with schizophrenia to those with a diagnosis of a Bipolar Disorder. Results indicated that there were no shifts in lateralized attentional deficits in schizophrenics. Further, CPT results could not differentiate the schizophrenic group from the Bipolar Disorder group, as both groups evidenced impairment overall on attentional measures relative to a normal control group. Addington and Addington (1998) also compared adults with schizophrenia to those with a Bipolar Disorder with similar results. Craig (1983) compared the performance of adults with schizophrenia (acute) on admission to that of adults diagnosed with Borderline Personality Disorder. Results indicated that both groups were impaired relative to the control group. Obiols et al. (1992) compared 39 adults with schizophrenia to 35 adults with Schizotypal Personality Disorder and 33 presumably healthy adults. The only significant difference found was between the schizophrenic group and the control group for sensitivity (d'); the performance of the schizotypal group was not significantly different from either group.

SUMMARY

Schizophrenia produces broad deficits in CPT performance that tend to be the most severe of those seen across many diagnostic groups, excluding acute, severe TBI patients and moderate mental retardation (and disorders that include mental retardation). Family members of individuals with schizophrenia tend to perform more poorly on many CPT variables relative to normal controls, but perform quite a bit better than the family member with schizophrenia. Even adults with a history of schizophrenia designated as in remission at the time of testing show clear deficits on most CPT paradigms, supporting the involvement of a common underlying neural system, or at least shared components, to schizophrenia and attentional and executive control processes. On the other hand, the presence of Schizotypal Personality Disorder does not predict CPT deficits.

CPTs AND BIPOLAR DISORDER

Several studies have examined the CPT performance of patients diagnosed with a Bipolar Disorder, but with differing results. As already mentioned, Addington and Addington (1998) compared a group of 40 adults with Bipolar Disorder to same-sized groups of adults with schizophrenia and a normal control group. Although the bipolar group scored between the performance levels of the schizophrenic group and the normal group, the only significant difference occurred between the schizophrenic group and the control group. In contrast, Fleming (1991) compared 17 adults with Bipolar Disorder who were in a manic phase to 16 age-matched control subjects. In this study, the bipolar individuals had significantly lower overall hit rates, lower sensitivity scores (d'), and made more commission errors than the control group. When manic states were in remission, CPT scores improved. Results are thus somewhat mixed for adults with Bipolar Disorder, with the implication that CPT performance is impaired during manic episodes. Impairment during psychotic episodes would be expected based on the overall body of literature specific to schizophrenia.

CPTs AND THE DEMENTIAS

A few studies have assessed the CPT performance of myriad individuals with dementia. Several used clearly defined diagnostic groups; another used a melange of individuals simply designated as demented. Designation has mattered very little in the outcome of the studies thus far. Given the overall broad deficits that are produced by nearly all types of dementia and the severity with which they can afflict higher cognitive functions, one would naturally anticipate a variety of impairments in the CPT performance of adults with dementia. Generally, this has been found. Attentional mechanisms that also are affected adversely in normal aging (e.g., Faust & Balota, 1997) seem particularly affected in adults with dementia. As early as 1973 (D. Alexander), a heterogeneous group of adults with senile dementia demonstrated increased inaccuracies relative not only to normal controls but to a group of heterogeneous psychiatric patients as well. More recently, Mendez et al. (1997) reported increased error rates and slower reaction times among adults with Alzheimer's and a more general dementia group relative to a control group that was more than three years older than the general dementia group. Attentional deficits in several conditions were noted for older adults even with very mild early-stage dementia of the Alzheimer's type (Faust & Balota, 1997).

One study (Hart, Wade, Calabrese, & Colenda, 1998) compared a group of patients with Parkinson's disease (PD) to a group of normal controls and a group of older subjects with a diagnosis of Major Depressive Disorder. As with schizophrenia, one component of the underlying pathophysiology of PD is the dopaminergic system (although the form of pathology differs radically); another component is the basal ganglia. With the involvement of the basal ganglia, PD produces resting tremors and motor incoordination. In some cases, PD also produces an early, but then static, dementia. In other cases, the Parkinsonian dementia is progressive. Not all individuals with PD develop a concomitant dementia, however. Based on the Hart et al. study with a visual AX-CPT, the PD group made more errors of commission than either the depressed group or the normal control group, but made fewer errors of omission than the depressed group. However, before one can draw clear conclusions regarding the association of PD to CPT performance, groups of adult with PD with and without an accompanying dementia must be studied, and those with static versus progressive dementias must be contrasted. Given the motor incoordination and tremors associated with PD, further study of differences in reaction time and the frequency of multiple responses as CPT variables may be useful. The association of various medications in the treatment of PD involving multiple psychoactive drugs requires study (e.g., an individual with PD may be taking amantadine, sinemet, haloperidol, and an antidepressant drug along with beta blockers or other cardiovascular agents, all of which may influence CPT performance). Several CPT paradigms should be employed as well, particularly an auditory paradigm.

CPTs AND TBI IN ADULTS

The two most common complaints of individuals with closed head injury or TBI are deficits in attention and concentration and in memory. As noted in Chapter 5, CPT paradigms are sensitive to the attentional deficits of individuals with dementia. In the six studies of adult TBI patients found in our review, deficits associated with TBI status occurred in all six studies whether the study used an X- or an AX-CPT. For example, Burg et al. (1995) reported mild to moderate deficits on vigilance and distractibility tasks using the AX-CPT. Ringholz (1989), also using the AX-CPT paradigm, reported that adults with focal TBI (a dorsolateral group and an orbital group) performed more poorly on all CPT variables except vigilance. Rosvold et al. (1956) tested adults with TBI on both an X- and an AX-CPT task; results indicated that their TBI group performed more poorly on all CPT variables, with worsening of performance by the TBI group when going from the X- to the AX-CPT. Overall, their TBI group performed more poorly on both tasks than two groups of adults with mental retardation (an organic group and an idiopathic group).

Rueckert and Grafman (1996) compared adults with focal right and left frontal TBI on an X-CPT task and found both to have performance decrements, although the right frontal group was found to be more impaired than the left. Gribble (1989) compared two TBI groups (ataxic and nonataxic) to each other and a normal control sample on an X-CPT task.

The two TBI groups did not differ from each other, but both groups demonstrated slower reaction time relative to the control group. Arcia and Gualtieri (1994), also using an X-CPT, found their TBI group to display significantly slower reaction time than a control group and an adult ADHD group. The TBI group also made more total errors (omission plus commission) than the normal control group.

Based on these studies, it appears that the attentional deficits of individuals with TBI are either more pronounced or more readily detectable as the complexity of the CPT paradigm increases. As such, the CPT may be useful in evaluating threshold effects of TBI. Head injury is obviously a widely varying phenomenon with multiple levels of severity and outcome. Although difficult to apply cleanly and clearly in every case, there are criteria for classification of TBI cases into categories such as mild, moderate, and severe (Raymond, Bennett, Hartlage, & Cullum, 1999). It would be useful to study the performance of individuals with TBI across these different classifications on multiple CPT paradigms. Correlations with other variables such as Glasgow Coma Scale scores (Teasdale & Jennett, 1974) would also be of interest in these studies. We suspect that CPTs may be sensitive not only to persistent attentional deficits so common among TBI cases but also to the slowed processing in the form of increased delays in reaction time that is common in the early, acute phases of recovery.

CPTs AND ENVIRONMENTAL NEUROTOXIC EXPOSURE

With the complexity of the functional systems that subserve attention and executive function, it is likely that any neurotoxin that could potentially result in a compromise to the CNS could result in impairment on CPTs as well. A few studies have examined the CPT performance of adults with a history of exposure to one or more environmental neurotoxins. One needs to be particularly careful in interpreting this research due to the poor quality of the designs and issues with proper control groups and specific exposure agents. Studies of adults exposed to neurotoxins do report abnormal CPT performance, but the types of abnormalities are inconsistent from study to study and only a few studies appear in the literature.

Estrin et al. (1987), using a visual X-CPT, compared a group of eight individuals with a history of ethylene oxide exposure and eight age-matched controls. They found that the exposed group had lower levels of CPT performance overall relative to the controls. Despite the very small *n* of eight, they go on to report a significant negative dose-response relationship (i.e., as exposure increased, CPT performance decreased). Morrow, Robin, Hodgson, and Kamis (1992) also used an X-CPT to assess a larger, more heterogeneous group of adults with neurotoxic exposure ($n = 40$). They reported slower reaction time and decreased sensitivity (d') of the exposed group relative to the control group. A vigilance decrement was noted as well, such that the exposure group tended to perform progressively more poorly as the CPT progressed. Tsai and Chen (1996) employed an X-CPT as in the studies noted above. In their study of styrene-exposed individuals only CPT scores, when entered into a regression equation, contributed significantly to discriminating between the exposed group and the nonexposed controls. Morrow (1994) employed an interesting design that intermingled X- and AX-CPT paradigms with a group of 47 individuals with histories of chronic exposure to organophosphates (principally, aromatic and aliphatic hydrocarbons). All individuals in their exposed group met criteria for a mild toxic encephalopathy prior to being tested. Results indicated slower reaction times for the exposed group, which, due to the pattern of slowing seen across the mixed CPT tasks, was interpreted as a disruption of the initial orienting component of attentional processes.

Neurotoxins certainly have the potential to disrupt attention and related self-regulatory mechanisms of the brain, as seen on CPT paradigms. However, the different components of CPT performance that are evidenced as impaired across studies, the small number of studies, and the lack of variety in CPT paradigms applied as yet lead us to be cautious about what latent neural structures are being affected. Careful attention needs to be given to the specific neurotoxin under study and results need to be reported in more detail than has been provided in these studies. That the variables assessed by CPTs can undergo significant disruption as a function of toxic exposure seems evident. At the same time, however, CPTs are sensitive to a host of disorders that must be ruled out in these cases, and careful screening of exposed groups for other potential problems, especially those occurring premorbidly, is necessary to draw appropriate conclusions about the effects of the neurotoxins.

CPTs AND RENAL DISEASE

Medical disorders that lead to CNS compromise and related symptoms will likely impact CPT performance as well. For example, several studies have examined the performance of adults on hemodialysis using two CPT paradigms but with conflicting outcomes. L. Alexander et al. (1980) assessed 28 adults on dialysis (ages 18 to 69 years) using an X-CPT paradigm. They reported a main effect for reaction time, with their dialysis group performing more slowly than the control group. There were no differences in errors of omission or commission across groups. In contrast to these results, Umans and Pliskin (1998) used a not-X-CPT paradigm to compare adults on dialysis to a same-age control group. They found no differences on any CPT variable and interpreted this to reflect an absence of neurocognitive deficits in adults with renal failure who are receiving dialysis. Although neither study had an impressive sample size, Umans and Pliskin had a substantially smaller *n* than did L. Alexander and colleagues, with only 10 per group (dialysis vs. controls) compared to 28 per group. Small sample sizes obviously make it more difficult to detect effects. However, Umans and Pliskin and L. Alexander et al. also used different CPT paradigms and, as we have seen in other research, different CPT paradigms and variables can produce different results. Renal failure certainly has implications for cognitive function. Dialysis may ameliorate the neurocognitive deficits associated with renal failure, but it also may induce a variety of symptoms including problems associated with psychotic symptoms (Sadock & Sadock, 2000). There are a variety of reasons to suspect that dialysis patients may show impairment on at least some CPT paradigms but to what extent and on which variables remains unclear. This is another avenue of fruitful exploration for CPT-related research.

CPTs AND OTHER GROUPS

A number of other studies suggest impaired CPT performance by a number of different groups. The findings of these studies may provide suggestions of other issues that could have an impact on CPT performance; however, many of these studies are old and use what are now archaic terms and diagnostic categories. For example, D. Byrne (1976) compared a then-termed neurotic depression group and a psychotic depression group to a control sample using an auditory AXB-CPT paradigm (a rarely used CPT paradigm). In this study, both depressed groups performed more poorly than the control group. The neurotic group, although impaired, outperformed the psychotic group on some variables but not others. The neurotic group actually had more errors of commission than the psychotic group, and the psychotic group's performance deteriorated more over time. More recent studies (e.g., J.D. Cohen, Barch, Carter, & Servan-Schreiber, 1999) failed to find impairment among groups diagnosed with Major Depressive Disorder. Neither of these latter studies, however, included depressed individuals with psychotic features.

As discussed in Chapters 5 and 6, individuals with seizure disorder tend to be consistently impaired on multiple CPT paradigms. For adults, Goldstein et al. (1997) and Mirsky et al. (1960) reported decreases in CPT performance on both visual X- and AX-CPTs. In general, the seizure disorder groups have slower reaction times and make more errors. Type of seizure disorder matters, such that nonfocal seizures seem to produce larger and more pervasive deficits on both X- and AX-CPTs.

Other groups that tend to be impaired on various CPT paradigms include adults with Chronic Fatigue syndrome, mental retardation, metachromatic leukodystrophy, and Borderline Personality Disorder. We

Table 7.1

CPT Studies with Groups of Adults

Study	CPT Type	N	Age Range or Mean (SD) in Years	Sample Types	Results
Addington & Addington, 1998	X-Visual	40 40 40	32.6 (9.2) 38.5 (11.0) 32.6 (11.3)	Schizophrenic Bipolar Control	The schizophrenic group obtained significantly lower sensitivity (d') scores relative to the control group. Although the bipolar group d' score was also lower than the control group, the difference was not significant.
D.D. Alexander, 1973	X-Visual AX-Visual	14 40 20	60–70	Dementia Controls Psychiatric control	The senile dementia group performed comparable to the other two groups on the X-CPT, but accuracy was impaired for the dementia group on the AX-CPT relative to the other groups.
L. Alexander et al., 1980	X-Visual	28 28	18–69	Dialysis patients Control	There was a main effect for group for reaction time only with the dialysis group performing significantly slower than the control group. There was also a main effect for age. No between-group differences were found for correct hits, commission errors, or total errors.
Arcia & Gualtieri, 1994	X-Visual	26 23 25	29.93 (11.02) 23.42 (9.30) 27.12 (9.80)	Closed head injury (CHI) ADD Control	The CHI group had a significantly slower reaction time relative to the controls. The ADD group was quicker than the CHI group, but slower than the control group; differences were not significant. For total errors, both the CHI and ADD groups demonstrated impaired performance relative to the control group.
Asarnow & MacCrimmon, 1978	X-Visual	20 20 20	37.0 42.8 35.1	Schizophrenic: acute Schizophrenic: remitted Control	Both acute and remitted schizophrenics made more errors of omission and commission than controls (p < .02). There was no difference between the acute versus remitted groups on omission or commission. In the distractor conditions, the remitted group demonstrated more impairment than either the acute or the control group (p < .10).
Barkley et al., 1996	Not-X-Visual	25 23	25	ADHD Control	The ADHD group had significantly more omission and commission errors, lower sensitivity (d'), and greater variability relative to the control group.
Bergman et al., 1995	IP-Visual	9 16	18.6. (3.7) 38.4 (10.5)	Schizophrenic: young Schizophrenic: chronic	Both groups had poorer performance in distraction condition. The chronic group demonstrated improvement with medication, but the younger group did not.

Study	Task	N	Age (SD)	Group	Results
Bowen et al., 1994	X-Visual	30 15	36.0 (8.6) 31.0 (10.7)	Schizophrenic Control	There were significant between-group differences on CPT with standard and degraded stimuli for omission errors.
Buchanan et al., 1997	X-Visual	20 56 27	34.0 (5.9) 34.8 (7.2) 36.1 (7.0)	Schizophrenic: deficit Schizophrenic: nondeficit Control	Significant main effect was found for the group due to decrease in ability to sustain attention. Sensitivity (d') was significantly lower in the deficit group and the control group than in the nondeficit group. No main effect of group on response bias (B) and no interaction effect was found with the main effect of time found for B with subjects being more conservative in the second half of the CPT. Significant group effect was found for reaction time with both deficit and nondeficit groups having longer reaction times than the control group.
Buchsbaum et al., 1990	X-Visual	13 18	28.0 (6.7) 26.2 (8.1)	Schizophrenic Control	The main effect for the group was found with CPT performance better in the control group than in the schizophrenic group.
Buchsbaum, Haier, et al., 1992	X-Visual	18 20	29.6 (7.12) 27.1 (6.4)	Schizophrenic Control	The schizophrenic group performed more poorly than controls based on SDT measures ($p < .034$). Correlations between hypofrontality ratios and sensitivity (d') were not significant for either group.
Burg et al., 1995	AX-Visual	30 25	40.0 41.0	Traumatic brain injury Controls	The TBI group demonstrated mild to moderate deficits on vigilance and distractibility tasks.
D.G. Byrne, 1976	AXB-Auditory	10 10 10	23–47	Depressed/neurotic Depressed/psychotic Control	The control group exhibited higher sensitivity (d') than both depressed groups. The neurotic group did significantly better than the psychotic group. The neurotic group made significantly more false positive errors than the other groups while the psychotic group had a significantly higher decrement rate over time as compared to the other groups.
Chen et al., 1998	X-Visual	60 148 20 42	30.7 (8.0) 46.9 (16.2) 32.3 (7.6) 38.4 (14.8)	Schizophrenic probands Relatives of schizophrenics Control probands Relatives of controls	The sensitivity scores (d') of the relatives of schizophrenics was lower than that of the relatives of controls, but higher than that of the schizophrenic probands. Depending on whether the CPT version used was standard or degraded, 45% to 63% of the schizophrenic group obtained d' with z-scores of −3.00, 19% to 34% of the relatives of schizophrenic group obtained d' with z-scores of −3.00. None of the control probands or relatives of control had z-scores of −3.00.

(continued)

Table 7.1 Continued

Study	CPT Type	N	Age Range or Mean (SD) in Years	Sample Types	Results
J.D. Cohen et al., 1999	AX-Visual	53 25 31	36.3 (8.7) 32.7 (10.0) 33.2 (7.7)	Schizophrenic Major depression Control	The schizophrenic group demonstrated impairment (misses, false alarms) relative to both other groups.
R.M. Cohen et al., 1987	X-Auditory	27 16	32.9 (12.2) 27.5 (6.6)	Control Schizophrenic	Overall, the schizophrenic group was impaired relative to the control group.
Cohler et al., 1977	X-Visual	26 14	31–35 26–30 26–30	Schizophrenic Depressed Control	No between-group differences in performance for omission or commission errors found.
Costa et al., 1997	X-Auditory XX-Auditory	11 11	33.I (5.8) 32.7 (6.0)	HIV+ Control	No between-group differences were found for accuracy or reaction time on either CPT.
Craig, 1983	X-Visual	14 14 12	25.1 (6.4) 26.0 (7.0) 23.9 (4.7)	Borderline Schizophrenic Normal	The borderline group was more impaired than the controls ($p < .05$) and better than the schizophrenic group (not significant) for all variables on admission. The schizophrenic group was more impaired than normals on all variables ($p < .05$) on admission. The reaction time standard deviation of the schizophrenic group differed from normals at $p < .01$. Differences at time of discharge had attenuated relative to admission with significant differences only for reaction time and reaction time standard deviation for both borderline and schizophrenic groups, and for late errors in the schizophrenic group.
Dalteg et al., 1997	X-Visual	50 39 34 24 14 12 33 25 96 101	25–52	Prisoners: Swedish Prisoners: Norwegian Schizophrenic: noncriminal Reading disability Brain lesion Schizophrenic: criminal Psychology students Arrested Control Previous prisoner group	There was a significant group and group-by-type-of-distractor effect for sensitivity (d′) as well as for speed (reaction time). The noncriminal schizophrenic and brain lesion groups were more accurate when letters were used as distractors. Psychology students had the fastest reaction times; the criminal schizophrenic group had the slowest reaction times; the reading disability group was slower than other groups as well. All prisoner groups were faster when the distractors were letters.
Downey et al., 1997	X-Visual	78	33.24 (11.39)	ADHD, ADHD with comorbid disorder	Omission errors were significantly higher relative to standardization sample for TOVA, but commission errors were within normal limits.

Study	Task	N	Age	Group	Findings
Earle-Boyer et al., 1991	X-Visual X-Auditory	17 17 19	31.12 (7.12) 31.64 (8.80) 28.40 (8.32)	Schizophrenic: unmedicated Schizophrenic: medicated Control	The control group's performance on the CPT was notably better with few errors. The unmedicated group made more commission errors on nonlexical stimuli than the control or medicated groups. Both schizophrenic groups had more errors on lexical stimuli.
Epstein et al., 1997	AX-Visual	91 52	18–71	ADHD Non-ADHD	The ADHD group had longer reaction time relative to the control group; reaction time increased as the ISI increased.
Epstein et al., 1998	Not-X-Visual	60 72	35 (11) 25 (10)	ADHD Control	The ADHD group made more omission and commission errors, and had lower sensitivity (d') scores. No difference was found for reaction time or variability of reaction time.
Estrin et al., 1987	X-Visual	8 8	54 52	Ethylene oxide exposure No exposure	The exposed group performance was lower on the CPT. There was a significant dose-response relationship associated with increased impairment on the CPT.
Faust & Balota, 1997	X-Visual	25 35 51	21.2 (2.6) 72.4 (7.3) 76.7 (8.6)	Younger control Alzheimer's Older control	Significant between-group differences were found for reaction time. The younger control group was significantly faster than both older groups.
Finkelstein et al., 1997	AX-Visual	24 20 44 14 15	29.0 (8.9) 32.4 (8.2) 27.8 (7.0) 28.6 (7.8) 30.5 (9.9)	Schizophrenic: neuroleptic naïve Schizophrenic: neuroleptic withdrawn Control Patients, siblings	There were significant overall group effects on sensitivity (d') and commission errors, but not for omission or response bias (B). The neuroleptic withdrawn group had lower d' scores and more commission errors than the neuroleptic naïve group; both the neuroleptic naïve and neuroleptic withdrawn groups had significantly lower d' at baseline and follow-up compared to controls. Both the neuroleptic naïve and neuroleptic withdrawn groups were more conservative (B) than controls. The neuroleptic withdrawn group had more commission errors than controls but the neuroleptic naïve group did not differ significantly from the controls. Both the neuroleptic naïve and controls made more errors of omission at baseline and follow-up. In comparison with other patients, siblings, and controls, schizophrenics had lower d' than controls but not siblings.

(continued)

Table 7.1 Continued

Study	CPT Type	N	Age Range or Mean (SD) in Years	Sample Types	Results
Fleming, 1991	X-Visual	17 16	34.1 (9.7) 33.7 (11.5)	Bipolar-manic Control	There was a main effect for group for hit rate and sensitivity ($p <$ .0001) with lower hit rate and d′ for bipolar group. There was also a main effect for commission errors by group ($p < .01$) and for group by time (manic state vs. remission).
Franke et al., 1994	IP-Visual	35 26 35	27.9 26.2 27.2	Schizophrenic Siblings Control	There was a significant main effect of group with the schizophrenic group showing poorer discriminative ability. There was also a main effect of stimulus type and task demand as well as an interaction with the schizophrenic group which was more impaired on shapes relative to numbers. The schizophrenic group also showed greater decline in performance with distraction. With the slow task, the schizophrenic group did not demonstrate the level of improvement evidenced by the controls. Although less pronounced, siblings also demonstrated poorer d′ than controls but this was not significant. Response bias (B) was significant with siblings demonstrating poorer performance with shapes when compared to controls.
B.D. Garfinkel et al., 1986	AX-Visual	22 22	19.2 (2.5)	ADD Control	At baseline, the ADD group made significantly more errors on the CPT.
Gilbert, 1995	X-Visual	20 20	64.5 (7.0) 60.7 (7.8)	Adult with child with schizophrenia Control	A significant difference was found in the proportion of poor attenders in the parents with a child with schizophrenia group as compared to control group for Blocks 3 and 4 based on sensitivity (d′).
Goldstein et al., 1997	X-Visual AX-Visual	15 19 19 20	31.7 (11.7) 35.3 (10.9) 28.2 (8.4) 33.1 (12.2)	Generalized seizures (GSP) Temporal lobe epilepsy (TLE) Schizophrenic Control	On the X-CPT, the GSP group had significantly fewer hits than either the control or schizophrenic group; on the AX-CPT, both the GSP and schizophrenic groups had fewer correct hits; the scores for the TLE group were not significantly different from the normal group on either task for correct hits. For both CPTs, the GSP and TLE groups had slower reaction times than normals; the schizophrenic group had slower reaction time than normals only on the AX-CPT.
Golier et al., 1997	IP-Visual	34 15	44.4 (2.2) 39.7 (7.3)	Posttraumatic Stress Disorder Control	No between-group differences were found for response style. Both groups demonstrated more conservative response style (lower B) with distraction and with numbers as compared to shapes as stimuli.

Study	CPT Type	N	Age (SD)	Group	Findings
Gribble, 1989	X-Visual	10 10 10	28.7 (6.47) 30.3 (6.94) 24.8 (4.04)	Ataxic TBI Nonataxic TBI Control	Both the ataxic and nonataxic TBI groups performed slower than the control group. There was no between-group difference found on commission or omission errors. All groups showed slight decrement in performance over time.
Grunebaum et al., 1978	X-Visual	12 18 22	Not reported	Affective psychosis (Unipolar) Schizophrenic Control	The mothers in the depressed group were more likely to have commission errors (false alarms), while the mothers in the schizophrenic group were more likely to make omission errors.
Guich et al., 1989	X-Visual	15 9	27 (6.4) 27.8 (8.9)	Schizophrenic Control	No significant between-group differences were found for sensitivity (d').
Hain et al., 1993	X-Visual	49 27	30.1 (10.8)	Schizophrenic Control	The schizophrenic group performed significantly worse than the control group.
Hart et al., 1998	AX-Visual	11 7 11	65.3 (5.4) 67.0 (10.2) 70.2 (6.6)	Parkinson's Major depression Control	The Parkinson's group demonstrated a greater number of commission errors as compared to the control and depressed groups. In contrast, the depressed group made more omission errors as compared to the control and Parkinson's groups.
Harvey et al., 1990	AX-Visual	14 14 15	39.10 (10.11) 38.00 (7.89) 37.86 (10.43)	Schizophrenic (medicated) Schizophrenic (no medication) Control	Significant differences found for errors of omission and d' suggesting attentional impairment for both schizophrenic groups.
Hazlett et al., 1993	X-Visual	6 6	27.0 (2.2) 26.0 (5.3)	Schizophrenic Control	The performance of the schizophrenic group as measured by sensitivity (d') was poorer than controls but the difference did not reach statistical significance.
Ito et al., 1997	X-Visual	49 43	40.9 (8.6) 40.7 (9.5)	Schizophrenic Control	The schizophrenic group demonstrated impaired performance on both the standard and degraded versions of the CPT for sensitivity (d'), correct hit rate, and commission errors.
M. Katz et al., 1996	X-Visual	18 22	30 (7) 28 (7)	Schizophrenic Control	The schizophrenic group had impaired performance on CPT relative to the control group. Based on PET, thalamic activity during CPT also differed significantly by group.

(continued)

Table 7.1 Continued

Study	CPT Type	N	Age Range or Mean (SD) in Years	Sample Types	Results
Keefe et al., 1997	AX-Visual	43 22	40.9 (11.3) 35.8 (10.3)	Schizophrenic Control	There was a main effect of group for CPT variables of omission, commission, sensitivity (d'), and reaction time. All CPT variables contributed to the discriminant function with 88.1% accuracy for schizophrenic classification and 68.2% for control classification.
Klee et al., 1986	AX-Visual	12 12	20.0 28.8	ADD Control	Significant group differences were found such that the ADD group made more omission errors and obtained a lower summary CPT score. The ADD group also made more commission errors but the difference was not significant.
Kornetsky & Orzack, 1978	X-Visual	25 25	48	Schizophrenic Alcoholic Control	The schizophrenic group demonstrated more impairment than the other groups with 44% of the schizophrenic sample making greater than 4% omission errors. The alcoholic group did not demonstrate impairment, but this may reflect a ceiling problem with the task.
Laidlaw, 1993	AX-Visual	21 21	27.85 24.32	CHI Control	CHI group differed significantly on CPT correct hits, misses, and false alarms as compared to the control group.
Lenzenweger et al., 1991	IP-Visual	32 43	Not reported	Schizotypic Control	The schizotypic group has lower sensitivity (d') scores than the control. Additional analyses revealed that this was the result of lower correct hits.
Mataix-Cols et al., 1997	IP-Visual	35 36	19.4 (2.6) 19.6 (2.2)	High obsessive compulsive Control	The Obsessive Compulsive group had a poorer performance when the CPT task used numbers as compared to letters for hit rate. There was a gender difference found in the high obsessive compulsive group for hits as well. There were no between-group differences found for response style (Beta), random commission errors, or reaction time.
N.F. McGrath, 1985	AX-Visual	25 14	35.4 (9.18) 34.3 (10.39)	Food sensitivity group Control	There were no significant between-group differences at baseline, but differences emerged with food allergy challenge by group and for specific individuals depending on the food.
Mendez et al., 1997	AX-Visual	30 30 30	69.6 72.2 72.9	Dementia Alzheimer's Control	Both dementia groups performed worse than the control group with more errors and slower reaction times.

Study	Task	N	Age	Group	Findings
Mirsky et al., 1960	X-Visual	5	26.20	Temporal lobe epilepsy	The nonfocal group tended to perform more poorly than the temporal lobe group, but the difference did not reach statistical significance.
		5	25.40	Nonfocal epilepsy	
	AX-Visual	39	31.03	Temporal lobe epilepsy	The nonfocal (centrencephalic) group had the poorest performance and was significantly below all other groups. When memory, IQ, and seizure frequency were controlled, continued significant difference was found for the AX-CPT ($p = .03$) with the nonfocal group still showing the most deficits.
		18	32.06	Frontal lobe epilepsy	
		19	28.16	Nonfocal Epilepsy	
		25	31.50	Control	
Mirsky, Ingraham, et al., 1995	AX-Visual	63	32	Adult children of schizophrenics	There was a significant difference between the schizophrenic group and the controls. The adult children were more accurate than the schizophrenic group, but not as accurate as the control group.
		31		Control	
		17		Schizophrenic	
Morrow, 1994	X-Visual	47	38.6 (8.0)	Neurotoxicity	The reaction time for the adults with mild solvent neurotoxicity was slower than the control group.
	AX-Visual	50	37.3 (10.9)	No Exposure	
Morrow et al., 1992	X-Visual	40	39.0	Neurotoxicity	Main effects for the group were found for reaction time and sensitivity (d'). The exposed group decreased in accuracy over time demonstrating a vigilance decrement not observed in the control group.
		40	37.2	Control	
Mussgay & Hertwig, 1990	X-Auditory	24	33.4	Schizophrenic	On all variations of the CPT, the schizophrenic group demonstrated lower sensitivity (d') relative to the alcoholic and control groups. No significant or consistent pattern was found for response style (Beta).
	X-Visual	12	35.8	Alcoholic	
	X-Auditory/Visual	12	35.8	Control	
Nelson et al., 1998	AX-Visual	13	32 (14)	Major depression: psychosis	The CPT performance of the depressed/psychosis and schizophrenic groups was impaired relative to the depressed: no psychosis and control groups. No significant difference was found between the depressed/psychosis and schizophrenic groups or between the depressed: no psychosis and control groups.
		14	34 (12)	Major depression: no psychosis	
		15	34 (10)	Schizophrenic	
		14	28 (11)	Control	
Nestor et al., 1990	X-Visual	22	39.9	Schizophrenic	Significant main effects were found for sensitivity (d') and response style (Beta) for group with the schizophrenic group demonstrating impairment. It was noted that the schizophrenic group demonstrated a significant vigilance decrement over time on task.
		21	39.9	Control	

(continued)

Table 7.1 Continued

Study	CPT Type	N	Age Range or Mean (SD) in Years	Sample Types	Results
Obiols et al., 1992	IP-Visual	39 35 33	27.1 (4.6) 20.4 (1.5) 21.2 (0.4)	Schizophrenic Schizotypic Control	The only significant difference was between the schizophrenic group and the control group for sensitivity (d').
Pandurangi et al., 1994	AX-Visual	41 28	30.02 (6.5) 29.25 (9.0)	Schizophrenic Control	The schizophrenic group had significantly higher mean commission and omission errors. These differences increased as interstimulus interval decreased.
Pass et al., 1980	X-Visual	17 16	28.58 (7.64) 29.06 (9.07)	Schizophrenic Nonschizophrenic	The schizophrenic group made more commission and omission errors and had a longer reaction time than the comparison group.
Pigache, 1996	X-Auditory	8 86	35–53	Schizophrenic Control	CPT results were not found to be good discriminators of schizophrenia.
Quillan, 1994	X-Visual AX-Visual	33 33 33 71	38.7 (9.7) 36.9 (11.3) 35.7 (11.5) 42.3 (11.9)	Medical control Chronic fatigue subsample Control Full chronic fatigue sample	The chronic fatigue group performance was significantly different from the medical control and general control group for mean hit rate and mean reaction time.
Ringholz, 1989	AX-Visual	29 28 25	24.1 (3.5) 26.3 (7.9) 23.2 (3.1)	CHI-dorsolateral CHI-orbital Control	Both CHI groups differed from the control group on all CPT variables except for the vigilance decrement.
Roitman et al., 1997	IP-Visual	30 35 36 20	37.9 (9.9) 39.3 (11.6) 39.9 (10.6) 37.7 (10.2)	Schizotypal Personality Disorder Other personality disorders Schizophrenia Control	The schizotypal group performed worse than all other groups for sensitivity (d'). The schizophrenic group performed worse than the control group on d'.
Rosvold et al., 1956	X-Visual AX-Visual	29 43 25 25	27.3 (8.1) 25.1 (7.8) 31.7 (12.1) 31.5 (13.9)	MR-organic MR-idiopathic Brain damaged Control	Individual's with identified brain damage performed more poorly on CPT. Differences increased from X-CPT to AX-CPT.
Roy et al., 1994	AX-Visual	68 62	35 (9) 32 (8)	Schizophrenia: familial Schizophrenia: sporadic	No significant difference found between groups on omission or commission errors.
Roy et al., 1995	AX-Visual	107 162	32.2 (10.0) 32.7 (10.7)	Schizophrenic: winter born Schizophrenic: nonwinter born	No significant difference was found between groups.

Study	Task type	N	Age (SD)	Group	Results
Roy-Bryne et al., 1997	Not-X-Visual	46 51 46	33.1 (9.7) 36.3 (9.4) 39.5 (11.2)	ADHD/LD Questionable ADHD Not ADHD	No group differences emerged for correct hits, standard error of the reaction time over the course of the test, or standard error across the varying ISI. The questionable ADHD group had a poorer CPT Index as compared to the not ADHD group. The ADHD/LD group did not differ significantly from the other two groups.
Rueckert & Grafman, 1996	X-Visual	11 10 16	45.2 46.6 50.9	Left frontal Right frontal Control	The right frontal group had longer reaction times and missed more targets than either of the other groups. They also demonstrated a greater vigilance decrement than the other groups.
Rund et al., 1992	X-Visual	28 19 17	32.2 (12.0) 38.9 (11.6) 32.2 (9.7)	Schizophrenic Affective Control	The schizophrenic group performance was significantly impaired (less correct hits) as compared to the control group, but there was not a significant difference between the schizophrenic and affective groups. No group differences were found for commission errors.
Sax, 1995	X-Visual	30 31	26 (8.4) 25 (6.4)	Psychiatric Control	The psychiatric group evidenced lower sensitivity (d') following their first psychotic episode as well as in remission. Response style (Beta) differed only when tested immediately following their first psychotic episode.
Sax, Strakowski, Keck, McElroy, et al., 1998	X-Visual	27 31	26 (9) 25 (6)	Affective psychosis Control	At the time of hospitalization, the adults with affective psychosis demonstrated significantly impaired performance relative to the control group. On retest, two months later (in remission), between-group differences no longer were evidenced.
Seidman et al., 1998	X-Visual	18 17 13	27–41 20–46 24–49	Schizophrenic Control ADD/LD	There was no significant between-group difference for response style (Beta) or commission errors. The schizophrenic group made significantly more omission errors and obtained lower sensitivity scores (d') on both the standard and degraded versions of the CPT. The ADD/LD group performance was consistently better than the schizophrenic group, but not as good as the control group; differences were not significant.
Serper et al., 1990	AX-Visual	4 4 4	38.25 (2.22) 39.25 (3.78) 33.75 (6.40)	Schizophrenic: medicated Schizophrenic: No medication Control	Both schizophrenic groups made more total errors than the control group. There was no difference between the two schizophrenic groups.

(continued)

Table 7.1 Continued

Study	CPT Type	N	Age Range or Mean (SD) in Years	Sample Types	Results
Servan-Schreiber et al., 1996	AX-Visual	11 6 21 11	25.7 26.3 32.2 36.6	Schizophrenic: no meds, first episode Schizophrenic: no meds, multiple Schizophrenic: medicated Psychiatric control	All schizophrenic groups demonstrated impaired performance as measured by sensitivity (d') relative to controls. The medicated schizophrenic group and the controls demonstrated improved performance when the ISI was increased (slower), however, this was not evident for the nonmedicated schizophrenic groups.
E.G. Shapiro et al., 1994	X-Visual	9	11–33	Metachromatic leukodystrophy	All subjects were significantly impaired on omission errors, reaction time, and variability on the TOVA.
Strauss et al., 1991	X-Visual AX-Visual	10 6 20	36.9 (8.2) 38.5 (15.5) 33.5 (10.3)	Schizophrenic Bipolar Control	Both the schizophrenic group and the bipolar group demonstrated impaired performance relative to the control group; there was no significant differences between the two clinical groups on CPT performance.
Suslow & Arolt, 1997	X-Visual	18 18 18	31.2 (7.5) 34.8 (11.4) 32.1 (7.5)	Schizophrenic Depressive Control	The schizophrenic group obtained significantly lower sensitivity (d') scores as compared to the control group. The depressed group's d' score was higher than that of the schizophrenic group and lower than the control group, but the differences were not significant.
Teixeira, 1993	AX-Auditory	20 20	19.3 (1.49) 19.1 (1.46)	Depressed Not depressed	No between-group difference was found for accuracy or commission errors.
Tsai & Chen, 1996	X-Visual	41 45	35.9 (9.6) 35.5 (8.9)	Styrene exposed Not exposed	CPT results were found to contribute to regression analysis at a significant level.
Umans & Pliskin, 1998	Not-X-Visual	10 10	61 (16) 62 (10)	Renal Disorder Control	No differences were found in CPT performance indicating an absence of neurocognitive deficits in adults with renal failure who are on hemodialysis.
Wagener et al., 1986	AX-Visual	25 25	24.5 51.2	Schizophrenic Mothers of schizophrenics	The schizophrenic group made significantly more omission errors than their mothers.
M. Wagner et al., 1989	X-Visual	14 14	25 (5) 29 (9)	Schizophrenic Control	The schizophrenic group made significantly more omission errors compared to the control group.
E. Walker & Green, 1982	AX-Visual	34 24	24 33.8	Schizophrenic Affective	The schizophrenic group was found to demonstrate significant attentional deficits relative to the affective group, however, performance was found to correlate significantly with motor proficiency.

Reference	CPT type	N	Age	Diagnostic groups	Results
E. Walker & Shaye, 1982	AX-Visual	12 12 12 12	29.27 28.92 30.10 27.53	Schizophrenic: familial Schizophrenic: nonfamilial Psychiatric control Control	The familial schizophrenic group had more errors than all other groups. For reaction time, the only significant difference was between the familial schizophrenic group and the psychiatric controls with the familial group having significantly slower reaction times.
Weinstein, 1996	AX-Visual	16 13 14	Over 40	Cluster A Personality Disorders Other clusters Control	There was no main effect for group or condition or an interaction effect.
Wohlberg & Kornetsky, 1973	AX-Visual	16 20	18–40	Schizophrenic: remitted Control	For omission errors, there was no significant between-group difference on the standard version, but the schizophrenic group made significantly more omission errors on the distraction condition. For both the standard and distraction conditions, the schizophrenic group made more commission errors.
Wolgin, 1994	X-Visual	24 36	40.01 23.69	Schizophrenic Control	A main effect for group emerged for variables of omission and commission errors, reaction time, and frequency of multiple responses.
Wu et al., 1992	Not described	4 11 15	29.8 (10.3) 30.8 (10.6)	Depressed responders Depressed nonresponders Control	Responders had significantly higher sensitivity (d') scores than both the nonresponders and the control group.

Notes: CPT = Continuous performance test; ADD = Attention Deficit Disorder; ADDH = Attention Deficit Disorder with hyperactivity; ADDWo = Attention Deficit Disorder without hyperactivity; ADHD = Attention-Deficit/Hyperactivity Disorder; CD = Conduct Disorder; LD = Learning disability; Meds = Medications.

assume many other groups would show impairment if the disorder involves higher cognitive deficits, especially if these deficits create or have characteristic attentional problems (of virtually any type) or self-regulating deficits that lead to disinhibitory problems; however, not all disorders were included in the available CPT literature.

SUMMARY

As we observed, based on studies with children and adolescents, CPTs of various types are highly sensitive to the presence of symptoms of a host of adult disorders. As discussed in Chapter 2, CPTs apparently measure multiple aspects of attention, including the initial orienting response, the ability to sustain attention, and the ability to resist distraction. CPTs detect disturbances in these cognitive processes rather well. The cognitive problems detected by the different CPT paradigms we have reviewed do not define a single adult syndrome. Rather, the symptoms detected are components of many disorders and these processes are disturbed in many of the psychopathologies listed in the *DSM-IV*. The diagnostic criteria for ADHD, for example, note the potential for attentional neglect (a disturbance principally of the initial orienting response of attention), inability to sustain attention, and ease of distractibility. Disturbances of various attentional mechanisms are noted also in the description of manic episodes of Bipolar Disorder and in descriptions of many of the anxiety disorders (e.g., PTSD, Acute Stress Disorder, and Generalized Anxiety Disorder), as well as some of the Cluster A personality disorders in the *DSM-IV*. Defects in attentional processes are reported widely in schizophrenia and other psychotic disorders. The various dementias produce broad defects in cognitive processes, including those assessed by CPTs. Medical disorders that impair cognition as well as licit and illicit drug use may have detrimental impact on attentional mechanisms (e.g., see Sadock & Sadock, 2000). The impact of licit and illicit drug use on CPTs is discussed in more depth in Chapter 8.

Table 7.2 has been compiled based solely on the available CPT literature. Comparable to Table 6.2, Table 7.2 lists the disorders that have been studied and shown to produce decrements in CPT performance. As noted above, the *DSM-IV* includes numerous disorders with attentional disturbance as a component. In addition, the *DSM-IV* lists numerous disorders that also include disturbances of impulse and volition that have not been studied via CPT performance (e.g., various phobias, anxiety disorders). Thus, there are likely many other mental disorders and medical conditions that are not listed in Table 7.2 that nevertheless may result in impaired performance on various CPT paradigms.

In contrast to the studies with children and adolescents, very few of the adult studies of CPT performance reported sensitivity and specificity

Table 7.2
Diagnostic Groups of Adults Showing Impairment
and Nonimpairment on CPTs

Impaired	Nonimpaired	Mixed Results/ No Clear Pattern
ADHD (all *DSM-IV* subtypes)	Affective disorders (without psychotic features)	Bipolar Disorder (without psychotic features)
Bipolar Disorder (active manic phase)	Alcoholism (without Korsakoff's disease)	Learning disabilities
Bipolar Disorder (with active psychosis)	Food allergy	Renal Disorder (on dialysis)
Borderline Personality Disorder	Major Depressive Disorder	Schizotypal Personality Disorder
Chronic fatigue syndrome	Posttraumatic Stress Disorder	
Dementia (all types)		
Mental retardation		
Metachromatic leukodystrophy		
Parkinson's disease		
Schizophrenia (all forms)		
Seizure disorders		
Traumatic brain injury		

Notes: ADHD = Attention-Deficit/Hyperactivity Disorder; CPT = Continuous performance test.

analyses. As we noted in the preceding chapter, such analyses, when restricted to one or two pathological groups and a normal control group, are of only minimal utility. In reviewing the many studies of CPT performance, it is clear that CPTs are highly sensitive to disturbances of attentional processes and to disinhibitory states, regardless of their cause. As with children, CPTs with adults are useful at ruling out disorders with characteristic disturbances of attention, impulse control, and volition. However, they are not useful in distinguishing among those many disorders that are characterized by these disturbances. Although it may be tempting to consider attentional deficits as measured by the CPT as a marker for the phenotype of schizophrenia, for example (Cornblatt & Keilp, 1994; Keefe et al., 1992), there are simply too many disorders that occur in adults to allow designation of a specific disorder based on a pattern of CPT performance. Thus, the essential conclusions reached at the end of Chapter 6 apply to adults and adult disorders and their relation to CPT performance as well—at least for now. In the last chapter, we discuss research that could test the utility of CPTs in differential diagnosis.

CHAPTER 8

Monitoring Medication
Effects with Continuous
Performance Tests

PREVIOUS CHAPTERS HAVE dealt with the use of the CPT paradigms in the diagnostic arena. Although diagnostic uses are important and have been the focus of much research, clinicians also need measures that can be used to monitor treatment outcomes reliably over time. Of the interventions available for a number of psychiatric disorders, pharmacotherapy is a frequently used option, regardless of whether or not the disorder involves components of attention and executive control. The use of pharmacotherapy to address, for example, ADHD, comes from implications that various neurotransmitters and neuromodulators are involved in attention and executive control. The use of pharmacotherapy as a treatment program is linked to the growing body of research on the biological etiology of learning and psychiatric disorders. As noted in Chapter 1, the role of catecholamines (i.e., dopamine, norepinephrine) has been emphasized (J. Cohen & Servan-Schreiber, 1992; Levy, 1991); other neurotransmitters, including serotonin, have been implicated to lesser degrees (Zubietka & Alessi, 1993).

The appropriateness of drug treatment with children and adolescents has been a continuing concern (Gadow, 1991). In the past 10 to 20 years, there has been an increase in the use of pharmacological treatment, particularly the use of stimulants, for a variety of disorders (Gadow, 1993; Safer & Krager, 1988, 1989; Safer, Zito, & Pine, 1996). This increase is due, at least in part, to the effectiveness of stimulant medications for individuals with ADHD (Greenhill, Halperin, & Abikoff, 1999). Attention and

Acknowledgment is given to Jennifer J. Moore for her assistance in preparation of this chapter.

258

executive control are not only behaviors often targeted for change, but are behaviors that may be impacted negatively (i.e., as a negative side effect) by a variety of medications. The potential for unforeseen effects on attention and executive control from pharmacotherapy underscores the need for monitoring of medication effects. As a result of the increased use of stimulant medication, the American Academy of Child and Adolescent Psychiatry (1997) advocated for systematic monitoring of medication effects across behavioral domains for children and youth with ADHD. With regard to the potential of pharmacotherapy to affect attention and executive control inadvertently and negatively, Brown and Sawyer (1998) asserted that there is a need for monitoring medication effects regardless of the medication or the disorder being treated. Specialty behavior rating scales (e.g., BASC Monitor for ADHD; Kamphaus & Reynolds, 1998) have been developed to monitor treatment effects, including those of psychopharmacotherapy in children and adolescents. However, the need for medication monitoring not only applies to children and youth, but extends into adulthood if optimal functioning is the desired outcome.

J. Swanson (1985) identified six measures that were found to be appropriate for monitoring pharmacological effects in children. He included objective laboratory measures of inattention as one type of information that can be used to monitor medication effects. The CPT is one group of paradigms for the evaluation of attention and, to a lesser degree, impulsivity that has been used for medication monitoring. The CPT has been described as the most sensitive measure for monitoring medication effects (e.g., Aman, 1978; Kornetsky, 1972). The usefulness of the CPT in monitoring medication effects has been researched extensively. Some advantages and disadvantages of using a CPT to monitor the effects of medication are described by Bergman, Winters, and Cornblatt (1991). One advantage they noted is excellent face validity in that the CPT appears to measure the ability of a person to concentrate on a single task for a certain length of time. Other advantages include the ease of administration, time required, and low cost (Bergman et al., 1991).

A review of the literature yielded a number of meta-analytic studies or qualitative reviews that have included research on specific effects of a single class of medication or of a single medication (e.g., Kavale, 1982, on stimulants; Losier, McGrath, & Klein, 1996, on methylphenidate; Moore, Riccio, Reynolds, & Lowe, 1998, on a variety of medications; Riccio, Moore, et al., 1999, in press, on methylphenidate and other substances). This chapter summarizes the extent to which the CPT has been used to monitor medication effects for the major classes of medication as well as leisure drugs, nicotine, and caffeine (see Table 8.1). Because, historically, it has been suggested that diet and sugars may affect attention (e.g., Feingold,

Table 8.1

Medications and Substances Included in CPT Studies

Psychostimulants	Antidepressants	Neuroleptics
Methylphenidate	Desipramine	Haloperidol
Pemoline	Imipramine	Thioridazine
Dextroamphetamine	MAO inhibitor—Type B	Chlorpromazine
	Venlafaxine	Thiothixene
	Buproprion	Carphenazine
	Fluoxetine	Quetiapine
		Phenothiazine
Anxiolytics (Antianxiety)	Antihypertensives	Anticonvulsants
Alprazolam	Guanfacine	Sodium Valproate
Buspirone	Clonodine	Carbamazepine
Other Medications	Nootropics	Antihistamines/Asthma
Fenfluramine	Oxiracetam	Astemizole
Lithium		Chlorpheniramine
Morphine		Prednizone
Methadone		
Leisure Drugs/ Substances		
Marijuana		
Lysergic acid diethy- lamide		
Caffeine		
Nicotine		
Carbohydrates/sugars		

Notes: MAO = Monamine oxidase.

1975), effects of sugars and carbohydrates on attention and executive control are included here as well.

PSYCHOSTIMULANTS

Of the medication effects on attention that have been studied, the psychostimulants have received the most extensive study (Riccio, Moore, et al., in press). Psychostimulants are believed to act on the catecholaminergic system, as they mimic the actions of dopamine and norepinephrine (Barkley, DuPaul, & Conner, 1999), both of which are believed to be involved in attentional processes (Clark, Geffen, & Geffen, 1987a, 1987b; Levy, 1991; Malone, Kershner, & Swanson, 1994; Pliszka, McCracken, & Maas, 1996). Prescribed psychostimulants generally include methylphenidate (Ritalin), pemoline (Cylert), dextroamphetamine (Dexedrine, d-amphetamine), methamphetamine (Desoxyn), and a combination of amphetamine and dextroamphetamine (Adderall). Psychostimulants or stimulant medications are the most frequently prescribed medication to address the behavioral complex of inattention, impulsivity, and hyperactivity associated with ADHD.

Kavale (1982) performed a meta-analysis on 135 studies to examine the efficacy of stimulant drug treatment for ADHD on 5,300 children. Attention and concentration (e.g., correct hits on the CPT) were found to improve with stimulant medication, and the number of error responses (e.g., commission errors) decreased with stimulant treatment. To monitor medication effects, Porteus Mazes (Porteus, 1959), a task on which impulsive responding and inattention increase error rates, was used in 16 studies with a mean *ES* of 0.54; the CPT was used in eight studies included in Kavale's meta-analysis with a mean *ES* of 0.56. Regardless of the measure of attention, improvement was comparable across studies with the introduction of stimulants (e.g., Aman, 1978; Barkley, 1977; Cantwell & Carlson, 1979; Klorman et al., 1990; Ross & Ross, 1976; Sandoval, 1977; Whalen & Henker, 1976). Consistent with the findings of Kavale, Losier and colleagues (1996) found significant improvement in attention as a result of the introduction of methylphenidate across studies specifically using the CPT.

In their review of 77 studies that addressed the effects of stimulant medications on CPT performance (see Tables 8.2 and 8.3), Riccio, Moore, and colleagues (in press) concluded that of the psychostimulants, methylphenidate is the most studied. Of the methylphenidate studies, the majority indicated improvement on some aspect of CPT performance following methylphenidate administration, and only five studies indicated no significant improvements. Results of studies using CPTs and other psychostimulants (i.e., dextroamphetamine) are generally positive as well. Depending on the stimulant and dosage and the type of CPT, improvement as evidenced by increased correct hits, decreased omission errors, or decreased commission errors. In a majority of studies, reaction time was decreased and, more important, was less variable with stimulant medication (e.g., Klorman et al., 1991). Notably, studies have been done with preschoolers with results similar to those found for older youth and adults (J. Byrne, Bawden, DeWolfe, & Beattie, 1998), suggesting that age is not a factor in assessing improvement with the CPT. Further, results of CPT monitoring over a two-year period continued to show positive effects of stimulant medication on CPT performance (Gadow, Sverd, Sprafkin, Nolan, & Grossman, 1999).

Electrophysiological research supports the belief that these changes in CPT performance reflect differences in CNS functioning (see Table 8.4). Associated changes in ERPs have been found such that methylphenidate resulted in increased magnitude of P3 to the target (e.g., Coons et al., 1981; Fitzpatrick et al., 1992; Klorman, Salzman, Pass,

Table 8.2

Psychostimulant Effects on CPT Performance for Normal/Control Groups

Study	CPT Type	Age Range or Mean (SD) in Years	N	Medication	Dose	Results
Aman et al., 1984	X-Visual	28.3	12	Methylphenidate[a]	0.3 mg/kg	No major effects were found for omission errors or reaction time; significant improvement was found for the commission errors with medication. It was concluded that possible effects were masked because the task was too easy.
Bergman et al., 1991	XX-Visual	6–12	29	Methylphenidate[b] Methylphenidate—SR20[b]	2–10 mg 10 mg	There was improvement in performance with medication.
Conners & Taylor, 1980	X-Visual	7–11	58	Methylphenidate[a] Pemoline[a]	10–60 mg 112.5 mg/day	There was no significant treatment effect for correct hits or commission errors.
Coons et al., 1981: Study 1	X-Visual AX-Visual	23.84 (2.85)	13	Methylphenidate[a]	0.28 mg/kg	For both versions of the CPT, the subjects demonstrated decreased omission and commission errors with medication, but differences were nonsignificant.
Coons et al., 1981: Study 2	X-Visual AX-Visual XX-Visual			Methylphenidate[a]	0.3 mg/kg	Although differences were found for omission and commission errors on all three versions, only the differences in errors on the XX-CPT were significant. This suggests that ceiling effects of the easier tasks may affect the results.
Fitzpatrick et al., 1992	XX-Visual	8.7 (1.33)	19	Methylphenidate[a]	Varied	Significant improvement (i.e., decreased omission and commission errors) was evident in the medication condition; reaction time was faster and less variable as well.
Garfinkel et al., 1986	AX-Visual	19.20 (2.50)	22	D-amphetamine[b]	10 mg	No improvement was noted in CPT performance with medication.
Loeb et al., 1965	X-Auditory	17–28	24	D-amphetamine[a]	10 mg	Sensitivity (d') significantly better with d-amphetamine.
Peloquin & Klorman, 1986	XX-Visual	11.39 (2.03)	18	Methylphenidate[a]	0.3 mg/kg	Significant improvements were found for correct hits, reaction time, and reaction time variability.
Rapoport et al., 1980	AX-Visual	1.10 (2.10) 22.50 (2.80) 22.20 (3.17)	14 15 16	D-amphetamine[b] D-amphetamine[b] D-amphetamine[b]	0.5 mg/kg 35 mg 17.5 mg	Significant improvement (decreased omission errors) was found for the higher doses of medication.

Study	Task	Age	N	Medication	Dose	Results
Riordan et al., 1999	AX-Visual	36.5 (10.8)	15	Methylphenidate[b]	0.5 mg/kg	There was no significant difference found for correct hits or reaction time.
Schechter & Timmons, 1985	AX-Visual	6–12	6	Low amphetamine[b] High amphetamine[b]	1.6 mg 5.0 mg	There was a positive change in omission errors with the low dose, however this was reversed with the high dose. In contrast, there was a positive change in reaction time with the high dose that was not evident with the low does.
Sostek et al., 1980	AX-Visual	10.1	14	Amphetamine[a]	0.5 mg/kg	CPT performance as measured by sensitivity (d′) and response style (Beta) improved with medication.
Weingartner et al., 1980	AX-Visual	10.1	14	Amphetamine[a]	0.5 mg/kg	Results indicated improved attention and better vigilance with treatment.

Notes: [a]Placebo versus medication; [b]Baseline versus medication; CPT = Continuous performance test; IP = Identical pairs; SR20 = Slow release.

Table 8.3

Psychostimulant Effects on CPT Performance for Clinical Populations

Study	CPT Type	Clinical Group	Age Range or Mean (SD) in Years	N	Medications	Dose	Results
Aman et al., 1991	X-Visual	Clinic Referrals	10.3	27	Methylphenidate[a]	0.3 mg/kg	Methylphenidate resulted in a significant decrease in omission errors.
Aman & Turbott, 1991	X-Visual	ADDH	8.3 (1.93)	26	Methylphenidate[b]	0.7 mg/kg	Both omission and commission errors were significantly improved with medication.
Aman et al., 1993	X-Visual	ADHD/MR	8.8	28	Methylphenidate[a]	0.4 mg/kg	Results indicated improvement in commission errors but not omission errors. Reaction time also improved.
K.C. Anderson, 1990	AX-Visual	ADHD	6–13	50	Methylphenidate[b]	NR	Significant improvement found for omission and commission errors with medication.
B.K. Baker, 1990	AX-Visual	CHI/ADHD	11.0 (2.73)	8	Methylphenidate[a]	0.6 mg/kg	Results indicated decreased omission errors and faster reaction times with medication.
Barkley et al., 1988	AX-Visual	ADHD	8.5 (2.3)	23	Methylphenidate[a]	0.3 mg/kg 0.5 mg/kg	At the low dose, no significant differences were found; at the higher dose, significant differences were found for correct hits, omission errors, and commission errors.
Barkley et al., 1989	AX-Visual	ADDH	8.3 (2.25)	74	Methylphenidate[a]	< 0.5 mg/kg	Results indicated significant improvement for commission errors only.
Barrickman et al., 1995	X-Visual	ADHD	11.8 (3.3)	18	Methylphenidate[b]	0.7 mg/kg	Significant improvement (decreased omission and commission errors) was found with medication.
Bawden, 1985	AX-Visual	CD	9.83	5	Methylphenidate[b]	10 mg	Medication resulted in improved performance for commission errors, but no omission errors.
Bawden et al., 1997	AX-Visual	Williams	11.41 (1.63)	3	Methylphenidate[b]	0.5 mg/kg	Results indicated improved performance with decreased omission errors and commission errors.
Bergman et al., 1991	IP-Visual	ADHD	6–12	42	Methylphenidate[b] Methylphenidate—SR20[b]	2–10 mg 10 mg	Results indicated improved performance with medication.
Brown & Sexson, 1988	AX-Visual	ADD	13.7	11	Methylphenidate[a] Methylphenidate[a] Methylphenidate[a]	0.15 mg/kg 0.3 mg/kg 0.5 mg/kg	CPT performance was improved for all dosage levels for commission errors; reaction time was improved for the two higher dosages; correct hits and omission errors were significantly improved at the highest dosage.

Study	CPT	Diagnosis	Age	N	Medication	Dose	Results
Coffey, 1993	AX-Visual	ADHD	7.33–11.92	24	Methylphenidate[a]	NR	Positive differences were found with medication for correct hits and commission errors.
Conners & Rothschild, 1968	X-Visual	Clinic referrals	NR	12	Methylphenidate[b]	NR	Significant improvement was found for commission errors with medication.
Coons et al., 1987	XX-Visual	ADD	14.8 (1.91)	19	Methylphenidate[a]	15–25 mg	Results indicated significant improvement in omission errors, reaction time, and sensitivity (d').
Fischer & Newby, 1991	AX-Visual	ADHD	8.9 (2.9)	160	Methylphenidate[b]	0.2 mg/kg 0.4 mg/kg	The higher dosage resulted in greater improvements (i.e., increased correct hits and decreased commission errors), but treatment effects were significant for both dosage levels.
Flansburg, 1986	AX-Visual	ADHD	8.51 (1.64)	15	Methylphenidate[b]	5–15 mg	Results indicated improved performance (increased correct hits and decreased omission errors).
Garfinkel et al., 1986	AX-Visual	ADD	19.2 (2.5)	22	D-amphetamine[b]	10 mg	Improved performance, as evidenced by commission errors, was found.
Hagerman et al., 1988	AX-Visual	Fragile X	7–9	15	Methylphenidate[a] D-amphetamine[a]	0.3 mg/kg 0.2 mg/kg	A comparison to placebo did not indicate significant improvement in CPT performance for either medication.
Hall & Kataria, 1992	AX-Visual	ADHD	7.7	21	Methylphenidate[b]	NR	Medication resulted in significant improvements in impulsive responding but not for vigilance.
Handen et al., 1990	X-Visual	ADHD/MR	6–9	12	Methylphenidate[a]	0.3 mg/kg 0.6 mg/kg	Higher dose resulted in greater improvement in performance (increased correct hits and decreased commission errors). Differences at the lower dose were nonsignificant.
Handen et al., 1992	X-Visual	ADHD/MR	9.1	14	Methylphenidate[a]	0.3 mg/kg 0.6 mg/kg	The higher dose resulted in increased correct hits, but subjects made less commission errors with the lower dose.
Jones, 1987	AX-Visual	ADHD	8.5	42	Placebo[b] Methylphenidate[b]	— 5 mg 10 mg 15 mg 20 mg	Performance (omission errors) improved with increasing dosage up through 15 mg, but the increase to 20 mg resulted in an increase in omission errors over other dose levels.

(continued)

Table 8.3 Continued

Study	CPT Type	Clinical Group	Age Range or Mean (SD) in Years	N	Medications	Dose	Results
R.W. Keith & Engineer, 1991	X-Auditory	ADHD	7–13	21	Methylphenidate[b]	4–25 mg	Results indicated increased correct hits and decreased commission errors with medication.
Klorman et al., 1979	X-Visual	ADDH	9.53 (1.38)	18	Methylphenidate[a]	0.3 mg/kg	Improvement found for commission errors but not omission errors.
Klorman et al., 1983	X-Visual XX-Visual	ADDH	8.34 (1.28)	41	Methylphenidate[a]	0.3–0.6 mg/kg	Medication resulted in improved performance (omission errors, commission errors, and reaction time).
Klorman et al., 1988	X-Visual XX-Visual	Clinic referrals	8.39 (1.52)	63	Methylphenidate[a]	0.3 mg/kg	Results indicated improvement on all CPT variables: omission and commission errors, reaction time, and sensitivity (d').
Klorman et al., 1991	XX-Visual	ADD	14.16 (1.70)	46	Methylphenidate[a]	0.64 mg/kg	Significant improvements were found on omission and commission errors as well as sensitivity (d').
Kupietz & Balka, 1976	AX-Auditory	ADDH	9.17 (1.5)	20	Methylphenidate[a]	40 mg	Medication resulted in increased correct hits as well as decreased commission errors.
Levy & Hobbes, 1988	X-Visual	ADDH	8.25	12	Methylphenidate[a]	0.3 mg/kg	Changes were evidenced on omission and commission errors, however, these improvements were not evident if the child also took haloperidol.
Levy & Hobbes, 1996	X-Visual	ADDH	5.58–12.33	10	Methylphenidate[a]	0.3 mg/kg	Changes were evidenced in reaction time, however, these differences were not evident if the child also took haloperidol.
Matier et al., 1992	AX-Visual	ADHD	8.2	24	Methylphenidate[a]	0.1–0.3 mg/kg	Inattention was improved with medication; impulsivity decreased only for the nonaggressive subjects.
Michael et al., 1981	X-Visual AX-Visual	ADDH	9.1	21	Methylphenidate[a]	0.3 mg/kg	Significant improvement was found for omission and commission errors.
Milich et al., 1989	AX-Visual	ADHD	8.8 (1.3)	26	Methylphenidate[a]	0.3 mg/kg	Results indicated improved performance on the CPT (omission and commission errors).
Musten et al., 1997	AX-Visual	ADHD	4.84 (0.54)	31	Methylphenidate[a]	0.3 mg/kg 0.5 mg/kg	Significant improvement was found for correct hits with both dosage levels; there was not a significant difference between results at the different dosage levels.

Study	Task	Group	Age (SD)	N	Medication	Dose	Results
Nigg et al., 1996	AX-Visual	ADHD	8.6 (1.74)	23	Methylphenidate[a]	0.3 mg/kg 0.6 mg/kg	Significant improvements were found for inattention, impulsivity, and dyscontrol indexes.
O'Toole et al., 1997	AX-Visual	ADHD	9.2	23	Methylphenidate[a]	0.3 mg/kg	Commission errors were significantly reduced with methylphenidate, however, omission errors were not affected.
Pelham et al., 1990	AX-Visual	ADHD	10.39 (1.38)	22	Methylphenidate[a] Methylphenidate-SR[a] Dextroamphet-SR[a] Pemoline[a]	10 mg 20 mg 10 mg 56.25 mg	All medications had similar positive effects on performance, with some indication that the long-acting stimulants were more effective than the standard dose.
Rapoport et al., 1980	AX-Visual	ADDH	9.44 (2.12)	15	D-amphetamine[b]	0.5 mg/kg	Significant differences were found on commission errors.
Rapport et al., 1986	AX-Visual	ADHD	7.75	14	Methylphenidate[a]	5–15 mg	Medication resulted in decreased omission and commission errors.
Rapport et al., 1993	AX-Visual XX-Visual	ADHD/MDD	9.83 (1.17)	16	Methylphenidate[a]	10–20 mg	Improvements in vigilance were found.
Rapport et al., 1987	AX-Visual	ADHD	8.5	42	Placebo Methylphenidate[b]	— 5 mg 10 mg 15 mg 20 mg	Based on omission errors, increased dosage was associated with improved performance up to 15 mg and then reversed.
Rapport et al., 1996	AX-Visual	ADHD	6	2	Methylphenidate[b]	0.29– 1.16 mg/kg	Dose related improvements were found in CPT performance for both subjects.
Riordan et al., 1999	AX-Visual	ADHD ADHD	31.8 (11.8) 32.7 (13.0)	19 17	Methylphenidate[b]	0.5mg/kg	Medication had the same effect on both groups with increased correct hits and faster reaction on the CPT.
Schechter & Timmons, 1985b	AX-Visual	ADDH	6–12	10	Low amphetamine[b] High amphetamine[b]	1.6 mg 5.0 mg	Results indicated positive effects for correct hits, omission errors, and commission errors.
Shekim et al., 1986	X-Visual	ADDH	9.75 (2.08)	22	D-amphetamine[b]	Varied	Significant improvement was found for omission and commission errors.

(continued)

Table 8.3 Continued

Study	CPT Type	Clinical Group	Age Range or Mean (SD) in Years	N	Medications	Dose	Results
Solanto et al., 1997	AX-Visual	ADHD	8.25	22	Methylphenidate[a]	0.6 mg/kg	Correct hits and sensitivity (d') improved with medication.
Sostek et al., 1980	AX-Visual	ADHD	6–9 10–12 9.4	5 10 15	Amphetamine[a]	0.5 mg/kg	Results indicated that both younger and older children showed improved sensitivity (d') but only the younger group showed improvement in response style (Beta).
Speech et al., 1993	AX-Visual	TBI	27.58 (5.6)	12	Methylphenidate[a]	0.3 mg/kg	No significant improvements in CPT performance were found.
M.O. Swartwood, 1994	X-Visual	ADHD	9–11	23	Methylphenidate[b]	5–20 mg	The only difference found was for variability of reaction time.
Sykes et al., 1971	X-Visual AX-Visual	ADDH	8.0 (1.75)	40	Methylphenidate[a]	30–40 mg	Medication resulted in improved performance.
Sykes et al., 1972	AX-Visual AX-Auditory	ADDH	8.42 (2.25)	24	Methylphenidate[a]	10–100 mg	Results indicated improved performance with medication.
Taylor et al., 1987	XX-Visual	ADDH	8.5	39	Methylphenidate[b]	0.5–1.4 mg/kg	Medication resulted in improved accuracy (decreased errors).
Tillery et al., 1998	X-Auditory	ADHD/CAPD	NR	32	Methylphenidate[a]	NR	Medication resulted in improved performance.
Verbaten et al., 1994	X-Visual	ADHD	11.2 (2.1)	12	Methylphenidate[a]	10 mg	Correct hits increased with medication; reaction time decreased.
Weingartner et al., 1980	AX-Visual	ADDH	9.4 (2.12)	15	Methylphenidate[a]	0.5 mg/kg	Improved attention and better vigilance were found with medication.
Werry & Aman, 1975	X-Visual	ADDH	7.9	24	Methylphenidate[a]	0.3 mg/kg	A small level of improvement in CPT performance was found.
Werry & Aman, 1984	X-Visual	Enuretic ADHD	8.4 8.5	16 16	Methylphenidate[a]	NR	For the combined samples, improvement was found for omission errors and reaction time.

Study	CPT	Disorder	Age	n	Medication	Dose	Results
Werry et al., 1980	X-Visual	ADDH	8.5	30	Methylphenidate[a]	0.4 mg/kg	Introduction of medication resulted in decreased omission and commission errors as well as increased (faster) reaction time.
Yepes et al., 1977	AX-Visual	ADHD	9.17	22	Methylphenidate[a]	39.1 mg	Results indicated significant improvement in omission and commission errors.

Notes: [a]Placebo versus medication; [b]Baseline versus medication; CPT = Continuous performance test; ADD = Attention Deficit Disorder; ADHD = Attention-Deficit/Hyperactivity Disorder; ADDH = Attention Deficit Disorder with hyperactivity; CAPD = Central Auditory Processing Disorder; CD = Conduct Disorder; CHI = Closed head injury; MDD = Major Depressive Disorder; MR = Mental retardation; NR = Not reported; SR = Slow release; TBI = Traumatic brain injury.

Table 8.4

Neurophysiological Correlates of Medication Effects on CPT Performance

Study	CPT Type	N	Groups	Medication	Results
Coons et al., 1981: Study 1	X-Visual AX-Visual	13	Adult controls	Methylphenidate	Results did not support effects on latency of ERP. It was concluded that medication only has a noticeable effect if the task requires additional attentional resources.
Coons et al., 1981: Study 2	X-Visual AX-Visual XX-Visual	23	Adult controls	Methlyphenidate	Effects found only for the XX-CPT for the late positive component such that the amplitude was increased in response to both target and nontarget with medication.
Coons et al., 1987	XX-Visual	19	Adolescents with ADD	Methylphenidate	Relative to baseline, there was an increase in P3 amplitude at central and parietal sites.
Fitzpatrick et al., 1992	XX-Visual	19	Child controls	Methylphenidate	P3 amplitude to targets was significantly larger with methylphenidate for both standard and slow release dosing.
Klorman et al., 1979	X-Visual	18	Children with ADDH	Methylphenidate	Using PET, amplitude of LPC was increased to within normal limits.
Klorman et al., 1988	X-Visual AX-Visual	53	Children: Clinic referrals	Methylphenidate	Drug effects were evident for amplitude of P3 only on the AX-CPT with increased amplitude.
Klorman et al., 1991	AX-Visual	46	Children with ADD	Methylphenidate	The amplitude of P3 was larger with methyl-phenidate particularly at Pz for nontargets. P3 latencies decreased as did the variability of P3 latencies for both targets and nontargets.

Michael et al., 1981	X-Visual AX-Visual	21	Children with ADDH	Methylphenidate	The amplitude of the parietal LPC for both the X- and AX-CPT was enhanced with medication. Similar drug effects were evident for LPC at the vertex.
Verbaten et al., 1994	X-Visual	12	Children with ADHD	Methylphenidate	Increases in P3 amplitude occurred concurrently with an increase in correct hits with administration of methylphenidate but in nonlinear manner; the same pattern was found for N2.

Notes: ADHD = Attention-Deficit/Hyperactivity Disorder; ADD = Attention Deficit Disorder; ADDH = Attention Deficit Disorder with hyperactivity; ERP = Event related potentials; LPC = Late positive component; PET = Positron emission tomography.

Borgstedt, & Dainer, 1979; Michael et al., 1981). Consistent with the decreased reaction time associated with stimulant treatment, there is also evidence of decreased latency of P3 to target stimuli with stimulant medication (e.g., Coons et al., 1981; Fitzpatrick et al., 1992; Klorman et al., 1979; Michael et al., 1981). For example, Fitzpatrick and colleagues investigated the effects of methylphenidate with 19 children with ADD. The age of the children ranged from 6.9 to 11.5 years with a mean of 8.7 years. Children received standard methylphenidate or the slow-release version (20 mg). Overall accuracy on the visual XX-CPT improved from baseline with methylphenidate; reaction time was faster and less variable as well. ERP results indicated that P3 amplitude to targets significantly increased with standard methylphenidate at 7.5 mg for children under 30 kg and 10 mg for children over 30 kg, and for the slow-release version. Similar findings of increased amplitude were found with presumably healthy adults by Peloquin and Klorman (1986).

Although outcome studies were generally positive, in some instances, significant pre-/posttreatment differences were evident only on a specific version of the CPT, but not on others. For example, in the study by Coons et al. (1981), results indicated a statistically significant decrease in errors for the XX-CPT but not for the X-CPT or the AX-CPT. In another study, a significant decrease in errors was found for the X-CPT but not the AX-CPT (Sykes et al., 1971). Thus, the interpretation of CPT performance may be a function not only of the medication, but of variations in the task that increase or decrease the sensitivity of the CPT to changes in the CNS. As noted in Chapter 2, additional research is needed with regard to the best CPT task parameters (score type, difficulty level, ISI, etc.) for appropriate evaluation of impact on CPT performance by psychostimulants.

Hale et al. (1998) identified four types of responses to methylphenidate based on dose effects. The linear response was characterized by improvement on cognitive and behavioral measures of increasing magnitude with increased doses of methylphenidate; the quadratic response was characterized by improvement in cognition and behavior with the low-dose (5 mg) condition, but no improvement or decline in the high-dose (10 mg) condition. The third type of response identified by Hale and colleagues was referred to as the "differential cognitive and behavioral" due to the differing impact of methylphenidate on cognitive level as opposed to behavior. With this differential response, the individual would be expected to show improvements on cognitive tasks (or behavioral ratings or both) in the low-dose condition; however, in the high-dose condition, the individual would show a very different pattern (e.g., if behavior was improved at a low dose, it would return to baseline and cognitive function improve). The fourth response style was that of no response. Hale and colleagues argued that there is a need for careful evaluation of stimulant response and titration given the potential differences in individuals' responses to methylphenidate. These findings need to be replicated with some consistent, objective measures such as the CPT. Given some indications that stimulant medication may have a negative impact on some children (e.g., Biederman, Faraone, Keenan, Steingard, & Tsuang, 1991; Handen, Feldman, Gosling, Breaux, & McAuliffe, 1991; J. Swanson et al., 1991), additional research to identify the characteristics of responders, nonresponders, and negative responders is needed as well. Simply put, dosage levels in mgs per kg of body weight produce different behavioral versus cognitive changes that may be nonlinear and may even be disordinal. Such effects are quite complicated and it is not known at present how to predict such responses on the basis of individual patient characteristics or other variables. This is crucial to understand, especially in recalcitrant cases and when there is comorbidity of ADHD and other learning and behavior disorders.

ANTIDEPRESSANTS

With the theoretical understanding of attention and executive control as subserved at least to some significant extent by the catecholamines, as noted already, most of the research on medication effects on attention is specific to the effects of stimulant medications. At the same time, there is a paucity of comprehensive research related to the effect(s) of other classes of medications and substances on attention and executive control. Primarily due to adverse reactions or weak responses to stimulant medication by some individuals with ADHD, the effectiveness of other classes of medication, including antidepressants, as an alternate treatment has been investigated (Barrickman, Noyes, Kuperman, Schumacher, & Verda, 1991). Notably, knowledge of the impact of antidepressant medications on attention may have implications for understanding changes in cognitive functioning regardless of the diagnosis (Wittenborn, Flaherty, McGough, Bossange, & Nash, 1976). There are four types of antidepressants: tricyclics (TCAs, which are primarily dopamine reuptake inhibitors), SSRIs, atypicals, and the selective and nonselective MAOIs. Depending on the type of antidepressant, neurotransmitters of norepinephrine, dopamine, and acetylcholine may be impacted as well as serotonin (Viesselman, 1999). Although not studied as often, serotonin modulation problems have been implicated in the attentional problems of some individuals (Zubietka & Alessi, 1993).

TRICYCLICS

Initially, the tricyclics were the most often used of the antidepressants for children and adults (DelMundo, Pumariega, & Vance, 1999). These include imipramine (Tofranil), desipramine (Noripramine), nortryptyline (Pamelor), and amitryptyline (Elavil). Imipramine, for example, acts primarily on the noradrenergic system, but also impacts the serotonergic system and has an anticholinergic effect (Viesselman, 1999). Imipramine often causes sedation along with other side effects such as dry mouth, weight gain, and some forms of hypotension because of its effects on neurotransmitters (DelMundo et al., 1999; Olvera, Pliszka, Luh, & Tatum, 1996). Presumably normal adults who were given imipramine made significantly more errors than individuals who were given a placebo or nomifensine (a compound with antidepressant characteristics) on the X-CPT and AX-CPT. Further, reports of drowsiness were higher for the imipramine group than for the placebo and nomifensine groups (Wittenborn et al., 1976). In contrast, for 30 children with ADHD, commission errors significantly improved with imipramine, but there was no improvement on omission errors or reaction time (Werry, Aman, & Diamond, 1980).

Relative to stimulant treatment in general, tricyclics have been found to result in improved performance on the CPT in some studies, but not to the same extent as has been found with stimulant medications. For example, when imipramine was compared to methylphenidate, the effect of imipramine was less pronounced than that of methylphenidate (Werry et al., 1980). Using a double-blind, placebo-controlled, crossover design and an AX- and an XX-CPT, Rapport, Carlson, Kelly, and Pataki (1993) examined the effects of another of the tricyclics, desipramine, by itself and in conjunction with methylphenidate for children with ADHD and Major Depressive Disorder (MDD). A significant main effect for medication was found for omission errors and commission errors on the XX-CPT; the differences were attributable solely to methylphenidate. The desipramine treatment by itself was not found to result in significant change in CPT performance. More important, at least one study (Wittenborn et al., 1976) suggested possible negative impacts on attention of imipramine with normal adults, likely due to the sedative effects of the medication.

MAOIs

Less commonly prescribed, MAOIs initially may produce a stimulant effect and this may be viewed as a positive effect on attentional problems (Viesselman, 1999). Although some MAOIs, such as tranylcypromine, resemble amphetamine in their chemical structure (Viesselman, 1999), the effect of these on attention as measured by CPT performance has not been studied extensively. In the one study that used a CPT to monitor effects on attention, Ernst et al. (1997) compared a selective MAOI type B at a low dose (20 mg/day) and at higher doses (60 mg/day). Results indicated dose-related improvements on correct hits, commission errors, and reaction time.

ATYPICAL ANTIDEPRESSANTS

Of the atypical antidepressants, venlafaxine (Effexor) and buproprion (Wellbutrin, also sold under the trade name of Zyban) have been studied. Using the Conners' CPT (Conners, 1995), Olvera et al. (1996) examined the effect of venlafaxine with 14 children with ADHD. Results failed to find any significant drug effects for reaction time, commission errors, or omission errors as a result of venlafaxine. Another atypical antidepressant, buproprion, is believed to act on the dopaminergic systems similar to the psychostimulants (Viesselman, 1999). As a treatment for ADHD, buproprion has been shown to be as effective as methylphenidate in improving commission and omission errors on specific versions of the CPT (Barrickman et al., 1995) but not on others (Conners et al., 1996). With the limited studies that have investigated the effects of atypical antidepressants, the results are at best equivocal, although buproprion looks promising.

SSRIs

The limited number of studies for specific drugs within the antidepressant group and limited clinical samples at various age levels in general leaves unanswered questions regarding the potential impact, positive or negative, of antidepressant medication on attention and executive control as a result. Treatment with SSRIs (e.g., Prozac, Zoloft, Paxil) appears to be increasing and replacing the use of tricyclics as a safer method of treating depression (DelMundo et al., 1999). Given this increase, together with the potential involvement of the serotonergic system on attention, it is particularly surprising that only one published CPT study (Barrickman et al., 1991) investigated the effects of SSRIs on attention. Individuals in the Barrickman et al. study were on fluoxetine (Prozac) and results suggested that SSRIs may result in improved attention as evidenced by fewer omission errors. At the same time, results indicated that Prozac may result in increased impulsivity, as evidenced by more commission errors. Thus, there is need for additional study of the impact of SSRIs on attention and executive control.

NEUROLEPTIC MEDICATIONS

As demonstrated in previous chapters, individuals with ADHD are not the only clinical group that evidences difficulty with attentional problems. The extent to which individuals with schizophrenia spectrum disorders have been characterized as having attentional deficits and demonstrate poor performance on the CPT was discussed in Chapter 7. The use of neuroleptics (antipsychotics), as opposed to stimulants or antidepressants, is a frequent treatment component for schizophrenia. In addition, neuroleptics may be used to treat some classes of stereotypic behaviors such as tics as well as explosive, aggressive, or violent behaviors (J. Johnson, Rasbury, & Siegel, 1997). The neuroleptic chlorpromazine (Thorazine) has been used for the treatment of hyperactivity as well (e.g., Weiss, Minde, Douglas, Werry, & Sykes, 1971). Neuroleptics vary in terms of the extent to which they act on various neurotransmitter receptors, but most are believed to be dopaminergic and serotonergic antagonists (Ernst et al., 1999). The most commonly prescribed medications in the neuroleptic (antipsychotic) family include thioridazine (Mellarill), chlorpromazine (Thorazine), clozapine (Clozaril), haloperidol (Haldol), thiothixene (Navane), pimozide (Orap), and risperidone (Risperdal) (J. Johnson et al., 1997).

Riccio, Moore, and colleagues (1999) reported on studies that examined the effects of neuroleptics on CPT performance, noting that they seemed to produce equivocal results (see Table 8.5). Results of some studies suggested that neuroleptics are not effective in improving attention in this population, but instead are more useful in treating clinical symptoms (Cornblatt, Obuchowski, Schnur, & O'Brien, 1997; Epstein, Keefe, Roitman, Harvey, & Mohs, 1996; Mirsky, Primac, & Bates, 1959). On the other hand, T. Goldberg and Weinberger (1995) suggested that high-potency neuroleptics can improve vigilance. Serper et al. (1990) found that schizophrenics who were treated with neuroleptics demonstrated better CPT performance than unmedicated schizophrenics. In contrast, Harvey et al. (1990) compared the performance of 14 medicated schizophrenics, 14 nonmedicated schizophrenics, and 15 controls on an AX-CPT. Medications were haloperidol (10 mg b.i.d.) and benztropine (1 mg b.i.d.). Both schizophrenic groups differed significantly from the control group on errors of omission and sensitivity (d'). In this study, medication did not seem to have an effect on any level of CPT performance (Harvey et al., 1990).

With many studies including subjects on different neuroleptic medications and dosing schedules, *ES* for omission errors ranged from 0.05 to 0.38 (Epstein et al., 1996; Erickson et al., 1984), with a number of studies reporting no significant effects for commission or omission errors as a result of neuroleptic treatment (Cornblatt et al., 1997; Finkelstein et al., 1997). Using measures from signal detection theory, larger *ES* were found for sensitivity (d') and response bias (Beta), with the largest effect found (*ES* = 1.49) by Epstein and colleagues for subjects on multiple medications and dosing schedules. Werry, Aman, and Lampen (1976) compared the efficacy of haloperidol (0.025mg/kg low and 0.05mg/kg high) to methylphenidate (0.3mg/kg) as treatments for hyperactivity and aggression. They found that methylphenidate was more effective at improving error rates on the CPT as compared to haloperidol. In addition, the results suggested that higher doses of haloperidol could impair

Table 8.5

Effects of Neuroleptics and Antipsychotics on CPT Results

Study	CPT Type	N	Medication(s)	Group(s)	Results
Aman et al., 1991	X-Visual	27	Thioridazine	Clinical sample	No effect of thioridazine on CPT performance was evident relative to placebo.
Bergman et al., 1995	IP-Visual	25	Haloperidol, Thiothixene, Trifluoperazine, Respiridone	Schizophrenic	There was a main effect for medication such that medication resulted in improved performance, however, this was specific to the chronic cases as opposed to the long-term cases.
Buchsbaum, Potkin, et al., 1992	X-Visual	25	Haloperidol	Schizophrenic	No significant improvement was found on CPT variables. Haloperidol was seen to have a normalizing effect on the metabolic rate of the striatum.
R.M. Cohen, Semple, Gross, Holcomb, et al., 1988	X-Auditory	24	Fluphenazine	Schizophrenic	Medication was associated with higher number of correct responses.
Cornblatt et al., 1997	XX-Visual	58	Haloperidol, Chlorpromazine, Trifluoperazine, Thioridazine, Fluphenazine	Schizophrenic	No improvement was found in CPT performance with medication.
Epstein et al., 1996	AX-Visual	38	Haloperidol, Thiothixene, Thioridazine	Schizophrenic	CPT performance was not significantly impacted by medication.
Erickson et al., 1984	AX-Visual	11	Thioridazine, Thiothixene	Schizophrenic	With medication, the reaction time was found to be significantly slower with a tendency for increased omission errors and decreased commission errors.
Harvey et al., 1990	AX-Visual	28	Haloperidol	Schizophrenic	CPT performance was not affected by medication.
E.D. Levin, Wilson, et al., 1996	Not-X-Visual	15	Haloperidol	Schizophrenic	In the no-nicotine condition, there was a haloperidol dose related impairment on the CPT.

(continued)

277

Table 8. 5 Continued

Study	CPT Type	N	Medication(s)	Group(s)	Results
Levy & Hobbes, 1988	X-Visual	12	Haloperidol	ADDH	Minimal changes were found in omission and commission errors, but they were not significant.
Levy & Hobbes, 1996	X-Visual	10	Haloperidol	ADDH	Haloperidol resulted in slowing of reaction time with no effect on omission or commission errors.
Mirsky et al., 1959	X-Visual AX-Visual	12 8	Chlorpromazine Chlorpromazine	Controls Controls	On X-CPT, chlorpromazine was found to result in impaired performance; on AX-CPT, with secobarbitol at peak levels, CPT performance was impaired as well.
Mirsky & Kornetsky, 1964	X-Visual AX-Visual	12	Chlorpromazine	Controls	Chlorpromazine was found to result in impaired performance on the CPT.
Nestor et al., 1991	X-Visual	25	Chlorpromazine	Schizophrenic	No difference was found between those on medication and those taken off medication on standard version. On degraded version, the group taken off medication were found to have a significantly higher rate of false alarms.
Orzak et al., 1967	X-Visual	18	Carphenazine	Schizophrenic	Medication resulted in significant improvement on CPT.
Primac et al., 1957	X-Visual AX-Visual	10	Chlorpromazine, Meperidine, Secobarbitol	Controls	Chlorpromazine was found to have significant negative and dose-related effect on CPT performance.
Sallee et al., 1994	AX-Visual	66	Haloperidol Pimozide	Tourette syndrome	Haloperidol was found to result in increased commission errors; pimozide resulted in decreased omission errors.
Sax et al., 1998	X-Visual	10	Quetiapine	Schizophrenic	Change significant for sensitivity (d') was found with medication.
Serper, 1991	AX-Visual	25	Haloperidol	Schizophrenic	There was no significant difference from baseline to week one, but after week two there were significant improvements as a result of medication.

Study	CPT	N	Medication	Population	Results
Serper et al., 1990	AX-Visual	8	Haloperidol	Schizophrenic	Medication resulted in improved CPT performance.
Spohn et al., 1977	X-Visual	40	Phenothiazine, Chlorpromazine	Schizophrenic	Omission errors were significantly reduced in the medicated group.
Van Putten et al., 1981	X-Visual	57	Thiothixene	Schizophrenic	Dysphoric responders did better on the CPT prior to receiving medication or at very low doses of the medication.
Werry & Aman, 1975	X-Visual	24	Haloperidol	ADDH	Haloperidol was not found to result in improved CPT performance.
Werry et al., 1976	X-Visual	29	Haloperidol	Clinic referrals	Haloperidol did not result in improved CPT performance and did result in negative side effects.

Notes: ADDH = Attention Deficit Disorder with hyperactivity; CPT = Continuous performance test.

cognitive functioning (Werry & Aman, 1975; Werry et al., 1976). Similarly, research by Levy and Hobbes (1996) suggested that when haloperidol (0.04 mg/kg) and methylphenidate (0.3 mg/kg) are used together, haloperidol blocks the effectiveness of methylphenidate and improved performance on the CPT was not evidenced.

Because of the various clinical groups that may receive neuroleptic treatment, CPT performance with these medications may be dependent on the population being treated, duration of the disorder, ratio of positive to negative symptoms, the specific neuroleptic prescribed, and dosage as well as the type of CPT. CPT performance of presumably healthy individuals was found to be impaired with neuroleptic treatment, and studies with haloperidol suggest impaired performance on CPTs for individuals with ADHD or TD. In contrast, phenothiazines seem to have positive effects in addressing the attentional deficits associated with schizophrenia based on improved CPT performance. As with antidepressants, taken together, the results of the studies reviewed suggest that there is a need to monitor medication effects of neuroleptics on attention if optimal functioning and levels of arousal are desired.

ANTIANXIETY (ANXIOLYTIC) AND ANTIHYPERTENSIVE MEDICATIONS

ANXIOLYTICS

The primary antianxiety medications include buspirone (BuSpar), alprozolam (Xanax), halcion (Triazolam), diazepam (Valium), and secobarbitol. Antianxiety drugs, especially the benzodiazepines (e.g., Xanax), have been used successfully as a treatment for anxiety disorders in adults. Although there is not much research on their effectiveness with children and adolescents, there is some support for their use (J. Johnson, Rasbury, & Siegel, 1997). Tolerances for anxiolytics develop quickly; as a result, increasingly higher doses are required to obtain symptomatic relief (J. Johnson et al., 1997) and addiction potential may be high. Some of the most common side effects found with anxiolytics, and the benzodiazepines in particular, include drowsiness, cognitive and performance decrements, and excessive behavioral disinhibition (DelMundo et al., 1999; J. Johnson et al., 1997; Werry & Aman, 1999). These negative side effects are believed to be due to depression of brain function. As such, the use of anxiolytics would be expected to have a negative impact on CPT performance. CPT performance of normal controls with antianxiety/antihypertensive medications has been studied, however, and their CPT performance was not impaired as a result of the medication (Bourke, Rosenberg, & Allen, 1984; McAuley, Reynolds, Kroboth, Smith, & Kroboth, 1995).

Of the anxiolytics, benzodiazepines act as CNS depressants and as a result are often used to treat anxiety disorders. Due to the CNS depression, benzodiazepines are known to produce behavioral side effects, impair reaction time, and decrease attentional capacity (Hart, Colenda, & Hamer, 1991). A popular intermediate-acting benzodiazepine used with normal elderly subjects is alprozolam (Xanax). Research by Hart et al. with the elderly did not report any significant drug effects (positive or negative) on CPT performance with alprozolam.

An atypical anxiolytic, buspirone (BuSpar), is commonly used to treat anxiety disorders and can be used as a treatment for people who become violently angry (Konopasek, 1997). Its chemical action is predominantly on the dopaminergic and serotonergic systems (Werry & Aman, 1999). Common side effects for buspirone include dizziness, anxiety, nausea, headaches, lightheadedness, restlessness, and possibly confusion, excitement, depression, or anger (J. Johnson et al., 1997). Compared to other anxiolytics, buspirone also acts on the adrenergic system and as a result is relatively less sedating (Konopasek, 1997; Werry & Aman, 1999). Buspirone was found to have a lesser effect on attentional capacity as compared to other anxiolytics, with the most negative effects occurring during absorption (Hart et al., 1991). No significant effects (positive or negative) were reported for buspirone as measured by CPT variables (Hart et al., 1991).

ANTIHYPERTENSIVES

Two common drugs in the antihypertensive subgroup are guanfacine (Tenex) and clonidine (Catapres). Clonidine is reported to stimulate the presynaptic autoreceptors with the effect of lowering the serotonin levels and increasing the dopamine levels. As such, it would be expected that clonidine would have positive effects on attention and executive control. In fact, there has been a significant increase in the use of clonidine for ADHD, TD, sleep problems, and other childhood disorders (J. Swanson et al., 1995), yet there is a lack of empirical data to support this increase (Werry & Aman, 1999). J. Swanson et al. (1995) reported a fivefold increase in the number of prescriptions for clonidine between 1992 and 1995 without sufficient empirical validation of its effectiveness in treating attention-related problems. In adults, clonidine has been used for a variety of behavioral problems, including aggression, anxiety, mania, tic disorders, and sleep problems as well as alcohol and substance withdrawal (Werry & Aman, 1999).

Guanfacine acts on the CNS in a manner similar to clonidine and is commonly used to treat high blood pressure and also heroin withdrawal. Side effects of both clonidine and guanfacine may include dizziness, drowsiness/fatigue, headaches, irritability, loss of appetite, and hypotension (Konopasek, 1997; Werry & Aman, 1999). Although clonidine may result in impaired cognitive function, guanfacine is believed to improve cognitive function (Horrigan & Barnhill, 1995). Guanfacine also has a longer half-life and fewer side effects as compared to clonidine (Horrigan & Barnhill, 1995). Recently, guanfacine has been used as an alternative medication for children with ADHD who are at risk for TD in hopes of vigilance and behavior improvements. This alternative is being implemented because stimulant medications such as methylphenidate, dextroamphetamine, and pemoline as well as clonidine may uncover or intensify tics in those children who are at risk for or who have TD (Chappell et al., 1995; Horrigan & Barnhill, 1995). Based on behavioral scales, guanfacine resulted in global improvement in a sample of boys with ADHD. However, only one study was found that used CPTs to evaluate the effects of guanfacine on attention (Horrigan & Barnhill, 1995). With children with ADHD and TD, CPTs were used to measure the effectiveness of guanfacine in improving attention and impulsivity. Reductions of commission errors were reported for both versions of the CPT used; however, improvement in omission errors was found only for the X-CPT and not the AX-CPT (Chappell et al., 1995).

   As with the other classes of medication, the effects of the anxiolytics and antihypertensive medications on CPT performance appears to be dependent on a variety of factors, including the disorder(s) of the individual and the type of CPT used. Dosage level, often dictated by the length of time the individual is in treatment, also appears to be a factor. Although not investigated by these studies, duration of the disorder may be a factor as well. Notably, only a minimal number of empirical studies with children or adults with ADHD have been completed with anxiolytics or antihypertensives despite increasing rates of prescription.

ANTICONVULSANTS/ANTIEPILEPTICS

It is estimated that 0.4% to 1.0% of children have a seizure disorder of some type that requires management through the use of medication (Hauser & Hesdorffer, 1990; Hunt, Arnsten, & Asbell, 1995); of those individuals with mental retardation who are institutionalized, approximately one-third take some form of anticonvulsant medication. Anticonvulsants alter brain excitability and, as a result, can have an impact on cognition, learning, and behavior (Vining, Carpenter, & Aman, 1999) as well as attention (Trimble & Reynolds, 1976). Although side effects vary depending on the drug and the dosage, some combination of drowsiness and lethargy as well as impaired cognition is often reported with anticonvulsant treatment. Since the 1970s, efforts have been made to achieve seizure control with fewer adverse affects on cognition and learning through the development of newer medications (e.g., carbamazepine). Currently, some of the anticonvulsants are being used in the treatment of disorders other than seizure-related disorders, including Bipolar Disorder, mania, and anxiety disorder (Sporn & Sachs, 1997; Vining et al.,1999; Walden, Hesslinger, vanCalker, & Berger, 1996). The anticonvulsants used in these ways include carbamazepine (Tegretol), valproate, and clonazepam (Klonopin). Other anticonvulsants include ethosurimide (Zarontin), phenobarbital, phenytoin (Dilantin), valproic acid (Depakote, Depakene), and lamotrigine (Lamictal).

Given the frequency with which seizure disorders occur, relatively few studies have looked at the impact of anticonvulsant medications on cognitive function (Duncan, Shorvon, & Trimble, 1990). Using a variety of measures to assess impact on attention, D. Smith et al. (1987) found that of the anticonvulsants, carbamazepine had the least negative effect on attention and primidone and phenobarbital had the most negative effects. Generally, studies have consistently indicated that anticonvulsants may impact negatively on cognitive functioning (Bennett & Krein, 1989; Calandre, Dominguez-Granados, Gomez-Rubio, & Molina-Font, 1990; Dodrill, 1988; Dorwen, Elger, Helmstaedter, & Penin, 1989). For example, there is evidence that phenobarbital significantly impairs cognitive functioning in some children (Farwell et al., 1990; Rodin, Schmaltz, & Twitty, 1986; Trimble & Corbette, 1980). To a lesser degree, carbamazepine has been found to impact memory (Forsythe, Butler, Berg, & McGuire, 1991). Of the newer medications available, lamotrigine is believed to produce fewer adverse effects on cognitive functioning than other antiepileptics (A. Cohen et al., 1985; M. Hamilton et al., 1993); however, there is need for additional study with each of these substances. In fact, despite the potential for anticonvulsants to impact attention, only four studies have used the CPT to measure the effects of anticonvulsants on attention.

Past research has been equivocal with regard to sodium valproate, an anticonvulsant often prescribed for absence seizures. Some simple reaction time research has suggested that sodium valproate improves reaction time and vigilance (Harding & Pullan, 1997). Other studies have indicated that sedation and even slower reaction times have been associated with the drug (Aman, Werry, Paxton, & Turbott, 1987). Aman and colleagues found significantly fewer errors in children with generalized epilepsy treated with low doses (15.85 mg/kg/day) of sodium valproate, whereas children with partial epilepsy demonstrated no significant drug effects. No main effect between low doses and high doses (27.1 mg/kg/day) of sodium valproate were reported (Aman et al., 1987). Aman et al. suggested that, based on their findings, the effects of sodium valproate on attention may be dependent on the type of seizure disorder.

In another study, Aman, Werry, Paxton, Turbott, and Stewart (1990) investigated the effects of carbamazepine in a group of 50 children with well-controlled seizures. With an X-CPT, results indicated that seizure type was not related to performance, but that concentration (peak or trough) of carbamazepine impacted performance. Peak-level performance was characterized by fewer errors of omission and commission as compared to trough level; however, the difference was significant only for commission errors.

OTHER MEDICATIONS

Many other medications, including fenfluramine, lithium, and various allergy/asthma medications (e.g., diphenydramine), have been studied to determine how they affect attention as measured by the CPT. Of these, fenfluramine (Pondimin, Ponderax) acts on the serotonergic system but is considered an amphetamine analog (Werry & Aman, 1999) and, therefore, would be expected to have an impact on attention and executive control. No longer available due to potentially lethal side effects, the most common minor side effects included weight loss, lethargy, sedation, and irritability. Fenfluramine has been found to reduce blood serotonin concentrations by approximately 50% and, as a result, it was most often used with children with autism (Aman & Kern, 1989; M. Campbell, 1988; M. Campbell et al., 1988). Changes in cognitive function and adaptive behavior in autism with fenfluramine were not supported fully in the literature, but inattention and distractibility were often improved (Werry & Aman, 1999). At the same time, Donnelly et al. (1989) found no improvements in vigilance performance in children with ADHD whose cognitive ability was within the average range.

LITHIUM

Lithium is a mood stabilizer that is commonly used to treat bipolar disorders (Kaskey et al., 1980). Lithium inhibits the release of norepinephrine and dopamine, with some indications of cognitive impairment as a result (Viesselman, 1999). Common side effects include slowed thinking and drowsiness (Konopasek, 1997), which can have detrimental effects on CPT performance. An investigation by Kaskey et al. with individuals with Manic Depressive Disorder reported interesting results on two versions of the CPT, the X-CPT and the AX-CPT. On the X-CPT, commission errors were significantly reduced with lithium treatment, but there were no significant effects for reaction time or omission errors. On the AX-CPT, although not statistically significant, commission errors were improved; however, omission errors increased and reaction times were significantly longer.

ANALGESICS

Only one study looked at the effects of analgesics on attention as measured by the CPT. Bourke et al. (1984) studied the effects of morphine combined with physostigmine and found no significant drug effects on CPT performance. An opiate, methadone, has analgesic properties as well. Tecce, Cole, Mayer, and Lewis (1979) investigated the effects of methadone on brain functioning expressed as vigilance. Methadone is used to wean addicts from morphine and heroin. The subjects were classified into two groups based on basal brain functioning; slow rise time and quick rise time were assessed. Results indicated significant group effects, with reaction time improving in the slow rise time group but increasing in the quick rise time group when methadone was administered (Tecce et al., 1979).

NOOTROPICS

Nootropics are believed to increase brain metabolic rate (Conners & Sparrow, 1999). Piracetam (Nootropil) is the nootropic most researched with humans. Oxiracetam (Neuromet), which is structurally related to piracetam, has been shown to improve memory and learning in studies with normal and cerebral-impaired animals (Banfi & Dorigotti, 1984). Villardita, Grioli, Lomeo, Cattaneo, and Parini (1992) looked at the effects of oxiracetam on attention in patients with Alzheimer's-type dementia and multi-infarct dementia. Both visual and auditory versions of the CPT were used, with significant improvements found to occur only on the auditory version.

ANTIHISTAMINES AND ASTHMA MEDICATIONS

Antihistamines are a class of drugs used for a variety of purposes, including sleep disorders or fussiness in infants and toddlers (Arnold, Janke, Waters, & Milch, 1999). Antihistamines are known to causes drowsiness and possibly lessen attention. At the same time, inattention is not infrequently associated with allergies (Kallam, Riccio, & Hynd, 1999). Shanon et al. (1993) investigated the effects of the antihistamine astemizole and chlorpheniramine on children with allergies and hay fever. In a crossover design, no significant drug effects were found for CPT performance.

A common medication for individuals with severe asthma, theophylline has been implicated as having a negative impact on cognition and attention (Arnold et al., 1999). The anti-inflammatory corticosteroids (e.g., prednisone) are used to treat asthma as well, with some indications that attention and memory may be impacted negatively (Arnold et al.,

1999; B. Bender, Lerner, & Kollasch, 1988). There has been little research on the effects of asthma treatments in children. When measured by the AX-CPT, no main drug effects for prednisone on attention were reported by B. Bender et al. (1988).

STUDIES WITH LEISURE DRUGS, CAFFEINE, NICOTINE, OR HIGH SUGARS

Unfortunately, the use of leisure drugs (i.e., alcohol, marijuana, lysergic acid diethylamide or LSD, heroin, cocaine) is not uncommon in today's society. The effects on the CNS differ depending on the leisure drug used. For example, alcohol is a CNS depressant, but may produce behavioral stimulation at lower levels, at least initially, whereas cocaine is a stimulant and acts on the CNS in much the same way as the psychostimulants. Heroin is an opiate and like other analgesics can result in sedation and a sense of euphoria. Marijauna is believed to result in impaired short-term memory and an altered perception of time. In contrast, LSD is believed to impact on many areas of CNS function and particularly on the serotonin receptors (Eisner & McClellan, 1999).

Vachon, Sulkowski, and Rich (1974) and Weil, Zinberg, and Nelson (1968) investigated the effects of firsthand use of marijuana by young adults. Neither study indicated drug effects (across dose level) for performance on the CPT. Similarly, the effects of LSD on attention with the X- and AX-CPTs have been investigated. Results indicated that LSD did not significantly impair CPT scores (Mirsky & Kornetsky, 1964; Primac, Mirsky, & Rosvold, 1957).

CAFFEINE AND NICOTINE

Caffeine and nicotine are both stimulant-type substances and it would seem reasonable to expect that intake of nicotine or caffeine would mimic the effects of stimulant medications. Results of studies that have investigated the effects of caffeine and nicotine, however, are equivocal or limited in scope (see Table 8.6). For example, Baer (1987) investigated the effects of caffeine on six normally developing 5-year-olds and found no significant differences on omission or commission errors for no cola, diet cola, or caffeine-free diet cola. Similarly, Schechter and Timmons (1985b) found no effect of caffeine on CPT performance of 10 children identified as hyperactive and 6 presumably normal children between the age of 6 and 10 years. Comparable studies with adults have not been completed.

Table 8.6

Effects of Other Stimulants on CPT Performance

Study	CPT Type	Clinical Group	Age Range or Mean (SD) in Years	N	Medication(s)	Dose	Results
Baer, 1987	X-Visual	Control	5	6	Caffeine[b]	1.6–2.5 mg/kg	No difference in performance was found.
Bernstein et al., 1994	X-Visual	ADHD	8–12	21	Caffeine[a]	2.5 mg/kg 5.0 mg/kg	With the higher dose, there was improvement but only for omission errors.
E.D. Levin, Conners, et al., 1996	Not-X-Visual	Smokers Nonsmokers	35	6 11	Nicotine[a]	21 mg	Nicotine resulted in a significant decrease in reaction time; for smokers, it also reduced the variability of reaction time.
E.D. Levin, Wilson, et al., 1996	Not-X-Visual	Schizophrenic	38.9	15	Nicotine[a] with Haloperidol	7 mg 14 mg 21 mg	At the highest dose of nicotine, there was improved rate of commission errors; at the lowest dose of nicotine, there was an improved rate for omission errors.
E.D. Levin et al., 1998	Not-X-Visual	Controls	23.3	11	Nicotine[a]	7 mg	Results indicated improved rate of commission errors with nicotine.
Schechter & Timmons, 1985b	X-Visual	ADDH Controls	6–12	10 6	Caffeine[b] Caffeine with amphetamine[b]	600 mg	Although both caffeine and caffeine with amphetamine resulted in improved performance (decreased commission errors) for the ADHD group, this was not the case with the control group or for other variables of the CPT.
Suzuki et al., 1995	X-Visual	Controls	20–21	21	Caffeine[b]	200 mg	No significant difference was found.

Notes: [a]Placebo versus substance; [b]Baseline versus substance; CPT = Continuous performance test; ADHD = Attention-Deficit/Hyperactivity Disorder; ADDH = Attention Deficit Disorder with hyperactivity; NR = Not reported.

Nicotine has been investigated in adult populations but not in children or adolescents. For example, E. Levin, Conners, et al. (1996), investigated the effect of nicotine by using a nicotine patch (21 mg/day) with 6 smokers and 11 nonsmokers on the Conners' (not-X) CPT. Results indicated that for smokers, there was an associated increase in reaction time and decreased variability of reaction time, neither of which were found in nonsmokers. At the same time, the introduction of nicotine to nonsmokers resulted in decreased variability across differing ISIs, which was not found to occur in smokers. In another study, E. Levin, Wilson, et al. (1996) found a trend toward decreased variability of reaction time with nicotine as well as increased reaction time with 21 mg of nicotine; no increase in reaction time was found with lower doses of nicotine. Notably, the study by Fried, Watkinson, and Gray (1992) suggested that children who were exposed to nicotine in utero were more likely to make commission errors as compared to children who were not exposed to nicotine in utero. Confounding this work, however, is the finding that adults with ADHD are 50% more likely to be smokers than non-ADHD adults (e.g., see Reynolds, 1999b). Studies using the nicotine patch in adults did not yield any significant difference in errors on the CPT (E. Levin, Conners, et al., 1996; E. Levin, Wilson, et al., 1996).

SUGARS AND CARBOHYDRATES

Historically, there have been theories implicating sugars and diet in ADHD (e.g., Feingold, 1975). At the same time, it is not uncommon to feel sleepy and less alert after a meal that is high in carbohydrates and low in protein. A few studies have investigated the effects of carbohydrate consumption on vigilance (e.g., Girardi et al., 1995; Robison, 1992). Using the AX-CPT, Girardi and colleagues investigated the effects of carbohydrates on children with ADD and presumably normal controls and found that the CPT performance of both groups of children declined significantly following carbohydrate ingestion. In contrast, Robison compared the effects of sugar with aspartame (a popular artificial sweetener) with young adults. Robison also used an AX-CPT, but unlike Girardi et al., Robison did not find any significant difference in performance associated with the ingestion of sugar. Further, there was no between-group difference (sugar, aspartame) on CPT performance. Thus, the results are equivocal with regard to the potential effect of carbohydrates on CPT performance.

SUMMARY

There is increasing use of medications for children and adults with behavioral and emotional disorders (DelMundo et al., 1999). Depending on the type of information provided to professionals, as well as the public, there is an increased perception that medications, particularly stimulants, can alleviate problems with minimal side effects (Borgschatz, Frankenberger, & Eder, 1999). All too often, medication for any number of disorders is administered and the effects—intended or not—on attention or other functions related to learning and memory are not monitored. A recent survey indicated that only 59% of pediatricians prescribing stimulant medication required follow-up office visits; no specific structure or outcome variable was identified (Murray et al., 1999). The American Academy of Child and Adolescent Psychiatry (AACAP, 1997) advocated for the use of multiple methods, including parent (and teacher for children and youth) input, for medication monitoring. Although their position was specific to medication for children, youth, and adults with ADHD, this same principle applies to medications used in the treatment of any disorder. Presumably, medications are prescribed with the intent of improving one's functional ability; negative impacts on attention can be detrimental to functioning and need to be considered as part of medical monitoring. Brown and Sawyer (1998) and DelMundo and colleagues (1999) also recommend that medication management be monitored over time. In addition to parent and, when appropriate, teacher input, CPTs provide a quick, relatively inexpensive, objective measure of the impact of medications on at least some components of attention as well as the impact on processing speed, as measured by reaction time, and executive control.

CPTs are an effective monitoring tool for the impact of a variety of substances (licit and illicit) on attention. CPTs may also be helpful in monitoring attentional impairment as a side effect of medication (e.g., antihistamines, anticonvulsant medications). Of categories of substances, psychostimulants most consistently resulted in improved CPT performance for both controls and clinical populations and have been researched most extensively. Impact of other medications on vigilance as measured by the CPT, based on this review, varied by population, medication and dosage, and CPT type. When auditory and visual AX-CPTs were compared, auditory CPTs were found to be more sensitive to apparent improvements (Sykes et al., 1972); at the same time, other studies with auditory versions found improvements with placebo as well as medication (Kupietz & Balka, 1976).

Notably, there is a plethora of research related to the psychostimulants and a paucity of research related to most other classes of medications as related to effects on attention, however measured. At the same time, there has been a tremendous increase in the extent to which pharmacotherapy is used for children (Gadow, 1991). Given the prevalence of children and adults being prescribed medication as treatment of one disorder or another, and the potential impact of attentional capacity on learning and memory, additional research is clearly needed. Without some formal research regarding the potential iatrogenic effects in addition to the beneficial effects on attention, it is not possible to conduct a comprehensive benefits (costs) analysis in determining the most appropriate treatment program. Additional research is needed with regard to the best CPT task parameters (score type, difficulty level, ISI, etc.) for appropriate evaluation of the impact on CPT performance by medications and other substances.

Finally, relatively few studies have investigated the effect on vigilance of commonly used substances such as caffeine and nicotine. Similarly, few studies have looked at the impact of sugar or carbohydrates on CPT performance. Given the equivocal results of the studies with caffeine, nicotine, and sugar, it would seem prudent to at least consider these differences when interpreting CPT performance. It is more difficult to control the intake of caffeine and nicotine in out-patient populations; requiring individuals to abstain from these substances may result in a measure of withdrawal as opposed to normal functioning. How to best address this issue, therefore, is not immediately apparent. However, it is possible to control for the potential impact of carbohydrate ingestion by scheduling the CPT at a time that does not immediately follow a meal or snack. The extent to which consumption of caffeine, sugars, or nicotine was controlled for during the standardization process for any of the commercially available CPTs is not detailed.

CHAPTER 9

CPTs in Monitoring Effectiveness of Other Treatment Approaches

As ALREADY DISCUSSED, attention and executive control problems are common complaints of a number of disorders, including the developmental disorders (e.g., ADHD), as well as following TBI regardless of the age of the individual affected (Beers, 1992; Donders, 1993; P. Kaufmann et al., 1993). Besides ADHD and TBI, there are numerous other disorders (e.g., schizophrenia, bipolar disorders) that include problems with attention and executive control as part of the cognitive sequelae to the disorder (see Chapters 6 and 7). Many of these disorders have high comorbidity rates as well.

The need for rehabilitation of attentional deficits is based on the premise that attention is a necessary prerequisite to an efficient processing system and, as such, a precursor to memory and other cognitive tasks. Attention is critical to successful everyday functioning (e.g., Ewing-Cobbs, Fletcher, & Levin, 1986; Klonoff, Clark, & Klonoff, 1993). Attention deficits pose impediments to other types of cognitive retraining or rehabilitation when the attentional difficulties include deficits in selective attention or focused attention (Wood, 1984). Problems with attention or executive control may not always be the predominant symptom reported by the client. In particular, it has been argued that deficits in memory may reflect underling deficits in attention (Sohlberg & Mateer, 1987).

In Chapter 8, we reviewed the literature available on the effects of various medications on attention and executive control as measured by CPTs. Although medication may be a frequent option for treatment of attentional deficits, other treatments are available for those individuals who

Acknowledgment is given to Christine L. French for her assistance in the preparation of this chapter.

291

either choose not to use medication or for whom medication is not a viable option. Mateer, Kerns, and Eso (1996) described three categories of alternative treatments for cognitive impairment, including deficits in attention: externally focused interventions (i.e., modifying the environment or providing accommodations to decrease the effects of the impairment); internally focused restorative interventions (i.e., modifying the individual's cognitive abilities); and internally focused compensatory approaches (i.e., teaching the individual strategies to compensate for the deficient processes). At the same time, due to the potential interaction of attention with other cognitive or emotional factors (e.g., stress, memory), alternative treatments that affect attention may have secondary attentional impacts as opposed to attention and executive control as the primary targets of intervention.

Either alone or in conjunction with medication, behavioral methods for modifying behavioral components of attention and executive control have been used most extensively with children. For children, the behavioral methods are generally more popular and less controversial than medical interventions (DuPaul, Guevremont, & Barkley, 1992). Modifications in the environment, for example, can include preferential seating, use of carrels or study rooms, frequent prompts, and decreasing extraneous stimuli in the environment. For children with ADHD, more structured behavioral programs in the classroom setting have been found to be successful in addressing problematic behaviors, including inattention, with subsequent improvements in academic performance (e.g., Atkins, Pelham, & White, 1990; DuPaul & Eckert, 1997; Kendall & Panichelli-Mindel, 1995; Rapport, Murphy, & Bailey, 1982; Reid & Maag, 1998). Such interventions are not designed to remediate attentional deficits but rather to subdue the impact of attentional deficits on learning, problem solving, and work in general and are unlikely to show up as improved CPT performance because the latent organic issues remain in disrepair.

Further, when attentional deficits are viewed in the context of cognitive deficits, it seems logical to make use of interventions to improve the underlying cognitive process (Mateer et al., 1996). Cognitive interventions have received the most attention in the context of rehabilitation for individuals who have sustained TBI (see Wood, 1984; Mateer & Mapou, 1996 for a review) or manifest attentional deficits in conjunction with postconcussional syndrome (Sbordone, 1986). Cognitive interventions also are recommended for children with ADHD (e.g., Ervin, Bankert, & DuPaul, 1996; Van der Krol, Oosterbaan, Weller, & Konig, 1998; Wilens et al., 1999; Young, 1999). Generally, intervention procedures of self-instructional strategy training, cognitive modeling, self-monitoring and self-evaluation, and other cognitive behavioral methods have been found to result in minimal to moderate short-term gains (see Abikoff, 1991).

Some of the methods reported in the literature to address attention or executive control include the Attention Training System (Gordon Systems, Inc., 1987b; Rapport & Gordon, 1987) the Captain's Log (Sanford & Browne, 1988), neurXercise (Podd & Seelig, 1989), Open Focus Attention Training (Fehmi, 1987), Attention Training (Wells, 1990), Attention Process Training (Sohlberg & Mateer, 1989a), Pay Attention! (Thomson, Seidenstrang, Kerns, Sohlberg, & Mateer, 1994), THINKable (Psychological Corporation, 1991), and Orientation Remedial Module (Ben-Yishay, Piasetsky, & Rattock, 1987), as well as other more generic attention training methods (e.g., self-instruction strategies, biofeedback) used by individual clinicians. The number and variety of attention programs is increasing rapidly, particularly programs that incorporate computer technology (Burda, Starkey, & Dominguez, 1991; Gianutsos, 1992; Larose, Gagnon, Ferland, & Pepin, 1989; Podd & Seelig, 1992). Many of these programs are intended to restore or rehabilitate the impaired components of attention and executive control through repeated practice and drill on tasks requiring these capabilities. The extent to which any of these alternatives have been developed and researched varies depending on the age and disorder of interest. Most of the research has focused on children with ADHD and adults with TBI (Mateer et al., 1996). In the face of a burgeoning number of treatment options, however, there is a paucity of empirical research available on many of these programs. Where attention is not the targeted behavior (i.e., memory is the targeted behavior), there are even fewer empirical data related to the specific components of attention and executive control that may be impacted by these programs. One of the factors associated with clinical efficacy of treatment programs involves the choice of outcome measures used across studies. The extent of empirical support for treatment programs that address attention and executive control, either as a primary or a secondary benefit, has been addressed elsewhere (see Abikoff, 1991; French & Riccio, 1999) and is reviewed briefly here with a focus on outcome measures.

STATUS OF EMPIRICAL SUPPORT FOR TREATMENT PROGRAMS

Regardless of the theoretical perspective underlying the intervention, or whether the behavioral or cognitive intervention is used in conjunction with or in place of medication, evaluation of treatment outcomes based on empirical data is imperative. Of the training packages for attentional deficits, one of the most researched is the Attention Training System (ATS). The ATS is a computerized response-cost system that enables a teacher to provide feedback to a child regarding on-task behavior. The ATS also provides for self-monitoring using a recording of beeps; the student records whether or not he or she is paying attention when the beep sounds and is rewarded for accurate self-monitoring. A third component of the system is a tape recording of messages that encourage the child to remain on task. Finally, a timer can be used to help the child complete work within a specified and agreed-on time frame (Detweiler, Hicks, & Hicks, 1995). A review of the literature, however, revealed that of the five studies that included the ATS, the results were reported in an anecdotal as opposed to a data-based format, and the size of the samples ranged from one to six children (e.g., DuPaul et al., 1992; J. Evans, Ferre, Ford, & Green, 1995; Gordon, Thomason, Cooper, & Ivers, 1991; Rapport et al., 1996).

Similarly, studies with other treatments reported minimal data and included small samples. Notably, French and Riccio (1999) found only 65 studies that addressed treatment alternatives for attentional deficits, and only 20 of these provided sufficient information for ES to be calculated. Among these 20 studies, there was very little consistency in the outcome measures used, further hindering the ability to compare results across studies. The lack of consistency in methods and measures is not unusual. In addition, most clinical efficacy studies tend to rely on single-case study methodologies, have small numbers if a group design, or have no control condition (Kerns, Eso, & Thomson, 1999). For example, Diller and Gordon (1981) found that only 20% of studies using cognitive retraining included a control group of any kind. In most studies, if there is a control group, it consists of individuals not receiving any treatment or contact other than pre- and posttesting; this does not eliminate the possibility that any type of interaction or activity could have had an effect.

CPT AS A PRE-/POSTINDEX OF EFFECTIVENESS

As noted elsewhere in this volume, CPTs represent only one family of paradigms for the assessment of attention and executive control. Of the studies on treatment programs that include the improvement of attention or executive control as target goals, only seven studies included CPT performance as a pre- and postmeasure; these are presented in Table 9.1. For example, Powanda (1995) reported on the outcome of 12 adults with mild or moderate mental retardation with the use of the Attention Process Training (APT) program. The APT is a multilevel program that addresses focused attention, sustained attention, selective attention, alternating attention, and divided attention (Sohlberg & Mateer, 1989a). One of the outcome measures used was the GDS. Following four to five training sessions, improvements were found for vigilance commission errors, distractibility commission errors, and vigilance correct responses. Of the CPT variables, the greatest improvement was noted on the vigilance correct responses, supporting improvements in selective attention.

Table 9.1

Efficacy Studies for Attention Training Methods with CPT Performance as Outcome Variables

Study	N	Age Range or Mean (SD) in Years	Clinical Group	Training Program	Results
Benedict et al., 1994	38	37.9 (10.8)	Schizophrenic	Generic	No significant differences found following treatment.
Fritcher, 1993	11	6–11	ADHD	Whole brain integration	Although improvement was noted, differences were not significant.
Hermanutz & Gestrich, 1991	30 30	31.5 27	Schizophrenic Normal control	Generic	Attention improved as a result of training.
Kerns et al., 1999	14	7–11	ADHD	Pay Attention!	On the CPT, no significant improvements were found for either total correct hits or commission errors. A possible ceiling effect of the task was offered as an explanation for the lack of significance.
Medalia et al., 1998	54	33/32	Schizophrenic	ORM	Attention training resulted in improved performance on the CPT based on correct hits, commission errors, and absolute commission errors. The treatment group also demonstrated greater improvement on the BPRS. There was no significant pre- or posttreatment differences for reaction time.

(continued)

295

Table 9.1 Continued

Study	N	Age Range or Mean (*SD*) in Years	Clinical Group	Training Program	Results
Rapport et al., 1996	2	6	ADHD	ATS; Methylphenidate	Ratings and direct observation indicated improved attention with attention training alone. CPT error rates were better under optimal levels of medication as compared to attentional training alone.
Slate et al., 1998	4	7–11	ADHD/SED	Captain's Log	All four participants demonstrated improved IVA scores and improved parent and teacher ratings. Differences on other measures were not significant. The child with the most success on the training program also demonstrated the greatest improvement on other measures.
L. Thompson & Thompson, 1998	98 13	5–17 18–63	ADD	Biofeedback, metacognitive strategies	Both groups demonstrated improved attention and impulsivity, as well as decreased variability in performance, on the TOVA.

Notes: ADD = Attention Deficit Disorder; ADHD = Attention-Deficit/Hyperactivity Disorder; ATS = Attention Training System; BPRS = Brief Psychiatric Rating Scale; GDS = Gordon Diagnostic System; IVA = Intermediate Variables of Attention; ORM = Orientation Remedial Module; SED = Severe emotional disturbance; TOVA Test of Variables of Attention.

In a study with 14 children, ages 7 to 11 years, Kerns and colleagues (1999) investigated the efficacy of the Pay Attention! program. The children were assigned to either the treatment group (mean age of 9.39 years) or the control group (mean age of 9.35 years). The Pay Attention! program was designed based on the APT materials, but specifically for use with children. Tasks included both visual and auditory stimuli with increasing difficulty by task order and with set criterion for moving forward in the materials. The program is intended to address both sustained and selective attention. In addition to other measures, the Children's Continuous Performance Test (CCPT; Kerns & Rondeau, 1998) was used to evaluate outcome. Results of the CCPT were not consistent with improved attentional ability; however, Kerns et al. indicated that the nonsignificant findings were most likely due to a ceiling effect in the pretreatment phase for both correct hits and commission errors.

Slate, Meyer, Burns, and Montgomery (1998) investigated the effectiveness of the Captain's Log program with four children, age 7 to 11 years, who were identified as severely emotionally disturbed (SED) with comorbid ADHD. Captain's Log is a computerized training program that includes five modules and a number of different tasks directed at improving attention, concentration, memory, and problem-solving skills. The tasks are arranged in levels of increasing difficulty (Tarnowski, 1988). In addition to other measures, the IVA was used as a pre- and postmeasure of attention and concentration. All four participants demonstrated improved IVA scores as well as improvements in other indices of inattention and hyperactivity/impulsivity; differences on other measures were not significant. Notably, the child who had the most success with the Captain's Log (i.e., attained the highest level of difficulty) also demonstrated the greatest improvement in attention (Slate et al., 1998).

Rapport and colleagues (1996) used an AX-CPT to compare the efficacy of the ATS to treatment with methylphenidate. The subjects in their study were dizygotic girls (age 6) who demonstrated significant problems with inattention, impulsivity, and overactivity. Both girls participated in the double-blind, placebo-controlled, within-subject reversal design with phases of medication (placebo and four dose levels) and ATS (administered twice), alternated with a return to baseline. With the total errors (omission plus commission errors) as the dependent variable, results indicated that although there was some improvement in CPT performance with the ATS, methylphenidate at optimal doses was significantly more effective than the ATS in improving CPT performance (Rapport et al., 1996).

Using a generic training program, Benedict et al. (1994) monitored the progress of 38 adults diagnosed with schizophrenia as well as the progress of a control group. The treatment program consisted of a mean of 14.4 sessions of practice with six video computer attention training tasks with an average of 648.7 minutes (SD = 61.3) of on-task practice. The training tasks selected had a high information-processing load and emphasized speed of information processing, vigilance, and selective attention. The six tasks included a choice reaction time task, a simultaneous attention task, a serial addition task, an immediate memory task, a word span of apprehension task, and a visual-motor task. During the training sessions, the participants received numerous verbal prompts for their participation and reinforcement for improvement in performance. Using signal detection methods and a visual X-CPT, the study yielded no significant pre- and posttreatment differences for sensitivity (d'). However, a significant difference was found for the experimental group for the sensitivity decrement, suggesting that the training resulted in improved ability to sustain attention over time.

L. Thompson and Thompson (1998) used a combination of metacognitive strategies (e.g., self-monitoring) and biofeedback to address attentional deficits associated with ADHD. Their sample of children (n = 98) ranged in age from 5 to 17 years; the adult participants (n = 13) ranged in age from 18 to 63. Based on the assumption that attentional deficits result from CNS dysfunction, the use of EEG biofeedback training to address attentional deficits has been studied with children with ADHD. The use of EEG biofeedback is derived from the initial hypothesis of Satterfield and colleagues (Satterfield & Dawson, 1971; Satterfield, Lesser, Saul, & Cantwell, 1973) that children with ADHD exhibit behaviors consistent with low arousal. The low arousal levels would be more consistent with increased theta activity as opposed to alpha (i.e., transition from sleep to wakefulness) or beta (i.e., alert) activity. The general focus of the training is to decrease theta or slow wave activity and increase beta activity (J.F. Lubar, 1991). From case studies and using direct observations as outcome measures, it has been concluded that EEG biofeedback training can result in changes in attention and executive control (see J.F. Lubar, 1991, for a review). According to Lubar, children with pure ADHD are the best candidates for successful treatment with EEG biofeedback training. Additional studies using biofeedback to decrease theta and increase beta activity have been conducted as well, all with children (e.g., J.L. Carter & Russell, 1985; Tansey, 1990; Tansey & Bruner, 1983; L. Thompson & Thompson, 1998). The L. Thompson and Thompson study supports previous research. Based on the results of the TOVA pre- and posttreatment, the combined treatments resulted in improved attention, decreased impulsivity, and decreased variability in response accuracy for both adults and children (L. Thompson & Thompson, 1998). The extent to which each of the treatments contributed to the improvements could not be determined, and the study did not include a control group. Similarly, methodological problems have been found to impede interpretation of other biofeedback studies (J.F. Lubar, 1991).

With a generic training program, Medalia, Aluma, Tryon, and Merriam (1998) found improvement for correct hits, commission errors, and percent correct for adults with schizophrenia. For their study, 27 adults with schizophrenia were assigned to a treatment group, and another 27 adults with schizophrenia provided a control group. The program Orientation Remedial Module (ORM) incorporates behavioral principles, practice, and computer exercises to address attentional deficits. The ORM is comprised of five modules, each of increasing difficulty. The tasks are intended to promote arousal and alertness, increase target detection, and facilitate rapid processing of auditory and visual stimuli with immediate feedback on task performance provided to the individual. Using the CPT as an outcome measure, the schizophrenic group that used ORM demonstrated significantly more improvement following treatment relative to the baseline as well as the control group (Medalia et al., 1998).

OTHER OUTCOME MEASURES

CPTs were not the only outcome measures used; in fact, a number of different measures were used with very little consistency across studies. A listing of these measures is provided in Table 9.2. Of these, direct observation was the most frequently used (DuPaul et al., 1992; J. Evans et al., 1995; Gordon et al., 1991; Rapport et al., 1996; Slate et al., 1998; I. Wagner, 1988). In the same way that direct behavioral observation still provides the best assessment of attention problems and executive control in the diagnostic process, direct observation provides the best method for monitoring, but it is very time- and cost-intensive, with reliability depending on the observational method used. For example, in the single case study designs using the ATS, Evans and colleagues used off-task behavior and time sampling data. DuPaul, Guevremont, and Barkley (1992) used the ATS and direct observation for the two children in their study as well. Notably, unlike DuPaul and colleagues, many of the studies did not specify the coding system or detail the methodology used in making their observations.

In other cases, the studies used other measures to reflect attention and executive control. Podd (1999) used the Paced Auditory Serial Addition Test (PASAT; Gronwall, 1977), Trails A and B (Reitan, 1958; Reitan & Wolfson, 1985), Rey Auditory Verbal Learning Test (RAVLT; Rey, 1964), and the Luria-Nebraska Neuropsychological Battery (LNNB; Golden, 1988). Podd reported on the progress of three adults with TBI using neurXercise. Like Captain's Log, neurXercise is a multilevel training program with increasing levels of difficulty. The neurXercise program also provides immediate feedback for most tasks as well as help screens in the event the individual needs assistance. The neurXercise program includes modules for attention, perception, memory, judgment, reasoning, and

Table 9.2

Other Measures Used in Treatment Outcome Studies

Measure	Studies
Academic performance (e.g., GPA, grades, work completion; achievement test)	DuPaul, Guevremont, et al., 1992; Kotwal et al., 1996; J.O. Lubar & Lubar, 1984; Slate et al., 1998; L. Thompson & Thompson, 1998; Valdés, 1985b, 1988
Attention Capacity Test (ACT), Weber & Segalowitz, 1990	Kerns et al., 1999
Behavioral points	Slate et al., 1998
Beck Anxiety Inventory (BAI), Beck et al., 1988	Papageorgiou & Wells, 1998
Brief Psychiatric Rating Scale (BPRS), Overall & Gorham, 1972	Hermanutz & Gestrich, 1991; Medalia et al., 1998
Block Span Learning Test, Milner, 1971	Niemann et al., 1990
Baking Tray Task	Robertson et al., 1995
Cancellation: type tasks	Kerns et al., 1999; Robertson et al., 1995; Semrud-Clikeman et al., 1998
Day-Night Stroop Task, Gerstadt et al., 1994	Kerns et al., 1999
Digit span (backward, forward or both)	Klein & Schwartz, 1979; Robertson et al., 1995
Direct observation	DuPaul, Anastopoulos, Shelton, & Guevremont, 1992; J.H. Evans et al., 1995; Gordon et al., 1991; Rapport et al., 1996; Slate et al., 1998; I. Wagner, 1988
Discriminant Judgement Task	Forsyth et al., 1970
Divided Attention Test	Niemann et al., 1990
Driver Education Tasks	Kewman et al., 1985
Electroencephalography/Theta-Beta Ratio	Kotwal et al., 1996; L. Thompson & Thompson, 1998
Geriatric Depression Scale, Yesavage et al., 1983	Papageorgiou & Wells, 1998
Global Assessment Scale	Hermanutz & Gestrich, 1991
Hidden objects	Hannon et al., 1989
Hooper Visual Organization Test, Hooper, 1983	Kerns et al., 1999
Labyrinth Task	Hermanutz & Gestrich, 1991
Line Orientation, Benton et al., 1983	Robertson et al., 1995

Table 9.2   Continued

Measure	Studies
Luria Nebraska Neuropsychological Battery, Golden, 1988	Podd, 1999
Matching Familiar Figures Test (MFFT), Kagan, 1966	Kerns et al., 1999
Matching Unfamiliar Figures Test (MUFT), Rapport et al., 1996	Rapport et al., 1996
Memory matrix	Hannon et al., 1989
Modality shift paradigm	Hermanutz & Gestrich, 1991
Paced Auditory Serial Addition Test (PASAT), Gronwall, 1977)	Gray et al., 1992; Niemann et al., 1990; Podd, 1999; Sohlberg & Mateer, 1987
Reaction Time Tasks (simple or choice)	Benedict & Harris, 1989; Hermanutz & Gestrich, 1991; Medalia et al., 1998
Remote Memory Task	Hannon et al., 1989
Rey Auditory Verbal Learning Test, Rey, 1964	Hannon et al., 1989; Niemann et al., 1990; Podd, 1999
Story recall	Hannon et al., 1989
Stress level assessment	Valdés, 1988
Structured clinical interview for *DSM III-R*	Papageorgiou & Wells, 1998
Span of Apprehension Test, Asarnow & MacCrimmon, 1978	Benedict et al., 1994
Tone counting	Robertson et al., 1995
Trail Making Task, Reitan & Wolfson, 1985	Niemann et al., 1990; Podd, 1999; Powanda, 1995; Slate et al., 1998
Various Rating Scales	DuPaul, Guevremont, et al., 1992; Kotwal et al., 1996; Powanda, 1995; Rapport et al., 1996; Slate et al., 1998; Thomson, 1995
Various subtests from ITPA	Klein & Schwartz, 1979
Various WISC-III or WAIS-R Subtests	Gray et al., 1992; Kerns et al., 1999; Kotwal et al., 1996; Slate et al., 1998; L. Thompson & Thompson, 1998
Visual Analogue Scale	Papageorgiou & Wells, 1998
Visual Search and Attention Test (VSAT), Trenerry et al., 1989	Powanda, 1995
Wisconsin Card Sorting Test, Heaton, 1981	Powanda, 1995
Word list recall	Benedict et al., 1994

Notes: DSM III-R = Diagnostic and Statistical Manual of Mental Disorders, 3rd ed.-Revised; GPA = Grade point average; WISC-III = Wechsler Intelligence Scale for Children-3rd ed.; WAIS-R = Wechsler Adult Intelligence Scale-Revised.

daily living skills. The attention tasks include selective or focused attention and sustained attention for visual, spatial, sequential, and emotional information in a game-like format. Related to attention and executive control, judgment tasks require the individual to avoid irrelevant distractions, to demonstrate cognitive flexibility, and to exercise response inhibition. Following training on neurXercise, greatest improvement was evidenced on Trails A and B and the RAVLT; differences on other measures were negligible (Podd, 1999).

Additional outcome measures used in the Kerns et al. (1999) study included selective subtests of the WISC-III (Wechsler, 1991), the Attentional Capacity Test (ACT; Weber & Segalowitz, 1990), selected cancellation-type tasks, the MFFT (Kagan, 1966), the Day-Night Stroop Test (Gerstadt, Hong, & Diamond, 1994), and the Hooper Visual Organization Test (VOT; Hooper, 1983). Results indicated significant improvement on the Mazes subtest of the WISC-III, the ACT, and cancellation-type tasks. In the Benedict et al. (1994) study, in addition to the CPT, outcome measures included interviews specific to negative and positive symptoms of schizophrenia, the Span of Apprehension Test (Asarnow & MacCrimmon, 1978), and a word-list recall task (Benedict et al., 1994). As evident from these examples and Table 9.2, there is very little consistency in the selection and administration of direct measures of attention and executive control used in efficacy studies. Notably, many of these measures (e.g., the Mazes subtest of the WISC-III) have limited psychometric properties and are not generally agreed-on measures of attention or executive function.

More frequently, studies with children used parent or teacher rating scales (e.g., Kotwal, Burns, & Montgomery, 1996). In some instances, rating scales did not reflect improvement in attention or executive control, whereas direct, laboratory measures did show improvement. This difference in findings may or may not reflect problems with the ecological validity of the attention tasks used. An alternative explanation may be that the lack of significant change on the rating scales reflects the sensitivity of the scales to detect change over short periods of time or the inclusion of multiple behaviors, albeit related to attention, that are not directly targeted by the treatment program. Many rating scales are intended to reflect behavior over the prior six months and report scores based on clusters of behavioral components as opposed to addressing single attentional or executive control components. In other studies, qualitative interviews with teachers or parents were used (e.g., Kerns et al., 1999; Kotwal et al., 1996) and indicated improvement in attention; the extent to which the reported improvement was a function of the respondents' knowledge that the child was in treatment is unknown.

In one study, a CPT was used as part of the training procedures rather than as an outcome variable. Hermanutz and Gestrich (1991) compared the effects of a computer-assisted attention training program, a cognitive training program, and no training for adults with schizophrenia and 30 presumed healthy adults. The attention training was accomplished through the use of a CPT, a simple reaction time task, an auditory discrimination task, a cancellation-type task, and the labyrinth task. For each of the tasks, the participants were provided with immediate feedback on their performance. The extent of improvement on most of these tasks, including the CPT, was not reported in the study. Outcome variables included rating scales, a modality shift reaction time paradigm, an attention stress test, and the labyrinth task.

A number of other studies that evaluated the outcomes of treatment programs included a variety of other outcome measures that do not directly reflect attention (e.g., Kotwal et al., 1996; Valdés, 1985a, 1985b, 1988). For example, Valdés (1985a, 1985b) used the Open Focus Attention Training program, which is based on the use of biofeedback to monitor and control the production of alpha and theta brain waves and the research of Lindsley (e.g., Lindsley et al., 1949; Weinberger, Yendall, & Lindsley, 1968). The program is designed to result in relaxation and normalization, which in turn enhance the attentional state and attentional flexibility of the individual (Fritz & Fehmi, 1983). Although referred to as an attention training program, Open Focus is usually used for stress reduction. As such, although there is believed to be an indirect effect on attention, outcome measures do not usually include a measure of attention or executive control (e.g., Valdés, 1985a, 1985b, 1988). The only pre- and postmeasure reported by Valdés (1985b) was the grade-point average (GPA) of the students in the study. Similarly, J.F. Lubar (1991) reported improvements in attention based solely on GPA and achievement testing from the use of EEG biofeedback training. Finally, in a study by Papageorgiou and Wells (1998), the Attention Training (ATT) program (Wells, 1990), which is described as an attention training program that consists of exercises in selective attention, attention switching, and divided attention, was used. The outcome measures used for this study, however, related specifically to anxiety, depression, and health worries; there were no measures of attention or executive control included.

SUMMARY

Clinical efficacy is a growing area of concern and there is increased emphasis on the need for evaluation of treatment programs and demonstration of positive outcomes. As noted by others (e.g., Kerns et al., 1999; Mateer et al., 1996), clinical efficacy studies are difficult, challenging, and time-consuming. Many of the studies in the literature are limited in that improvement is noted qualitatively as opposed to quantitatively and sample sizes are small. In some studies, more than one intervention was used simultaneously without the provision of control groups to allow for separation of specific treatment effects. In addition, results of studies have not been replicated across age levels or across disorders; in fact, most of the studies have been done with children with ADHD or with adults with TBI. Given the potential for deficits in attention and executive control across myriad disorders as well as across the life span, additional studies with differing populations and age levels are needed.

Intervention treatment programs to address deficits in attention and executive control are increasing rapidly. With increased access and availability of technology, as well as an emphasis on cost efficiency, there is sure to be an increase in the number of computer software programs available to address these deficits. Shaw and McKenna (1989) developed an evaluation format to evaluate software that is designed to provide attention training. The extent to which the evaluation provided by this format is consistent with actual outcome data on the software programs available still needs to be documented; however, the issues included in their format are relevant. Some of these issues include identifying the level of alertness required to complete the requisite tasks, complexity of the response required, rate of presentation, extent of anticipation, timing and time estimation required, and presence or absence of distractors (Shaw & McKenna, 1989). The extent to which the levels of difficulty based on these parameters can be manipulated allows for individualized design of the training program and the ability to gradually increase the difficulty of the tasks involved. Although the format provided by Shaw and McKenna was designed to evaluate computerized programs, similar questions may apply to noncomputerized programs as well. In addition to evaluating treatment programs based on the content and demands, computerized or not, it is important for clinicians to be able to evaluate the treatment programs based on empirical research.

The current trend to use empirically validated treatments advocates for more in-depth and extensive research in this area. Because attention is not a unitary construct, the issue of which components of attention are targeted (i.e., training specificity) needs to be addressed as well (Sturm, Willmes, Orgass, & Hartje, 1997). Whereas attention and executive control are core behaviors across life activities, increased knowledge of the efficacy of attention programs is important. As with medication, study of those characteristics that help to predict the success of a specific treatment for a specific individual (i.e., based on cognitive characteristics, behavioral variables such as in the BASC, demographic variables, etiology, and severity) are needed as well. To maximize the usefulness of the data generated and the generalizability of findings across studies, it is important that researchers employ similar (e.g., manualized) treatment programs as well as maintain at least some core consistent outcome measures across studies. Treatment programs and outcomes measures may need to be modified for use with children (Mateer et al., 1996); these modifications need to be identified and standardized to ensure treatment integrity across studies. Thus, future research needs to include comparable methods and outcome measures across studies to be able to evaluate program efficacy across programs and populations.

Given the complexity of attention and executive control, outcome measures need to address multiple components and levels of attention and executive control systems. It seems likely that the same measures identified as being most sensitive to medication effects (J.M. Swanson, 1985) and brain injury (Cicerone, 1997), including the CPT, would be appropriate for evaluation of alternative treatment outcomes. One method of demonstrating improvement could be the final level of success attained on the training materials themselves (Wood, 1984), as has been noted for those programs that have different difficulty levels (e.g., Captain's Log). At the same time, measures to assess the real-life outcome of treatment should be included (Kerns & Mateer, 1996). In the adult literature, there is preliminary evidence of positive outcomes on academics (e.g., Raskin & Mateer, 1993), memory (e.g., Mateer & Sohlberg, 1988), and work (Mateer, Sohlberg, & Yougman, 1990).

Regardless of the measures included, it is important that studies be conducted that provide sufficient information to attest to treatment integrity and provide for the possibility of study replication by other investigators as well as clinicians. Studies are needed with sufficient objective and reliable data to apply current single-subject design methodologies (see Franklin, Allison, & Gorman, 1996; Kratochwill & Levin, 1992; Reynolds & Willson, 1985) and sufficient participants to ensure that there can be a true control group and a treatment group with enough individuals in each group to decrease error in analyses. In many studies, outcome data are available only immediately posttreatment or within two weeks from the completion of the treatment program (e.g., Powanda, 1995); only in a limited number of studies are more long-term (i.e., six months or longer) data provided (e.g., Kotwal et al., 1996). Studies need to include outcome data to attest to the long-term maintenance, or lack thereof, of the improvements over time.

CHAPTER 10

Where Do We
Go from Here?

THE PREVIOUS CHAPTERS have provided a background on the constructs
and associated neural substrates of attention and executive control as well
as what is currently known about the increasingly popular paradigms
known as continuous performance tests. Attention and executive control
are multifaceted constructs that appear to be subserved by multiple brain
structures. With the complexity of attention and executive control systems, it is not possible to establish a clear-cut one-to-one correspondence
between specific deficits and brain structures. Disruption to any part or
parts of the functional systems responsible for attention and executive
control can impact some component(s) and yet leave other components intact. Because of the complexity of the functional systems of attention, it is
not surprising that behavioral symptoms associated with deficits in attention or executive control frequently occur with many neurological disorders or CNS dysfunction (R.A. Cohen et al., 1999; Mapou, 1999; Sadock
& Sadock, 2000; also see Luria, 1966, for a discussion of complex functional systems generally and with regard to attentional systems).

Taken together, various models of attention and executive control consistently suggest the involvement of cortical and subcortical structures as
well as the afferent and efferent pathways among the basal ganglia, thalamus, and frontal lobes. Also implicated in the functional systems subserving attention and executive control are multiple neurotransmitters,
particularly the catecholamines. Consistent with these models, various
components of the CPT tasks have been found to be associated with the
proposed neural substrates of attention and response inhibition. The extent to which the CPT parallels brain function is highlighted by the differences in physiological responses to targets and nontargets as well as
the extent to which age differences in brain activation during CPT performance parallel brain development.

The complexity of the constructs of attention and executive control suggests that no single measure can provide information that is sufficiently comprehensive to address all the components of interest. The best any single measure, including the CPT, can provide is data on specific aspects of attention and executive control. Used in conjunction with other information, the CPT can be useful in the diagnostic process and in the monitoring of the treatment and rehabilitation process. As others have pointed out (e.g., Bergman et al., 1991; Gordon & Mettelman, 1988), there are a number of advantages to the use of CPTs. These include the ease of administration, time required, cost of administration, and an abundant research base as evidenced by over 400 research articles on the CPT. There are, however, some concerns that need to be addressed if the use of the CPT in clinical practice is to meet the standards for technical adequacy as advocated by the American Educational Research Association (AERA), American Psychological Association (APA), and the National Council on Measurement in Education (NCME) in their renowned and respected joint *Standards for Educational and Psychological Testing* (AERA, 1999; APA, 1999; NCME, 1999). CPTs used in clinical settings need to be held to the same standards for technical adequacy and psychometric properties as any other measures used in clinical practice.

WILL THE REAL CPT PLEASE STAND UP?

The basic paradigm for the CPT was designed initially almost 50 years ago for the assessment of attention and, to a lesser degree, response inhibition or dyscontrol. Now there are numerous variations of the CPT, with potential combinations and permutations seeming nearly infinite. At the same time, different CPTs and different clinicians using a common CPT paradigm report a wide variety of scores for interpretation. Even research scientists report data differently within and among CPT paradigms. Notably, the effect of the permutations to the task and the effect of using different rubrics for scoring have not been investigated thoroughly. The extent to which the varying CPTs are measuring the same constructs has not been investigated either. In fact, the sheer number of CPTs in use and the extent of differences across CPTs suggests that, although CPTs may constitute a similar group of tasks with a common paradigm, they are also very distinct.

Different CPTs may place different demands on an individual's attention, executive, and memory systems; one cannot be substituted for another. Even when the same CPT paradigm is employed (e.g., visual AX-, X-, not-X), clinicians and researchers may vary presentations times, nature of the stimuli (e.g., shapes, letters, numbers), location of stimuli in a visual field, the ISI, and the ratio of correct to incorrect stimuli, to name only a few of the chameleonic variables. Research findings may not be generalizable across even minor variations in tasks, and generalizability across these variations cannot be assumed but must first be proven. Minor variations in test administration do alter score distributions and technical data such as reliability coefficients as well.

In a number of studies, there is concern with regard to possible ceiling effects. It is also conceivable that there may be floor problems for younger children (i.e., 5 years or younger) given the preponderance of CPTs that use letters and numbers as stimuli. Additional research is needed to ensure the appropriateness of the various CPTs available for different age levels. The possible ceiling and floor effects may well compound the CPT-IQ issues discussed in previous chapters. At the same time, although the meaning of very low scores (or poor performance) on CPTs is believed to be understood, what of very high scores? Additional research to investigate correlates of higher than normal scores may be of interest as well.

STANDARDIZATION
OF ADMINISTRATION

In the twenty-first century, it is incumbent on test developers and publishers to ensure that an appropriate level of technical information, at least consistent with the standards set by Kaufman and Kaufman (1983), is provided in test manuals. As such, CPT manuals should include detailed instructions for standardized administration, instructions for scoring, and guidelines for interpretation, as well as technical data, including reliability of the test scores and validity of the interpretation of scores obtained. The CPT manuals we have reviewed and the supporting research published to date do not meet these standards. In some cases, the instructions for administration do not include the details that are delineated in the description of how the standardization data were collected. For example, in some of the manuals, there is no specification regarding whether the examiner is to be present or absent, how directions are to be given, and so on. Yet, research studies have demonstrated that experimenter-manipulated variables, such as examiner presence, can impact the results of CPT-based evaluations (e.g., Ballard, 1996a; Leark et al., 1999; Sergeant & Scholten, 1985; Tupler, 1989). At the same time, the effect of additional experimenter-manipulated variables (e.g., use of space bar vs. mouse, type of mouse, use of laptop vs. PC, size of screen) have not been investigated and are likely to vary from one clinician to another. Moreover, although some programs provide an option for customizing the task, clinicians need to follow the standardized procedures if interpretation of the results is to be accurate. A clinician who chooses to customize the paradigm will not be able to make comparisons between an individual's performance and the performance of the normative group, thus providing little meaning to the results obtained (Reynolds, 1999a). As we noted in prior chapters (see especially 6 and 7), CPTs are very sensitive to changes in brain function and to changes in CPT paradigms. Small changes in the paradigm may have dramatic effects on an individual's performance.

TECHNICAL ADEQUACY

The current state of technical adequacy is best appreciated from the review of the manuals for the published versions of the CPT. The CPT normative samples do not meet current expectations or standards. If the test developers are to meet reasonable professional standards, the normative samples should be large enough to allow for stratification across a number of different demographic dimensions. The manuals should include detailed descriptions of the normative samples to allow comparisons across tasks. With the expected developmental trajectory of brain development and corresponding differences in CPT performance as a result of age, the normative data need to be partitioned into smaller (e.g., six-month to one-year) age-level increments through at least age 21, and then again at the other end of the trajectory, beginning at age 45. Without additional research, the use of 10-year age intervals at any point in the life span is not supported by research and is not appropriate.

Other demographic variables have been reported to have a possible effect on CPT performance. Only one study (Bauermeister et al., 1990) has investigated the possible issue of cultural bias in CPT performance, with some indications that there may be a cultural confound; the issue of possible cultural confounds needs to be addressed more extensively. Methods for such studies are described at length in Reynolds (in press). Given that the results of the existing studies on gender differences are equivocal, there needs to be increased effort to ensure that females and males are equally represented in the normative sample at all age levels, with additional study of gender as a potential confound. Further research specific to computer exposure and educational level as possible confounds is needed as well.

As mentioned previously, systematic studies are needed to address the validity of the interpretation of different CPT scores. To develop a better understanding of what the different CPT scores measure, researchers need to specify the CPT paradigms, indices, task parameters, environmental factors, samples, and other measures used in current and future research endeavors. A systematic approach with sound methodology as opposed to the shotgun approach used in the past is needed. The accumulation of evidence to support the validity of the interpretation of a given measure is a never-ending process as theories and constructs evolve. As this process moves forward for the CPTs, gradual movement away from the weak toward a strong approach of examining the construct validity is essential. Researchers have collected a substantial amount of information on the different CPT scores and scores on other measures. Even though the collection process has not been systematic or exhaustive due to the numerous permutations and combinations possible with the various CPTs available, attempts have been made to make sense of the relations among the different CPT scores and scores on other measures (weak approach). Correlational studies found strong associations between CPT performance and direct behavioral observations (e.g., Barkley, 1991; Garretson et al., 1990; Gordon, DiNiro, et al., 1989; Harper & Ottinger, 1992; Kupietz & Richardson, 1978), other measures of attention and executive control (e.g., Burg et al., 1995; Koelega et al., 1989; Slicker, 1991), and behavioral ratings of children (e.g., Klee & Garfinkel, 1983; Slicker, 1991).

In the future, it is recommended that researchers move beyond the basics toward the strong approach using confirmatory factor analytic (CFA) procedures in their investigations with the CPT. T. Keith and Witta (1997) viewed CFA as an excellent method for assessing the construct validity of, in this case, the interpretations of different CPT scores. Creation of rival hypotheses about what CPT scores might measure other than what these scores are supposed to measure and testing these hypotheses (strong approach) using advanced statistical techniques such as LISREL and EQS are suggested as well. Examination of CPT data using different CFA models such as path models (see Wilson, 1995), saturated models, constrained models, and factor analytic models in future research endeavors will improve our understanding of what the different CPT scores measure and, ultimately, the worth of the CPT to practitioners as a measure of inattention and executive control.

We reviewed the validity of the popular interpretations of CPT scores in the traditional vein for ease of understanding; however, some psychometricians, for example, Messick (1995), have condemned the traditional trinitarian conceptualization of validity (i.e., the three-category taxonomy for accumulating evidence of validity: construct validity, criterion-related validity, and content validity) as fragmented and incomplete. As R.J. Cohen and Swerdlik (1999) pointed out, Messick, along with other psychometricians who view validity from a more modernistic perspective, supported a unitarian conceptualization of validity. The unitarian view of validity goes beyond the magnitude of a simple correlation coefficient between test scores—in this case, CPT test scores and a purported criterion—and includes the interpretation and value implications of test scores as well as the relevance or utility and social consequences of test use (Messick, 1995). Examination of these validity issues in relation to the CPT is suggested now and in the future to develop a more comprehensive understanding of what the different CPT test scores measure as well as their salient value to clinical practice and society.

Another area in need of research is the reliability of the individual CPTs; few of the manuals included reliability studies. Studies addressing the comparative reliability of CPT scores across demographic variables and diagnostic groups are needed as well. Stability and comparability of scores and normative data across examiner-allowed changes in any aspect of a CPT presentation must be studied and results provided. Temporal reliability also warrants additional research. The lack of evidence for temporal stability calls into question the use of the CPT in clinical contexts as well as research contexts. The need for temporal stability is particularly important if CPTs are to be used routinely to monitor the effects of treatment and if, as represented, they measure traits, not states.

SENSITIVITY AND SPECIFICITY

Regardless of the version of the CPT used, results clearly substantiate Rosvold et al.'s (1956) contention that CPTs are sensitive to brain damage or dysfunction. Studies of individuals with identifiable brain damage suggest a direct relationship between impairment on the CPT and the extent to which the damage/dysfunction is diffuse as opposed to focal, regardless of the etiology of that damage. Studies also consistently demonstrate sensitivity to CNS dysfunction in those individuals where the brain damage is presumed rather than identifiable (e.g., ADHD, schizophrenia).

Since compromise to any of the brain structures or pathways implicated in the attentional system may lead to attentional deficits, the specificity of attention problems as a diagnostic consideration for any one disorder is suspect, and the presence of attention problems may be suggestive of any one of a number of disorders. The CPT then does not provide useful information about the presence or absence of a specific disorder, but rather provides information about symptoms of disorders involving the self-regulatory system of the brain. As a diagnostic tool, it may be more useful in ruling out a diagnosis than ruling in a diagnosis. At the same time, the same sensitivity to changes in CNS function that make it nonspecific serve the CPT well as a measure for use in monitoring the effects of treatment or the gradual effects of neurological disease or disorder over time.

WHY USE THE CPT?

Given the current state of the art and the need for additional research and standardized administration related to the CPT, one might ask, "Why use the CPT?" As pointed out at the beginning of this chapter, there are a number of advantages to the CPT. As research continues to grow in this area, publishers increase the quality of the manuals and clinicians become more knowledgeable of the strengths and weaknesses of the many CPT paradigms; the CPT may grow in importance as a component to neuropsychological evaluation, especially as a method of assessing attention and executive control. Although not specific to a single disorder, the various CPT paradigms have consistently demonstrated sensitivity to a variety of neurological and psychiatric disorders in both adults and children. It is, however, only one measure and multiple sources of information and multiple measures are needed to develop a comprehensive picture and attain a better understanding of what is going on with any individual. Given the various types and locations of brain dysfunction that can potentially impact attention and executive control systems, impaired CPT performance may be interpreted best simply as evidence of CNS dysfunction.

Although less seductive, a viable use of the CPT is for monitoring outcome of various treatments on aspects of attention and executive control. There is overwhelming agreement that the use of medication for attention problems in children should be monitored (AACAP, 1997; Brown & Sawyer, 1998; Kamphaus & Reynolds, 1998). Often overlooked, there is a need to monitor the effects of medications prescribed for other purposes (e.g., seizures, schizophrenia) as well. The need to monitor medication effects is particularly important given the increasing use of medications to treat behavioral and emotional disorders for both children and adults (DelMundo et al., 1999) and the apparent lack of structured follow-up or an identified outcome variable by many pediatricians (Murray et al., 1999). For many medications other than the stimulants, there is a paucity of research on the effects of medications on attention and executive control. The CPT provides a quick, relatively inexpensive, objective measure of the impact of medications on at least some components of attention as well as processing speed.

Although medication may be a frequent option for treatment of attentional deficits, other treatments are available and treatment planning should include some means of objective monitoring. There are currently a number of commercially available programs that purport to improve attentional skills, yet the empirical base to support these programs collectively is abysmal. At the same time, there are numerous generic programs, with multiple variations, and single research studies that have addressed outcome efficacy with myriad outcome variables. The lack of sufficient empirical data to support the use of any of these programs in a day and age where best practice demands the use of empirically supported programs is a definite problem to be addressed. As with medication monitoring, the use of the CPT as a pre-/postmeasure to attention training programs with replication is a cost- and time-efficient objective method of generating this research base.

The CPT may also provide an excellent vehicle for objective, quantifiable, and carefully calibrated data about the course of CNS disease and related conditions that have an adverse impact on higher cognitive skills. Repeated testing with CPTs of adults suffering from dementia, multiple sclerosis, and Alzheimer's disorder, adults who have been exposed to toxic substances, and many others can provide useful information about the nature and course of such problems that can be associated with quantitative imaging techniques to gain new insights into neurocognitive functioning.

WHERE TO FROM HERE?

Diagnostic algorithms for the CPT do not exist currently. Those who would use the CPT as a definitive diagnostic tool are acting with a naïveté that belies proper clinical practice. Third-party payors who promote such applications can no longer be seen as acting in good faith, but rather as having been ill-advised or misinformed. There is just too much contradictory information to support continued classification/diagnostic decisions on the basis of a CPT.

Impairments in CPT performance must be viewed as general deficits, not specific to a singular diagnosis (much as psychomotor slowing is a general deficit appearing in many disorders, but taken as solely diagnostic of none; see Sadock & Sadock, 2000, Chapter 3). D. Siegel (2000) discussed at length the many problems inherent in attempting to correlate complex cognitive findings with clinical presentations in which he highlighted the distinctions between general and specific deficits. As he noted, careful and creative design of experiments is needed to distinguish the two. It is past time for such careful and creative designs to be applied to the CPT paradigms.

The use of CPTs as one component of the assessment process as well as a tool for monitoring treatment effects and the course of neurological disorder holds tremendous promise. This promise, however, is sorely compromised by the need for additional research on the effects of using different paradigms, appropriate normative samples, comparative studies across disorders with differing paradigms and task demands, and so on. It is imperative that research studies be conducted using strict adherence to standardized procedures and controlling for myriad confounds, including relevant historical variables (e.g., illness, developmental disorders, prenatal compromise, licit and illicit drug use, vegetative symptoms, and occupational hazards, to name a few).

A large-sample, multisite study using a common CPT paradigm (or the same combination of CPTs) and multiple groups with relevant psychopathologies is direly needed. Such a study would have to include samples of individuals diagnosed with rigorous, common criteria, with ADHD (preferably by subtype), schizophrenia, TBI, Bipolar Disorder, dementia (if studying adults), medical controls, and a general mental health clinic referral sample as a control at a bare minimum. Through such studies, it may be possible to determine whether CPT variables (and which ones) can discriminate among these groups simultaneously. Is it not difficult in most clinics to distinguish normal from abnormal, yet this is the task of the CPT in most research. The problem is to differentiate adequately among the various psychopathologies that present to us. The CPT may be helpful in this regard, or it may not. It may be that algorithms can be devised from CPT variables to classify referrals into diagnostic categories quite well—or perhaps not. Even in the latter case, the CPT is still a good tool for assessment of *symptoms* associated with disturbances of attention and executive control. As such, the CPT may be a useful tool for monitoring effects of treatments (intended and unintended) on self-regulatory mechanisms.

References

Achenbach, T.M., & Edelbrock, C.S. (1986a). *Child Behavior Checklist*. Burlington, VT: University of Vermont, Department of Psychiatry.

Achenbach, T.M., & Edelbrock, C.S. (1986b). *Teacher Report Form*. Burlington, VT: University of Vermont, Department of Psychiatry.

Addington, J., & Addington, D. (1998). Facial affect recognition and information processing in schizophrenia and bipolar disorder. *Schizophrenia Research, 32,* 171–181.

Addington, J., McCleary, L., & Munroe-Blum, H. (1998). Relationship between cognitive and social dysfunction in schizophrenia. *Schizophrenia Research, 34,* 59–66.

Alexander, D.D. (1973). Attention dysfunction in senile dementia. *Psychological Reports, 32,* 229–230.

Alexander, L., Hightower, M.G., Anderson, R.P., & Snow, N.E. (1980). Suitability of vigilance test data as a neurobehavioral measure of uremic status. *Perceptual and Motor Skills, 50,* 131–135.

Ali, N.J., Pitson, D., & Strading, J.R. (1996). Sleep disordered breathing: Effects of adenotonsillectomy on behavior and psychological functioning. *European Journal of Pediatrics, 155,* 56–62.

Allen, L.F. (1993). *Developmental delay of frontal lobe functioning: A possible cause of attention deficits in children*. Unpublished doctoral dissertation, Texas A&M University, College Station.

Aman, M.G. (1978). Drugs, learning, and the psychotherapies. In J.S. Werry (Ed.), *Pediatric psychopharmacology: The use of behavior modifying drugs in children* (pp. 79–108). New York: Brunner/Mazel.

Aman, M.G., & Kern, R.A. (1989). Review of fenfluramine in the treatment of the developmental disabilities. *Journal of the American Academy of Child and Adolescent Psychiatry, 28,* 549–565.

Aman, M.G., Kern, R.A., McGhee, D.E., & Arnold, L.E. (1993). Fenfluramine and methylphenidate in children with mental retardation and attention deficit hyperactivity disorder: Laboratory effects. *Journal of Autism and Developmental Disorders, 23,* 491–506.

Aman, M.G., Marks, R.W., Turbott, S.H., Wilsher, L.P., & Merry, S.N. (1991). Methylphenidate and thiroidazine in the treatment of intellectually subaverage children: Effects on cognitive-motor performance. *Journal of the American Academy of Child and Adolescent Psychiatry, 30,* 816–824.

Aman, M.G., & Mayhew, J.M. (1980). Consistency of cognitive and motor performance measures over two years in reading retarded children. *Perceptual and Motor Skills, 50,* 1059–1065.

Aman, M.G., & Turbott, S.H. (1991). Prediction of clinical response in children taking methylphenidate. *Journal of Autism and Developmental Disorders, 21,* 211–228.

Aman, M.G., Vamos, W., & Werry, J.S. (1984). Effects of methylphenidate in normal adults with reference to drug action in hyperactivity. *Australian and New Zealand Journal of Psychiatry, 18,* 86–88.

Aman, M.G., Werry, J.S., Paxton, J.W., & Turbott, S.H. (1987). Effects of sodium valproate on psychomotor performance in children as a function of dose fluctuations in concentration and diagnosis. *Epilepsia, 28,* 115–124.

Aman, M.G., Werry, J.S., Paxton, J.W., Turbott, S.H., & Stewart, A.W. (1990). Effects of carbamazepine on psychomotor performance in children as a function of drug concentration, seizure type, and time of medication. *Epilepsia, 31,* 51–60.

American Academy of Child and Adolescent Psychiatry. (1997). Summary of the practice parameters for the assessment and treatment of children, adolescents, and adults with ADHD. *Journal of the American Academy of Child and Adolescent Psychiatry, 36,* 1311–1317.

American Educational Research Association. (1999). *Standards for educational and psychological testing.* Washington, DC: Author.

American Psychiatric Association. (1980). *Diagnostic and statistical manual of mental disorders* (3rd ed.). Washington, DC: Author.

American Psychiatric Association. (1994). *Diagnostic and statistical manual of mental disorders* (4th ed.). Washington, DC: Author.

American Psychological Association. (1999). *Standards for educational and psychological testing.* Washington, DC: American Educational Research Association.

Anastasi, A. (1988). *Psychological testing* (6th ed.). New York: Macmillan.

Anastopoulos, A.D., & Costabile, A.A. (1994). The Conners' Continuous Performance Test: A preliminary examination of its diagnostic utility. *ADHD Report,* 2(5), 7–8.

Anderson, K.C. (1990). *Assessment and treatment outcomes of medicated and unmedicated groups of children with attention deficit hyperactivity disorder.* Unpublished doctoral dissertation, Georgia State University, Atlanta.

Anderson, V.E., Siegel, F.S., Fisch, R.O., & Wirt, D. (1969). Response of phenylketonuric children on a continuous performance test. *Journal of Abnormal Psychology, 74,* 358–362.

Arcia, E., & Gualtieri, C.T. (1994). Neurobehavioral performance of adults with closed head injury, adults with attention deficit, and controls. *Brain Injury, 8,* 395–404.

Arcia, E., & Roberts, J.E. (1993). Otitis media in early childhood and its association with sustained attention in structured situations. *Developmental and Behavioral Pediatrics, 14,* 181–183.

Arnold, L.E., Janke, I., Waters, B., & Milch, A. (1999). Psychoactive effects of medical drugs. In J.S. Werry & M.G. Aman (Eds.), *Practitioner's guide to psychoactive drugs for children and adolescents* (2nd ed., pp. 387–412). New York: Plenum Press.

Arruda, J.E. (1994). *Confirmatory factor analyses of quantified electroencephalogram measured during a continuous performance test: A confirmation of neurocognitive systems.* Unpublished doctoral dissertation, University of Rhode Island, Providence.

Asarnow, R.F., & MacCrimmon, D.J. (1978). Residual performance deficit in clinically remitted schizophrenia: A marker of schizophrenia? *Journal of Abnormal Child Psychology, 87,* 597–608.

Asarnow, R.F., Steffy, R., MacCrimmon, D.J., & Cleghorn, J.M. (1977). An attentional assessment of foster children at risk for schizophrenia. *Journal of Abnormal Child Psychology, 86,* 267–275.

Assemany, A.E., & McIntosh, D.E. (1999, April). *The relationship between CPT and WISC-III performance of children with ADHD.* Paper presented at the annual meeting of the National Association of School Psychologists, Las Vegas, NV.

Atkins, M.S., Pelham, W.E., & White, K.J. (1990). Hyperactivity and attention deficit disorders. In M. Hersen & V.B. Vanhasselt (Eds.), *Psychological aspects of developmental and physical disabilities: A casebook* (pp. 137–156). Newbury Park, CA: Sage.

Atkins, M.S., Stoff, D.M., Osborne, M.L., & Brown, K. (1993). Distinguishing instrumental and hostile aggression: Does it make a difference? *Journal of Abnormal Child Psychology, 21,* 355–365.

August, G.J., & Garfinkel, B.D. (1989). Behavioral and cognitive subtypes of ADHD. *Journal of the American Academy of Child and Adolescent Psychiatry, 28,* 739–748.

Aylward, G., Gordon, M., & Verhulst, S. (1997). Relationships between continuous performance task scores and other cognitive measures: Causality or commonality? *Assessment, 4,* 325–336.

Aylward, G., Verhulst, S., & Bell, S. (1990). Individual and combined effects of attention deficits and learning disabilities on computerized ADHD assessment. *Journal of Psychoeducational Assessment, 8,* 497–508.

Baer, R.A. (1987). Effects of caffeine on classroom behavior, sustained attention, and a memory task in preschool children. *Journal of Applied Behavior Analysis, 20,* 225–234.

Baker, B.K. (1990). *The effect of methylphenidate on the attending behavior of children with closed-head injuries.* Unpublished doctoral dissertation, University of Utah, Salt Lake City.

Baker, D.B., Taylor, C.J., & Leyva, C. (1995). Continuous performance tests: A comparison of modalities. *Journal of Clinical Psychology, 51,* 548–551.

Baker, L., & Cantwell, D.P. (1990). The association between emotional/behavior disorders and learning disorders in children with speech/language disorders. *Advances in Learning and Behavioral Disabilities, 6,* 27–46.

Ballard, J.C. (1996a). Computerized assessment of sustained attention: Interactive effects of task demand, noise, and anxiety. *Journal of Clinical and Experimental Neuropsychology, 18,* 864–882.

Ballard, J.C. (1996b). Computerized assessment of sustained attention: A review of factors affecting vigilance performance. *Journal of Clinical and Experimental Neuropsychology, 18,* 843–863.

Banfi, S., & Dorigotti, L. (1984). Experimental behavioral studies with oxiracetam on different types of chronic cerebral impairment. *Clinical Neuropharmacology, 7,* 768–769.

Barbas, H., & Mesulam, M.M. (1981). Organization of afferent input of subdivisions of area 8 in the rhesus monkey. *Journal of Comparative Neurology, 200,* 407–431.

Barkley, R.A. (1977). A review of stimulant drug research with hyperactive children. *Journal of Child Psychology and Psychiatry, 18,* 137–155.

Barkley, R.A. (1990). *Attention deficit hyperactivity disorder: A handbook for diagnosis and treatment.* New York: Guilford Press.

Barkley, R.A. (1991). The ecological validity of laboratory and analogue assessment methods of ADHD symptoms. *Journal of Abnormal Child Psychology, 19,* 149–178.

Barkley, R.A. (1995). Sex differences in ADHD. *ADHD Report, 3*(1), 1–4.

Barkley, R.A. (1997a). Attention-deficit/hyperactivity disorder. In E.J. Mash & L.G. Terdal (Eds.), *Assessment of childhood disorders* (3rd ed., pp. 71–129). New York: Guilford Press.

Barkley, R.A. (1997b). Attention-deficit/hyperactivity disorder, self-regulation, and time: Toward a more comprehensive theory. *Developmental and Behavioral Pediatrics, 18,* 271–279.

Barkley, R.A. (1998). *Attention deficit hyperactivity disorder: A handbook for diagnosis and treatment* (2nd ed.). New York: Guilford Press.

Barkley, R.A., Anastopoulos, A.D., Guevremont, D.C., & Fletcher, K.E. (1991). Adolescents with ADHD: Patterns of behavioral adjustment, academic functioning, and treatment utilization. *Journal of the American Academy of Child and Adolescent Psychiatry, 30,* 752–761.

Barkley, R.A., DuPaul, G.J., & Connor, D.F. (1999). Stimulants. In J.S. Werry & M.G. Aman (Eds.), *Practitioner's guide to psychoactive drugs for children and adolescents* (2nd ed., pp. 213–248). New York: Plenum Press.

Barkley, R.A., DuPaul, G.J., & McMurray, M.B. (1990). Comprehensive evaluation of attention deficit disorder with and without hyperactivity as defined by research criteria. *Journal of Consulting and Clinical Psychology, 58,* 775–789.

Barkley, R.A., Fischer, R.F., Newby, R.F., & Breen, M.J. (1988). Development of a multimethod clinical protocol for assessing stimulant drug response in children with attention deficit disorder. *Journal of Clinical Child Psychology, 17,* 14–24.

Barkley, R.A., & Grodzinsky, G.M. (1994). Are tests of frontal lobe functions useful in the diagnosis of attention deficit disorders? *Clinical Neuropsychologist, 8,* 121–139.

Barkley, R.A., Grodzinsky, G.M., & DuPaul, G. (1992). Frontal lobe functions in attention deficit disorder with and without hyperactivity: A review and research report. *Journal of Abnormal Child Psychology, 20,* 163–188.

Barkley, R.A., McMurray, M.B., Edelbrock, C.S., & Robbins, K. (1989). The response of aggressive and non-aggressive attention deficit and hyperactivity disorder children to two doses of methylphenidate. *Journal of the American Academy of Child and Adolescent Psychiatry, 28,* 873–881.

Barkley, R.A., Murphy, K., & Kwasknik, D. (1996). Psychological adjustment and adaptive impairment in young adults with ADHD. *Journal of Attention Disorders, 1,* 41–54.

Barrickman, L., Noyes, R., Kuperman, S., Schumacher, E., & Verda, M. (1991). Treatment of ADHD with fluoxetine: A preliminary trial. *Journal of the American Academy of Child and Adolescent Psychiatry, 30,* 762–767.

Barrickman, L.L., Perry, P.J., Allen, A.J., Kuperman, S., Arndt, S.V., Hermann, K.J., & Schumacker, E. (1995). Buproprion versus methylphenidate in the treatment of attention-deficit hyperactivity disorder. *Journal of the American Academy of Child and Adolescent Psychiatry, 34,* 649–657.

Bauermeister, J.J., Berrios, V., Jimenez, A.L., Acevedo, L., & Gordon, M. (1990). Some issues and instruments for the assessment of attention deficit hyperactivity disorder in Puerto Rican children. *Journal of Clinical Child Psychology, 19*(1), 9–16.

Bawden, H.N. (1985). *Cognitive and behavioral effects of methylphenidate on conduct disorder in boys.* Unpublished doctoral dissertation, Carleton University, Ottowa, Ontario, Canada.

Bawden, H.N., MacDonald, W., & Shea, S. (1997). Treatment of children with William's syndrome with methylphenidate. *Journal of Clinical Neurology, 12,* 248–252.

Beale, I.L., Matthew, P.J., Oliver, S., & Corballis, M.C. (1987). Performance of disabled and normal readers on the continuous performance test. *Journal of Abnormal Child Psychology, 15,* 229–238.

Beck, A.T., Epstein, N., Brown, G., & Steer, R.A. (1988). An inventory for measuring clinical anxiety: Psychometric properties. *Journal of Consulting and Clinical Psychology, 56,* 893–897.

Becker, L.E. (1993). *Comprehensive auditory visual attention assessment system.* Fort Wayne, IN: Becker & Associates.

Becker, M.G., Isaac, W., & Hynd, G.W. (1987). Neuropsychological development of nonverbal behaviors attributed to "frontal lobe" functioning. *Developmental Neuropsychology, 3,* 275–298.

Bedi, G.C., Halperin, J.M., & Sharma, V. (1994). Investigation of modality specific distractibility in children. *International Journal of Neuroscience, 74,* 79–85.

Beers, S.R. (1992). Cognitive effects of mild head injury in children and adolescents. *Neuropsychology Review, 3,* 281–320.

Beery, K.D. (1982). *Developmental test of visual motor integration.* Chicago: Follett Educational Corporation.

Bender, B.G., Lerner, J.A., & Kollasch, E. (1988). Mood and memory changes in asthmatic children receiving corticosteroids. *Journal of the American Academy of Child and Adolescent Psychiatry, 27,* 720–725.

Bender, L. (1938). *A visual motor Gestalt test and its clinical use.* New York: American Orthopsychiatric Association.

Benedict, R.H., & Harris, A.E. (1989). Remediation of attention deficits in chronic schizophrenia patients: A preliminary study. *British Journal of Clinical Psychology, 28,* 187–188.

Benedict, R.H., Harris, A.E., Markow, T., McCormick, J.A., Nuechterlein, K.H., & Asarnow, R.F. (1994). The effects of attention training on information processing in schizophrenia. *Schizophrenia Bulletin, 20,* 537–546.

Benedict, R.H., Lockwood, A.H., Shucard, J.L., Shucard, D.W., Wack, D., & Murphy, B.W. (1998). Functional neuroimaging of attention in the auditory modality. *Neuroreport, 9,* 121–126.

Bennett, T.L., & Krein, L.K. (1989). The neuropsychology of epilepsy: Psychological and social impact. In C.R. Reynolds & E. Fletcher-Jantzen (Eds.), *Handbook of clinical child neuropsychology* (pp. 419–441). New York: Plenum Press.

Benton, A.L., Hamsher, K.D., Varney, N., & Spreen, O. (1983). *Contributions to neuropsychological assessment.* Oxford, England: Oxford University Press.

Benton, A.L., & Joynt, R.J. (1958). Reaction time in unilateral cerebral disease. *Confinia Neurologica, 19,* 247–256.

Ben-Yishay, Y., Piasetsky, E.B., & Rattock, J. (1987). A systematic method for ameliorating disorders in basic attention. In M.J. Meyer, A.L. Benton, & L. Diller (Eds.), *Neuropsychological rehabilitation* (pp. 165–181). Edinburgh, Scotland: Churchill.

Berch, D.B., & Kanter, D.R. (1984). Individual differences. In J.S. Warm (Ed.), *Sustained attention in human performance* (pp. 143–178). New York: Wiley.

Bergman, A., O'Brien, J., Osgood, G., & Cornblatt, B. (1995). Distractibility in schizophrenia. *Psychiatry Research, 57,* 131–140.

Bergman, A., Winters, L., & Cornblatt, B. (1991). Methylphenidate: Effects on sustained attention. In L.L. Greenhill & B.B. Osman (Eds.), *Ritalin: Theory and management* (pp. 223–232). New York: Mary Ann Liebert.

Bernstein, G.A., Carroll, M.E., Crosby, R.D., Perwien, A.R., Go, F.S., & Benowitz, N.L. (1994). Caffeine effects on learning, performance, and anxiety in normal school-age children. *Journal of the American Academy of Child and Adolescent Psychiatry, 33,* 407–415.

Biederman, J., Faraone, S.V., Keenan, K., Steingard, R., & Tsuang, M.T. (1991). Familial association between attention deficit disorder and anxiety disorders. *American Journal of Psychiatry, 148,* 251–256.

Bock, R.D. (1982). *The role of arousal in Tourette syndrome.* Unpublished doctoral dissertation, New York University, New York City.

Boivin, M.J., Chounramany, C., Giordani, B., Xaisida, S., Choulamountry, L., Pholsena, P., Crist, C.L., & Olness, K. (1996). Validating a cognitive ability testing protocol with Lao children for community development applications. *Neuropsychology, 10,* 588–599.

Borgschatz, H., Frankenberger, W., & Eder, R. (1999). Effects of information on perceptions of stimulant medication efficacy for treatment of attention-deficit hyperactivity disorder. *Psychology in the Schools, 36,* 515–522.

Bourke, D.L., Rosenberg, M., & Allen, P.D. (1984). Physostigmine: Effectiveness as an antagonist of respiratory depression and psychomotor effects caused by morphine or diazepam. *Anesthesiology, 61,* 523–528.

Bowen, L., Wallace, C.J., Glynn, S.M., Nuechterlein, K.H., Lirtzker, J.R., & Keuhnel, T.G. (1994). Schizophrenic individuals' cognitive functioning and performance in interpersonal interactions and skills training procedures. *Journal of Psychiatric Research, 28,* 289–301.

Brandt, J. (1984). Defective stimulus set attention in generalized epilepsy. *Brain and Cognition, 3,* 140–151.

Breen, M.J. (1989). Cognitive and behavioral differences in ADHD boys and girls. *Journal of Child Psychology and Psychiatry, 30,* 711–716.

Bremer, D.A. (1989). Mini–CPT: A continuous performance test program for the Tandy PC–8 pocket computer. *Behavior Research Methods, Instruments, and Computers, 21,* 11–14.

Broadbent, D.E. (1953). Noise, paced performance, and vigilance tasks. *British Journal of Psychology, 44,* 295–303.

Broadbent, D.E. (1957). A mechanical model for human attention and immediate memory. *Psychological Review, 64,* 205–215.

Brown, R.T., Coles, C.D., Smith, I.E., Platzman, K.A., Silverstein, J., Erickson, S., & Falek, A. (1991). Effects of prenatal alcohol exposure at school age: II. Attention and behavior. *Neurotoxicology and Teratology, 13,* 369–376.

Brown, R.T., & Ivers, C.E. (1999). Gilles de la Tourette syndrome. In S. Goldstein & C.R. Reynolds (Eds.), *Handbook of neurodevelopmental and genetic disorders in children* (pp. 185–215). New York: Guilford Press.

Brown, R.T., & Sawyer, M.G. (1998). *Medications for school-age children.* New York: Guilford Press.

Brown, R.T., & Sexson, S.B. (1988). A controlled trial of methylphenidate in Black adolescents. *Clinical Pediatrics, 27,* 74–81.

Bruininks, R.H. (1978). *Bruininks-Oseretsky Test of Motor Proficiency: Examiner's manual.* Circle Pines, MN: American Guidance Service.

Brumm, V.L. (1994). *Neuropsychological and psychological correlates of marital violence in a clinical sample.* Unpublished doctoral dissertation, University of Southern California, San Diego.

Brunner, R.L., & Berry, H.K. (1987). Phenylketonuria and sustained attention: The continuous performance test. *International Journal of Clinical Neuropsychology, 9,* 68–70.

Brunton, T.L. (1983). On the nature of inhibition, and the reaction of drugs upon it. *Nature, 27,* 419–422.

Buchanan, R.W., Strauss, M.E., Breier, A., Kirkpatrick, B., & Carpenter, W.T. (1997). Attentional impairments in deficit and nondeficit forms of schizophrenia. *American Journal of Psychiatry, 154,* 363–370.

Buchsbaum, M.S., Haier, R.J., Potkin, S.G., Nuechterlein, K.H., Bracha, S.H., Lohr, J., Wu, J.C., Lottenberg, S., Jerabeck, P.A., Trenary, M., Tafalla, R., Reynolds, C.R., & Bunney, W.E. (1992). Frontostriatal disorder of cerebral metabolism in never-medicated schizophrenics. *Archives of General Psychiatry, 49,* 935–942.

Buchsbaum, M.S., Haier, R.J., Sostek, A.J., Weingartner, H., Zahn, T.P., Silver, L.J., Murphy, D.L., & Brody, L. (1985). Attention dysfunction and psychopathology in college men. *Archives of General Psychiatry, 42,* 354–359.

Buchsbaum, M.S., & Hazlett, E. (1989). Relative metabolic rate in frontal lobes of normals and schizophrenics assessed by positron emission tomography. In S.C. Schulz & C.A. Tammiga (Eds.), *Schizophrenia: Scientific progress* (pp. 247–259). New York: Oxford University Press.

Buchsbaum, M.S., Lee, S., Haier, R., Wu, J.C., Green, M., & Tang, S.W. (1988). Effects of amoxapine and imipramine on evoked potentials in the continuous performance test in patients with affective disorder. *Neuropsychobiology, 20,* 15–22.

Buchsbaum, M.S., Nuechterlein, K.H., Haier, R.J., Wu, J.C., Sicotte, N., Hazlett, E., Asarnow, R.F., Potkin, S.G., & Guich, S.M. (1990). Glucose metabolic rate in normals and schizophrenics during the continuous performance test assessed by positron emission tomography. *British Journal of Psychiatry, 156,* 216–227.

Buchsbaum, M.S., Potkin, S.G., Siegel, B.V., Lohr, J., Katz, M., Gottschalk, L.A., Gulasekaram, B., Marshall, J.F., Lottenberg, S., Teng, C.Y., Abel, L., Plon, L., & Bunney, W.E. (1992). Striatal metabolic rate and clinic response to neuroleptics in schizophrenia. *Archives of General Psychiatry, 49,* 966–974.

Buchsbaum, M.S., Siegel, B.V., Wu, J.C., Hazlett, E.A., Sicotte, N., Haier, R.J., Tanguay, P., Asarnow, R., Cadorette, T., Donoghue, D., Lagunas-Solar, M., Lott, I., Paek, J., & Sabalesky, D. (1992). Brief report: Attention performance in autism and regional brain metabolic rate assessed by positron emission tomography. *Journal of Autism and Developmental Disorders, 22,* 115–125.

Buchsbaum, M.S., & Sostek, A.J. (1980). An adaptive-rate continuous performance test: Vigilance characteristics and reliability for 400 male students. *Perceptual and Motor Skills, 51,* 707.

Burda, P.C., Starkey, T.W., & Dominguez, F. (1991). Computer administered treatment of psychiatric inpatients. *Computers in Human Behavior, 7,* 1–5.

Burg, J.S., Burright, R.G., & Donovick, P.J. (1995). Performance data for traumatic brain injured subjects on the Gordon Diagnostic System (GDS) tests of attention. *Brain Injury, 9,* 395–403.

Burland, S.G. (1985). *A multimethod assessment of attention in school-aged boys.* Unpublished doctoral dissertation, University of Waterloo, Waterloo, Ontario, Canada.

Byrne, D.G. (1976). Vigilance and arousal in depressive states. *British Journal of Social and Clinical Psychology, 15,* 267–274.

Byrne, J.M., Bawden, H.N., DeWolfe, N.A., & Beattie, T.L. (1998). Clinical assessment of psychopharmacological treatment of preschoolers with ADHD. *Journal of Clinical and Experimental Neuropsychology, 20,* 613–627.

Calandre, E.P., Dominguez-Granados, R., Gomez-Rubio, M., & Molina-Font, J.A. (1990). Cognitive effects of long term treatment with phenobarbital and valproic acid in school children. *Acta Neurologica Scandinavica, 81,* 504–506.

Campanelli, P.A. (1970). Sustained attention in brain damaged children. *Exceptional Children, 36,* 317–327.

Campbell, J.W., D'Amato, R.C., Raggio, D.J., & Stephens, K.D. (1991). Construct validity of the computerized continuous performance test with measures of intelligence, achievement, and behavior. *Journal of School Psychology, 29,* 143–150.

Campbell, K.B., Courchesne, E., Picton, T.W., & Squires, K.C. (1979). Evoked potential correlates of human information processing. *Biological Psychiatry, 8,* 45–68.

Campbell, M. (1988). Annotation: Fenfluramine treatment of autism. *Journal of Child Psychology and Psychiatry, 29,* 1–10.

Campbell, M., Adams, P., Small, A.M., Curren, E.L., Overall, J.E., Anderson, L.T., Lynch, N., & Perry, R. (1988). Efficacy and safety of fenfluramine in autistic children. *Journal of the American Academy of Child and Adolescent Psychiatry, 27,* 434–439.

Cantwell, D.P., & Carlson, G.A. (1979). Stimulants. In J.S. Werry (Ed.), *Pediatric psychopharmacology* (pp. 171–207). New York: Brunner/Mazel.

Carter, C.S., Krener, P., Chaderjian, M., Northcutt, C., & Wolfe, V. (1995). Abnormal processing of irrelevant information in attention deficit hyperactivity disorder. *Psychiatry Research, 56,* 59–70.

Carter, C.S., Perlstein, W., Ganguli, R., Brar, J., Mintan, M., & Cohen, J.D. (1998). Functional hypofrontality and working memory dysfunction in schizophrenia. *American Journal of Psychiatry, 155,* 1285–1287.

Carter, J.D. (1992). *The relationship between intelligence and attention in kindergarten children.* Unpublished doctoral dissertation, University of British Columbia, Vancouver, Canada.

Carter, J.L., & Russell, H.L. (1985). Use of EMG biofeedback procedures with learning disabled children in a clinical setting. *Journal of Learning Disabilities, 18,* 213–216.

Cenedela, M. (1996). *TOVA: Test of Variables of Attention user's manual: IBM/PC version 7.0.* Los Alamitos, CA: Universal Attention Disorders.

Chadwick, O., Rutter, M., Brown, G., Shafer, D., & Traub, M. (1981). A prospective study of children with head injuries: II. Cognitive sequelae. *Psychological Medicine, 11,* 49–61.

Chae, P.K. (1999). Correlation study between WISC-III scores and TOVA performance. *Psychology in the Schools, 36,* 179–185.

Chappell, P.B., Riddle, M.A., Scahill, L., Lynch, K.A., Schultz, R., Arnsten, A., Leckman, J.F., & Cohen, D.J. (1995). Guanfacine treatment of comorbid attention deficit hyperactivity disorder and Tourette's syndrome: Preliminary clinical experience. *Journal of the American Academy of Child and Adolescent Psychiatry, 34,* 1140–1145.

Chee, P., Logan, G., Schachar, R., Lindsay, P., & Wachsmuth, R. (1989). Effects of event rate and display time on sustained attention in hyperactive, normal, and control children. *Journal of Abnormal Child Psychology, 17,* 371–391.

Chelune, G.J., & Baer, R.A. (1986). Developmental norms for the Wisconsin Card Sorting Test. *Journal of Clinical and Experimental Neuropsychology, 8,* 219–228.

Chen, W.J., Hsiao, C.K., Hsiao, L.L., & Hwu, H.G. (1998). Performance of the continuous performance test among community samples. *Schizophrenia Bulletin, 24,* 163–174.

Chugani, H.T. (1999). PET scanning studies of human brain development and plasticity. *Developmental Neuropsychology, 16,* 379–381.

Cicerone, K.D. (1997). Clinical sensitivity of four measures of attention to mild traumatic brain injury. *Clinical Neuropsychologist, 11,* 266–272.

Clark, C.R., Geffen, G.M., & Geffen, L.B. (1987a). Catecholamines and attention: I. Animal and clinical studies. *Neuroscience and Biobehavioral Reviews, 11,* 341–352.

Clark, C.R., Geffen, G.M., & Geffen, L.B. (1987b). Catecholamines and attention: II. Pharmacological studies in normal humans. *Neuroscience and Biobehavioral Reviews, 11,* 353–364.

Clure, C., Brady, K.T., Saladin, M.E., Johnson, D., Waid, R., & Rittenbury, M. (1999). Attention deficit/hyperactivity disorder and substance use: Symptom pattern and drug choice. *American Journal of Drug and Alcohol Abuse, 25,* 441–448.

Coffey, L.D. (1993). *The effects of methylphenidate on self-regulatory speech of children with attention deficit hyperactivity disorder.* Unpublished doctoral dissertation, Indiana State University, Terre Haute.

Cohan, M.F. (1995). *Validity investigation of the Conners' Continuous Performance Test.* Unpublished doctoral dissertation, State University of New York, Albany.

Cohen, A.F., Ashby, L., Crowley, D., Land, G., Peck, A.W., & Miller, A.A. (1985). Lamotrigine, a potential anticonvulsant: Effects on the central nervous system in comparison to phenytoin and diazepam. *British Journal of Clinical Pharmacology, 29,* 619–629.

Cohen, J.D., Barch, D.M., Carter, C., & Servan-Schreiber, D. (1999). Context processing deficits in schizophrenia: Converging evidence from three theoretically motivated cognitive tasks. *Journal of Abnormal Psychology, 108,* 120–133.

Cohen, J.D., & Servan-Schreiber, D. (1992). Context, cortex, and dopamine: A connectionist approach to behavior and biology in schizophrenia. *Psychological Review, 99,* 45–47.

Cohen, J.D., & Servan-Schreiber, D. (1993). A theory of dopamine function and its role in cognitive deficits in schizophrenia. *Schizophrenia Bulletin, 19,* 85–104.

Cohen, M.J., Riccio, C.A., & Gonzalez, J.J. (1994). Methodological differences in the diagnosis of attention-deficit hyperactivity disorder: Impact on prevalence. *Journal of Emotional and Behavioral Disorders, 2,* 31–38.

Cohen, R.A. (1993a). Attentional control: Subcortical and frontal lobe influences. In R.A. Cohen (Ed.), *The neuropsychology of attention* (pp. 219–254). New York: Plenum Press.

Cohen, R.A. (1993b). Introduction. In R.A. Cohen (Ed.), *The neuropsychology of attention* (pp. 3–10). New York: Plenum Press.

Cohen, R.A. (1993c). Neural mechanisms of attention. In R.A. Cohen (Ed.), *The neuropsychology of attention* (pp. 145–176). New York: Plenum Press.

Cohen, R.A. (1993d). Neuropsychological assessment of attention. In R.A. Cohen (Ed.), *The neuropsychology of attention* (pp. 307–328). New York: Plenum Press.

Cohen, R.A. (1993e). Toward an integrated neuropsychological framework of attention. In R.A. Cohen (Ed.), *The neuropsychology of attention* (pp. 459–482). New York: Plenum Press.

Cohen, R.A., Malloy, P.F., & Jenkins, M.A. (1999). Disorders of attention. In P.J. Snyder & P.D. Nussbaum (Eds.), *Clinical neuropsychology* (pp. 541–572). Washington, DC: American Psychological Association.

Cohen, R.A., & O'Donnell, B.F. (1993a). Attentional dysfunction associated with psychiatric illness. In R.A. Cohen (Ed.), *The neuropsychology of attention* (pp. 275–305). New York: Plenum Press.

Cohen, R.A., & O'Donnell, B.F. (1993b). Models and mechanisms of attention: A summary. In R.A. Cohen (Ed.), *The neuropsychology of attention* (pp. 177–188). New York: Plenum Press.

Cohen, R.A., & O'Donnell, B.F. (1993c). Neuropsychological models of attentional dysfunction. In R.A. Cohen (Ed.), *The neuropsychology of attention* (pp. 329–349). New York: Plenum Press.

Cohen, R.A., & O'Donnell, B.F. (1993d). Physiological substrates of attention. In R.A. Cohen (Ed.), *The neuropsychology of attention* (pp. 115–144). New York: Plenum Press.

Cohen, R.J., & Swerdlik, M.E. (1999). *Psychological testing and assessment: An introduction to tests and measurement* (4th ed.). Mountain View, CA: Mayfield.

Cohen, R.M., Semple, W.E., Gross, M., Holcomb, H.H., Dowling, S.M., & Nordahl, T.E. (1988). Functional localization of sustained attention. *Neuropsychology and Behavioral Neurology, 1,* 3–20.

Cohen, R.M., Semple, W.E., Gross, M., Nordahl, T.E., DeLise, L.E., Holcomb, H.H., King, A.C., Morihisa, J.M., & Pickar, D. (1987). Dysfunction in a prefrontal substrate of sustained attention in schizophrenia. *Life Sciences, 40,* 2031–2039.

Cohen, R.M., Semple, W.E., Gross, M., Nordahl, T.E., Holcomb, H.H., Dowling, M.S., & Pickar, D. (1988). The effect of neuroleptics on dysfunction in a prefrontal substrate of sustained attention in schizophrenia. *Life Sciences, 44,* 1141–1150.

Cohler, B.J., Grunebaum, H.U., Weiss, J.L., Gamer, E., & Gallant, D.H. (1977). Disturbance of attention among schizophrenic, depressed and well mothers and their children. *Journal of Child Psychology and Psychiatry, 18,* 115–135.

Colby, L. (1991). The neuroanatomy and neurophysiology of attention. *Journal of Child Neurology, 6*(Suppl.), S90–S118.

Congalton, A.A. (1969). *Status and prestige in Australia.* Chesire, Australia: Author.

Conners, C.K. (1992). *Conners' Continuous Performance Test user's manual.* Toronto, Canada: Multi-Health Systems.

Conners, C.K. (1995). *Conners' Continuous Performance Test user's manual.* Toronto, Canada: Multi-Health Systems.

Conners, C.K. (1999). *Kiddie Continuous Performance Test.* Toronto, Canada: Multi-Health Systems.

Conners, C.K., Casat, C.D., Gualtieri, T., Weller, E., Reader, M., Reiss, A., Weller, R.A., Khayrallah, M., & Ascher, J. (1996). Bupropion hydrochloride in attention deficit disorder with hyperactivity. *Journal of the American Academy of Child and Adolescent Psychiatry, 34,* 1314–1321.

Conners, C.K., & Rothschild, G.H. (1968). Drugs and learning in children. *Learning Disorders, 3,* 193–218.

Conners, C.K., & Sparrow, E.P. (1999). Nootropics and foods. In J.S. Werry & M.G. Aman (Eds.), *Practitioner's guide to psychoactive drugs for children and adolescents* (2nd ed., pp. 413–432). New York: Plenum Press.

Conners, C.K., & Taylor, E. (1980). Pemoline, methylphenidate, and placebo in children with minimal brain dysfunction. *Archives of General Psychiatry, 37,* 922–930.

Coons, H.W., Klorman, R., & Borgstedt, A.D. (1987). Effects of methylphenidate on adolescents with a childhood history of attention deficit disorder: II. Information processing. *Journal of the American Academy of Child and Adolescent Psychiatry, 26,* 368–374.

Coons, H.W., Peloquin, L.J., Klorman, R., Bauer, L.O., Ryan, R.M., Perlmutter, R.A., & Salzman, L.F. (1981). Effects of methylphenidate on young adults' vigilance and event-related potentials. *Electroencephalography and Clinical Neurophysiology, 51*, 373–387.

Corbetta, M., Miezen, F.M., Dobmeyer, S., Shulman, G.L., & Petersen, S.E. (1993). Selective and divided attention during visual discrimination of shape, color, and speed: Functional anatomy by positron emission tomography. *Journal of Neuroscience, 11*, 2383–2402.

Corbetta, M., Miezen, F.M., Shulman, G.L., & Petersen, S.E. (1991). A PET study of visuospatial attention. *Journal of Neuroscience, 13*, 1202–1226.

Corkum, P.V., Schachar, R.J., & Siegel, L.S. (1996). Performance on the continuous performance task and the impact of reward. *Journal of Attention Disorders, 1*, 163–172.

Corkum, P.V., & Siegel, L.S. (1993). Is the continuous performance task a valuable research tool for use with children with attention deficit hyperactivity disorder? *Journal of Child Psychology and Psychiatry, 34*, 1217–1239.

Cornblatt, B.A., & Keilp, J.G. (1994). Impaired attention, genetics, and pathophysiology of schizophrenia. *Schizophrenia Bulletin, 20*, 31–46.

Cornblatt, B.A., Lenzenweger, M.F., & Erlenmeyer-Kimling, L. (1989). The Continuous Performance Test, Identical Pairs version (CPT-IP): II. Contrasting attentional profiles in schizophrenia and depressed patients. *Psychiatry Research, 29*, 65–85.

Cornblatt, B.A., Obuchowski, M., Schnur, D.B., & O'Brien, J.D. (1997). Attention and clinical symptoms in schizophrenia. *Psychiatric Quarterly, 68*, 343–359.

Cornblatt, B.A., Risch, N.J., Faris, G., Friedman, D., & Erlenmeyer-Kimling, L. (1988). The Continuous Performance Test, Identical Pairs version (CPT-IP): I. New findings about sustained attention in normal families. *Psychiatry Research, 26*, 223–238.

Cornblatt, B.A., Winters, L., & Erlenmeyer-Kimling, L. (1989). Attentional markers of schizophrenia: Evidence from the New York high risk study. In S.C. Schulz & C.A. Tamminga (Eds.), *Schizophrenia: Scientific progress* (pp. 83–92). New York: Oxford University Press.

Costa, L., Arruda, J.E., Stern, R.A., Somerville, J.A., & Valentino, D. (1997). Asymptomatic HIV-infected women: Preliminary study of quantitative EEG activity and performance on a continuous performance test. *Perceptual and Motor Skills, 85*, 1395–1408.

Craig, S. (1983). *Sustained attention in hospitalized borderline patients.* Unpublished doctoral dissertation, Boston University, Boston.

Crocker, L., & Algina, J. (1986). *Introduction to classical and modern test theory.* Orlando, FL: Harcourt Brace Jovanovich.

Crosby, K.G. (1972). Attention and distractibility in mentally retarded and intellectually average children. *American Journal of Mental Deficiency, 77*, 46–53.

Dahl, R., White, R.F., Weihe, P., Sorensen, N., Letz, R., Hudnell, H.K., Otto, D.A., & Grandjean, P. (1996). Feasibility and validity of three computer-assisted neurobehavioral tests in 7-year-old children. *Neurotoxicology and Teratology, 18*, 413–419.

Dainer, K.B., Klorman, R., Salzman, L.F., Hess, D.W., Davidson, P.W., & Michael, R.L. (1981). Learning-disordered children's evoked potentials during sustained attention. *Journal of Abnormal Child Psychology, 9,* 79–94.

Dalteg, A., Rasmussen, K., Jensen, J., Persson, B., Lindgren, M., Lundquist, A., Wirsen-Meurling, A., Ingvar, D.H., & Levander, S. (1997). Prisoners use an inflexible strategy in a continuous performance test: A replication. *Personality and Individual Differences, 23,* 1–7.

Damasio, A.R., Damasio, H., & Chang Chui, H. (1980). Neglect following damage to frontal lobes or basal ganglia. *Neuropsychologia, 18,* 123–132.

Das, J.P., Snyder, J.J., & Mishra, R.K. (1992). Assessment of attention: Teachers' rating scales and measures of selective attention. *Journal of Psychoeducational Assessment, 10,* 37–46.

Davies, A.D.M., & Davies, D.R. (1975). The effects of noise and time of day upon age differences in performance at two checking tasks. *Ergonomics, 18,* 321–336.

Davies, D.R., & Parasuraman, R. (1977). Cortical evoked potentials and vigilance: A decision theory analysis. In R.R. Mackie (Ed.), *Vigilance: Theory, operational performance, and physiological correlates* (pp. 285–306). New York: Plenum Press.

Dee, H.L., & van Allen, M.W. (1973). Speed of decision-making processes in patients with unilateral cerebral disease. *Archives of Neurology, 28,* 163–166.

DelMundo, A.S., Pumariega, A.J., & Vance, H.R. (1999). Psychopharmacology in school-based mental health services. *Psychology in the Schools, 36,* 437–450.

Denckla, M.B. (1996). Biological correlates of learning and attention: What is relevant to learning disabilities and attention deficit hyperactivity disorder? *Journal of Developmental and Behavioral Pediatrics, 17,* 114–119.

Dennis, M., Wilkinson, M., Koski, L., & Humphries, R.P. (1995). Attention deficits in the long term after childhood head injury. In S.H. Broman & M.E. Michel (Eds.), *Traumatic head injury in children* (pp. 165–187). New York: Oxford University Press.

Deragotis, L.R. (1986). *Manual for the Symptom Checklist 90–Revised (SCL-90-R).* Baltimore: Author.

DeRenzi, E., & Faglioni, P. (1965). The comparative efficiency of intelligence and vigilance tests in detecting hemispheric change. *Cortex, 1,* 410–433.

Detweiler, R.E., Hicks, A.P., & Hicks, M.R. (1995). The multi-modal diagnosis and treatment of attention deficit hyperactivity disorder. *Therapeutic Care and Education, 4,* 4–9.

Diller, L., & Gordon, W.A. (1981). Interventions for cognitive deficits in brain-injured adults. *Journal of Consulting and Clinical Psychology, 49,* 822–834.

Dodrill, C.B. (1988). Effects of anti-epileptic drugs on abilities. *Journal of Clinical Psychiatry, 49*(Suppl.), S31–S34.

Donders, J. (1993). Memory functioning after traumatic brain injury in children. *Brain Injury, 7,* 431–437.

Donnelly, M., Rapoport, J.L., Potter, W.Z., Oliver, J., Keysor, C.S., & Murphy, D.L. (1989). Fenfluramine and dextroamphetamine treatment of childhood hyperactivity: Clinical and biochemical findings. *Archives of General Psychiatry, 46,* 205–212.

Dorwen, H.F., Elger, C.E., Helmstaedter, C., & Penin, H. (1989). Circumscribed improvement of cognitive performance in temporal lobe epilepsy patients with intractable seizures following reduction of anti-convulsant medication. *Journal of Epilepsy, 2,* 147–152.

Downey, K.K., Stetson, F.W., Pomerleau, O.F., & Giordani, B. (1997). Adult attention deficit hyperactivity disorder: Psychological profile in a clinical population. *Journal of Nervous and Mental Disease, 185,* 32–38.

Draeger, S., Prior, M., & Sanson, A. (1986). Visual and auditory attention performance in hyperactive children: Competence or compliance. *Journal of Abnormal Child Psychology, 14,* 411–424.

Driscoll, S.M. (1994). *The development and evaluation of objective auditory and visual attention instruments.* Unpublished doctoral dissertation, Northwestern University, Evanston, IL.

Dumont, R., Tamborra, A., & Stone, B. (1995). Continuous performance tests: The TOVA, Conners' CPT, and IVA. *Communique, 21*(1), 22–24.

Dumont, R., Tamborra, A., & Stone, B. (1999, April 13). *Continuous performance tests* (1–8). Available: http://www.plattsburgh.edu/faculty/dumontr/homepage/cpt_review.htm

Duncan, J.S., Shorvon, S.D., & Trimble, M.R. (1990). Effects of the removal of phenytoin, carbamazepine, and valproate on cognitive function. *Epilepsia, 31,* 584–591.

Dunn, L.M., & Dunn, L.M. (1981). *Peabody Picture Vocabulary Test–Revised.* Circle Pines, MN: American Guidance Service.

Dunn, L.M., & Markwardt, F.C. (1970). *Peabody Individual Achievement Test manual.* Circle Pines, MN: American Guidance Service.

DuPaul, G.J., Anastopoulos, A.D., Shelton, T.L., Guevremont, D.C., & Metevia, L. (1992). Multimethod assessment of attention deficit hyperactivity disorder: The diagnostic utility of clinic-based tests. *Journal of Clinical Child Psychology, 21,* 394–402.

DuPaul, G.J., & Eckert, T.L. (1997). The effects of school-based interventions for attention deficit hyperactivity disorder: A meta-analysis. *School Psychology Review, 26,* 5–27.

DuPaul, G.J., Guevremont, D.C., & Barkley, R.A. (1992). Behavioral treatment of attention-deficit hyperactivity disorder in the classroom: The use of the attention training system. *Behavior Modification, 16,* 204–225.

Dupuy, T.R. (1995). *The prevalence of attention deficit disorder in a sample of at risk middle school students.* Unpublished doctoral dissertation, California State University, Northridge.

Dykman, R.A., & Ackerman, P.T. (1991). Attention deficit disorder and specific reading disability: Separate but often overlapping disorders. *Journal of Learning Disabilities, 24,* 96–103.

Dykman, R.A., & Ackerman, P.T. (1993). Behavioral subtypes of attention deficit disorder. *Exceptional Children, 60,* 132–141.

Earle-Boyer, E.A., Serper, M.R., Davidson, M., & Harvey, P.D. (1991). Continuous performance tests in schizophrenic patients: Stimulus and medication effects on performance. *Psychiatry Research, 37,* 47–56.

Ebert, J. (1995). Review of attention-deficit/hyperactivity disorder: Implications for identification and management. *Journal of Psychological Practice, 1,* 81–98.

Edley, R.S., & Knopf, I.J. (1987). Sustained attention as a predictor of low academic readiness in a preschool population. *Journal of Psychoeducational Assessment, 4,* 340–352.

Edwards, G. (1998). Determining the role of a new continuous performance test in the diagnostic evaluation for ADHD. *ADHD Report, 6*(3), 11–13.

Eisner, A., & McClellan, J. (1999). Drugs of abuse. In J.S. Werry & M.G. Aman (Eds.), *Practitioner's guide to psychoactive drugs for children and adolescents* (2nd ed., pp. 329–353). New York: Plenum Press.

Eliason, M.J. (1988). Neuropsychological patterns: Neurofibromatosis compared to developmental learning disorders. *Neurofibromatosis, 1,* 17–25.

Eliason, M.J., & Richman, L.C. (1987). The continuous performance test in learning disabled and nondisabled children. *Journal of Learning Disabilities, 20,* 614–619.

Eliason, M.J., & Richman, L.C. (1988). Behavior and attention in LD children. *Learning Disability Quarterly, 11,* 360–369.

Ellis, C.R. (1991). *The utility of a computerized assessment battery to evaluate cognitive functioning and attention.* Unpublished doctoral dissertation, College of William and Mary, Williamsburg, VA.

Enander, A. (1987). Effects of moderate cold on performance of psychomotor and cognitive tasks. *Ergonomics, 30,* 1431–1445.

Endicott, J., Spitzer, R.L., Fleiss, J.L., & Cohen, J. (1976). The Global Assessment Scale: A procedure for measuring overall severity of psychiatric disturbance. *Archives of General Psychiatry, 33,* 766–771.

Epstein, J.N., Conners, C.K., Erhardt, D., March, J.S., & Swanson, J.M. (1997). Asymmetrical hemispheric control of visual-spatial attention in adults with attention deficit hyperactivity disorder. *Neuropsychology, 11,* 467–473.

Epstein, J.N., Conners, C.K., Sitarenios, G., & Erhardt, D. (1998). Continuous performance test results of adults with attention deficit hyperactivity disorder. *Clinical Neuropsychologist, 12,* 155–168.

Epstein, J.N., Keefe, R.S.E., Roitman, S.L., Harvey, P.D., & Mohs, R.C. (1996). Impact of neuroleptic medications on continuous performance test measures in schizophrenia. *Biological Psychiatry, 39,* 902–905.

Erickson, W.D., Yellin, A.M., Hopwood, J.H., Realmuto, G.M., & Greenberg, L.M. (1984). The effects of neuroleptics on attention in adolescent schizophrenics. *Biological Psychiatry, 19,* 745–753.

Erkwoh, R., Sabri, O., Willmes, K., Steinmeyer, E.M., Buell, U., & Sass, H. (1999). Active and remitted schizophrenia: Psychopathological and regional cerebral blood flow findings. *Psychiatric Research: Neuroimaging, 90,* 17–30.

Erlenmeyer-Kimling, L., & Cornblatt, B. (1978). Attentional measures in a study of children at high risk for schizophrenia. *Journal of Psychiatric Research, 14,* 93–98.

Ernst, M., Liebenauer, L.L., Tebeka, D., Jons, P.H., Eisenhofer, G., Murphy, D.L., & Zametkin, A.J. (1997). Selegiline in ADHD adults: Plasma monamines and monamine metabolites. *Neuropsychopharmacology, 16,* 276–284.

Ernst, M., Malone, R.P., Rowan, A.B., George, R., Gonzalez, N.M., & Silva, R.R. (1999). Antipsychotics (neuroleptics). In J.S. Werry & M.G. Aman (Eds.), *Practitioner's guide to psychoactive drugs for children and adolescents* (2nd ed., pp. 297–329). New York: Plenum Press.

Ernst, M., Zametkin, A.J., Phillips, R.L., & Cohen, R.M. (1998). Age-related changes in brain glucose metabolism in adults with attention-deficit/hyperactivity disorder and control subjects. *Journal of Neuropsychiatry and Clinical Neurosciences, 10,* 168–177.

Ervin, R.A., Bankert, C.L., & DuPaul, G.J. (1996). Treatment of attention-deficit/hyperactivity disorder. In M.A. Reinecke, F.M. Dattilio, & A. Freeman (Eds.), *Cognitive therapy with children and adolescents: A casebook for clinical practice* (pp. 38–61). New York: Guilford Press.

Estrin, W.J., Cavalieri, S.A., Wald, P., Becker, C.E., Jones, J.R., & Cone, J.E. (1987). Evidence of neurologic dysfunction related to long-term ethylene oxide exposure. *Archives of Neurology, 44,* 1283–1286.

Estrin, W.J., Moore, P., Letz, R., & Wasch, H.H. (1988). The P-300 event-related potential in experimental nitrous oxide exposure. *Clinical Pharmacology & Therapeutics, 43,* 86–90.

Evans, C.A. (1988). *A study of vigilance, memory processing speed, cognitive ability and the prediction of academic achievement in children 6–14 years old.* Unpublished doctoral dissertation, Ohio State University, Columbus.

Evans, J.H., Ferre, L., Ford, L.A., & Green, J.L. (1995). Decreasing attention deficit hyperactivity disorder symptoms utilizing an automated classroom reinforcement device. *Psychology in the Schools, 32,* 210–219.

Ewing-Cobbs, L., Fletcher, J.M., & Levin, H.S. (1986). Neurobehavioral sequelae following head injury in children: Educational implications. *Journal of Head Trauma Rehabilitation, 14,* 57–65.

Ewing-Cobbs, L., Prasad, M., Fletcher, J.M., Levin, H.S., Miner, M.E., & Eisenberg, H.M. (1998). Attention after pediatric traumatic brain injury: A multidimensional assessment. *Child Neuropsychology, 4,* 35–38.

Fallgatter, A.J., Brandeis, D., & Strik, W.K. (1997). A robust assessment of the no go anteriorization of P300 microstates in a cued continuous performance test. *Brain Topography, 9,* 295–302.

Fallgatter, A.J., & Strik, W.K. (1997). Right frontal activation during the continuous performance test assessed with near-infrared spectroscopy in healthy subjects. *Neuroscience Letters, 233,* 89–92.

Fallgatter, A.J., Wiesbeck, G.A., Weijers, H-G., Boening, J.Y., & Strik, W.K. (1998). Event-related correlates of response suppression as indicators of novelty seeking in alcoholics. *Alcohol and Alcoholism, 33,* 475–481.

Farwell, J.R., Lee, Y.J., Hirtz, D.G., Suizbacher, S.I., Ellenberg, J.H., & Nelson, K.B. (1990). Phenobarbital for febrile seizures: Effects on intelligence and on seizure recurrence. *New England Journal of Medicine, 322,* 264–368.

Faust, M.E., & Balota, D.A. (1997). Inhibition of return and visuospatial attention in healthy adults and individuals with dementia of the Alzheimer type. *Neuropsychology, 11,* 13–29.

Fehmi, L. (1987). Biofeedback assisted attention training: Open Focus Workshop. *Psychotherapy in Private Practice, 5,* 47–49.

Feingold, B. (1975). *Why your child is hyperactive.* New York: Random House.

Finkelstein, J.R.J., Cannon, T.D., Gur, R.E., Gur, R.C., & Moberg, P. (1997). Attentional dysfunctions in neuroleptic naïve and neuroleptic withdrawn schizophrenic patients and their siblings. *Journal of Abnormal Psychology, 106,* 203–212.

Fischer, M., Barkley, R., Edelbrock, C., & Smallish, L. (1990). The adolescent outcome of hyperactive children diagnosed by research criteria: II. Academic, attentional, and neuropsychological status. *Journal of Consulting and Clinical Psychology, 58,* 580–588.

Fischer, M., & Newby, R.F. (1991). Assessment of stimulant response in ADHD children using a refined multimethod clinical protocol. *Journal of Clinical Child Psychology, 20,* 232–244.

Fischer, M., Newby, R.F., & Gordon, M. (1995). Who are the false negatives on continuous performance tests? *Journal of Clinical Child Psychology, 24,* 427–433.

Fitzpatrick, P.A., Klorman, R., Brumaghim, J.T., & Borgstedt, A.D. (1992). Effects of sustained release and standard preparations of methylphenidate on attention deficit disorder. *Journal of the American Academy of Child and Adolescent Psychiatry, 31,* 226–234.

Flansburg, M.W. (1986). *Validation of the Gordon Diagnostic System and the WISC-R in the diagnosis of attention deficit disorder.* Unpublished doctoral dissertation, University of Nebraska, Lincoln.

Flavell, J.H. (1971). First discussant's comments: What is memory development the development of? *Human Development, 14,* 272–278.

Fleming, K.L. (1991). *Visual information processing deficits in mania: Vulnerability or episode indicators?* Unpublished doctoral dissertation, California School of Professional Psychology, Fresno.

Fleming, K.L., Goldberg, T.W., & Gold, J.M. (1994). Applying working memory constructs to schizophrenic cognitive impairment. In. A.S. David & J.C. Cutting (Eds.), *The neuropsychology of schizophrenia* (pp. 197–213). Hillsdale, NJ: Erlbaum.

Floyd, R.G. (1999, August). *Convergent and divergent validity of the preschool checking task.* Paper presented at the annual convention of the American Psychological Association, Boston.

Forbes, G.B. (1998). Clinical utility of the Test of Variables of Attention (TOVA) in the diagnosis of attention deficit hyperactivity disorder. *Journal of Clinical Psychology, 54,* 461–476.

Forsyth, G.A., Forsyth, P.D., & Pinsince, J. (1970). Dimensional salience as a function of educational attainment and method of discrimination training. *Perception and Psychophysics, 7,* 345–347.

Forsythe, I., Butler, R., Berg, I., & McGuire, R. (1991). Cognitive impairment in new cases of epilepsy randomly assigned to carbamazepine, phenytoin, and sodium valproate. *Developmental Medicine and Child Neurology, 33,* 524–534.

Franke, P., Maier, W., Hardt, J., Hain, C., & Cornblatt, B.A. (1994). Attentional abilities and measures of schizotypy: Their variation and covariation in schizophrenic patients, their siblings, and normal control subjects. *Psychiatry Research, 54,* 259–272.

Franklin, R.D., Allison, D.B., & Gorman, B.S. (Eds.). (1996). *Design and analysis of single-case research.* Hillsdale, NJ: Erlbaum.

French, C.L., & Riccio, C.A. (1999). *Efficacy of programs to remediate attention.* Paper presented at the 19th annual National Academy of Neuropsychology Conference, San Antonio, TX.

Fried, P.A., Watkinson, B., & Gray, R. (1992). A follow-up study of attentional behavior in 6-year-old children exposed prenatally to marihuana, cigarettes, and alcohol. *Neurotoxicology and Teratology, 14,* 299–311.

Friedman, D., Boltri, J., Vaughan, H., Jr., & Erlenmeyer-Kimling, L. (1985). Effects of age and sex on the endogenous brain potential components during two continuous performance tests. *Psychophysiology, 22,* 440–452.

Friedman, D., Cornblatt, B., Vaughan, H., Jr., & Erlenmeyer-Kimling, L. (1986). Event-related potentials in children at risk for schizophrenia during two versions of the continuous performance test. *Psychiatry Research, 18,* 161–177.

Friedman, D., Erlenmeyer-Kimling, L., & Vaughan, H., Jr. (1985). Auditory event-related potentials in children at risk for schizophrenia revisited: Re-diagnosis of the patient parents and inclusion of the psychiatric control group. *Psychophysiology, 22,* 590.

Friedman, D., Vaughan, H.G., Jr., & Erlenmeyer-Kimling, L. (1978). Stimulus and response related components of the late positive complex in visual discrimination tasks. *Electroencephalography and Clinical Neurophysiology, 45,* 319–330.

Friedman, D., Vaughan, H.G., Jr., & Erlenmeyer-Kimling, L. (1981). Multiple late positive potentials in two visual discrimination tasks. *Neurophysiology, 18,* 635–649.

Fritcher, M.K. (1993). *The effect of whole brain integration on ADD/ADHD.* Unpublished thesis, Texas A&M University, College Station.

Fritz, G., & Fehmi, L. (1983). *The open focus handbook.* Englewood Cliffs, NJ: Biofeedback Computers.

Fuster, J.M. (1980). *The prefrontal cortex.* New York: Raven Press.

Fuster, J.M. (1989). *The prefrontal cortex: Anatomy, physiology, and neuropsychology of the frontal lobe* (2nd ed.). New York: Raven Press.

Gadow, K. (1991). Clinical issues in child and adolescent psychopharmacology. *Journal of Consulting and Clinical Psychology, 59,* 842–852.

Gadow, K. (1993). Prevalence of drug therapy. In J.S. Werry & M.G. Aman (Eds.), *Practitioner's guide to psychoactive drugs for children and adolescents* (pp. 57–74). New York: Plenum Press.

Gadow, K.D., Sverd, J., Sprafkin, J., Nolan, E.E., & Grossman, S. (1999). Long-term methylphenidate therapy in children with comorbid attention-deficit hyperactivity disorder and chronic multiple tic disorder. *Archives of General Psychiatry, 56,* 330–336.

García-Sánchez, C., Estévez-Gonzáles, A., Suárez-Romero, E., & Junqué, C. (1997). Right hemisphere dysfunction in subjects with attention-deficit disorder with and without hyperactivity. *Journal of Child Neurology, 12,* 107–115.

Garfinkel, B.D., Brown, W.A., Klee, S.H., Braden, W., Beauchesnes, H., & Shapiro, S.K. (1986). Neuroendocrine and cognitive responses to amphetamine in adolescents with a history of attention deficit disorder. *Journal of the American Academy of Child and Adolescent Psychiatry, 25,* 503–508.

Garfinkel, B.D., & Klee, S.H. (1983). A computerized assessment battery for attention deficits. *Psychiatry Hospitals, 14,* 163–166.

Garretson, H.B., Fein, D., & Waterhouse, L. (1990). Sustained attention in children with autism. *Journal of Autism and Developmental Disorders, 20,* 101–114.

Gerstadt, C.L., Hong, Y.J., & Diamond, A. (1994). The relationship between cognition and action: Performance of children on a Stroop-like daylight test. *Cognition, 53,* 129–153.

Gevins, A.S., Bressler, S.L., Morgan, N.H., Cutillo, B.A., White, R.M., Greer, D.S., & Illes, J. (1989). Event-related covariances during a bimanual visuomotor task: I. Methods and analysis of stimulus- and response-locked data. *Electroencephalography and Clinical Neuropsychology, 74,* 58–75.

Gianutsos, R. (1992). The computer in cognitive rehabilitation: It's not just a tool anymore. *Journal of Head Trauma Rehabilitation, 7,* 26–35.

Giaquinto, S., & Fiori, M. (1992). THINKable, a computerized cognitive remediation: First results. *Acta Neurologica, 14,* 547–560.

Gilbert, P.F. (1995). *Sustained attention among mothers of individuals with schizophrenia.* Unpublished doctoral dissertation, University of Houston, TX.

Girardi, N.L., Shaywitz, S.E., Marchione, K., Fleischman, S.J., Jones, T.W., & Tamborlane, W.V. (1995). Blunted catecholamine responses after glucose ingestion in children with attention deficit disorder. *Pediatric Research, 38,* 539–542.

Goldberg, J.O., & Konstanareas, M.M. (1979). Vigilance in hyperactive and normal children on a self-paced operant task. *Journal of Child Psychology and Psychiatry, 22,* 55–63.

Goldberg, T.W., & Weinberger, D.R. (1995). Thought disorder, working memory and attention: Interrelationships and the effects of neuroleptic medications. *International Clinical Psychopharmacology, 10*(Suppl. 3), 99–104.

Golden, C.J. (1975). The relationship of the Stroop color and word tests for the presence and localization of brain dysfunction. *Dissertation Abstracts International, 36*(5-B), 2470.

Golden, C.J. (1988). *Luria-Nebraska Neuropsychological Battery.* Los Angeles: Western Psychological Service.

Goldman-Rakic, P.S. (1988). Topography of cognition: Parallel distributed networks in primate association cortex. *Annual Review of Neuroscience, 11,* 137–156.

Goldstein, P.C., Rosenbaum, G., & Taylor, M.J. (1997). Assessment of differential attention mechanisms in seizure disorders and schizophrenia. *Neuropsychology, 11,* 309–317.

Golier, J., Yehuda, R., Cornblatt, B., Harvey, P., Gerber, D., & Levengood, R. (1997). Sustained attention in combat-related posttraumatic stress disorder. *Integrative Physiological and Behavioral Science, 32,* 52–61.

Gordon, M. (1983). *The Gordon Diagnostic System.* DeWitt, NY: Gordon Systems.

Gordon, M. (1986a). How is a computerized attention test used in the diagnosis of attention deficit disorder? *Journal of Children in Contemporary Society, 19,* 53–64.

Gordon, M. (1986b). Microprocessor-based assessment of attention deficit disorders. *Psychopharmacology Bulletin, 22,* 288–290.

Gordon, M. (1987). *The Attention Training System (ATS) user's manual.* New York: Gordon Systems.

Gordon, M., DiNiro, D., & Mettelman, B.B. (1988). Effect upon outcome of nuances in selection criteria for ADHD/hyperactivity. *Psychological Reports, 62,* 530–544.

Gordon, M., DiNiro, D., Mettelman, B.B., & Tallmadge, J. (1989). Observations of test behavior, quantitative scores and teacher ratings. *Journal of Psychoeducational Assessment, 7,* 141–147.

Gordon, M., McClure, F.D., & Aylward, G.P. (1996). *Gordon Diagnostic System interpretive guide.* DeWitt, NY: Gordon Systems.

Gordon, M., & Mettelman, B.B. (1988). The assessment of attention: I. Standardization and reliability of a behavior-based measure. *Journal of Clinical Psychology, 44,* 682–690.

Gordon, M., Mettelman, B.B., & DiNiro, D. (1989). *Are continuous performance tests valid in the diagnosis of ADHD/hyperactivity?* Paper presented at the 97th annual convention of the American Psychological Association, New Orleans, LA.

Gordon, M., Mettelman, B.B., & Irwin, M. (1994). Sustained attention and grade retention. *Perceptual and Motor Skills, 78,* 555–560.

Gordon, M., Thomason, D., & Cooper, S. (1990). To what extent does attention affect K-ABC scores? *Psychology in the Schools, 27,* 144–147.

Gordon, M., Thomason, D., Cooper, S., & Ivers, C.L. (1991). Nonmedical treatment of ADHD/hyperactivity: The attention training system. *Journal of School Psychology, 29,* 151–159.

Gordon Systems, Inc. (1986). *Technical manual for the Gordon Diagnostic System.* DeWitt, NY: Author.

Gordon Systems, Inc. (1987a). *Interpretive manual for the Gordon Diagnostic System.* DeWitt, NY: Author.

Gordon Systems, Inc. (1987b). *Attention training system.* DeWitt, NY: Author.

Gordon Systems, Inc. (1991). *Administration manual for the Gordon Diagnostic System.* DeWitt, NY: Author.

Gorenstein, E.E., & Newman, J.P. (1980). Disinhibitory psychopathology: A new perspective and a model for research. *Psychological Review, 87,* 301–315.

Goyette, C.H., Conners, C.K., & Ulrich, R.F. (1978). Normative data on the revised Conners' Parent and Teacher Rating Scales. *Journal of Abnormal Child Psychology, 6,* 222–236.

Grant, M.L., Ilai, D., Nussbaum, N.L., & Bigler, E.D. (1990). The relationship between continuous performance tasks and neuropsychological tests in children with attention-deficit hyperactivity disorder. *Perceptual and Motor Skills, 70,* 435–445.

Grassi, J.R. (1970). Auditory vigilance performance in brain-damaged, behavior disordered and normal children. *Journal of Learning Disabilities, 3,* 6–9.

Gray, J.M., Robertson, I., Pentland, B., & Anderson, S. (1992). Microcomputer-based attentional retraining after brain damage: A randomized group-controlled trial. *Neuropsychological Rehabilitation, 2,* 97–115.

Green, M.F., Satz, P., Ganzell, S., & Vaclav, J.F. (1992). Wisconsin Card Sorting Test performance in schizophrenia: Remediation of a stubborn deficit. *American Journal of Psychiatry, 149,* 62–67.

Greenberg, L.M. (1988–1999). *The Test of Variables of Attention (TOVA).* Los Alamitos, CA: Universal Attention Disorders.

Greenberg, L.M. (1996–1999). *The Test of Variables of Attention-Auditory (TOVA-A).* Los Alamitos, CA: Universal Attention Disorders.

Greenberg, L.M. (1998). Anticipatories and TOVAs. *TOVA News,* 4(1), 1–2.

Greenberg, L.M., & Crosby, R.D. (1992a). *Specificity and sensitivity of the Test of Variables of Attention (TOVA).* Unpublished manuscript available from Universal Attention Disorders, Los Alamitos, CA.

Greenberg, L.M., & Crosby, R.D. (1992b). *A summary of developmental normative data on the TOVA ages 4 to 80+.* Unpublished manuscript. Available from Universal Attention Disorders, Los Alamitos, CA.

Greenberg, L.M., & Kindschi, C.L. (1996). *TOVA Test of Variables of Attention: Clinical guide.* St. Paul, MN: TOVA Research Foundation.

Greenberg, L.M., Kindschi, C.L., & Corman, C.L. (1999). *TOVA Test of Variables of Attention: Clinical guide* (2nd ed.). Los Alamitos, CA: Universal Attention Disorders.

Greenberg, L.M., & Waldman, I.D. (1993). Developmental normative data on the Test of Variables of Attention (TOVA). *Journal of Child Psychology and Psychiatry, 34,* 1019–1030.

Greene, R. (1982). *The relationship of family communication deviance and attention dysfunction in schizophrenia.* Unpublished doctoral dissertation, Florida Institute of Technology, Melbourne.

Greenhill, L.L., Halperin, J.M., & Abikoff, H. (1999). Stimulant medications. *Journal of the American Academy of Child and Adolescent Psychiatry, 38,* 503–512.

Gribble, M.W. (1989). *Ataxia, attention deficit, and diffuse axonal injury following closed head injury.* Unpublished doctoral dissertation, Ohio State University, Columbus.

Gridley, B.E., Hinds, P., & Hall, J. (2000, March). *Teacher ratings vs. the TOVA for intervention planning.* Paper presented at the annual meeting of the National Association of School Psychologists, New Orleans, LA.

Griffiths, P., Campbell, R., & Robinson, P. (1998). Executive function in treated phenylketonuria as measured by the one-back and two-back versions of the continuous performance test. *Journal of Inherited Metabolic Disorders, 21,* 125–135.

Grodzinsky, G.M., & Barkley, R.A. (1999). Predictive power of frontal lobe tests in the diagnosis of attention-deficit hyperactivity disorder. *Clinical Neuropsychologist, 13,* 12–21.

Grodzinsky, G.M., & Diamond, R. (1992). Frontal lobe functioning in boys with attention deficit hyperactivity disorder. *Developmental Neuropsychology, 8,* 427–445.

Gronwall, D. (1977). Paced auditory serial addition task: A measure of recovery from concussion. *Perceptual Motor Skills, 44,* 367–373.

Grooms, T. (1998). A review of the Conners' Continuous Performance Test as a clinical tool. *Child Assessment News,* 6(5), 9–12.

Grunebaum, H., Cohler, B.J., Kauffman, C., & Gallant, D. (1978). Children of depressed and schizophrenic mothers. *Child Psychiatry and Human Development, 8,* 219–228.

Grunebaum, H., Weiss, J.L., Gallant, D., & Cohler, B.J. (1974). Attention in young children of psychotic mothers. *Journal of Psychiatry, 131,* 887–891.

Guich, S.M., Buchsbaum, M.S., Burgwald, L., Wu, J., Haier, R.J., Asarnow, R., Nuechterlein, K., & Potkin, S. (1989). Effects of attention on frontal distribution of delta activity and cerebral metabolic rate in schizophrenia. *Schizophrenia Research, 2,* 439–448.

Häger, F., Volz, H-P., Gaser, C., Mentzel, H-J., Kaiser, W.A., & Sauer, H. (1998). Challenging the anterior attentional system with a continuous performance task: A functional magnetic imaging approach. *European Archives of Psychiatry and Clinical Neuroscience, 248,* 161–170.

Hagerman, R.J., Murphy, M.A., & Wittenberger, M.D. (1988). A controlled trial of stimulant medication in children with the Fragile X syndrome. *American Journal of Medical Genetics, 30,* 377–392.

Hain, C., Maier, W., Klinger, T., & Franke, P. (1993). Positive/negative symptomatology and experimental measures of attention in schizophrenic patients. *Psychopathology, 26,* 62–68.

Hale, J.B., Hoeppner, J.A.B., DeWitt, M.B., Coury, D.L., Ritacco, D.G., & Trommer, B. (1998). Evaluating medication response in ADHD: Cognitive, behavior, and single-subject methodology. *Journal of Learning Disabilities, 31,* 595–607.

Hall, C.W., & Kataria, S. (1992). Effects of two treatment techniques on delay and vigilance tasks with attention deficit hyperactive disordered (ADHD) children. *Journal of Psychology, 126,* 17–25.

Halperin, J.M. (1991). The clinical assessment of attention. *International Journal of Neuroscience, 50,* 171–182.

Halperin, J.M., Matier, K., Bedi, G., Sharma, V., & Newcorn, J.H. (1992). Specificity of inattention, impulsivity, and hyperactivity to the diagnosis of attention deficit hyperactivity disorder. *Journal of the American Academy of Child and Adolescent Psychiatry, 31,* 190–196.

Halperin, J.M., Newcorn, J.H., Matier, K., Bedi, G., Hall, S., & Sharma, V. (1995). Impulsivity and the initiation of fights in children with disruptive behavior disorders. *Journal of Child Psychology and Psychiatry, 36,* 1199–1211.

Halperin, J.M., Newcorn, J.H., Matier, K., Sharma, V., McKay, K.E., & Schwartz, S. (1993). Discriminant validity of attention-deficit hyperactivity disorder. *Journal of the American Academy of Child and Adolescent Psychiatry, 32,* 1038–1043.

Halperin, J.M., Newcorn, J.H., Sharma, V., Healey, J.M., Wolf, L.E., Pascualvaca, D.M., & Schwartz, S. (1990). Inattentive and noninattentive ADHD children: Do they constitute a unitary group? *Journal of Abnormal Child Psychology, 10,* 437–440.

Halperin, J.M., O'Brien, J.D., Newcorn, J.H., Healey, J.M., Pascualvaca, D.M., Wolf, L.E., & Young, J.G. (1990). Validation of hyperactive, aggressive, and mixed hyperactive/aggressive childhood disorders: A research note. *Journal of Child Psychology and Psychiatry, 31,* 455–459.

Halperin, J.M., Sharma, V., Greenblatt, E., & Schwartz, S.T. (1991). Assessment of the continuous performance test: Reliability and validity in a non-referred sample. *Psychological Assessment, 3,* 803–808.

Halperin, J.M., Wolf, L.E., Greenblatt, E., & Young, J.G. (1991). Subtype analysis of commission errors on the continuous performance test in children. *Developmental Neuropsychology, 7,* 207–217.

Halperin, J.M., Wolf, L.E., Pascualvaca, D.M., Newcorn, J.H., Healey, J.M., O'Brien, J.D., Morganstein, A., & Young, J.G. (1988). Differential assessment of attention and impulsivity in children. *Journal of the American Academy of Child and Adolescent Psychiatry, 27,* 326–329.

Halstead, W. (1947). *Brain and intelligence.* Chicago: University of Chicago Press.

Hamilton, J.A., Haier, R.J., & Buchsbaum, M.S. (1984). Intrinsic enjoyment and boredom coping scales: Validation with personality, evoked potentials, and attention measures. *Personality and Individual Differences, 5,* 183–193.

Hamilton, M.J., Cohen, A.F., Yuen, A.W.C., Harkin, N., Lang, G., Weatherley, B.C., & Peck, A.W. (1993). Carbamazepine and lamotrigine in healthy volunteers: Relevance to tolerance and clinical trial dosages. *Epilepsia, 34,* 166–173.

Hancock, P.S. (1984). Environmental stressors. In J.S. Warm (Ed.), *Sustained attention in human performance* (pp. 103–142). Chichester, England: Wiley.

Hancock, P.S., & Warm, J.S. (1989). A dynamic model of stress and sustained attention. *Human Factors, 31,* 519–537.

Handen, B.L., Breaux, A.M., Gosling, A., Ploof, D.L., & Feldman, H. (1990). Efficacy of methylphenidate among mentally retarded children with attention deficit hyperactivity disorder. *Pediatrics, 86,* 922–930.

Handen, B.L., Breaux, A.M., Janosky, J., McAuliffe, S., Feldman, H., & Gosling, A. (1992). Effects and noneffects of methylphenidate in children with mental retardation and ADHD. *Journal of the American Academy of Child and Adolescent Psychiatry, 31,* 455–461.

Handen, B.L., Feldman, H., Gosling, A., Breaux, A.M., & McAuliffe, S. (1991). Adverse side effects of methylphenidate among mentally retarded children with ADHD. *Journal of the American Academy of Child and Adolescent Psychiatry, 30,* 241–245.

Hannon, R., de la Cruz-Schmedel, D.E., Cano, T.C., Moreira, K., & Nasuta, R. (1989). Memory retraining with male alcoholics. *Archives of Clinical Neuropsychology, 4,* 227–232.

Hara, H., & Fukuyama, Y. (1992). Partial imitation and partial sensory agnosia in mentally normal children with convulsive disorders. *Acta Paediatrica Japonica, 34,* 416–425.

Harding, G.F.A., & Pullan, J.J. (1997). The effect of sodium valproate on the EEG, the photosensitive range, the CNV, and reaction time. *Electroencephalography and Clinical Neurophysiology, 43,* 465.

Harper, G.W., & Ottinger, D.R. (1992). The performance of hyperactive and control preschoolers on a new computerized measure of visual vigilance: The preschool vigilance task. *Journal of Child Psychology and Psychiatry, 33,* 1365–1372.

Harris, E.L., Schuerholz, L.J., Singer, H.S., Reader, M.J., Brown, J.E., Cox, C., Mohr, J., Chase, G.A., & Denckla, M.B. (1995). Executive function in children with Tourette syndrome and/or attention deficit hyperactivity disorder. *Journal of the International Neuropsychological Society, 1,* 511–516.

Hart, R.P., Colenda, C.C., & Hamer, R.M. (1991). Effects of buspirone and alprazolam on the cognitive performance of normal elderly subjects. *American Journal of Psychiatry, 148,* 73–77.

Hart, R.P., Wade, J.B., Calabrese, V.P., & Colenda, C.C. (1998). Vigilance performance in Parkinson's disease and depression. *Journal of Clinical and Experimental Neuropsychology, 20,* 111–117.

Harter, M.R., Aine, C.J., & Schroeder, C. (1982). Hemispheric differences in the neural processing of stimulus location and type: Effects of selective attention on visual evoked potentials. *Neuropsychologia, 20,* 421–438.

Harvey, P.D., Keefe, R.S., Moskowitz, J., Putnam, K.M., Mohs, R.C., & Davis, K.L. (1990). Attentional markers of schizophrenia: Performance of medicated and unmedicated patients and normals. *Psychiatry Research, 33,* 179–188.

Hassler, R. (1978). Striatal control of locomotion, intentional actions, and of integrating and perceptive activity. *Journal of the Neurological Sciences, 36,* 187–224.

Hauser, W.A., & Hesdorffer, D.C. (1990). *Epilepsy: Frequency, causes, and consequences.* New York: Demos.

Hazlett, E.A., Dawson, M.E., Buchsbaum, M.S., & Nuechterlein, K.H. (1993). Reduced regional brain glucose metabolism assessed by positron emission tomography in electrodermal nonresponder schizophrenics. *Journal of Abnormal Psychology, 1,* 39–46.

Healey, J.M., Newcorn, J.H., Halperin, J.M., Wolf, L.E., Pascualvaca, D.M., Schmeidler, J., & O'Brien, J.D. (1993). Factor structure of ADHD items in *DSM-III-R:* Internal consistency and external validation. *Journal of Abnormal Child Psychology, 21,* 441–453.

Heaton, R.K. (1981). *A manual for the Wisconsin Card Sorting Test.* Odessa, FL: Psychological Assessment Resources.

Hebb, D.O. (1958). *A textbook of psychology.* Philadelphia: Saunders.

Heilman, K.M., & van den Abell, T. (1979). Right hemisphere dominance for attention: The mechanism underlying hemispheric asymmetries in inattention (neglect). *Neurology, 30,* 327–330.

Heilman, K.M., Voeller, K.K.S., & Nadeau, S.E. (1991). A possible pathophysiological substrate of attention deficit hyperactivity disorder. *Journal of Child Neurology, 6*(Suppl.), S76–S81.

Heilman, K.M., Watson, R.T., & Valenstein, E. (1985). Neglect and related disorders. In K.M. Heilman & E. Valenstein (Eds.), *Clinical neuropsychology* (2nd ed., pp. 243–293). New York: Oxford University Press.

Hermanutz, M., & Gestrich, J. (1991). Computer-assisted attention training in schizophrenics: A comparative study. *European Archives of Psychiatry and Clinical Neuroscience, 240,* 282–287.

Herrera, J., Keilp, J.G., Cornblatt, B.A., Lee, H., Stritzke, P., Valance, J., Wielgus, M., Duval, J., & Davis, K. (1991). Hemispheric dysfunction in schizophrenia. *Biological Psychiatry, 29,* 84A.

Hickey, J.E., Suess, P.E., Newlin, D.B., & Spurgeon, L. (1995). Vagal tone regulation during sustained attention in boys exposed to opiates in utero. *Addictive Behaviors, 2,* 43–59.

Hillyard, S.A., & Munte, T.F. (1984). Selective attention to color and location: An analysis with event-related potentials. *Perception and Psychophysics, 36,* 185–198.

Hoerig, D.C., D'Amato, R.C., Raggio, D.J., & Martin, J.D. (1998, November). *Comparing the TOMAL, CPT, and WISC-III: Are memory, attention, and intelligence related?* Paper presented at the annual meeting of the National Academy of Neuropsychology, Washington, DC.

Hoffman, R.E., Buchsbaum, M.S., Escobar, M.D., Makuch, R.W., Nuechterlein, K.H., & Guich, S.M. (1991). EEG coherence of prefrontal areas in normal and schizophrenic males during perceptual activation. *Journal of Neuropsychiatry and Clinical Neurosciences, 3,* 169–175.

Holcomb, P.J., Ackerman, P.T., & Dykman, R.A. (1985). Cognitive event-related potentials in children with attention and reading deficits. *Psychophysiology, 22,* 656–667.

Hollingshead, A.B., & Redlich, F.C. (1958). *Social class and mental illness: A community study.* New York: Wiley.

Hooks, K., Milich, R., & Lorch, E.P. (1994). Sustained and selective attention in boys with attention deficit hyperactivity disorder. *Journal of Clinical Child Psychology, 23,* 69–77.

Hooper, H.E. (1983). *Hooper Visual Organization Test.* Los Angeles: Western Psychological Services.

Horn, W.F., Wagner, A.E., & Ialongo, N. (1989). Sex differences in school aged children with pervasive attention deficit hyperactivity disorder. *Journal of Abnormal Child Psychology, 17,* 109–125.

Horrigan, J.P., & Barnhill, L.J. (1995). Guanfacine for treatment of attention deficit hyperactivity disorder in boys. *Journal of Child and Adolescent Psychopharmacology, 5,* 215–223.

Howes, D.H., & Boller, F. (1975). Simple reaction time: Evidence for focal impairment from lesions of the right hemisphere. *Brain, 98,* 317–332.

Hoy, E., Weiss, G., Minde, K., & Cohen, N. (1978). The hyperactive child at adolescence: Cognitive, emotional, and social functioning. *Journal of Abnormal Child Psychology, 6,* 311–324.

Huberty, T.J. (1996). Integrating interviews, observations, questionnaires, and test data: Relationships among assessment, placement, and intervention. In M.J. Breen & C.R. Friedler (Eds.), *Behavioral approach to assessment of youth with emotional/behavioral disorders: A handbook for school-based practitioners* (pp. 631–679). Austin, TX: ProEd.

Hunt, R.D., Arnsten, A.F.T., & Asbell, M. (1995). An open trial of guanfacine in the treatment of attention deficit hyperactivity disorder. *Journal of the American Academy of Child and Adolescent Psychiatry, 34,* 50–54.

Hynd, G.W., Hern, K.L., Novey, E.S., Eliopolus, D., Marshall, R., Gonzalez, J.J., & Voeller, K.K. (1991). Attention-deficit hyperactivity disorder (ADHD) and asymmetry of the caudate nucleus. *Journal of Child Neurology, 8,* 339–347.

Hynd, G.W., Morgan, A.E., Edmonds, J.E., Black, K., Riccio, C.A., & Lombardino, L. (1995). Reading disabilities, comorbid psychopathology, and the specificity of neurolinguistic deficits. *Developmental Neuropsychology, 11,* 311–322.

Hynd, G.W., & Willis, W.G. (1988). *Pediatric neuropsychology.* New York: Grune & Stratton.

Ingvar, D.H. (1985). Memory of the future: An essay on the temporal organization of conscious awareness. *Human Neurobiology, 4,* 127–136.

Ito, M., Kanno, M., Mori, Y., & Niwa, S-I. (1997). Attention deficits assessed by continuous performance test and span of apprehension test in Japanese schizophrenic patients. *Schizophrenia Research, 23,* 205–211.

Jastak, S., & Wilkinson, G.S. (1984). *Wide Range Achievement Test–Revised.* Wilmington, DE: Author.

Jensen, A.R. (1982). Reaction time and psychometric *g.* In H.J. Eysenck (Ed.), *A model for intelligence* (pp. 93–132). Berlin, Germany: Springer-Verlag.

Johnson, B.D. (1993). Attention deficit hyperactivity disorder and undifferentiated attention deficit disorder: A study of neuropsychological differences. Unpublished master's thesis, University of Iowa, Iowa City.

Johnson, J.H., Rasbury, W.C., & Siegal, L.J. (1997). *Approaches to child treatment: Introduction to theory, research, and practice* (2nd ed.). New York: Allyn & Bacon.

Johnson, T.N., Rosvold, H.E., & Mishkin, M. (1968). Projections from behaviorally defined sectors of the prefrontal cortex to the basal ganglia, septum, and diencephalon of the monkey. *Experimental Neurology, 21,* 20.

Jones, J.T. (1987). *Attention deficit disorder and methylphenidate: Molar and molecular level analyses of dose effects on attention in clinic and classroom settings.* Unpublished doctoral dissertation, University of Rhode Island, Providence.

Kagan, J. (1966). *The Matching Familiar Figures Test.* Cambridge, MA: Harvard University Press.

Kagan, J., Rosman, B., Day, D., Albert, J., & Phillips, W. (1964). Information processing in the child: Significance of analytic and reflective attitudes. *Psychological Monographs, 78*(1, Whole No. 578).

Kallam, A.C., Riccio, C.A., & Hynd, G.W. (1999). *Allergy and behavioral symptomology in children.* Unpublished manuscript, Fort Hayes State University, Hays, KS, Department of Psychology.

Kamphaus, R.W., & Frick, P. (1994). *Clinical assessment of child and adolescent personality and behavior.* Boston: Allyn & Bacon.

Kamphaus, R.W., & Reynolds, C.R. (1998). *The BASC monitor for ADHD.* Circle Pines, MN: American Guidance Service.

Kandel, E.R. (1985). Cellular mechanisms of learning and the biological basis of individuality. In E.R. Kandel & J.H. Schwartz (Eds.), *Principles of Neural Science* (2nd ed., pp. 816–833). New York: Elsevier.

Kardell, E.G. (1994). *Evaluation of the WISC-III in the assessment of attention and concentration processes in children.* Unpublished doctoral dissertation, Pace University, New York, New York City.

Karper, L.P., Freeman, G.K., Grillon, C., Morgan, C.A., Charney, D.S., & Krystal, J.H. (1996). Preliminary evidence of an association between sensorimotor gating and distractibility in psychosis. *Journal of Neuropsychiatry and Clinical Neurosciences, 8,* 60–66.

Kashden, J., Fremouw, W.J., Callahan, T.S., & Franzen, M.D. (1993). Impulsivity in suicidal and nonsuicidal adolescents. *Journal of Abnormal Child Psychology, 21,* 339–351.

Kaskey, G.B., Salzman, L.F., Ciccone, J.R., & Klorman, R. (1980). Effects of lithium on evoked potentials and performance during sustained attention. *Psychiatry Research, 3,* 281–289.

Katz, K.S., Dubowitz, L.M.S., Henderson, S., Jongmans, M., Kay, G.G., Nolte, C.A., & de Vries, L.C. (1996). Effect of cerebral lesions on continuous performance test responses of school age children born prematurely. *Journal of Pediatric Psychology, 21,* 841–855.

Katz, M., Buchsbaum, M.S., Siegal, B.V., Wu, J.C., Haier, R.J., & Bunney, W.E. (1996). Correlational patterns of cerebral glucose metabolism in never-medicated schizophrenics. *Neuropsychobiology, 33,* 1–11.

Kaufman, A.S. (1994). *Intelligent testing with the WISC-III.* New York: Wiley Interscience.

Kaufman, A.S., & Kaufman, N.L. (1983). *Interpretive manual for Kaufman Assessment Battery for Children.* Circle Pines, MN: American Guidance Service.

Kaufman, A.S., & Kaufman, N.L. (1985). *Manual for Kaufman Test of Educational Achievement.* Circle Pines, MN: American Guidance Service.

Kaufmann, J. (1983). *Sustained attention in children: A comparison of performance on vigilance and continuous performance test measures.* Unpublished doctoral dissertation, Emory University, Atlanta, GA.

Kaufmann, P.M., Fletcher, J.M., Levin, H.S., & Miner, M.E. (1993). Attentional disturbance after pediatric closed head injury. *Journal of Child Neurology, 8,* 348–353.

Kavale, K. (1982). The efficacy of stimulant drug treatment for hyperactivity: A meta-analysis. *Journal of Learning Disabilities, 15,* 280–289.

Kaye-Swift, M. (1992). *An exploration of the modulation of aggression and impulsivity in preschool children with developmental language disorders.* Unpublished doctoral dissertation, Pace University, New York, New York City.

Keefe, R.S.E., Silverman, J.M., & Cornblatt, B.A. (1992). Refining phenotype characteristics in genetic linkage studies of schizophrenia. *Social Biology, 38,* 197–218.

Keefe, R.S.E., Silverman, J.M., Mohs, R.C., Siever, L.J., Harvey, P.D., Friedman, L., Roitman, S.E.L., DuPre, R.L., Smith, C.J., Schmeidler, J., & Davis, K.L. (1997). Eye tracking, attention, and schizotypal symptoms in nonpsychotic relatives of patients with schizophrenia. *Archives of General Psychiatry, 54,* 169–176.

Keilp, J.G., Herrera, J., Stritzke, P., & Cornblatt, B.A. (1997). The Continuous Performance Test, Identical Pairs version (CPT-IP): III. Brain functioning during performance of numbers and shapes subtasks. *Psychiatry Research: Neuroimaging Section, 74,* 35–45.

Keith, R.W. (1994). *The Auditory Continuous Performance Test manual.* San Antonio, TX: Psychological Corporation.

Keith, R.W., & Engineer, P. (1991). Effects of methylphenidate on the auditory processing abilities of children with attention deficit-hyperactivity disorder. *Journal of Learning Disabilities, 24,* 630–636.

Keith, T.Z., & Witta, E.L. (1997). Hierarchical and cross-age confirmatory factor analysis of the WISC-III: What does it measure? *School Psychology Quarterly, 12,* 89–107.

Kendall, P.C., & Panichelli-Mindel, S.M. (1995). Cognitive behavioral treatments. *Journal of Abnormal Child Psychology, 23,* 107–124.

Kerns, K.A., Eso, K., & Thomson, J. (1999). Investigation of a direct intervention for improving attention in young children with ADHD. *Developmental Neuropsychology, 16,* 273–295.

Kerns, K.A., & Mateer, C.A. (1996). Walking and chewing gum: The impact of attentional capacity on everyday activities. In R.J. Sbordone & C.L. Long (Eds.), *Ecological validity of neuropsychological testing* (pp. 147–170). Delray Beach, FL: St. Lucie Press.

Kerns, K.A., & Rondeau, L.A. (1998). Development of a continuous performance test for preschool children. *Journal of Attention Disorders, 2,* 229–238.

Kewman, D.G., Seigerman, C., Kintner, H., Chu, S., Henson, D., & Reeder, C. (1985). Simulation training of psychomotor skills: Teaching the brain-injured to drive. *Rehabilitation Psychology, 30,* 11–27.

Keys, B.A., & White, B.A. (2000). Exploring the relationship between age, executive abilities, and psychomotor speed. *Journal of the International Neuropsychological Society, 6,* 76–82.

King, C.M. (1996). *An evaluation of a continuous performance test for the differential diagnosis of attention deficit/hyperactivity disorder.* Unpublished master's thesis, Stephen F. Austin University, Nacogdoches, TX.

Kintslinger, G. (1987). *The use of the Gordon Diagnostic System for assessing attention deficit disorders as compared with traditional adaptive behavior measures in the public schools.* Unpublished doctoral dissertation, University of Nebraska, Lincoln.

Kirchner, G.L. (1976). Differences in the vigilance performance of highly active and normal second grade males under four experimental conditions. *Journal of Educational Psychology, 68,* 696–701.

Kirchner, G.L., & Knopf, I.J. (1974). Differences in the vigilance performance of second grade children as related to sex and achievement. *Child Development, 45,* 490–495.

Klee, S.H., & Garfinkel, B.D. (1983). A computerized continuous performance task: A new measure of inattention. *Journal of Abnormal Child Psychology, 11,* 487–496.

Klee, S.H., Garfinkel, B.D., & Beauchesne, H. (1986). Attention deficits in adults. *Psychiatric Annals, 16,* 52–56.

Klein, P.S., & Schwartz, A.A. (1979). Effects of training auditory sequential memory and attention on reading. *Journal of Special Education, 13,* 365–374.

Klonoff, H., Clark, C., & Klonoff, P.S. (1993). Long term outcome of head injuries: A 23 year follow-up study of children with head injuries. *Journal of Neurology, Neurosurgery, and Psychiatry, 56,* 410–415.

Klorman, R., Brumaghim, J.T., Fitzpatrick, P.A., & Borgstedt, A.D. (1990). Clinical effects of a controlled trial of methylphenidate on adolescents with attention deficit disorder. *Journal of the American Academy of Child and Adolescent Psychiatry, 29,* 701–709.

Klorman, R., Brumaghim, J.T., Fitzpatrick, P.A., & Borgstedt, A.D. (1991). Methylphenidate speeds evaluation processes of attention deficit disorder adolescents during a continuous performance test. *Journal of Abnormal Child Psychology, 19,* 263–283.

Klorman, R., Brumaghim, J.T., Salzman, L.F., Strauss, J., Borgstedt, A.D., McBride, M.C., & Loeb, S. (1988). Effects of methylphenidate on attention-deficit hyperactivity disorder with and without aggressive/noncompliant features. *Journal of Abnormal Psychology, 97,* 413–422.

Klorman, R., Salzman, L.F., Bauer, L.O., Coons, H.W., Borgstedt, A.D., & Halpern, W.I. (1983). Effects of two doses of methylphenidate on cross-situational and borderline hyperactive children's evoked potentials. *Electroencephalography and Clinical Neurophysiology, 56,* 169–185.

Klorman, R., Salzman, L.F., Pass, H.L., Borgstedt, H.L., & Dainer, K.B. (1979). Effects of methylphenidate in hyperactive children's evoked responses during passive and active observation. *Psychophysiology, 16,* 23–29.

Koelega, H.S., Brinkman, J.A., Hendriks, L., & Verbaten, M.N. (1989). Processing demands, effort and individual differences in four vigilance tasks. *Human Factors, 31,* 45–62.

Kohn, M., & Rosman, B.L. (1973). Cross-situational and longitudinal stability of social-emotional functioning in young children. *Child Development, 44,* 721–727.

Konopasek, D.E. (1997). *Medication fact sheet 1998 edition.* Anchorage, AK: Arctic Tern.

Koppitz, E.M. (1970). The Visual and Aural Digit Span Test with elementary school children. *Journal of Clinical Psychology, 26,* 349–353.

Koppitz, E.M. (1977). Strategies for diagnosis and identification of children with behavior and learning problems. *Behavioral Disorders, 2*(3), 136–140.

Koriath, U., Gualtieri, T., van Bourgondien, M., Quade, D., & Werry, J. (1985). Construct validity of clinical diagnosis in pediatric psychiatry: Relationship among measures. *Journal of the American Academy of Child and Adolescent Psychiatry, 24,* 429–436.

Kornetsky, C. (1972). The use of a simple test of attention as a measure of drug effects in schizophrenic patients. *Psychopharmacologia, 24,* 99–106.

Kornetsky, C., & Orzack, M.H. (1978). Physiological and behavioral correlates of attention dysfunction in schizophrenic patients. *Journal of Psychiatric Research, 14,* 69–79.

Kotwal, D.B., Burns, W.J., & Montgomery, D.D. (1996). Computer-assisted cognitive training for ADHD: A case study. *Behavior Modification, 20,* 85–96.

Kratochwill, T.R., & Levin, J.R. (1992). *Single-case research design and analysis: New directions for psychology and education.* Hillsdale, NJ: Erlbaum.

Kupietz, S.S. (1976). Attentiveness in behaviorally deviant and nondeviant children: I. Auditory vigilance performance. *Perceptual and Motor Skills, 43,* 1095–1101.

Kupietz, S.S. (1990). Sustained attention in normal and reading disabled youngsters with and without ADDH. *Journal of Abnormal Child Psychology, 18,* 357–372.

Kupietz, S.S., & Balka, E.B. (1976). Alterations in vigilance performance of children receiving amitriptyline and methylphenidate pharmacotherapy. *Psychopharmacology, 50,* 29–33.

Kupietz, S.S., & Richardson, E. (1978). Children's vigilance performance and inattentiveness in the classroom. *Journal of Child Psychology and Psychiatry, 19,* 145–154.

Kurlan, R. (1994). Hypothesis: II. Tourette's syndrome is part of a clinical spectrum that includes normal brain development. *Archives of Neurology, 51,* 1145–1150.

Laidlaw, T.M. (1993). Hypnosis and attention deficits after closed head injury. *International Journal of Clinical and Experimental Hypnosis, 41,* 97–111.

Lam, C.M., & Beale, I.L. (1991). Relations among sustained attention, reading performance, and teachers' ratings of behavior problems. *Remedial and Special Education (RASE), 12,* 40–47.

Lambert, N., & Sandoval, J. (1980). The prevalence of learning disabilities in a sample of children considered hyperactive. *Journal of Abnormal Child Psychology, 8,* 33–50.

Lansdell, H., & Mirsky, A.F. (1964). Attention in focal and centrencephalic epilepsy. *Experimental Neurology, 9,* 463–469.

Larose, S., Gagnon, S., Ferland, C., & Pepin, M. (1989). Psychology of computers: XIV. Cognitive rehabilitation through computer games. *Perceptual and Motor Skills, 69,* 851–858.

Lassiter, K.S., D'Amato, R.C., Raggio, D.J., Whitten, J.C.M., & Bardos, A.N. (1994). The construct specificity of the continuous performance test: Does inattention relate to behavior and achievement? *Developmental Neuropsychology, 10,* 179–188.

Leark, R.A., Dixon, D., Hoffman, T., & Huynh, D. (1999, November). *The effects of malingering on the Test of Variables of Attention (TOVA).* Paper presented at the annual meeting of the National Academy of Neuropsychology, San Antonio, TX.

Leark, R.A., Dupuy, T.R., Greenberg, L.M., Corman, C.L., & Kindschi, C.L. (1996). *TOVA Test of Variables of Attention: Professional manual version 7.0.* Los Alamitos, CA: Universal Attention Disorders.

Leavell, C.A., Leavell, J.A., Kramer, S., & Entwistle, P. (1999, August). *Variations on continuous performance testing in children with attention, hyperactivity, and other concerns.* Paper presented at the annual convention of the American Psychological Association, Boston.

Lenzenweger, M.F., Cornblatt, B.A., & Putnick, M. (1991). Schizotypy and sustained attention. *Journal of Abnormal Psychology, 100,* 84–89.

Leung, W.L., & Luk, S.L. (1988). Differences in attention control between "clinic-observable" and "reported" hyperactivity: A preliminary report. *Child Care, Health and Development, 14,* 199–211.

Leuthold, H., & Sommer, W. (1993). Stimulus presentation rate dissociates sequential effects in event-related potentials and reaction times. *Psychophysiology, 30,* 510–517.

Levav, M. L. (1991). *Attention performance in children affected with absence epilepsy and their first degree relatives.* Unpublished doctoral dissertation, University of Maryland, College Park.

Levin, E.D., Conners, C.K., Silva, D., Hinton, S.C., Meck, W.H., March, J., & Rose, J.E. (1998). Transdermal nicotine effects on attention. *Psychopharmacology, 140,* 135–141.

Levin, E.D., Conners, C.K., Sparrow, E., Hinton, S.C., Erhardt, D., Meek, W.H., Rose, J.E., & March, J. (1996). Nicotine effects on adults with attention-deficit/hyperactivity disorder. *Psychopharmacology, 123,* 55–63.

Levin, E.D., Wilson, W., Rose, J.E., & McEvoy, J. (1996). Nicotine-haloperidol interactions and cognitive performance in schizophrenics. *Neuropsychopharmacology, 15,* 429–436.

Levin, H.S., Culhane, K.A., Hartmann, J., Evankovich, K., Mattson, A.J., Harward, H., Ringholz, G., Ewing-Cobbs, L., & Fletcher, J.M. (1991). Developmental changes in performance on tests of purported frontal lobe functioning. *Developmental Neuropsychology, 7,* 377–395.

Levin, H.S., Peters, B.H., Kalisky, Z., High, W.M., Jr., von Laufen, A., Eisenberg, H.M., Morrison, D.P., & Gary, H.E. (1986). Effects of oral physostigmine and lecithin on memory and attention in closed head-injured patients. *Central Nervous System Trauma, 3,* 333–342.

Levy, F. (1980). The development of sustained attention (vigilance) and inhibition in children: Some normative data. *Journal of Child Psychology and Psychiatry, 21,* 77–84.

Levy, F. (1991). The dopamine theory of attention deficit hyperactivity disorder (ADHD). *Australian and New Zealand Journal of Psychiatry, 25,* 277–283.

Levy, F., & Hobbes, G. (1979). The influence of social class and sex on sustained attention (vigilance) and motor inhibition in children. *Australian and New Zealand Journal of Psychiatry, 13,* 321–324.

Levy, F., & Hobbes, G. (1981). The diagnosis of attention deficit disorder (hyperactivity) in children. *Journal of the American Academy of Child and Adolescent Psychiatry, 20,* 376–384.

Levy, F., & Hobbes, G. (1988). The action of stimulants in attention deficit disorder with hyperactivity: Dopaminergic, noradrenergic, or both. *Journal of the American Academy of Child and Adolescent Psychiatry, 27,* 802–805.

Levy, F., & Hobbes, G. (1996). Does haloperidol block methylphenidate? Motivation or attention? *Psychopharmacology, 126,* 70–74.

Levy, F., & Hobbes, G. (1997). Discrimination of attention deficit hyperactivity disorder by the continuous performance test. *Journal of Pediatric Child Health, 33,* 384–387.

Levy, F., Horn, K., & Dalglish, R. (1987). Relation of attention deficit and conduct disorder to vigilance and reading lag. *Australian and New Zealand Journal of Psychiatry, 21,* 242–245.

Lewis, T.M. (1993). *Attention deficit subtypes in ADHD and their relationship to cognitive functioning and historical variables.* Unpublished doctoral dissertation, Drexel University, Philadelphia.

Lindsley, D.B., Bowden, J.W., & Magoun, H.W. (1949). Effect upon the EEG of acute injury to the brainstem activating system. *Electroencephalography and Clinical Neurophysiology, 1,* 475–486.

List, M.A. (1985). *A developmental study of distractibility in the school aged child.* Unpublished doctoral dissertation, University of Waterloo, Waterloo, Ontario, Canada.

Liu, S.K., Hwu, H., & Chen, W.J. (1997). Clinical symptom dimensions and deficits on the continuous performance test in schizophrenia. *Schizophrenia Research, 25,* 211–219.

Llorente, A.M., Amado, A.J., Voigt, R.G., Berretta, M.C., Fraley, J.K., Jensen, C.L., & Heird, W.C. (2000). Internal consistency, temporal stability, and reproducibility of individual index scores on the Tests of Variables of Attention (TOVA) in children with attention-deficit/hyperactivity disorder (AD/HD). *Archives of Clinical Neuropsychology, 15,* 1–12.

Loeb, M., Hawkes, G.R., Evans, W.D., & Alluishi, E.A. (1965). The influence of d-amphetamine, benactzinc, and chlorpromazine on performance in an auditory vigilance task. *Psychonomic Science, 3,* 29–30.

Loge, D., Staton, D., & Beatty, W. (1990). Performance of children with ADHD on tests sensitive to frontal lobe dysfunction. *Journal of the American Academy of Child and Adolescent Psychiatry, 29,* 540–545.

Loiselle, D.L., Stamm, J.S., Matinsky, S., & Whipple, S. (1980). Evoked potential and behavior signs of attentive dysfunction in hyperactive boys. *Psychophysiology, 17,* 193–201.

Loken, W.J., Thornton, A.E., Otto, R.I., & Long, C.J. (1995). Sustained attention after severe closed head injury. *Neuropsychology, 9,* 592–598.

Loney, J., & Milich, R. (1982). Hyperactivity, inattention, and aggression in clinical practice. *Advances in Developmental and Behavioral Pediatrics, 3,* 113–147.

Lordon, J.F., Rickert, E.J., Dawson, R., & Pellymounter, M.A. (1980). Forebrain norepinephrine and the selective processing of information. *Brain Research, 190,* 569.

Losier, B.J., McGrath, P.J., & Klein, R.M. (1996). Error patterns of the continuous performance test in non-medicated and medicated samples of children with and without ADHD: A meta-analytic review. *Journal of Child Psychology and Psychiatry, 37,* 971–987.

Lou, H.C., Henrikson, L., & Bruhn, P. (1984). Focal cerebral hypoperfusion in children with dysphasia and/or attention deficit disorder. *Archives of Neurology, 41,* 825–829.

Lou, H.C., Henrikson, L., Bruhn, P., Borner, H., & Nielsen, J.B. (1989). Striatal dysfunction in attention deficit and hyperkinetic disorder. *Archives of Neurology, 46,* 48–52.

Lovejoy, M.C., & Rasmussen, N.H. (1990). The validity of vigilance tasks in differential diagnosis of children referred for attention and learning problems. *Journal of Abnormal Child Psychology, 18,* 671–681.

Lowe, P.A., & Reynolds, C.R. (1999). Age, gender, and education may have little influence on error patterns in the assessment of set-shifting and rule induction among normal elderly. *Archives of Clinical Neuropsychology, 14,* 303–315.

Lowe, P.A., Reynolds, C.R., Riccio, C.A., & Moore, J.J. (2000). *Psychometric characteristics of continuous performance tests (CPT).* Manuscript in preparation.

Lubar, J.F. (1991). Discourse on the development of EEG diagnostics and biofeedback for attention deficit hyperactivity disorders. *Biofeedback and Self-Regulation, 16,* 201–225.

Lubar, J.F., Bianchini, K.J., Calhoun, W.H., Lambert, E.W., Brody, A.H., & Shabsin, H.S. (1985). Spectral analysis of EEG differences between children with and without learning disabilities. *Journal of Learning Disabilities, 18,* 403–408.

Lubar, J.O., & Lubar, J.F. (1984). Electroencephalographic biofeedback of SMR and beta for the treatment of attention deficit disorders in a clinical setting. *Biofeedback and Self-Regulation, 9,* 1–23.

Luk, S.L., Leung, D.W.L., & Yuen, J. (1991). Clinic observations in the assessment of pervasiveness of childhood hyperactivity. *Journal of Child Psychology and Psychiatry, 32,* 833–850.

Luria, A.R. (1966). *Higher cortical functions in man.* New York: Basic Books.

Luria, A.R. (1973). *The working brain.* London: Penguin Press.

Luria, A.R. (1980). *Higher cortical functions in man* (2nd ed.). New York: Basic Books.

Maas, J.W., & Leckman, J.F. (1983). Relationship between central nervous system noradrenergic function and plasma and urinary MHPG and other norepinephrine metabolites. In J.W. Maas (Ed.), *MHPG: Basic mechanisms in psychopathology* (pp. 33–43). New York: Academic Press.

Mahan, S.M. (1996). *Relationships among measures used in the assessment of attention-deficit hyperactivity disorder.* Unpublished doctoral dissertation, Indiana State University, Terre Haute.

Maier, W., Franke, P., Hain, C., Kopp, B., & Rist, F. (1992). Neuropsychological indicators of the vulnerability to schizophrenia. *Progress in Neuropsychopharmacology and Biological Psychiatry, 16,* 703–716.

Malone, M.A., Kershner, J.R., & Swanson, J.M. (1994). Hemispheric processing and methylphenidate effects in attention deficit hyperactivity disorder. *Journal of Child Neurology, 9,* 181–189.

Mangone, C.A., Hier, D.B., Gorelick, P.B., Ganellen, R.J., Langenberg, P., Boarman, R., & Dollear, W.C. (1991). Impaired insight in Alzheimer's disease. *Journal of Geriatric Psychiatry and Neurology, 4,* 189–193.

Mann, J.B. (1997). *Assessment of ADHD: Does the addition of continuous performance tests, memory tests and direct behavioral observations enhance informants' ratings of the child?* Unpublished doctoral dissertation, California School of Professional Psychology, San Diego.

Mansour, C.S., Haier, R.J., & Buchsbaum, M.S. (1996). Gender comparisons of cerebral glucose metabolic rate in healthy adults during a cognitive task. *Personality and Individual Differences, 20,* 183–191.

Mapou, R.L. (1995). A cognitive framework for neuropsychological assessment. In R.L. Mapou & J. Spector (Eds.), *Clinical neuropsychological assessment: A cognitive approach* (pp. 295–337). New York: Plenum Press.

Mapou, R.L. (1999, November). *Clinical assessment of attention: Models and methods.* Paper presented at the annual meeting of the National Academy of Neuropsychology, San Antonio, TX.

Margolis, J.S. (1972). *Academic correlates of sustained attention.* Unpublished doctoral dissertation, University of California, Los Angeles.

Mariani, M.A., & Barkley, R.A. (1997). Neuropsychological and academic functioning in preschool boys with attention deficit hyperactivity disorder. *Developmental Neuropsychology, 13*(1), 111–129.

Marks, D.J., Himelstein, J., Newcorn, H.H., & Halperin, J.M. (1999). Identification of ADHD subtypes using laboratory-based measures: A cluster analysis. *Journal of Abnormal Child Psychology, 27,* 167–175.

Markwardt, F.C. (1989). *The Peabody Individual Achievement Test–Revised.* Circle Pines, MN: American Guidance Service.

Marshall, R.M., Hynd, G.W., Handwerk, M.J., & Hall, J. (1997). Academic underachievement in ADHD subtypes. *Journal of Learning Disabilities, 30,* 635–642.

Maruish, M.E. (1999). Symptom Assessment-45 Questionnaire (SA-45). In M.E. Maruish (Ed.), *The use of psychological testing for treatment planning and outcomes assessment* (2nd ed., pp. 725–757). Mahwah, NJ: Erlbaum.

Mason, S.T., & Fibiger, H.C. (1978). Noradrenaline and spatial memory. *Brain Research, 156,* 382–386.

Mataix-Cols, D., Junqué, C., Vallejo, J., Sánchez-Turet, M., Verger, K., & Barrios, M. (1997). Hemispheric functional imbalance in a sub-clinical obsessive-compulsive sample assessed by the Continuous Performance Test, Identical Pairs version. *Psychiatry Research, 72,* 115–126.

Mateer, C.A., Kerns, K.A., & Eso, K.L. (1996). Management of attention and memory disorders following traumatic brain injury. *Journal of Learning Disabilities, 29,* 618–632.

Mateer, C.A., & Mapou, R. (1996). Understanding, evaluation, and managing attention disorders following traumatic brain injury. *Journal of Head Trauma Rehabilitation, 11,* 1–16.

Mateer, C.A., & Sohlberg, M.M. (1988). A paradigm shift in memory rehabilitation. In H. Whitaker (Ed.), *Neuropsychological studies of nonfocal brain injury: Dementia and closed head injury* (pp. 202–225). New York: Springer-Verlag.

Mateer, C.A., Sohlberg, M.M., & Yougman, P. (1990). The management of acquired attention and memory disorders following mild closed head injury. In R. Wood (Ed.), *Cognitive rehabilitation in perspective* (pp. 68–95). London: Taylor & Francis.

Matier, K., Halperin, J.M., Sharma, V., Newcorn, J.H., & Sathaye, N. (1992). Methylphenidate response in aggressive and non-aggressive ADHD children: Distinction on laboratory measures of symptoms. *Journal of the American Academy of Child and Adolescent Psychiatry, 31,* 219–225.

Matier-Sharma, K., Perachio, N., Newcorn, J.H., Sharma, V., & Halperin, J.M. (1995). Differential diagnosis of ADHD: Are objective measures of attention, impulsivity, and activity level helpful? *Child Neuropsychology, 1,* 118–127.

Matosich, C.G. (1988). *Cognitive processing and personality similarities between attention deficit disordered children and their parents.* Unpublished doctoral dissertation, California School of Professional Psychology, Fresno.

Mattes, J.A. (1980). The role of frontal lobe dysfunction in childhood hyperkinesis. *Comprehensive Psychiatry, 21,* 358–369.

Mayes, S.D., & Calhoun, S.L. (1999). Discriminative validity of the Gordon Diagnostic System (GDS). *ADHD Report, 7*(6), 11, 14.

Mayes, S.D., Calhoun, S.L., & Crowell, E.W. (1998, November). *Clinical validity and interpretation of the Gordon Diagnostic System in ADHD assessments.* Paper presented at the annual meeting of the National Academy of Neuropsychology, Washington, DC.

McAuley, J.W., Reynolds, I.J., Kroboth, F.J., Smith, R.B., & Kroboth, P.D. (1995). Orally administered progesterone enhances sensitivity to triazolam in postmenopausal women. *Journal of Clinical Pharmacology, 15,* 3–10.

McClure, F.D., & Gordon, M. (1984). The performance of disturbed hyperactive and nonhyperactive children on an objective measure of hyperactivity. *Journal of Abnormal Child Psychology, 12,* 561–572.

McGrath, N.F. (1985). *Neuropsychological dysfunction in food-sensitive subjects and controls: An experimental study.* Unpublished doctoral dissertation, Northwestern University, Evanston, IL.

McLaren, T.R. (1990). *Assessing attentional disorders using cognitive and neuropsychological measures.* Unpublished doctoral dissertation, Ball State University, Muncie, IN.

Medalia, A., Aluma, M., Tryon, W., & Merriam, A.E. (1998). Effectiveness of attention training in schizophrenia. *Schizophrenia Bulletin, 24,* 147–152.

Meier, S.T. (1999). Training the practitioner-scientist: Bridging case conceptualization, assessment, and intervention. *Counseling Psychologist, 27,* 846–869.

Melnyk, L., & Das, J.P. (1992). Measurement of attention deficit: Correspondence between rating scales and tests of sustained and selective attention. *American Journal of Mental Retardation, 96,* 599–606.

Mendez, M.F., Cherrier, M.M., & Perryman, K.M. (1997). Differences between Alzheimer's disease and vascular dementia on information processing measures. *Brain and Cognition, 34,* 301–310.

Merola, J.L., & Leiderman, J. (1985). The effect of task difficulty upon the extent to which performance benefits from between hemisphere division of inputs. *International Journal of Neuroscience, 51,* 35–44.

Messick, S. (1995). Standards of validity and the validity of standards in performance assessment. *Educational Measurement: Issues and Practice, 14*(4), 5–8.

Mesulam, M.M. (1981). A cortical network for directed attention and unilateral neglect. *Annals of Neurology, 10,* 309–325.

Mesulam, M.M. (1985a). Attention, confusional states and neglect. In M.M. Mesulam (Ed.), *Principles of behavioral neurology* (pp. 125–168). Philadelphia: Davis.

Mesulam, M.M. (1985b). *Principles of behavioral neurology.* Philadelphia: Davis.

Michael, R.L., Klorman, R., Salzman, L.F., Borgstedt, A.D., & Dainer, K.B. (1981). Normalizing effects of methylphenidate on hyperactive children's vigilance performance and evoked potentials. *Psychophysiology, 18,* 665–677.

Michaels, K.L. (1996). *Differentiating attentional functions in children with ADHD, anxiety, and depression.* Unpublished doctoral dissertation, University of Georgia, Athens.

Milich, R., Licht, B.G., Murphy, D.A., & Pelham, W.E. (1989). Attention-deficit hyperactivity disordered boys' evaluations of and attributions for task performance on medication versus placebo. *Journal of Abnormal Psychology, 98,* 280–284.

Miller, J.M. (1996). *Patterns of attentional impairment in children with generalized and partial epilepsy.* Unpublished doctoral dissertation, Washington University, St. Louis, MO.

Milner, B. (1963). Effects of different brain lesions on card sorting. *Archives of Neurology, 9,* 90–100.

Milner, B. (1964). Some effects of frontal lobectomy in man. In J.M. Warren & K. Akert (Eds.), *The frontal granular cortex and behavior* (pp. 313–334). New York: McGraw-Hill.

Milner, B. (1971). Interhemispheric differences in the localization of psychological processes in man. *British Medical Bulletin, 27,* 272–277.

Mirsky, A.F. (1987). Behavioral and psychophysiological markers of disordered attention. *Environmental Health Perspectives, 74,* 191–199.

Mirsky, A.F. (1989). The neuropsychology of attention: Elements of a complex behavior. In E. Perecman (Ed.), *Integrating theory and practice in neuropsychology* (pp. 75–91). Hillsdale, NJ: Erlbaum.

Mirsky, A.F., Anthony, B.J., Duncan, C.C., Ahearn, M.B., & Kellam, S.G. (1991). Analysis of the elements of attention: A neuropsychological approach. *Neuropsychology Review, 2,* 109–145.

Mirsky, A.F., Fantie, B.D., & Tatman, J.E. (1995). Assessment of attention across the lifespan. In R.L. Mapou & J. Spector (Eds.), *Clinical neuropsychological assessment: A cognitive approach* (pp. 17–48). New York: Plenum Press.

Mirsky, A.F., Ingraham, L.J., & Kugelmass, S. (1995). Neuropsychological assessment of attention and its pathology in the Israeli cohort. *Schizophrenia Bulletin, 21,* 193–204.

Mirsky, A.F., & Kornetsky, C. (1964). On the dissimilar effects of drugs on the digit symbol substitution and continuous performance tests. *Psychopharmacologia, 5,* 161–177.

Mirsky, A.F., Primac, D.W., & Bates, R. (1959). The effects of chlorpromazine and secobarbital on the CPT. *Journal of Nervous and Mental Diseases, 128,* 12–17.

Mirsky, A.F., Primac, D.W., Marsan, C.A., Rosvold, H.E., & Stevens, J.R. (1960). A comparison of the psychological test performance of patients with focal and nonfocal epilepsy. *Experimental Neurology, 2,* 75–89.

Mirsky, A.F., & Van Buren, J.M. (1965). On the nature of "absence" in centrencephalic epilepsy: A study of some behavioral, electroencephalographic and autonomic factors. *Electroencephalography and Clinical Neurophysiology, 18,* 334–348.

Mitchell, T.V., & Quittner, A.L. (1996). Multimethod study of attention and behavior problems in hearing impaired children. *Journal of Clinical Child Psychology, 25,* 83–96.

Mitchell, W.G., Chavez, J.M., Baker, S.A., Guzman, B.L., & Azen, S.P. (1990). Reaction time, impulsivity, and attention in hyperactive children and controls: A video game technique. *Journal of Child Neurology, 5,* 195–204.

Moore, J.J., Riccio, C.A., Reynolds, C.R., & Lowe, P.A. (1998, November). *How drug use affects CPT outcomes: Diagnosis and misdiagnosis in the presence of licit and illicit substances.* Paper presented at the National Academy of Neuropsychology, Washington, DC.

Morgan, A.E., Hynd, G.W., Riccio, C.A., & Hall, J. (1996). Validity of *DSM-IV* ADHD predominantly inattentive and combined types: Relationship to previous *DSM* diagnoses/subtype differences. *Journal of the American Academy of Child and Adolescent Psychiatry, 35,* 325–333.

Morrow, L.A. (1994). Cuing attention: Disruptions following organic solvent exposure. *Neuropsychology, 8,* 471–476.

Morrow, L.A., Robin, N., Hodgson, M.J., & Kamis, H. (1992). Assessment of attention and memory efficiency in persons with solvent neurotoxicity. *Neuropsychologia, 30,* 911–922.

Moruzzi, G., & Magoun, H.W. (1949). Brainstem reticular formation and activation of the EEG. *Electroencephalography and Clinical Neurophysiology, 1,* 455–473.

Murray, K., May, D., Kundert, D., Potenza, E., DeJong, E., & Kelly, E. (1999, August). *Pediatrician's practices for the treatment of children with ADHD.* Paper presented at the annual convention of the American Psychological Association, Boston.

Mussgay, L., & Hertwig, R. (1990). Signal detection indices in schizophrenics on a visual, auditory, and bimodal continuous performance test. *Schizophrenia Research, 3,* 303–310.

Musten, L.M., Firestone, P., Pisterman, S., Bennett, S., & Mercer, J. (1997). Effects of methylphenidate on preschool children with ADHD: Cognitive and behavioral functions. *Journal of the American Academy of Child and Adolescent Psychiatry, 36,* 1407–1415.

Näätänen, R. (1992). Selective attention and evoked potentials in humans: A critical review. *Biological Psychiatry, 2,* 237–307.

National Council on Measurement in Education. (1999). *Standards for educational and psychological testing.* Washington, DC: Author.

Nelson, E.B., Sax, K.W., & Strakowski, S.M. (1998). Attentional performance in patients with psychotic and nonpsychotic major depression and schizophrenia. *American Journal of Psychiatry, 155,* 137–139.

Nestor, P.G., Faux, S.F., McCarley, R.W., Sands, S.F., Horvath, T.B., & Peterson, A. (1991). Neuroleptics improve sustained attention in schizophrenia. *Neuropsychopharmacology, 4,* 145–149.

Nestor, P.G., Faux, S.F., McCarley, R.W., Shenton, M.E., & Sands, S.F. (1990). Measurement of visual sustained attention in schizophrenia using signal detection analysis and a newly developed computerized CPT task. *Schizophrenia Research, 3,* 329–332.

Newcorn, J.H., Halperin, J.M., Healey, J.M., O'Brien, J.D., Pascualvaca, D.M., Wolf, L.E., Morganstein, A., Sharma, V., & Young, G. (1989). Are ADDH and ADHD the same or different? *Journal of the American Academy of Child and Adolescent Psychiatry, 285,* 734–738.

Newcorn, J.H., Halperin, J.M., Schwartz, S., Pascualvaca, D.M., Wolf, L.E., Schmeidler, J., & Sharma, V. (1994). Parent and teacher ratings of attention-deficit hyperactivity disorder symptoms: Implications for case identification. *Journal of Developmental and Behavioral Pediatrics, 15,* 86–91.

Niemann, H., Ruff, R.M., & Baser, C.A. (1990). Computer-assisted attention re-training in head-injured individuals: A controlled efficacy study of an outpatient program. *Journal of Consulting and Clinical Psychology, 58,* 811–817.

Nigg, J.T., Hinshaw, S.P., & Halperin, J.M. (1996). Continuous performance test in boys with attention deficit hyperactivity disorder: Methylphenidate dose response and relations with observed behaviors. *Journal of Clinical Child Psychology, 25,* 330–340.

Norman, D.A., & Shallice, T. (1985). Attention to action: Willed and automatic control of behavior. In R.J. Davidson, G.E. Schwartz, & D. Shapiro (Eds.), *Consciousness and self regulation: Advances in research* (Vol. 4, pp. 1–17). New York: Plenum Press.

Nuechterlein, K.H. (1983). Signal detection in vigilance tasks and behavioral attributes of schizophrenic mothers and among hyperactive children. *Journal of Abnormal Psychology, 92,* 4–28.

Nuechterlein, K.H. (1991). Vigilance in schizophrenia and related disorders. In S.R. Steinhauer & J.H. Gruzelier (Eds.), *Neuropsychology, psychophysiology, and information processing: Handbook of schizophrenia* (Vol. 5, pp. 397–433). Amsterdam: Elsevier Science.

Nuechterlein, K.H., & Dawson, M.E. (1984). Information processing and attentional functioning in the developmental course of schizophrenic disorders. *Schizophrenia Bulletin, 10,* 160–202.

Nuechterlein, K.H., Edell, W.S., Norris, M., & Dawson, M.E. (1986). Attentional vulnerability indicators, thought disorders, and negative symptoms. *Schizophrenia Bulletin, 12,* 408–426.

Nurss, J.R., & McGauvran, D. (1976). *Metropolitan Readiness Tests.* San Antonio, TX: Psychological Corporation.

Nussbaum, N.L., & Bigler, E.D. (1990). *Identification and treatment of attention deficit disorder.* Austin, TX: ProEd.

Nussbaum, N.L., & Bigler, E.D. (1997). Halstead–Reitan neuropsychological batteries for children. In C.R. Reynolds & E. Fletcher-Jantzen (Eds.), *Handbook of clinical child neurology* (2nd ed., pp. 219–236). New York: Plenum Press.

Obiols, J.E., Clos, M., Corberó, García-Domingo, M., de Trinchería, I., & Doménech, E. (1992). Sustained attention deficit in young schizophrenic and schizotypic men. *Psychological Reports, 71,* 1131–1136.

O'Brien, J.D., Halperin, J.M., Newcorn, J.H., Sharma, V., Wolf, L.E., & Morganstein, A. (1992). Psychometric differentiation of conduct disorder and attention deficit disorder with hyperactivity. *Developmental and Behavioral Pediatrics, 13,* 274–277.

O'Dougherty, M., Berntson, G.G., Boysen, S.T., Wright, F.S., & Teske, D. (1988). Psychophysiological predictors of attentional dysfunction in children with congenital heart defects. *Psychophysiology, 25,* 305–315.

O'Dougherty, M., Nuechterlein, K.H., & Drew, B. (1984). Hyperactive and hypoxic children: Signal detection, sustained attention, and behavior. *Journal of Abnormal Psychology, 93,* 178–191.

Okada, Y.C., Kaufman, L., & Williamson, S.J. (1983). The hippocampal formation as a source of the slow endogenous potentials. *Electroencephalography and Clinical Neurophysiology, 55,* 417–426.

Olvera, R.L., Pliszka, S.R., Luh, J., & Tatum, R. (1996). An open trial of venlafaxine in the treatment of attention-deficit/hyperactivity disorder in children and adolescents. *Journal of Child and Adolescent Psychopharmacology, 6,* 241–250.

Oppenheimer, P.M. (1986). *A comparison of methods for assessing attention deficit disorders with hyperactivity in emotionally disturbed, learning disabled and normal children.* Unpublished doctoral dissertation, University of Virginia, Charlottesville.

Orzack, M.H., Kornetsky, C., & Freeman, H. (1967). The effects of daily administration of carphenazine on attention in the schizophrenic patient. *Psychopharmacologia, 11,* 31–38.

O'Toole, K., Abramowitz, A., Morris, R., & Dulcan, M. (1997). Effects of methylphenidate on attention and nonverbal learning in children with attention-deficit hyperactivity disorder. *Journal of the American Academy of Child and Adolescent Psychiatry, 36,* 531–538.

Overall, J.E., & Gorham, D.R. (1972). The brief psychiatric rating scale. *Psychological Reports, 10,* 799–812.

Oyler, R.G., Rosenhagen, K.M., & Michael, M.L. (1998). Sensitivity and specificity of Keith's Auditory Continuous Performance Test. *Language, Speech, and Hearing Services in the Schools, 29,* 180–185.

Ozolins, D.A., & Anderson, R.P. (1980). Effects of feedback on the vigilance task performance of hyperactive and hypoactive children. *Perceptual and Motor Skills, 50,* 415–424.

Pandurangi, A.K., Sax, K.W., Pelonero, A.L., & Goldberg, S.C. (1994). Sustained attention and positive formal thought disorder in schizophrenia. *Schizophrenia Research, 13,* 109–116.

Pantle, M.L., Ebner, D.L., & Hynan, L.S. (1994). The Rorschach and the assessment of impulsivity. *Journal of Clinical Psychology, 50,* 633–638.

Papageorgiou, C., & Wells, A. (1998). Effects of attention training on hypochondriasis: A brief case series. *Psychological Medicine, 28,* 193–200.

Papanicolaua, A.C., Loring, D.W., Raz, N., & Eisenberg, H.M. (1985). Relationship between stimulus intensity and the P300. *Psychophysiology, 22,* 326–329.

Parasuraman, R. (1979). Memory load and event rate control sensitivity decrements in sustained attention. *Science, 205,* 924–927.

Parasuraman, R. (1984a). The psychobiology of sustained attention. In J.S. Warm (Ed.), *Sustained attention in human performance* (pp. 61–100). New York: Wiley.

Parasuraman, R. (1984b). Sustained attention in detection and discrimination. In R. Parasuraman & D.R. Davies (Eds.), *Varieties of attention* (pp. 243–271). Orlando, FL: Academic Press.

Parasuraman, R., & Davies, D.R. (1977). A taxonomic analysis of vigilance performance. In R.R. Mackie (Ed.), *Vigilance theory, operational performance, and physiological correlates* (pp. 559–574). New York: Plenum Press.

Parasuraman, R., & Giambra, L. (1991). Skill development in vigilance: Effects of event rate and age. *Psychology and Aging, 6,* 155–169.

Parasuraman, R., Mutter, S.A., & Molloy, R. (1991). Sustained attention following mild closed-head injury. *Journal of Clinical and Experimental Neuropsychology, 13,* 789–811.

Parr, H.D. (1995). *The effect of age on a clinical test of attention.* Unpublished master's thesis, University of Iowa, Iowa City.

Parrila, R.K., Äystö, S., & Das, J.P. (1994). Development of planning in relation to age, attention, simultaneous, and successive processing. *Journal of Psychoeducational Assessment, 12*, 212–227.

Pascualvaca, D.M., Anthony, B.J., Arnold, L.E., Rebok, G.W., Ahearn, M.B., Kellam, S.G., & Mirsky, A.F. (1997). Attention performance in an epidemiological sample of urban children: The role of gender and verbal intelligence. *Child Neuropsychology, 3*, 13–27.

Pass, H.L., Klorman, K., Salzman, L.F., Klein, R.H., & Kaskey, G.B. (1980). The late positive component of the evoked response in acute schizophrenia during a test of sustained attention. *Biological Psychiatry, 15*, 9–20.

Passler, M.A., Isaac, W., & Hynd, G.W. (1985). Neuropsychological development of behavior attributed to frontal lobe functioning in children. *Developmental Neuropsychology, 1*, 349–370.

Pelham, W.E., Greenslade, K.E., Voale-Hamilton, M., Murphy, D.A., Greenstein, J.J., Gnagy, E.M., Guthrie, K.J., Hoover, M.D., & Dahl, R.E. (1990). Relative efficacy of long acting stimulant on children with attention deficit and hyperactivity disorder: A comparison of standard methylphenidate, sustained-release methylphenidate, sustained release dextroamphetamine and pemoline. *Pediatrics, 86*, 226–237.

Pelham, W.E., Milich, R., Murphy, D.A., & Murphy, H.A. (1989). Normative data on the IOWA Conners' Teacher Rating Scale. *Journal of Clinical Child Psychology, 18*, 259–262.

Peloquin, L.J., & Klorman, R. (1986). Effects of methylphenidate and performance in memory scanning and vigilance. *Journal of Abnormal Psychology, 95*, 88–98.

Perry, A.R., & Laurie, C.A. (1993). Sustained attention and the Type A behavior pattern: The effect of daydreaming on performance. *Journal of General Psychology, 119*, 217–228.

Petersen, S.E., Fox, P.T., Posner, M.I., Mintur, M., & Raichle, M.E. (1989). Positron emission tomographic studies of the cortical anatomy of single word processing. *Nature, 331*, 585–589.

Pigache, R.M. (1996). Auditory sustained attention in schizophrenia: A comparison of the continuous performance test and the Pigache attention task. *Psychiatry Research, 60*, 155–165.

Pliszka, S.R. (1992). Comorbidity of attention-deficit hyperactivity disorder and overanxious disorder. *Journal of the American Academy of Child and Adolescent Psychiatry, 31*, 197–203.

Pliszka, S.R., McCracken, J.T., & Maas, J.W. (1996). Catecholamines in attention deficit hyperactivity disorder: Current perspectives. *Journal of the American Academy of Child and Adolescent Psychiatry, 35*, 264–272.

Plomin, R., & Foch, T.T. (1981). Hyperactivity and pediatrician diagnoses, parental ratings, specific cognitive abilities, and laboratory measures. *Journal of Abnormal Child Psychology, 9*, 55–64.

Podd, M.H. (1999). *Effectiveness of the neurXercise cognitive remediation program: Three case studies.* Unpublished manuscript available from M.H. Podd, National Naval Medical Center, Bethesda, MD.

Podd, M.H., & Seelig, D.P. (1989). *NeurXercise* [Computer software]. Fort Washington, MD: Authors.

Podd, M.H., & Seelig, D.P. (1992). Computer-assisted cognitive remediation of attention disorders following mild closed head injuries. In C.J. Long & L.K. Ross (Eds.), *Handbook of head trauma: Acute care to recovery* (pp. 231–244). New York: Plenum Press.

Pogge, D.L., Stokes, J., & Harvey, P.D. (1992). Psychometric vs. attentional correlates of early onset alcohol and substance abuse. *Journal of Abnormal Child Psychology, 20*, 151–162.

Poley, J.A. (1995). *Effects of classroom cognitive behavioral training with elementary school ADHD students: A pilot study.* Unpublished doctoral dissertation, Indiana University of Pennsylvania, Indiana.

Polich, J. (1990). P300, probability, and interstimulus interval. *Psychophysiology, 27*, 396–403.

Ponsford, J., & Kinsella, G. (1992). Attentional deficits following closed-head injury. *Journal of Clinical and Experimental Neuropsychology, 14*, 822–838.

Porrino, L.J., & Goldman-Rakic, P.S. (1982). Brain stem innervation of prefrontal and anterior cingulate cortex in the rhesus monkey revealed by retrograde transport of HRP. *Journal of Comparative Neurology, 205*, 63–76.

Porrino, L.J., Rapoport, J.L., Behar, D., Sceery, W., Ismond, D., & Bunney, W.E. (1983). A naturalistic assessment of the motor activity of hyperactive boys. *Archives of General Psychiatry, 40*, 681–687.

Porteus, S.D. (1959). *The maze test and clinical psychology.* Palo Alto: Pacific Books.

Porteus, S.D. (1965). *Porteus Maze Tests: Fifty years of application.* Palo Alto, CA: Pacific Books.

Posner, M.I. (1978). *Chronometric explorations of mind.* Hillsdale, NJ: Erlbaum.

Posner, M.I. (1988). Structures and functions of selective attention. In T. Boll & B. Bryant (Eds.), *Master lectures in clinical neuropsychology* (pp. 173–202). Washington, DC: American Psychological Association.

Posner, M.I., & Boies, S.J. (1971). Components of attention. *Psychological Review, 78*, 391–408.

Posner, M.I., & Cohen, Y. (1984). Components of performance. In H. Bouma & D. Bowhuis (Eds.), *Attention and performance* (pp. 531–556). Hillsdale, NJ: Erlbaum.

Posner, M.I., Inhoff, A.W., & Fredrich, F.S. (1987). Isolating attentional systems: A cognitive-anatomical analysis. *Psychobiology, 15*, 107–121.

Posner, M.I., & Petersen, S.E. (1990). The attention system of the human brain. *Annual Review of Neuroscience, 13*, 25–42.

Posner, M.I., Petersen, S.E., Fox, P.T., & Raichle, M.E. (1988). Localization of cognitive operations in the human brain. *Science, 240*, 1627–1631.

Posner, M.I., & Raichle, M.E. (1994). *Images of the mind.* New York: Scientific American Books.

Powanda, C.B. (1995). *Attention training in persons with mental retardation.* Unpublished doctoral dissertation, University of New Orleans, LA.

Power, T.J. (1992). Contextual factors in vigilance testing of children with ADHD. *Journal of Abnormal Child Psychology, 20*, 579–593.

Pribram, K.H., & McGuinness, D. (1975). Arousal, activation, and effort in the control of attention. *Psychological Review, 82,* 116–149.

Primac, D.W., Mirsky, A.F., & Rosvold, H.E. (1957). Effects of centrally acting drugs on two tests of brain damage. *Archives of Neurology and Psychiatry, 77,* 328–332.

Prinz, R.J., Myers, D.R., Holden, E.W., Tarnowski, K.J., & Roberts, W.A. (1983). Marital disturbance and child problems: A cautionary note regarding hyperactive children. *Journal of Abnormal Child Psychology, 11,* 393–399.

Psychological Corporation. (1991). *THINKable Rehabilitation System* [Computer program]. San Antonio, TX: Author.

Psychological Corporation. (1992). *Wechsler Individual Achievement Test.* San Antonio, TX: Author.

Quillan, R.E. (1994). *Neuropsychological functioning in chronic fatigue syndrome.* Unpublished doctoral dissertation, Miami University, Oxford, OH.

Raggio, D.J. (1991). *Raggio Evaluation of Attention Deficit Disorder computerized test.* Jackson: University of Mississippi Medical Center, Infant and Child Development Clinic.

Raggio, D.J. (1992, November). *Relationship of the continuous performance test with intelligence, academic achievement, and neurological impairment.* Paper presented at the annual conference of the National Academy of Neuropsychology, Pittsburgh, PA.

Raggio, D.J. (1993, April). *Utilization of the READD/continuous performance test for the diagnosis of attention deficit hyperactivity disorder.* Paper presented at the annual conference of the National Association of School Psychologists, Washington, DC.

Raggio, D.J., & Whitten, J.M. (1994). *Raggio Evaluation of Attention Deficit Disorder READD manual.* Unpublished manuscript available from D.J. Raggio, University of Mississippi Medical Center, Department of Pediatrics, Jackson.

Raggio, D.J., Whitten, J.D., & Shine, A.E. (1994, November). *Neuropsychological deficit of ADHD children based on analysis of the continuous performance test.* Paper presented at the 14th annual meeting of the National Academy of Neuropsychology, Orlando, FL.

Ramsey, M., & Reynolds, C.R. (2000). Does smoking by pregnant women influence IQ, birth weight, and developmental disabilities in their infants? A methodological review and multivariate analysis. *Neuropsychology Review, 10,* 1–40.

Rapoport, J.L., Buchsbaum, M.S., Weingarten, H., Zahn, T.P., Ludlow, C., & Mikkelsen, E.J. (1980). Dextroamphetamine: Its cognitive and behavioral effects in normal and hyperactive boys and normal men. *Archives of General Psychiatry, 37,* 933–943.

Rapport, M.D., Carlson, G.A., Kelly, K.L., & Pataki, C. (1993). Methylphenidate and desipramine in hospitalized children: I. Separate and combined effects on cognitive function. *Journal of the American Academy of Child and Adolescent Psychiatry, 32,* 333–342.

Rapport, M.D., DuPaul, G.J., Stoner, G., & Jones, J.T. (1986). Comparing classroom and clinic measures of attention deficit disorder: Differential, idiosyncratic, and dose-response effects of methylphenidate. *Journal of Consulting and Clinical Psychology, 54,* 334–341.

Rapport, M.D., & Gordon, M. (1987). *The Attention Training System (ATS).* DeWitt, NY: Gordon Systems.

Rapport, M.D., Jones, J.T., DuPaul, G.J., Kelly, K.L., Gardner, M.J., Tucker, S.B., Shea, M.S. (1987). Attention deficit disorder and methylphenidate: Group and single subject analyses of dose effects on attention in clinic and classroom settings. *Journal of Clinical Child Psychology, 16,* 329–338.

Rapport, M.D., Loo, S., Isaacs, P., Goya, S., Denney, C., & Scanlan, S. (1996). Methylphenidate and attentional training: Comparative effects on behavior and neurocognitive performance in twin girls with attention-deficit/hyperactivity disorder. *Behavior Modification, 20,* 428–450.

Rapport, M.D., Murphy, A., & Bailey, J.S. (1982). Ritalin vs. response cost in the control of hyperactive children: A within-subject comparison. *Journal of Applied Behavior Analysis, 15,* 205–216.

Rasbury, W.C., Fennell, R.S., Eastman, B.G., Garin, E.H., & Richards, G. (1979). Cognitive performance of children with renal disease. *Psychological Reports, 45,* 231–239.

Rasile, D., Burg, J.S., Burright, R.G., & Donovick, P.J. (1995). The relationship between performance on the Gordon Diagnostic System and other measures of attention. *International Journal of Psychology, 30,* 35–45.

Raskin, S., & Mateer, C.A. (1993, June). *Cognitive rehabilitation of the functional reading deficits following traumatic brain injury.* Paper presented at the meeting of the American College of Rehabilitation Medicine, Denver, CO.

Raymond, M.J., Bennett, T.L., Hartlage, L.C., & Cullum, C.M. (1999). *Mild traumatic brain injury.* Austin, TX: ProEd.

Reader, M.J., Harris, E.L., Schuerholz, L.J., & Denckla, M.B. (1994). Attention deficit hyperactivity disorder and executive dysfunction. *Developmental Neuropsychology, 10,* 493–512.

Reichenbach, L.L., Halperin, J.M., Sharma, V., & Newcorn, J.H. (1992). Children's motor activity: Reliability and relationship to attention and behavior. *Developmental Neuropsychology, 8,* 87–97.

Reid, R., & Maag, J.W. (1998). Functional assessment: A method for developing classroom-based accommodations and interventions for children with ADHD. *Reading and Writing Quarterly: Overcoming Learning Difficulties, 14,* 9–42.

Reitan, R.M. (1958). Validity of the Trail Making Tests as an indicator of organic brain damage. *Perceptual and Motor Skills, 8,* 271–276.

Reitan, R.M. (1969). *Manual for administering and scoring the Reitan–Indiana Neuropsychological Battery for Children (aged 5 through 8).* Indianapolis: Indiana University Medical Center.

Reitan, R.M. (1974). Psychological effects of cerebral lesions in children in early school age. In R.M. Reitan & L.A. Davison (Eds.), *Clinical neuropsychology: Current status and applications.* Washington, DC: Winston.

Reitan, R.M., & Wolfson, D. (1985). *Halstead-Reitan Neuropsychological Test Battery: Theory and clinical interpretation.* Tucson, AZ: Neuropsychology Press.

Rey, A. (1964). *L'examen clinique en psychologie [The clinical exam in psychology].* Paris: Presses Universitaires de France.

Reynolds, C.R. (1997). Measurement and statistical problems in neuropsychological assessment of children. In C.R. Reynolds & E. Fletcher-Janzen (Eds.), *Handbook of clinical child neuropsychology* (2nd ed., pp. 296–319). New York: Plenum Press.

Reynolds, C.R. (1999a). Fundamentals of measurement and assessment. In C.R. Reynolds (Ed.), *Assessment, Vol. 4: Comprehensive clinical psychology* (pp. 33–56). Oxford, England: Elsevier Science.

Reynolds, C.R. (1999b). The influence of causality between smoking and low birth weight: Good science or good politics? *Journal of Forensic Neuropsychology, 1,* 55–87.

Reynolds, C.R. (in press). Methods for detecting and evaluating cultural bias in neuropsychological tests. In E. Fletcher-Janzen, T. Strickland, & C.R. Reynolds (Eds.), *Handbook of cross-cultural neuropsychology.* New York: Plenum Press.

Reynolds, C.R., & Bigler, E.D. (1994). *Manual for the Test of Memory and Learning.* Austin, TX: ProEd.

Reynolds, C.R., & Kamphaus, R.W. (1992). *Manual for the Behavioral Assessment System for Children (BASC).* Circle Pines, MN: American Guidance Service.

Reynolds, C.R., Lowe, P.A., Moore, J.J., & Riccio, C.A. (1998, November). *Sensitivity and specificity of CPT in the diagnosis of ADHD: Much of one and none of the other.* Paper presented at the annual meeting of the National Academy of Neuropsychology, Washington, DC.

Reynolds, C.R., Lowe, P.A., & Saenz, A.L. (1999). The problem of bias in psychological assessment. In C.R. Reynolds & T.B. Gutkin (Eds.), *The handbook of school psychology* (3rd ed., pp. 549–596). New York: Wiley.

Reynolds, C.R., & Willson, V. (1985). *Methodological and statistical advances in the study of individual differences.* New York: Plenum Press.

Rezai, K., Andreasen, N.C., Alliger, R., Cohen, G., Swayze, V., II, & O'Leary, D.S. (1993). The neuropsychology of the prefrontal cortex. *Archives of Neurology, 50,* 636–642.

Riccio, C.A., Cohen, M.J., Hynd, G.W., & Keith, R.W. (1996). Validity of the Auditory Continuous Performance Test in differentiating central processing auditory disorders with and without ADHD. *Journal of Learning Disabilities, 29,* 561–566.

Riccio, C.A., & Jemison, S. (1998). ADHD and emergent literacy: Influence of language factors. *Reading and Writing Quarterly, 14,* 43–58.

Riccio, C.A., Moore, J.J., Lowe, P.A., & Reynolds, C.R. (1998, November). *The Continuous Performance Test: A window on the neural substrates of attention?* Paper presented at the annual meeting of the National Academy of Neuropsychology, Washington, DC.

Riccio, C.A., Moore, J.J., Reynolds, C.R., & Lowe, P.A. (1999). *Various medications and other substances: Implications for CPT use and interpretation.* Unpublished manuscript, Texas A&M University, Department of Educational Psychology, College Station.

Riccio, C.A., Moore, J.J., Reynolds, C.R., & Lowe, P.A. (in press). Effects of stimulants on the continuous performance test (CPT): Implications for CPT use and interpretation. *Journal of Neuropsychiatry and Clinical Neuroscience.*

Riccio, C.A., Reynolds, C.R., Lowe, P.A., & Moore, J.J. (in press). The Continuous Performance Test: A window on the neural substrates of attention? *Archives of Clinical Neuropsychology.*

Richards, G.P., Samuels, S.J., Turnure, J.E., & Ysseldyke, J.E. (1990). Sustained and selective attention in children with learning disabilities. *Journal of Learning Disabilities, 23,* 129–136.

Richman, J.E. (1986). Use of a sustained visual attention task to determine children at risk for learning problems. *Journal of the American Optometric Association, 57,* 20–26.

Ringholz, G.M. (1989). *Inconsistent attention in chronic survivors of severe closed head injury.* Unpublished doctoral dissertation, University of Houston, TX.

Riordan, H.J., Flashman, L.A., Saykin, A.J., Frutiger, S.A., Carroll, K.E., & Huey, L. (1999). Neuropsychological correlates of methylphenidate treatment in adult ADHD with and without depression. *Archives of Clinical Neuropsychology, 14,* 217–233.

Risser, A.H., & Hamsher, K. (1990, February). *Vigilance and distractibility on a continuous performance test by severely head injured adults.* Paper presented at the 18th annual meeting of the International Neuropsychological Society, Orlando, FL.

Roberts, L.W., Rau, H., Lutzenberger, W., & Birbaumer, N. (1994). Mapping P300 waves onto inhibition: Go/no-go discrimination. *Electroencephalography and Clinical Neurophysiology, 92,* 44–55.

Robertson, I.H., Tegner, R., Tham, K., Lo, A., & Nimmo-Smith, I. (1995). Sustained attention training for unilateral neglect: Theoretical and rehabilitation implications. *Journal of Clinical and Experimental Neuropsychology, 17,* 416–430.

Robins, P.M. (1992). A comparison of behavioral and attentional functioning in children diagnosed as hyperactive or learning disabled. *Journal of Abnormal Child Psychology, 20,* 65–82.

Robison, M. (1992). *The effect of refined carbohydrates on alertness, sleepiness, and sustained attention in men and women.* Unpublished doctoral dissertation, California School of Professional Psychology, Fresno.

Rodenburgh, J. (in press). *Comprehensive Attention Battery CPT.* Greensboro, NC: Neuropsychworks.

Rodin, E.A., Schmaltz, S., & Twitty, G. (1986). Intellectual functions of patients with childhood onset epilepsy. *Developmental Medicine and Child Neurology, 28,* 25–33.

Roitman, S.E.L., Keefe, R.S.E., Harvey, P.D., Siever, L.J., & Mohs, R.C. (1997). Attentional and eye tracking deficits correlate with negative symptoms in schizophrenia. *Schizophrenia Research, 26,* 139–146.

Romans, S.M., Roeltgen, D.P., Kushner, H., & Ross, J.L. (1997). Executive function in girls with Turner's syndrome. *Developmental Neuropsychology, 13,* 23–40.

Rosenberg, R.J. (1980). *The effects of irrelevant visual stimuli on visual attention in learning disabled boys.* Unpublished doctoral dissertation, Emory University, Atlanta, GA.

Ross, D.A., & Ross, S.A. (1976). *Hyperactivity: Research, theory, action.* New York: Wiley.

Rosvold, H.E., Mirsky, A., Sarason, I., Bransome, E.D., Jr., & Beck, L.H. (1956). A continuous performance test of brain damage. *Journal of Consulting Psychology, 20,* 343–350.

Rourke, B.P. (1989). *Nonverbal learning disabilities: The syndrome and the model.* New York: Guilford Press.

Roy, M.A., Flaum, M., & Andreasen, N.C. (1995). No difference found between winter- and non-winter-born schizophrenic cases. *Schizophrenia Research, 17,* 241–248.

Roy, M.A., Flaum, M.A., Gupta, S., Jaramillo, L., & Andreasen, N.C. (1994). Epidemiological and clinical correlates of familial and sporadic schizophrenia. *Acta Psychiatrica Scandinavica, 89,* 324–328.

Roy-Byrne, P., Scheele, L., Brinkley, J., Ward, N., Wiatrak, C., Russo, J., Tounes, B., & Varley, C. (1997). Adult attention-deficit hyperactivity disorder: Assessment guidelines based on clinical presentation to a specialty clinic. *Comprehensive Psychiatry, 38*(3), 133–148.

Rueckert, L., & Grafman, J. (1996). Sustained attention deficits in patients with right frontal lesions. *Neuropsychologia, 34,* 953–963.

Rueckert, L., & Grafman, J. (1998). Sustained attention deficits in patients with lesions of posterior cortex. *Neuropsychologia, 36,* 653–660.

Rumble, S.R. (1984). *An examination of the psychological variables of attention deficit behavior in children.* Unpublished doctoral dissertation, Indiana State University, Terre Haute.

Rund, B.R., Orbeck, A.L., & Landro, N.I. (1992). Vigilance deficits in schizophrenics and affectively disturbed patients. *Acta Psychiatrica Scandinavica, 86,* 207–212.

Rund, B.R., Zeiner, P., Sundet, K., Oie, M., & Bryhn, G. (1998). No vigilance deficit found in either young schizophrenic or ADHD subjects. *Scandinavian Journal of Psychology, 39,* 101–107.

Rutschmann, J., Cornblatt, B., & Erlenmeyer-Kimling, L. (1977). Sustained attention in children at risk for schizophrenia: Report on a continuous performance test. *Archives of General Psychiatry, 34,* 571–575.

Rutter, M. (1981). Psychological sequelae of brain damage in children. *American Journal of Clinical Neuropsychology, 138,* 1533–1544.

Sadock, B.I., & Sadock, V.A. (2000). *Kaplan and Sadock comprehensive textbook of psychiatry* (7th ed.). Baltimore: Lippincott.

Safer, D.J., & Krager, J.M. (1988). A survey of medication treatment for hyperactive/inattentive students. *Journal of the American Medical Association, 260,* 2256–2258.

Safer, D.J., & Krager, J.M. (1989). Hyperactivity and inattentiveness: School assessment of stimulant treatment. *Clinical Pediatrics, 28,* 216–221.

Safer, D.J., Zito, J.M., & Pine, E.M. (1996). Increased methylphenidate usage for attention deficit disorders in the 1990s. *Pediatrics, 98,* 1084–1088.

Salazar, A.M., Grafman, A., Schlesselman, S., Vance, S.C., Mohr, J.P., Carpenter, M., Pevsner, P., Ludlow, C., & Weingartner, H. (1986). Penetrating war injuries of the basal forebrain: Neurology and cognition. *Neurology, 36,* 459–465.

Sallee, F.R., Sethuraman, G., & Rock, C.M. (1994). Effects of pimozide on cognition in children with Tourette syndrome: Interaction with comorbid attention deficit hyperactivity disorder. *Acta Psychiatrica Scandinavica, 90,* 4–9.

Samuels, I. (1959). Reticular mechanisms and behavior. *Psychological Bulletin, 56,* 1–25.

Sandford, J.A. (1994). *A reliability study of IVA: Preliminary report.* Richmond, VA: BrainTrain.

Sandford, J.A., & Browne, R.J. (1988). *Captain's Log* [Computer software]. Richmond, VA: BrainTrain.

Sandford, J.A., Fine, A.H., & Goldman, L. (1995a, August). *Validity study of the IVA: A visual and auditory CPT.* Paper presented at the 1995 annual convention of the American Psychological Association, New York.

Sandford, J.A., Fine, A.H., & Goldman, L. (1995b, November). *A comparison of auditory and visual processing in children with ADHD using the IVA Continuous Performance Test.* Paper presented at the 1995 annual convention of CHADD, Washington, DC.

Sandford, J.A., & Turner, A. (1994–1999). *Integrated Visual and Auditory (IVA) Continuous Performance Test.* Richmond, VA: BrainTrain.

Sandford, J.A., & Turner, A. (1995). *Manual for the Integrated Visual and Auditory (IVA) Continuous Performance Test.* Richmond, VA: BrainTrain.

Sandoval, J. (1977). The measurement of hyperactive syndrome in children. *Review of Educational Research, 47,* 293–318.

Satterfield, J.H., & Dawson, M.E. (1971). Electrodermal correlates of hyperactivity in children. *Psychophysiology, 8,* 191.

Satterfield, J.H., Lesser, L.I., Saul, R.E., & Cantwell, D.P. (1973). Response to stimulant drug treatment in hyperactive children: Prediction from EEG and neurological findings. *Journal of Autism and Childhood Schizophrenia, 3,* 36–48.

Sax, K.W. (1995). *The relationship between attention and psychotic symptoms in patients with first episode psychosis during hospitalization and two-months later.* Unpublished doctoral dissertation, Virginia Commonwealth University, Richmond.

Sax, K.W., Strakowski, S.M., & Keck, P.E., Jr. (1998). Attentional improvement following quetiapine fumarate treatment in schizophrenia. *Schizophrenia Research, 33,* 151–155.

Sax, K.W., Strakowski, S.M., Keck, P.E., Jr., McElroy, S.L., West, S.A., & Stanton, S.P. (1998). Symptom correlates of attentional improvements following hospitalization for a first episode of affective psychosis. *Biological Psychiatry, 44,* 784–786.

Sax, K.W., Strakowski, S.M., McElroy, S.L., Keck, P.E., Jr., & West, S.A. (1995). Attention and normal thought disorder in mixed and pure mania. *Biological Psychiatry, 37,* 420–423.

Sax, K.W., Strakowski, S.M., Zimmerman, M.E., DelBello, M.P., Keck, P.E., Jr., & Hawkins, J.M. (1999). Frontosubcortical neuroanatomy and the continuous performance test in mania. *American Journal of Psychiatry, 156,* 139–141.

Sbordonne, R.J. (1986). Does computer assisted cognitive rehabilitation work? A case study. *Psychotherapy in Private Practice, 4,* 51–61.

Schachar, R., Logan, G., Wachsmuth, R., & Chajczyk, D. (1988a). Attaining and maintaining preparation: A comparison of hyperactive, normal, and disturbed control children. *Journal of Abnormal Child Psychology, 16,* 361–378.

Schachar, R., Logan, G., Wachsmuth, R., & Chajczyk, D. (1988b). An examination of attention, arousal, and learning dysfunctions of hyperkinetic children. *Psychological Bulletin, 85,* 689–715.

Schechter, M.D., & Timmons, G.D. (1985a). Objectively measured hyperactivity: I. Comparison with normal controls. *Journal of Clinical Pharmacology, 25,* 269–275.

Schechter, M.D., & Timmons, G.D. (1985b). Objectively measured hyperactivity: II. Caffeine and amphetamine effects. *Journal of Clinical Pharmacology, 25,* 276–280.

Schein, J.D. (1962). Cross-validation of the continuous performance test for brain damage. *Journal of Consulting Psychology, 26,* 115–118.

Schröeder, J., Buchsbaum, M.S., Siegel, B.V., Geider, F.J., Haier, R.J., Lohr, J., Wu, J.C., & Potkin, S.G. (1994). Patterns of cortical activity in schizophrenia. *Psychological Medicine, 24,* 947–955.

Schupp, H.T., Lutzenberger, W., Rau, H., & Birbaumer, N. (1994). Positive shifts of event-related potentials: A state of cortical disfacilitiation as reflected by the startle reflex probe. *Electroencephalography and Clinical Neurophysiology, 90,* 135–144.

Seabrook, S.H. (1995). *An assessment of attention deficit hyperactivity disorder and undifferentiated attention deficit disorder using the Raggio Evaluation of Attention Deficit Disorder, the Conners' Parent Rating Scale and the ADD-H Comprehensive Teachers' Rating Scale.* Unpublished doctoral dissertation, Mississippi State University, Starkville.

Seckler, P., Burns, W., Montgomery, D., & Sandford, J.A. (1995, November). *A reliability study of IVA: Intermediate Visual and Auditory Continuous Performance Test.* Paper presented at the 1995 annual convention of CHADD, Washington, DC.

Seidel, W.T. (1989). Assessment of attention in children. *Dissertation Abstracts International, 50*(5-B), 2166.

Seidel, W.T., & Joschko, M. (1990). Evidence of difficulties in sustained attention in children with ADDH. *Journal of Abnormal Child Psychology, 18,* 217–229.

Seidel, W.T., & Joschko, M. (1991). Assessment of attention in children. *Clinical Neuropsychologist, 5,* 53–66.

Seidman, L.J., Biederman, J., Faraone, S., Milberger, S., Norman, D., Seiverd, K., Benedict, K., Guite, J., Mick, E., & Kiely, K. (1995). Effects of family history and comorbidity on the neuropsychological performance of children with ADHD: Preliminary findings. *Journal of the American Academy of Child and Adolescent Psychiatry, 34,* 1015–1024.

Seidman, L.J., Biederman, J., Faraone, S.V., Weber, W., & Oeullette, C. (1997). Toward defining a neuropsychology of attention deficit-hyperactivity disorder:

Performance of children and adolescents from a large clinically referred sample. *Journal of Consulting and Clinical Psychology, 65,* 150–160.

Seidman, L.J., Van Manen, K-J., Turner, W.M., Gamser, D.M., Faraone, S.V., Goldstein, J.M., & Tsuang, M.T. (1998). The effects of increasing resource demand on vigilance performance in adults with schizophrenia or developmental attentional/learning disorders: A preliminary study. *Schizophrenia Research, 34,* 101–112.

Selemon, L.D., & Goldman-Rakic, P.S. (1990). Topographic intermingling of striatonigral and striatopallidal neurons in the rhesus monkey. *Journal of Comparative Neurology, 297,* 359–370.

Semrud-Clikeman, M., Harrington, K., Clinton, A., Connor, R.T., & Sylvester, L. (1998, February). *Attention functioning in two groups of ADHD children with and without attention training interventions.* Paper presented at the 26th annual International Neuropsychological Society Conference, Honolulu, HI.

Sergeant, J.A., & Scholten, C.A. (1985). On resource strategy limitations in hyperactivity: Cognitive impulsivity reconsidered. *Journal of Child Psychology and Psychiatry, 26,* 97–109.

Serper, M.R. (1991). *The temporal relationship of attentional and clinical changes during neuroleptic treatment of schizophrenia: A descriptive study.* Unpublished doctoral dissertation, State University of New York, Binghamton.

Serper, M.R., Bergman, R.L., & Harvey, P.D. (1990). Medication may be required for the development of automatic information processing in schizophrenia. *Psychiatry Research, 32,* 281–288.

Servan-Schreiber, D., Cohen, J.D., & Steingard, S. (1996). Schizophrenic deficits in the processing of context. *Archives of General Psychiatry, 53,* 1105–1112.

Shanon, A., Feldman, W., Leiken, L., Pong, A.H., Peterson, R., & Williams, V. (1993). Comparison of CNS adverse effects between astemizole and chlorpheniramine in children: A randomized, double-blind study. *Developmental Pharmacology and Therapeutics, 20,* 239–246.

Shapiro, E.G., Lockman, L.A., Knopman, D., & Krivit, W. (1994). Characteristics of the dementia in late-onset metachromatic leukodystrophy. *Neurology, 44,* 662–665.

Shapiro, M.B., Morris, R.D., Morris, M.K., Flowers, C., & Jones, R.W. (1999). A neuropsychologically based assessment model of the structure of attention in children. *Developmental Neuropsychology, 14,* 657–677.

Shapiro, S.K., & Garfinkel, B.D. (1986). The occurrence of behavior disorders in children: The interdependence of attention deficit disorder and conduct disorder. *Journal of the American Academy of Child and Adolescent Psychiatry, 25,* 809–819.

Shapiro, S.K., & Herod, L.A. (1994). Combining visual and auditory tasks in the assessment of attention-deficit hyperactivity disorder. In D.K. Routh (Ed.), *Disruptive behavior disorders in childhood* (pp. 87–107). New York: Plenum Press.

Sharma, V., Halperin, J.M., Newcorn, J.H., & Wolf, L.E. (1991). The dimension of focussed attention: Relationship to behavior and cognitive functioning in children. *Perceptual and Motor Skills, 72,* 787–793.

Shaw, C., & McKenna, K. (1989). Microcomputer activities for attention training. *Cognitive Rehabilitation, 7,* 18–21.

Shekim, W.O., Bylund, D.B., Alexson, J., Glaser, R.D., Jones, S.B., Hodges, K., & Perdue, S. (1986). Platelet MAO and measurements of attention and impulsivity in boys with attention deficit disorder and hyperactivity. *Psychiatry Research, 18,* 179–188.

Sheslow, D., & Adams, W. (1990). *Examiner's manual for the Wide Range Assessment of Memory and Learning.* Wilmington, DE: Jastak.

Shiffrin, R.M., & Schneider, W. (1977). Controlled and automatic human information processing: II. Perceptual learning, automatic attending, and a general theory. *Psychology Review, 84,* 127–190.

Shucard, D.W., Benedict, R.H.B., Tekok-Kilic, A., & Lichter, D.G. (1997). Slowed reaction time during a continuous performance test in children with Tourette's syndrome. *Neuropsychology, 11,* 147–155.

Siegel, B.V., Jr., Nuechterlein, K.H., Abel, L., Wu, J.C., & Buchsbaum, M.S. (1995). Glucose metabolic correlates of continuous performance test performance in adults with a history of infantile autism, schizophrenics, and controls. *Schizophrenic Research, 17,* 85–94.

Siegel, D.J. (2000). Perception and cognition. In B. Sadock & V. Sadock (Eds.), *Kaplan and Sadock's comprehensive textbook of psychiatry* (7th ed., pp. 386–402). New York: Lippincott.

Silverstein, M.L., Weinstein, M., Turnbull, A., & Nadar, T. (1999, August). *Target frequency in a vigilance attention task.* Paper presented at the annual convention of the American Psychological Association, Boston.

Simson, R., Vaughan, H.G., Jr., & Ritter, W. (1977a). The scalp topography of potentials associated with missing visual or auditory stimuli. *Electroencephalography and Clinical Neurophysiology, 42,* 528–535.

Simson, R., Vaughan, H.G., Jr., & Ritter, W. (1977b). The scalp topography of potentials in auditory and visual go/no-go tasks. *Electroencephalography and Clinical Neurophysiology, 43,* 864–875.

Slate, S.E., Meyer, T.L., Burns, W.J., & Montgomery, D.D. (1998). Computerized cognitive training for severely emotionally disturbed children with ADHD. *Behavior Modification, 22,* 415–437.

Slicker, E.K. (1991). *Validation of an objective measure of perseveration in children with attention deficit hyperactivity disorder.* Unpublished doctoral dissertation, Texas A&M University, College Station.

Smith, D.B., Mattson, R.H., Cramer, J.A., Collins, J.F., Novelly, R.A., Craft, B., & Veterans Administration Epilepsy Cooperative Study Group. (1987). Results of a nationwide Veterans Administration cooperative study comparing the efficacy and toxicity of carbamazapine, phenobarbital, phenytoin, and primidone. *Epilepsia, 28*(Suppl. 3), S50–S58.

Sohlberg, M.M., & Mateer, C.A. (1987). Effectiveness of an attention-training program. *Journal of Clinical and Experimental Neuropsychology, 9,* 117–130.

Sohlberg, M.M., & Mateer, C.A. (1989a). *Attention process training.* Puyallup, WA: Association for Neuropsychological Research and Development.

Sohlberg, M.M., & Mateer, C.A. (1989b). *Introduction to cognitive rehabilitation.* New York: Guilford Press.

Solanto, M.V., Wender, E.H., & Bartell, S.S. (1997). Effects of methylphenidate and behavioral contingencies on sustained attention in attention deficit hyperactivity disorder: A test of the reward dysfunction hypothesis. *Journal of Child and Adolescent Psychopharmacology, 7,* 123–136.

Sostek, A.J., Buchsbaum, M.S., & Rapoport, J.L. (1980). Effects of amphetamine on vigilance performance in normal and hyperactive children. *Journal of Abnormal Child Psychology, 8,* 491–500.

Speech, T.J., Rao, S.M., Osman, D.C., & Sperry, L T. (1993). A double-blind controlled study of methylphenidate treatment in closed head injury. *Brain Injury, 7,* 333–338.

Spence, S.A., Hirsch, S.J., Brooks, D.J., & Grasby, P.M. (1998). Prefrontal cortex activity in people with schizophrenia and control subjects: Evidence from positron emission tomography for remission of "hypofrontality" with recovery from acute schizophrenia. *British Journal of Psychiatry, 172,* 316–323.

Spohn, H.E., Lacoursiere, R.B., Thompson, R.N., & Coyne, L. (1977). Phenothiazine effects on psychological and psychophysiological dysfunction in chronic schizophrenia. *Archives of General Psychiatry, 34,* 633–644.

Sporn, J., & Sachs, G. (1997). The anticonvulsant lamotrigine in treatment of resistant manic-depressive illness. *Journal of Clinical Psychopharmacology, 17,* 185–189.

Spreen, O., Risser, A.H., & Edgell, D. (1995). *Developmental neuropsychology.* London: Oxford University Press.

Sprinkle, B.J. (1992). *The role of affect in the diagnosis of attentional disorders: Assessment of comorbidity.* Unpublished doctoral dissertation, Texas A&M University, College Station.

Squires, N.K., Halgren, E., Wilson, C., & Crandall, P. (1983). Human endogenous limbic potentials: Cross-modality and depth surface comparisons in epileptic subjects. In A.W.K. Gaillard & W. Ritter (Eds.), *Tutorials in event-related potential research: Endogenous components* (pp. 217–232). New York: North Holland.

Stamm, J., Birbaumer, N., Lutzenberger, W., Elbert, T., Rockstroh, B., & Schlottke, P. (1982). Event-related potentials during a continuous performance test vary with attentive capacities. In A. Rothberger (Ed.), *Event-related potentials in children* (pp. 273–294). Amsterdam: Elsevier.

Stankov, L. (1988). Aging, attention, and intelligence. *Psychology and Aging, 3,* 59–74.

Stein, M.A., Szumowski, E., Sandoval, R., Nadelman, D., O'Brien, T., Krasowski, M., & Phillips, W. (1994). Psychometric properties of the Children's Atypical Development Scale. *Journal of Abnormal Child Psychology, 22,* 167–176.

Steinhauer, S.R., Locke, J., & Hill, S. (1997). Vigilance and iconic memory in children at high risk for alcoholism. *Journal of Studies in Alcoholism, 58,* 428–434.

Strandburg, R.J., Marsh, J.T., Brown, W.S., Asarnow, R.F., Guthrie, D., & Higa, J. (1990). Event-related correlates of impaired attention in schizophrenic children. *Biological Psychiatry, 27,* 1103–1115.

Strandburg, R.J., Marsh, J.T., Brown, W.S., Asarnow, R.F., Higa, J., & Guthrie, D. (1994). Continuous processing related ERPs in schizophrenic and normal children. *Biological Psychiatry, 35,* 525–538.

Strauss, M.E., Buchanan, R.W., & Hale, J. (1993). Relations between attentional deficits and clinical symptoms in schizophrenic out-patients. *Psychiatry Research, 47,* 205–213.

Strauss, M.E., Novakovic, T., Tien, A.Y., Bylsma, F., & Pearlson, G.D. (1991). Disengagement of attention in schizophrenia. *Psychiatry Research, 37,* 139–146.

Sturm, W., Willmes, K., Orgass, B., & Hartje, W. (1997). Do specific attention deficits need specific training? *Neuropsychological Rehabilitation, 7,* 81–106.

Stuss, D.T., & Benson, D.F. (1984). Neuropsychological studies of the frontal lobes. *Psychological Bulletin, 95,* 3–28.

Stuss, D.T., & Benson, D.F. (1986). *The frontal lobes.* New York: Raven Press.

Suslow, T., & Arolt, V. (1997). Paranoid schizophrenia: Non-specificity of neuropsychological vulnerability markers. *Psychiatry Research, 72,* 103–114.

Suslow, T., Junghanns, K., Weitzsch, C., & Arolt, V. (1998). Relations between neuropsychological vulnerability markers and negative symptoms in schizophrenia. *Psychopathology, 31,* 178–187.

Sutton, S., Braren, M., Zubin, J., & John, E.R. (1965). Evoked potential correlates of stimulus uncertainty. *Science, 150,* 1187–1188.

Suzuki, M., Araki, R., Suzuki, M., Haki, N., & Yoshida, K. (1995). Effects of caffeine on human performance: Analysis with a computer-based neurobehavioral evaluation system. *Research Communications in Biological Psychology and Psychiatry, 20,* 29–42.

Swanson, H.L. (1981). Vigilance deficit in learning disabled children: A signal detection analysis. *Journal of Child Psychology and Psychiatry, 22,* 393–399.

Swanson, H.L. (1983). A developmental study of vigilance in learning-disabled and non-disabled children. *Journal of Abnormal Child Psychology, 11,* 415–429.

Swanson, H.L., & Cooney, J.B. (1989). Relationship between intelligence and vigilance in children. *Journal of School Psychology, 27,* 141–153.

Swanson, J.M. (1985). Measures of cognitive functioning appropriate for use in pediatric psychopharmacological research studies. *Psychopharmacology Bulletin, 21,* 887–890.

Swanson, J.M., Cantwell, D.P., Lerner, M., McBurnett, K., & Hanna, G. (1991). Effects of stimulant medication on learning in children with ADHD. *Journal of Learning Disabilities, 24,* 219–230.

Swanson, J.M., Flockhart, D., Udrea, D., Cantwell, D.P., Connor, D., & Williams, L. (1995). Clonidine in the treatment of ADHD: Questions about safety and efficacy. *Journal of Child and Adolescent Psychopharmacology, 5,* 301–304.

Swartwood, J.N. (1994). *An assessment of neurophysiological, behavioral, and performance differences between ADHD and non-ADHD children.* Unpublished doctoral dissertation, University of Tennessee, Knoxville.

Swartwood, M.O. (1994). *An assessment of the effects of methylphenidate on electrophysiological, behavioral, and performance measures.* Unpublished doctoral dissertation, University of Tennessee, Knoxville.

Swets, J.A. (1964). *Signal detection and recognition by human observers.* New York: Wiley.

Swets, J.A. (1973). The relative operating characteristic in psychology. *Science, 182,* 990–1000.

Swets, J.A. (1984). Mathematical models of attention. In R. Parasuraman & D.R. Davies (Eds.), *Varieties of attention* (pp. 183–242). New York: Academic Press.

Sykes, D.H., Douglas, V.I., & Morganstern, G.L. (1972). The effect of methylphenidate (Ritalin) on sustained attention in hyperactive children. *Psychopharmacologia, 25,* 262–274.

Sykes, D.H., Douglas, V.I., & Morganstern, G.L. (1973). Sustained attention in hyperactive children. *Journal of Child Psychology and Psychiatry, 14,* 213–220.

Sykes, D.H., Douglas, V.I., Weiss, G., & Minde, K.M. (1971). Attention in hyperactive children and the effects of methylphenidate (Ritalin). *Journal of Child Psychology and Psychiatry, 12,* 129–139.

Tansey, M.A. (1990). Righting the rhythms of reason: EEG biofeedback training as a therapeutic modality in a clinical office setting. *Medical Psychotherapy, 3,* 57–68.

Tansey, M.A., & Bruner, R.L. (1983). EMG and EEG biofeedback training in the treatment of a 10-year-old hyperactive boy with a developmental reading disorder. *Biofeedback and Self-Regulation, 8,* 25–37.

Tarnowski, K.J. (1988). Cognitive assessment and intervention: Captain's Log. *Research in Developmental Disabilities, 9,* 101–104.

Tarnowski, K.J., Prinz, R.J., & Nay, S.M. (1986). Comparative analysis of attentional deficits in hyperactive and learning disabled children. *Journal of Abnormal Psychology, 95,* 341–345.

Tartaglione, A., Bino, G., Manzino, M., Spadevecchia, L., & Favale, E. (1986). Simple reaction-time changes in patients with unilateral brain damage. *Neuropsychologia, 24,* 649–658.

Taylor, E., Schachar, R., Thorley, G., Wieselberg, H.M., Everitt, B., & Rutter, H. (1987). Which boys respond to stimulant medication? A controlled trial of methylphenidate in boys with disruptive behavior *Psychological Medicine, 17,* 121–143.

Teasdale, G., & Jennett, B. (1974). Glasgow Coma Scale. *Lancet, 2,* 81–84.

Tecce, J.J., Cole, J.O., Mayer, J., & Lewis, D.C. (1979). Methadone effects on brain functioning and type A and B CNV shapes. *Psychopharmacology, 65,* 21–25.

Teicher, M.H., Ito, Y., Glod, C.A., & Barber, N.I. (1996). Objective measurement of hyperactivity and attentional problems in ADHD. *Journal of the American Academy of Child and Adolescent Psychiatry, 35,* 334–342.

Teixeira, L.C.H. (1993). *Comparison of EEG of depressed and nondepressed college students during an attention task.* Unpublished doctoral dissertation, University of Rhode Island, Providence.

Thompson, L., & Thompson, M. (1998). Neurofeedback combined with training in metacognitive strategies: Effectiveness in students with ADD. *Applied Psychophysiology and Biofeedback, 23,* 243–263.

Thompson, R.W., & Nichols, G.T. (1992). Correlations between scores on a continuous performance test and parent ratings of attention problems and impulsivity in children. *Psychological Reports, 70,* 739–742.

Thompson, T.L. (1988). *Attention-deficit hyperactivity disorder: Search for an objective diagnostic measure.* Unpublished doctoral dissertation, Texas A&M University, College Station.

Thomson, J.B. (1995, February). *Rehabilitation of individuals with traumatic brain injury (TBI) through utilization of an attention training program.* Paper presented at the 23rd annual International Neuropsychological Society Conference, Seattle, WA.

Thomson, J.B., Seidenstrang, L., Kerns, K.A., Sohlberg, M.M., & Mateer, C.A. (1994). *Pay attention!* Puyallup, WA: Association for Neuropsychological Research and Development.

Tillery, K.L., Katz, J.K., & Keller, W.D. (1998). *Central auditory processing and auditory continuous performance tests in children with attention deficit hyperactivity and central auditory processing disorders under Ritalin and placebo conditions.* Manuscript submitted for publication, State University of New York, Fredonia.

Timmermans, S.R., & Christensen, B. (1991). The measure of attention deficits in TBI children and adolescents. *Cognitive Rehabilitation, 9*(4), 26–31.

Trenerry, M.R., Crosson, B., DeBoe, J., & Leber, W.R. (1989). *Visual Search and Attention Test (VSAT).* Odessa, FL: Psychological Assessment Resources.

Trimble, M.R., & Corbette, J.A. (1980). Behavioral and cognitive disturbance in epileptic children. *Irish Medical Journal, 73,* 21–28.

Trimble, M.R., & Reynolds, E.H. (1976). Anticonvulsant drugs and mental symptoms: A review. *Psychological Medicine, 6*(2), 69–78.

Trommer, B.L., Hoeppner, J.B., Lorber, R., & Armstrong, K. (1988). Pitfalls in the use of a continuous performance test as a diagnostic tool in attention deficit disorder. *Journal of Developmental and Behavioral Pediatrics, 9,* 339–345.

Tsai, S.Y., & Chen, J.D. (1996). Neurobehavioral effects of occupational exposure to low-level styrene. *Neurotoxicology and Teratology, 18,* 463–469.

Tucker, D.M. (1986). Hemispheric specialization: A mechanism for unifying anterior and posterior brain regions. In D. Ottosm (Ed.), *Duality and unity of the brain: Unified functioning and specialization of the hemispheres* (pp. 75–128). New York: Plenum Press.

Tucker, D.M., & Williamson, P.A. (1984). Asymmetric neural control systems in human self-regulation. *Psychological Review, 91,* 185–215.

Tucker, R.L. (1990). *The ability of the Gordon Diagnostic System to differentiate between attention-deficit hyperactivity disorder and specific developmental disorders in children.* Unpublished doctoral dissertation, University of Toledo, OH.

Tupler, L.A. (1989). *The role of attentional resources in the memory performance of elderly adults: An investigation of the integration deficit hypothesis.* Unpublished doctoral dissertation, Emory University, Atlanta, GA.

Turner, A., & Sandford, J.A. (1995a, November). *Developmental age and sex differences in auditory and visual processing using the IVA Continuous Performance Test.* Paper presented at the 1995 annual convention of CHADD, Washington, DC.

Turner, A., & Sandford, J.A. (1995b, August). *A normative study of IVA: Integrated Visual and Auditory Continuous Performance Test.* Paper presented at the 1995 annual convention of the American Psychological Association, New York.

Umans, J.G., & Pliskin, N.H. (1998). Attention and mental processing speed in hemodialysis patients. *American Journal of Kidney Diseases, 32,* 749–751.

Vachon, L., Sulkowski, A., & Rich, E. (1974). Marihuana effects on learning, attention, and time estimation. *Psychopharmacologia, 39,* 1–11.

Valdés, M.R. (1985a). Biofeedback in private practice, and stress reduction in a college population using biofeedback and open focus technique. *Psychotherapy in Private Practice, 3,* 43–55.

Valdés, M.R. (1985b). Effects of biofeedback-assisted attention training in a college population. *Biofeedback and Self-Regulation, 10,* 315–324.

Valdés, M.R. (1988). A program in stress management in a college setting. *Psychotherapy in Private Practice, 6,* 43–54.

Valentino, D.A., Arruda, J.E., & Gold, S.M. (1993). Comparison of QEEG and response accuracy in good vs. poorer performers during a vigilance task. *International Journal of Psychophysiology, 15,* 123–133.

van den Bosch, R.J. (1984). Eye tracking impairment: Attentional and psychometric correlates in psychiatric patients. *Journal of Psychiatric Research, 18,* 277–286.

van den Broek, A., Mattis, K., & Golden, C. (1997, November). *Intelligence, memory, and attention in children: A correlational study.* Paper presented at the annual conference of the National Academy of Neuropsychologists, Las Vegas, NV.

Van der Krol, R.J., Oosterbaan, H., Weller, S.D., & Koning, A.E. (1998). Attention-deficit hyperactivity disorder. In P.J. Graham (Ed.), *Cognitive-behaviour therapy for children and families* (pp. 32–44). New York: Cambridge University Press.

van der Meere, J.J., & Stemerdink, B.A. (1999). The development of state regulation in normal children: An indirect comparison with children with ADHD. *Developmental Neuropsychology, 16,* 213–225.

van der Meere, J.J., Stemerdink, B.A., & Gunning, W.B. (1995). Effect of presentation rate of stimuli on response inhibition in ADHD children with and without tics. *Journal of Perceptual and Motor Skills, 81,* 259–262.

van Leeuwen, T.H., Steinhausen, H-C., Overtoom, C.C.E., Pascual-Marqui, R.D., van't Klooster, B., Rothenberger, A., Sergeant, J.A., & Brandeis, D. (1998). The continuous performance test revisited with neuroelectric mapping: Impaired orienting in children with attention deficits. *Behavioural Brain Research, 94,* 97–110.

Van Putten, T., May, P.R.A., Marder, S.R., & Wittmann, L.A. (1981). Subjective response to antipsychotic drugs. *Archives of General Psychiatry, 38,* 187–190.

van Zomeran, A.H., & Brouwer, W.H. (1994). *Clinical neuropsychology of attention.* New York: Oxford University Press.

Verbaten, M.N., Overtoom, C.C.E., Koelega, H.S., Swaab-Barneveld, H., van der Gaag, R.J., Buitelaare, J., & van Engeland, H. (1994). Methylphenidate influences on both early and late ERP waves of ADHD children in a continuous performance test. *Journal of Abnormal Child Psychology, 22,* 561–578.

Vernon, P.A. (1989). The heritability of measures of speed of information processing. *Personality and Individual Differences, 10,* 573–576.

Viesselman, J.O. (1999). Anti-depressant and antimaniac drugs. In J.S. Werry & M.G. Aman (Eds.), *Practitioner's guide to psychoactive drugs for children and adolescents* (2nd ed., pp. 249–296). New York: Plenum Press.

Vigil, R. (1996). *The Vigil Continuous Performance Test.* San Antonio, TX: Psychological Corporation.

Villardita, C., Grioli, S., Lomeo, C., Cattaneo, C., & Parini, J. (1992). Clinical studies with oxiracetam in patients with dementia of Alzheimer type and multi-infarct dementia of mild to moderate degree. *Neuropsychobiology, 25,* 24–28.

Vining, E.P.G., Carpenter, R.O., & Aman, M.G. (1999). Antiepileptics (anticonvulsants). In J.S. Werry & M.G. Aman (Eds.), *Practitioner's guide to psychoactive drugs for children and adolescents* (2nd ed., pp. 355–385). New York: Plenum Press.

Vitiello, B., Stoff, D., Atkins, M., & Mahoney, A. (1990). Soft neurological signs and impulsivity in children. *Journal of Developmental and Behavioral Pediatrics, 11,* 112–115.

Voeller, K.K.S. (1991). Toward a neurobiologic nosology of attention deficit hyperactivity disorder. *Journal of Clinical Neurology, 65,* 52–58.

Vygotsky, L.S. (1980). *Mind in society: The development of higher psychological process.* Cambridge, MA: Harvard University Press.

Wagener, D.K., Hogarty, G.E., Goldstein, M.J., Asarnow, R.F., & Browne, A. (1986). Information processing and communication deviance in schizophrenic patients and their mothers. *Psychiatry Research, 18,* 365–377.

Wagner, A.E. (1987). *Gender differences in hyperactive school-age children.* Unpublished master's thesis, Michigan State University, East Lansing.

Wagner, I. (1988). Attention training with individuals, groups, and classes. *School Psychology International, 9,* 277–283.

Wagner, M., Kurtz, G., & Engel, R.R. (1989). Normal P300 in acute schizophrenics during a continuous performance test. *Biological Psychiatry, 25,* 792–795.

Waisbren, S.E. (1999). Phenylketonuria. In S. Goldstein & C.R. Reynolds (Eds.), *Handbook of neurodevelopmental and genetic disorders in children* (pp. 433–458). New York: Guilford Press.

Walden, J., Hesslinger, B., vanCalker, D., & Berger, M. (1996). Addition of lamotrigine to valproate may enhance efficacy in the treatment of bipolar affective disorder. *Pharmacopsychiatry, 29,* 193–195.

Walker, E., & Green, M. (1982). Motor proficiency and attentional task performance by psychotic patients. *Journal of Abnormal Psychology, 91,* 261–268.

Walker, E., & Shaye, J. (1982). A predictor of neuromotor and attentional abnormalities in schizophrenia. *Archives of General Psychiatry, 39,* 1153–1156.

Walker, P.S. (1993). *Motivation, sustained attention and cardiac reactivity in school-aged boys exposed to opiates in utero.* Unpublished doctoral dissertation, University of Maryland, College Park.

Walton, P., Halliday, R., Naylor, H., & Calloway, J. (1986). Stimulus intensity, contrast and complexity have additive effects on P3 latency. In. J.W. Rohrbaugh, R. Johnson, & R. Parasuraman (Eds.), *Eighth international conference on event related potentials of the brain* (pp. 409–411). Stanford, CA: Stanford University Press.

Weber, A.M., & Segalowitz, S.J. (1990). A measure of children's attentional capacity. *Developmental Neuropsychology, 6,* 13–23.

Wechsler, D. (1974). *The Wechsler Intelligence Scale for Children–Revised.* San Antonio, TX: Psychological Corporation.

Wechsler, D. (1981). *The Wechsler Adult Intelligence Scale–Revised.* San Antonio, TX: Psychological Corporation.

Wechsler, D. (1989). *The Wechsler Preschool and Primary Scale of Intelligence Children–Revised.* San Antonio, TX: Psychological Corporation.

Wechsler, D. (1991). *The Wechsler Intelligence Scale for Children–III.* San Antonio, TX: Psychological Corporation.

Wechsler, D. (1997). *The Wechsler Adult Intelligence Scale* (3rd ed.). San Antonio, TX: Psychological Corporation.

Weil, A.T., Zinberg, N.E., & Nelson, J.M. (1968). Clinical and psychological effects of marihuana in man. *Science, 162,* 1234–1242.

Weiler, M.D. (1992). *A measurement model for spectral analyzed EEG.* Unpublished doctoral dissertation, University of Rhode Island, Providence.

Weinberger, N., Yendall, L., & Lindsley, D.B. (1968). EEG correlates of reinforced behavioral inhibition. *Psychonomic Science, 10,* 11–12.

Weingartner, H., Rapoport, J.L., Buchsbaum, M.S., Bunney, W.E., Jr., Ebert, M.H., Mikkelson, E.J., & Caine, E.D. (1980). Cognitive processes in normal and hyperactive children and their response to amphetamine treatment. *Journal of Abnormal Psychology, 89,* 25–37.

Weinstein, J.A. (1996). *Neuromotor and attentional functioning in schizophrenia spectrum disorders.* Unpublished doctoral dissertation, Emory University, Atlanta, GA.

Weiss, G., Minde, K., Douglas, V., Werry, J., & Sykes, D. (1971). Comparison of the effects of chlorpromazine, dextroamphetamine and methylphenidate on the behavior and intellectual functioning of hyperactive children. *Canadian Medical Association Journal, 104,* 20–25.

Wells, A. (1990). Panic disorder in association with relaxation induced anxiety: An attentional training approach to treatment. *Behaviour Therapy, 21,* 273–280.

Welsh, M.C., & Pennington, B.F. (1988). Assessing frontal lobe functioning in children: Views from developmental psychology. *Developmental Neuropsychology, 4,* 199–230.

Welsh, M.C., Pennington, B.F., & Grossier, D.B. (1991). A normative developmental study of executive function: A window on the prefrontal function in children. *Developmental Neuropsychology, 7,* 131–139.

Werry, J.S., & Aman, M.G. (1975). Methylphenidate and haloperidol in children: Effects on attention, memory, and activity. *Archives of General Psychiatry, 32,* 790–795.

Werry, J.S., & Aman, M.G. (1984). Methylphenidate in hyperactive and enuretic children. In L. Greenhill & B. Shopsin (Eds.), *The psychobiology of childhood* (pp. 183–195). Jamaica, NY: Spectrum.

Werry, J.S., & Aman, M.G. (1999). Anxiolytics, sedatives, and miscellaneous drugs. In J.S. Werry & M.G. Aman (Eds.), *Practitioner's guide to psychoactive drugs for children and adolescents* (2nd ed., pp. 433–470). New York: Plenum Press.

Werry, J.S., Aman, M.G., & Diamond, E. (1980). Imipramine and methylphenidate in hyperactive children. *Journal of Child Psychology and Psychiatry, 21,* 27–35.

Werry, J.S., Aman, M.G., & Lampen, E. (1976). Haloperidol and methylphenidate in hyperactive children. *Acta Paedopsychiatrica, 42,* 26–40.

Werry, J.S., Elkind, G.S., & Reeves, J.C. (1987). Attention deficit, conduct, oppositional, and anxiety disorders in children: III. Laboratory differences. *Journal of Abnormal Child Psychology, 15,* 409–428.

Whalen, C.K., & Henker, B. (1976). Psychostimulants and children: A review and analysis. *Psychological Bulletin, 83,* 1113–1130.

Wherry, J., Paal, N., Jolly, J., Balkozar, A., Holloway, C., Everett, B., & Vaught, L. (1993). Concurrent and discriminant validity of the Gordon Diagnostic System: A preliminary study. *Psychology in the Schools, 30,* 29–36.

Whyte, J. (1992). Attention and arousal: Basic science aspects. *Archives of Physical Medicine and Rehabilitation, 73,* 940–949.

Wilens, T.E., McDermott, S.P., Biederman, J., Brantes, A., Hahesy, A., & Spencer, T.J. (1999). Cognitive therapy in the treatment of adults with ADHD: A systematic chart review of 26 cases. *Journal of Cognitive Psychotherapy, 13,* 215–226.

Willson, V.L., & Reynolds, C.R. (1982). Methodological and statistical problems in determining membership in clinical populations. *Clinical Neuropsychology, 4,* 134–138.

Wilson, J.S. (1995). *Attention, attachment, and motivation in schizotypy: A review and extension of research with the continuous performance test.* Unpublished doctoral dissertation, Duke University, Durham, NC.

Wilson, J.S., & Costanzo, P.R. (1996). A preliminary study of attachment, attention, and schizotypy in early adulthood. *Journal of Social and Clinical Psychology, 15,* 231–260.

Wittenborn, J.R., Flaherty, C.F., McGough, W.E., Bossange, K.A., & Nash, R.J. (1976). A comparison of the effect of imipramine, nomifensine, and placebo on the psychomotor performance of normal males. *Psychopharmacology, 51,* 85–90.

Wohlberg, G., & Kornetsky, C. (1973). Sustained attention in remitted schizophrenics. *Archives of General Psychiatry, 28,* 533–537.

Wolfe, N., Linn, R., Babikian, V.L., Knoefel, J.E., & Albert, M.L. (1990). Frontal systems impairment following multiple lacunar infarcts. *Archives of Neurology, 47,* 129–132.

Wolgin, D.M. (1994). *The effect of auditory distractors on variables of attention in schizophrenia.* Unpublished doctoral dissertation, University of Houston, TX.

Wood, R.L. (1984). Management of attention disorders following brain injury. In B.A. Wilson & N. Moffat (Eds.), *Clinical management of memory problems* (pp. 148–170). Rockville, MD: Aspen Press.

Wu, J.S., Gillin, J.C., Buchsbaum, M.S., Hershey, T., Hazlett, E., Sicotte, N., & Bunney, W.E., Jr. (1992). Effect of sleep deprivation on cerebral glucose metabolic rate in normal humans assessed with positron emission tomography. *Sleep, 14,* 155–162.

Wu, J.S., Gillin, J.C., Buchsbaum, M.S., Hershey, T., Johnson, J.C., & Bunney, W.E., Jr. (1991). Effect of sleep deprivation on brain metabolism of depressed patients. *American Journal of Psychiatry, 149,* 538–543.

Yepes, L.E., Balka, E.B., Winsberg, B.G., & Bialer, I. (1977). Amitriptyline and methylphenidate treatment of behaviorally disordered children. *Journal of Child Psychology and Psychiatry and Allied Disciplines, 18,* 39–52.

Yesavage, J.A., Brink, T.L., Rose, T.L., Lum, O., Huang, V., Adey, M.B., & Leirer, V.O. (1983). Development and validation of a geriatric depression screening scale: A preliminary report. *Journal of Psychiatric Research, 17,* 37–49.

Young, S. (1999). Psychological therapy for adults with attention deficit hyperactivity disorder. *Counseling Psychology Quarterly, 12,* 183–190.

Zametkin, A.J., & Rapoport, J.L. (1987). Neurobiology of attention deficit disorder with hyperactivity: Where have we come in 50 years? *Journal of the American Academy of Child and Adolescent Psychiatry, 26,* 676–686.

Zemishlany, Z., Alexander, G.E., Prohovnik, I., Goldman, R.G., Mukheijee, S., & Sackheim, H. (1996). Cortical blood flow and negative symptoms in schizophrenia. *Neuropsychobiology, 33,* 127–131.

Zentall, S.S. (1986). Effects of color stimulation on performance and activity of hyperactive and nonhyperactive children. *Journal of Educational Psychology, 78,* 159–165.

Zentall, S.S., & Meyer, M.J. (1987). Self-regulation of stimulation for ADD-H children during reading and vigilance task performance. *Journal of Abnormal Child Psychology, 15,* 519–536.

Zubietka, J.K., & Alessi, N.E. (1993). Is there a role of serotonin in the disruptive behavior disorders? *Journal of Child and Adolescent Psychopharmacology, 3,* 11–35.

Zubin, J. (1975). Problem of attention in schizophrenia. In M.L. Kietzman, S. Sutton, & J. Zubin (Eds.), *Experimental approaches to psychopathology* (pp. 139–166). New York: Academic Press.

About the Authors

Cynthia A. Riccio, PhD received her doctoral degree in Educational Psychology from The University of Georgia in 1993 under the leadership of Dr. George W. Hynd with a major in School Psychology and minor in Child Neuropsychology. She completed her predoctoral internship in the Department of Neurology, Section of Pediatric Neurology, at the Medical College of Georgia. She completed postdoctoral training at the Center for Clinical and Developmental Neuropsychology at The University of Georgia. Dr. Riccio is currently an Associate Professor at Texas A&M University. Prior to joining the Texas A&M University faculty in 1997, she was a faculty member at the University of Alabama, where she served as Program and Training Coordinator for the School Psychology program.

Dr. Riccio's primary research interests include learning disabilities, Attention-Deficit/Hyperactivity Disorder, neuropsychology, and individual assessment. She has published in such journals as the *Journal of Learning Disabilities, Developmental Neuropsychology, Journal of Psychoeducational Assessment, School Psychology Review,* and *Journal of the American Academy of Child and Adolescent Psychiatry.* She also has coauthored a number of book chapters. Dr. Riccio is an active member in many professional organizations, such as the American Psychological Association (Divs. 16, 40, 53, 54), National Association of School Psychologists, National Academy of Neuropsychologists, International Neuropsychological Society, the Council for Learning Disabilities, and Children and Adults with ADD. She serves on review boards for four professional journals. Dr. Riccio was a 1999 recipient of the Lightner Witmer Award from APA Division 16 (School Psychology) in recognition of her early career accomplishments.

Cecil R. Reynolds, PhD, ABPN, ABPP, earned his doctoral degree from the University of Georgia in 1978 under the tutelage of Dr. Alan S. Kaufman, with a major in School Psychology and minors in Statistics and Clinical Neuropsychology. He served an internship divided between the Medical College of Georgia and the Rutland Center for Severely Emotional Disturbed Children. He is a Professor of Educational Psychology and Distinguished Research Scholar in the College of Education at Texas A&M University and a charter member of the Texas A&M University

Faculty of Neuroscience. Prior to joining the Texas A&M University faculty in 1981, Dr. Reynolds was a faculty member at the University of Nebraska-Lincoln, where he served as Associate Director and Acting Director of the Buros Institute of Mental Measurement, after writing the grants and proposals to move the Institute to Nebraska following the death of its founder, Oscar Buros. His primary research interests are in all aspects of psychological assessment, with particular emphasis on assessment of memory, emotional and affective states and traits, and issues of cultural bias in testing. He is the author of more than 300 scholarly publications and author or editor of 33 books including *Handbook of School Psychology, Encyclopedia of Special Education,* and *Handbook of Clinical Child Neuropsychology.* He is the author of several widely used tests of personality and behavior, including the Behavior Assessment System for Children and the Revised Children's Manifest Anxiety Scale. He is also senior author of the Test of Memory and Learning and coauthor of several computerized test interpretation systems.

Dr. Reynolds holds a diplomate in Clinical Neuropsychology from the American Board of Professional Neuropsychology, of which he is also past president. He is a diplomate in School Psychology of the American Board of Professional Psychology and is a diplomate of the American Board of Forensic Examiners. He is a past president of the National Academy of Neuropsychology, APA Division 5 (Evaluation, Measurement, and Statistics), and APA Division 40 (Clinical Neuropsychology). He is a Fellow of APA Divisions 1, 5, 15, 16, and 40. Dr. Reynolds teaches courses primarily in the areas of psychological testing and diagnosis and in neuropsychology in addition to supervising clinical practica in testing and assessment. He is editor in chief of *Archives of Clinical Neuropsychology,* the official journal of the National Academy of Neuropsychology, and serves on the editorial boards of 11 other journals in the field. Dr. Reynolds has received multiple national awards recognizing him for excellence in research, including the Lightner Witmer Award and the early career awards from APA Divisions 5 and 15. He is a corecipient of the Society for the Psychological Study of Social Issues Robert Chin Award and a MENSA best research article award. He received the ABPN Distinguished Achievement Award for Research and also for Service in 1998. More recently, Dr. Reynolds received the Senior Scientist Award from APA Division 16 (School Psychology) in 1999 and was the 2000 recipient of the National Academy of Neuropsychology Distinguished Clinical Neuropsychologist Award. His service to the profession and to society has been recognized as well through the President's Gold Medal for Service to the National Academy of Neuropsychology and the University of North Carolina at Wilmington Razor Walker Award.

Patricia A. Lowe, PhD earned her doctoral degree in School Psychology with a Clinical Child Emphasis with minors in Neuropsychology and Child and Family in the Department of Educational Psychology at Texas A&M University in 2000 under Dr. Cecil R. Reynolds. Currently, she is a postdoctoral resident at the Warm Springs Counseling Center and Training Institute in Boise, Idaho.

Dr. Lowe's primary research interests include measurement issues, personality assessment, neuropsychology, school reentry issues, outcome research, and Attention-Deficit/Hyperactivity Disorder. She has coauthored journal articles in *Archives of Clinical Neuropsychology, Educational and Psychological Measurement,* and *Journal of School Psychology.* She also coauthored a book chapter in *Handbook of School Psychology* and is a coauthor of the Adult Manifest Anxiety Scales, the upward extension of the Revised Children's Manifest Anxiety Scale. She is a member of the American Psychological Association Division 16 (School Psychology) and National Association of School Psychologists. She also is a member of the Kappa Delta Phi International Honor Society in Education, Psi Chi National Honor Society in Psychology, and Phi Kappa Phi Honor Society. She was the recipient of the Lechner Graduate Merit Fellowship at Texas A&M University and is recognized in *Who's Who in American Colleges and Universities.*

Author Index

Subject Index

ABX-type CPT, 211, 213, 243, 244
Accelerating format (AF), 44
Acetylcholine, 273
Achievement, 100, 108–110, 113, 117–119, 127–131, 152
Activation system, 11, 12
Activation task, 113
Actometer, 115
Adaptive rate ISI, 42, 53, 160, 179
Adderall, 261
ADDH Comprehensive Teachers Rating Scale (ACTeRS), 136
Adenotonsillectomy, 229
Adjustment disorder, 231
Adolescents (and CPTs), 66, 70, 75, 77, 87, 190–232
Adrenergic system, 281
Adults (and CPTs), 66, 70, 75, 77, 87, 116, 125, 134, 233–257
Affective disorders, 84, 170, 190, 232, 249, 253, 257
Afferent pathways, 6, 160, 306
Age effects, 46, 81, 82, 107, 116, 126, 157, 187, 236, 237
Aggression, 46, 276, 281
Alcohol, 70, 172, 193, 229, 250, 251, 257, 281, 286
Alertness, 3, 7, 8, 10, 49, 169, 298, 299
Alertness, indicators of, 48, 49
Allergy medications, 284
Alpha waves, 169, 298, 303
Alprozolam, 260, 280, 281
Alternate forms reliability, 93, 96, 99, 250
Alzheimer's disease, 1, 15, 100, 105, 239, 247, 285, 313
Amitryptyline, 274
Amphetamine, 261, 263, 267, 268, 274, 284
Amygdala, 179
Analgesics, 285, 286
Angular gyrus, 179
Anhedonia, 150, 151
Anoxia, 230

Antagonistic inhibition, 13
Anterior network, 9
Anterior-posterior gradient, 10, 169–180, 182, 185, 188
Antianxiety medications. *See* Anxiolytics
Anticholinergic effect, 274
Anticipatory errors, 52, 89
Anticipatory responses, 88
Anticonvulsants, 260, 282–284, 289
Antidepressants, 260, 273–275, 280
Antihistamines, 260, 286, 289
Antihypertensives, 260, 280–282
Antipsychotics, 275, 276
Anxiety, 134, 145, 281, 303
Anxiety disorders, 191, 200, 208, 212, 219, 221, 228, 230, 256, 280, 281, 283
Anxiolytics, 260, 280–282
Arousal, 2, 3, 5–8, 10, 12, 13, 17, 45, 49, 51, 68, 179, 182, 280, 298, 299
Arousal system, 12, 179
Arousal theory, 2, 5
Ascending pathways, 10, 188
Aspartame, 288
Astemizole, 260, 285
Asthma medications, 260, 284–286
Ataxia, 164, 240, 249
Attention, asymmetry of, 12, 182–184
Attention, components of, 1, 3, 4, 8, 15
Attention, conceptualization of, 2, 3, 7
Attention, developmental issues of, 7, 14
Attention, divided, 3, 17, 18, 294, 303
Attention, focused, 2, 3, 6, 9, 12, 13, 17, 18, 49, 111, 160, 295, 302
Attention, models of, 2–14
Attention, neurobiology of, 5–13
Attention, selective, 2, 3, 6–8, 10, 13–15, 17, 18, 45, 48, 49, 66, 111, 146, 160, 161, 295, 297, 298, 302, 303
Attention, shifting of, 2–4, 9, 11, 49, 111, 303
Attention, sustained, 2–4, 7, 8, 10, 11, 17, 18, 44, 45, 49–51, 66, 146, 159, 180, 182, 295, 297, 302